JUDICIAL PROCESS AND JUDICIAL POLICYMAKING

JUDICIAL PROCESS AND JUDICIAL POLICYMAKING

G. Alan Tarr
Rutgers University (Camden)

WEST PUBLISHING COMPANY

St. Paul • New York • Los Angeles • San Francisco

Production, Prepress, Printing and Binding by West Publishing Company.

 TEXT IS PRINTED ON 10% POST CONSUMER RECYCLED PAPER

Library of Congress Cataloging-in-Publication Data

Tarr, G Alan (George Alan)
  Judicial process and judicial policy making / G. Alan Tarr
      p.   cm.
  Includes index
  ISBN 0-314-022775-0 (softcover)
  1. Courts—United States.   2. Judicial process—United States.
I. Title.
KF8700.T37 1994
347.73'1—dc20
[347.3071]

                                                    93-27984
                                                         CIP

CONTENTS

ix

PREFACE

Judicial Process and Judicial Policymaking is designed as a basic text for courses on the judicial process, the American legal system, or law and politics. Its approach to these subjects is based on four major premises.

First, courts in the United States have always played an important role in governing, and that role has increased in recent decades. Various factors have been suggested to explain this judicial involvement in governing, including the common-law system imported from England and modified in response to American conditions and beliefs, the institution of judicial review, and the legalistic and litigious orientation of the American populace. Whatever its causes, the phenomenon of judicial participation in governing makes understanding the processes and consequences of judicial policymaking essential for understanding American government.

Second, judicial policymaking is distinctive. Judges develop public policy in the course of resolving disputes. They bring to the task of policymaking a particular training and orientation. The institutional constraints they operate under differ considerably from those on legislators or administrators. Together, these factors affect the way that judges view problems and the policies they develop. They also highlight why understanding the judicial process and the participants in it is crucial for understanding judicial policymaking. Therefore, Chapters 2 through 8 are devoted to examining the processes by which courts operate and the participants in those processes.

Third, courts make policy in a variety of ways. Sometimes, a court announces a landmark decision with national implications. More frequently, however, judicial policymaking occurs through less heralded rulings or series of rulings. At times this policymaking brings courts into conflict with other branches of government, as when a court strikes down a statute as unconstitutional. But often judicial policymaking complements policymaking by another branch, as when courts choose between competing understandings of the law through statutory interpretation. At other times judicial policymaking may be altogether independent of the actions of other branches, as when judges elaborate the common law. To provide a sense of this diversity, Chapter 9 surveys the various forms of judicial policymaking, and Chapters 10 and 11 provide detailed case studies of the development and consequences of important judicial policies.

Finally, courts may be the objects of public policy, as well as its creators. Reformers have attacked various features of the administration of justice in the United States, including the insanity defense, the adversarial system, plea bargaining, and the jury system. Sometimes they have succeeded in enacting their reforms into law. Even when they have not, their criticisms require us to consider how effectively the judicial process in the United States promotes justice and what effects the proposed reforms would have on the administration of justice. Throughout the book, therefore, we discuss and assess these various reform proposals. We also survey legal practices and institutions in other nations, so readers can consider how other countries have dealt with common legal problems.

A number of people contributed to the completion of this project. At West Publishing Company, Clark Baxter was involved in the project from the outset, providing just the right mix of editorial insistence and encouragement, and Andrea Peters guided the manuscript through production. At Rutgers-Camden, Nancy McClain completed the typing, xeroxing, and other secretarial work for the book with her usual cheerfulness and efficiency, and Mauricio Paez proved to be a resourceful research assistant. Mary Cornelia Porter read portions of the manuscript and offered excellent suggestions on how to improve it. A number of reviewers—Lauren Bowen, John Carroll University; John C. Domino, Sam Houston State University; Larry Elowitz, Georgia College; Sheldon Goldman, University of Massachusetts; Jona Goldschmidt, Northern Arizona University; A.J. Goubler, Delgado Community College; Phillip M. Simpson, Cameron University; Ken R. Stockholm, University of Alaska—also provided useful comments and rescued me from various errors of fact or interpretation. Henry Glick, Craig Emmert, Sheldon Goldman, Frank Coffin, Barbara Curran, James Eisenstein, Herbert Jacob, Jeffrey Segal, Harold Spaeth, Stephen Halpern, and Charles Lamb all graciously consented to my reprinting material from their research Any errors that remain are, of course, solely my responsibility. Finally, I would like to thank my wife Susan for her loving support and my sons Bobby and Andy, to whom this book is dedicated.

For Bobby and Andy

1 COURTS AND LAW

Today the United States has almost 800,000 lawyers, one for about every 360 Americans, and its law schools annually graduate over 43,000 more.[1] In 1990 the nation's state and federal courts resolved over one hundred million cases, more than one for every three Americans, and the courts' caseloads increase with each passing year.[2] Impressive as these figures are, even they do not capture the full impact of law and the courts in the United States. Scan a newspaper, and one is immediately struck by how often Americans call upon judges to resolve important policy disputes. Judicial rulings affect everything from prayers at school graduations to conditions in jails and prisons, from the disposal of radioactive wastes to the relocation of sports franchises.[3] Many judicial decisions, of course, affect only the parties to the dispute. But as the United States Supreme Court's rulings on school desegregation and abortion illustrate, others may focus public attention on issues and encourage broad societal changes.[4] Thus, courts do not merely resolve large numbers of disputes; they also actively participate in governing.

It is hardly surprising, therefore, that Americans have a fascination with law, lawyers, and legal institutions. We indulge that interest through bestsellers, like *The Firm* and *Presumed Innocent*, and through television shows, like *L.A. Law* and *The People's Court*.[5] We incorporate legal terms, such as "taking the Fifth" and "the right to privacy," into our everyday conversations. We even tend to think about political issues from a legal perspective.[6] Ours is truly a law-permeated society.

Combined with our fascination with the legal order, however, is often a concern about the law and about American legal institutions. This concern extends both to the ways in which courts operate and to the decisions they render. It underlies the frequent, often biting jokes we tell about lawyers: "What do you have when you have a lawyer buried up to his neck in the sand? Not enough sand." It is reflected more directly in poll data expressing public dissatisfaction with courts. A Gallup poll conducted in 1989, for example, found that almost three-quarters of the respondents had little or no confidence in "the ability of courts to convict and properly sentence criminals."[7] Two years earlier, a Louis Harris poll had found that 54 percent of Americans believed that the nation's civil justice imposed unreasonable costs on society.[8] The sense that Americans are angry about excessive and costly litigation prompted George Bush to attack greedy lawyers during his unsuccessful 1992 presidential campaign.[9] In 1991 the Executive Branch's Council on Competitiveness addressed these concerns in a lengthy report that documented problems with the American legal system and proposed fundamental reforms.[10] Simply put, there is a widespread perception that American legal institutions are not working very well.

Whether this perception is correct is, of course, a matter of some controversy. Some commentators deny that there is a crisis in the courts and view the criticisms as exaggerated, an attempt to justify fundamental changes in the administration of justice.[11] It is also noteworthy that the attacks on the courts come from widely divergent perspectives and reflect a variety of perspectives. Following the not-guilty verdict in the police-brutality case that sparked the Los Angeles riots, critics charged that American courts were guilty of racism. This complaint differed markedly from the concerns about excessive and drawn-out litigation found in the Council on Competitiveness's "Agenda for Civil Justice Reform in America" and from popular concerns about excessive leniency by the courts in criminal cases. Yet although the grounds for complaint may vary, the chorus of criticism raises serious questions about how effective American courts and legal institutions are in promoting justice.

This volume seeks to provide readers with the information and the range of perspectives they need to arrive at their own assessment of the American legal system. To do so, it first describes the nation's legal structures and the participants—judges, lawyers, and litigants—in the judicial process. Next, it examines the processes by which courts—from trial courts to the United States Supreme Court—resolve the cases that come before them and the ways in which judges reach their decisions. Finally, it surveys how courts participate in policymaking and analyzes the consequences of this judicial involvement in governing.

Throughout the book, we analyze various reform proposals, such as eliminating plea bargaining and permitting the use of illegally seized evidence at trial, so that readers may consider the likely consequences of their adoption. We also draw comparisons with the legal systems of other countries. These comparisons highlight what is distinctive about the American legal system and also show how other countries have dealt with similar legal problems.

Before proceeding with this analysis, we begin with an overview of legal systems and of the law and consider certain common misconceptions about law and the courts.

LEGAL SYSTEMS

Legal scholars group the legal systems of the world into "legal families," based on the legal systems' common origins and on similarities in their law and their legal institutions (see Table 1-1).[12] The most influential families of legal systems—

TABLE 1-1 FAMILIES OF LEGAL SYSTEMS

The Common Law Family
  Origins: England, beginning in the twelfth century.
  Geographic area: England, former English colonies, and other countries with strong political ties to England. North America: the United States and Canada (with the exception of Quebec); Africa: Nigeria, Kenya, and Uganda, among others; Asia: India and Pakistan; and Australia and New Zealand.
  Distinguishing feature: Judges decide cases through inductive reasoning, relying heavily on precedent.

The Civil Law (Romano-Germanic) Legal Family
  Origins: European universities, during the twelfth and thirteenth centuries, which adapted the Code of Justinian to new circumstances.
  Geographic area: Most countries in continental Europe and in Latin America, as well as former French colonies in North America (Quebec and Louisiana) and the former Belgian and French colonies in Africa (e.g., Rwanda and Burundi). Some other legal systems (e.g., Algeria, Morocco, and Indonesia) contain elements of the civil-law and of other legal traditions.
  Distinguishing feature: Judges decide cases through the application of legal principles, which are often drawn from a legal code.

The Socialist Law Family
  Origins: The Soviet Union, in the aftermath of the Russian Revolution of 1917.
  Geographic area: Formerly, all Communist countries in Europe, such as the Soviet Union, Yugoslavia, and Bulgaria; today, with the collapse of European communism, a few countries that continue as communist, such as Cuba and Vietnam.
  Distinguishing feature: Its primary objective is to move society toward communism in accordance with Marxist-Leninist theory.

The Islamic Law Family
  Origins: The founding of Islam in the sixth century.
  Geographic area: Most Muslim nations in North Africa, the Middle East, and Asia base their law, at least in part, on Islamic law.

Distinguishing feature: Islamic law is religious law, understood by believers as divinely revealed and inseparable from the religion of Islam.

The Hindu Law Family

Origins: Sacred texts known as the *dharmasastras*, written between 800 B.C. and 200 A.D.

Geographic area: While Hindu law imposes obligations on all Hindus, it primarily affects the national law of India.

Distinguishing feature: Hindu law is religious law, regulating virtually all aspects of life for believers.

The Far Eastern Legal Family

Origins: The traditional Chinese notion of social order, exemplified by the writings of Confucius (551-479 B.C.).

Geographic area: Historically, China, Japan, Korea, and Indochina; today, despite communism in China and Vietnam and changes in Japanese law associated with its economic development, it still influences the law in all those countries.

Distinguishing feature: Far Eastern legal systems encourage the resolution of disputes by compromise, settlement, or other mechanisms rather than by the rule of law.

The African Legal Family

Origins: Custom within various African tribes.

Geographic area: Although some African states (e.g., Senegal and Tanganyika) have sought since independence to collect and codify tribal customs, the influence of those customs on the law of modern African states has been minimal.

Distinguishing feature: Traditional African law stresses custom and tradition as authoritative.

SOURCES: Information for this table is drawn from Rene David and John Brierley, *Major Legal Systems in the World Today*, 2nd ed. (London: Stevens & Sons, 1978), and Konrad Zweigert and Hein Kotz, *Introduction to Comparative Law*, 2nd ed. (Oxford: Clarendon Press, 1987).

the common-law and civil-law (or Romano-Germanic) families—originated in Europe. These legal systems have spread their influence throughout the world through colonialism and through the process of modernization in non-European countries. Nevertheless, many countries in Africa and Asia have also retained elements of their indigenous legal systems.

The legal system of the United States belongs to the family of common-law legal systems. So too do the legal systems of other former British colonies, such as Australia, Nigeria, and India. Most legal systems on the European continent belong to the civil-law (Romano-Germanic) family, as do the legal systems of most Latin American countries and of the former French and Belgian colonies in Africa and Asia. Some legal systems, such as that of Japan, defy easy categorization into a legal family, because they have derived elements from French, German, English, and American law.[13]

The Common-Law Legal Family

Although each country within the common-law legal family has developed its own legal institutions and bodies of law, common-law legal systems resemble each other in the general organization of their courts, in the rules of evidence and procedure they employ, and in the legal doctrines they have developed. Because these features of common-law systems derive from English law and legal practice, an understanding of the historical origins of the common law in England is crucial to understanding common-law legal systems, including that of the United States.

The Development of the Common Law[14]

The Norman conquest of England in 1066 under William the Conqueror laid the groundwork for the development of the common law. In order to extend royal authority over this dominion, William's successors created permanent courts, staffed by judges appointed by the King, to administer the law of the realm. From the twelfth century onward, the English monarchs also dispatched "travelling justices" to rule in the King's name in the county courts.[15] By the thirteenth century, the kings had succeeded in establishing a common set of legal procedures and legal standards throughout England.

But what legal procedures were the royal judges to follow in deciding cases, and what legal principles were they to employ? The judges could not rely upon parliamentary enactments for guidance—Parliament's emergence as a legislative body was still several centuries in the future. Nor could they rely much upon royal edicts, for these did not extend to many of the legal problems confronting the judges. Rather, as William Blackstone observed in his famous treatise on the common law, the judges looked to a body of "unwritten law," the common law, for guidance.[16] In speaking of the common law as "unwritten," Blackstone did not mean that it was transmitted by word of mouth. Rather, he was emphasizing that the doctrines of the common law, unlike legislative enactments, "are not set down in any written statute or ordinance, but depend merely upon immemorial usage." Judges served as the "depositories of the law," and their decisions served as "the principal and most authoritative evidence that can be given of the existence of such a custom as shall form a part of the common law."[17] Thus, the common law originated in judicial decisions, which enunciated authoritative legal principles, presumably drawn from the customs and practices of the society, in the course of resolving disputes between litigants.

As these judicial decisions accumulated, they comprised a body of law that judges could draw upon to resolve the cases coming before them. Recurrence to precedent—that is, to the judges' own earlier decisions, or to those of their predecessors or colleagues—facilitated judicial decisionmaking by giving judges standards that they could rely upon in deciding the cases before them. Initially, "there was merely a tendency to establish a procedure, and perhaps adopt a few substantive principles which, taken together, constituted the custom of the court" and provided a standard for judicial decisions.[18] Over time, however, as the practice of publishing written reports of judicial decisions developed, judges could easily consult the rulings of other courts. Over time too, the authority of these precedents increased. This is reflected in the judges' acceptance of the doctrine of *stare decisis et non quieta movere* (to stand by precedents and not to disturb settled points). Common-law judges under this doctrine of *stare decisis* are obliged to conform their decisions to those reached by prior judges deciding similar cases.

Despite the proliferation of legislation and administrative regulations over the last two centuries, judge-made law continues to govern important areas of life in common-law countries. Moreover, as Roscoe Pound has observed, the common law provides "a mode of treating legal problems rather than a fixed body of definite rules."[19] Thus, in dealing with statutes and other enactments, judges in common-law systems usually employ the same approaches to decision-making, such as reliance on precedent, that they had developed for dealing with the common law. Recent legal developments have therefore not altered the basic character of common-law legal systems.

The Common Law in the United States

During the seventeenth century, most colonists emigrated to America from England, and they brought the English legal system with them when they came to North America. When the United States declared its independence from England, the new states retained their common-law legal systems. Thus, like their English counterparts, American judges have had to enunciate legal standards in the absence of legislation in order to resolve disputes between litigants. This in turn has guaranteed American judges a major role in law-making.

American courts have nevertheless modified the body of common law that they received from England in several important respects. In the decades following Independence, American judges expunged aspects of the common law that reflected the aristocratic character of English society and were therefore inappropriate for the more democratic society being created in the United States.[20]   During the nineteenth century, they also adapted common-law doctrines that originated in an agrarian society in order to encourage economic development and accommodate industrialization.[21]   Finally, although they have generally adhered to precedent, American judges have never viewed precedent as binding to the same extent as did their English counterparts. They therefore have shown greater willingness to overrule earlier decisions and to alter the common law in response to changing circumstances.

The Civil-Law (Romano-Germanic) Legal Family

The other major family of legal systems is the civil-law (or Romano-Germanic family. Civil-law legal systems are found on the European continent, throughout South America, and in various countries in Africa and Asia. The origins of the civil law, however, can be traced to the rediscovery of Roman law during the Middle Ages in Europe.

The Rediscovery of Roman Law

The creation of civil-law legal systems began with the intellectual revival during the twelfth and thirteenth centuries in Western Europe.[22] The founding of universities and the spread of learning during this period led to the rediscovery of the highly developed body of law that had governed ancient Rome. This Roman law, which was collected in the Emperor Justinian's *Corpus juris civilis*, a systematic compilation (or code) of law dealing with relations between private persons, became the subject of law studies in major European universities. The study of Roman law both promoted the notion that society should be governed by formal law and provided the vocabulary, categories, and concepts that were needed for the construction of a modern body of law.

This is not to say that European monarchs seized upon Roman law in order to impose it on their subjects. For one thing, because of the political fragmentation in Europe, rulers were rarely in a position to impose much law on anyone. For another, societal changes had rendered parts of the Roman law obsolete—for example, those sections dealing with slavery. Other elements of the Roman law—for example, family law—were already dealt with by the canon law established by the Church. As a result, the law which came to prevail in Europe reflected local, non-Roman sources. Nevertheless, jurists and practitioners alike drew their conceptions of law, as well as their legal terminology and their approach to legal reasoning, from the tradition of Roman law.

The Napoleonic Code

The influence of Roman law scholars on civil-law legal systems, especially on their approach to law and on their terminology, continued from the Middle Ages to the nineteenth century.[23] For modern civil-law systems, the decisive event was probably the formulation of the Napoleonic Code (or *Code civil*) in 1804. This Code, developed by legal experts in France with the active participation of Napoleon himself, immediately became the law in France. French conquests in Europe under Napoleon spread the Code throughout the continent, and various European countries quickly developed codes modeled on Napoleon's, either under pressure from France or out of respect for the country's military prowess. Even after the defeat of Napoleon, his Code continued to influence law throughout much of Europe and became the basis for legal codes in Central America and South America.

Developed in the aftermath of the French Revolution, the Napoleonic Code destroyed the remaining vestiges of feudalism and replaced them with a body of modern law. It recognized the legal equality of all citizens, freed economic enterprise from traditional constraints, and secularized family law. Equally important, it demonstrated the advantages of systematizing the national law and provided a model for other countries.

Civil Law vs. Common Law

Civil-law legal systems differ from their common-law counterparts in more than their historical roots.[24] Some differences involve the structure and operation of legal institutions, such as the role of judge and attorney at trial and the forms of legal procedure. (These differences are discussed in Chapters 3 and 4 of this volume.) Others involve the characteristic source of law. In common-law systems, it is the judge, enunciating law in the course of resolving disputes. In civil-law systems, it is the legislative authority, announcing governing legal principles or, in the case of the Napoleonic Code, a more or less comprehensive body of law. Perhaps the most important difference, however, relates to what might be called the legal frame of mind. Legal thinking in common-law systems emphasizes the concrete rather than the general and places its faith in experience rather than in abstractions. In contrast, legal thinking in civil-law systems reasons from principles to particular instances and has an inclination toward systematizing. As one commentator has put it, a civil-law "system differs from a common-law system much as rationalism differs from empiricism or deduction from induction."[25]

LAW

A speed limit is law; so too are wills, regulations established by the Environmental Protection Agency, congressional statutes, trial court rulings, and business contracts. The length of the list (and it is hardly comprehensive!) illustrates the diversity of law. In order to make sense of this diversity, practitioners and scholars have devised various ways of categorizing law.

Private Law/Public Law

Legal scholars often distinguish between *private law* and *public law*. This distinction is particularly important in civil-law legal systems, such as those of France and Argentina. In fact, France has established a separate set of courts which only hears cases involving public law.

Private law is concerned with relations among private citizens and/or private organizations. Often these private parties enter into legal agreements (contracts) to order their affairs and to prevent disputes from arising. Yet these efforts are not always effective. Disputes between tenants and landlords over the payment of rent, between neighbors over a noisy pet, and between family members over an inheritance are all examples of private law disputes. So too are suits by consumers injured by unsafe products, by patients accusing physicians of medical malpractice, and by retailers claiming that their suppliers had failed to deliver merchandise as promised. These disputes may arise out of legal obligations voluntarily assumed by the parties, as in contracts. Or the applicable law may be found in statutes or in judicial decisions. Whatever its source, in the realm of private law, "the sole function of the government [is] the recognition and enforcement of private rights."[26] Table 1-2 identifies important fields of private law.

Public law, in contrast, involves relations between private citizens or organizations and the government. Thus public law includes statutes outlawing murder or fraud, setting auto emissions standards, and taxing capital gains. It also encompasses Supreme Court rulings protecting constitutional rights, such as the freedom of speech, and administrative regulations governing airline safety.

Two major branches of public law are *constitutional law* and *administrative law*. Constitutional law is the fundamental law within a political unit, embodied in the constitution itself and in the decisions of courts and other bodies interpreting that document. The constitution establishes the government and

TABLE 1-2 SOME CATEGORIES OF PRIVATE LAW

Type of Law	What Does It Address?	Who Makes It?
Contract law	The enforcement of those promises for the breach of which the law provides a remedy	State law (primarily state courts through the decision of cases at common law)
Tort law	Legal wrongs committed upon a person or property, other than the breach of contract, and the award of damages for such torts	State law, primarily state common law, but more recently legislation as well
Family law	Relationships between husband and wife and between parent and child, with the rights and duties arising from those relationships	Chiefly state legislation; also federal legislation (social welfare and taxation) and judicial rulings (e.g., abortion)
Commercial law	Aspects of business, such as the sale of goods, bank deposits and collections, investment services, etc.	State law (especially the Uniform Commercial Code, legislation adopted by almost all state legislatures)
Business enterprises law	The formation and conduct of business enterprises (corporations, partnerships, etc.)	State law primarily (e.g., incorporation), but also congressional enactments

prescribes how the public business shall be conducted. More specifically, it creates the major offices within a government, determines how they shall be filled, distributes governmental power among those offices, defines the procedures by which government shall operate, and establishes limitations on the scope of governmental power. The United States has fifty-one constitutions. The Federal Constitution establishes the national government and governs its operations, while state constitutions do the same for the governments of the fifty states.

Courts in the United States, both federal and state, participate in the development of constitutional law through the exercise of judicial review. Because the United States Constitution is the "supreme law of the land," actions of the national or state governments that conflict with the Constitution are invalid, and persons affected by those actions can challenge them in court.[27] (Similarly, litigants may challenge state or local actions that they believe violate the state constitution.) When a litigant claims that the government has acted unconstitutionally, the judge must determine whether the government has exceeded its power or violated rights guaranteed by the Constitution. Altogether, the United States Supreme Court has struck down over 125 federal statutes and over 1000 state statutes as unconstitutional.[28]

Administrative law is concerned with the powers and procedures of governmental bodies that exercise power delegated to them by the legislature. Within the United States government, these bodies include government departments such as the Department of Agriculture, administrative agencies such as the Environmental Protection Agency, and independent regulatory commissions such as the Securities and Exchange Commission. These institutions establish rules and regulations that have the force of law. They also hold hearings and adjudicate disputes, such as over the termination of welfare benefits. In addition, these institutions decide on the award or withdrawal of government grants—recall the controversy in the early 1990's over the National Endowment for the Arts' denial of grants to artists whose works were alleged to be obscene. Finally, they control the distribution of other government benefits—for example, the broadcast licenses awarded by the Federal Communications Commission to radio and television stations. Administrative law largely deals with the processes by which public officials discharge their responsibilities and with the oversight of administrative action by the courts.[29]

Criminal Law/Civil Law

Law is also sometimes categorized based on the relationships that it regulates.[30] The *criminal law* establishes what actions are offenses against the political society and prescribes the punishment to be imposed for such conduct. The criminal law thus is a branch of public law. The parties in a criminal case are always the government, which prosecutes the case, and the defendant, who is charged with the criminal violation. Although they may have an interest in the outcome of a prosecution, victims of crime are not parties to the litigation. The criminal offense is understood as a violation of the public order, not as an offense against a particular person. Familiar crimes include murder, arson, fraud, and burglary.

All other law is classified as *civil law*. (Note that this is different from the distinction between common-law and civil-law legal systems discussed earlier.) Civil law is concerned with private rights and obligations and with legal remedies when those rights are violated or those obligations unmet. It usually involves legal relationships between private persons and/or organizations.

Rights and obligations at civil law may arise from voluntary agreements, as in the case of a contract between a borrower and a lender. They may also result from legislation or administrative action. A law establishing tax rates, a statute permitting victims of sex discrimination to sue for damages, a regulation of the Environmental Protection Agency setting auto-emission levels—all involve civil law. Finally, rights and obligations at civil law may be established by judicial decisions interpreting the common law. For example, if you are involved in an automobile accident because your car malfunctions, you may sue the manufacturer for damages. The obligation of manufacturers to produce safe and serviceable products—and their legal liability when they fail to do so—is established by the common law.

Substantive Law/Procedural Law

The distinction between substance and procedure, between substantive law and procedural law, cuts across the previous classifications into public law and private law, criminal law and civil law.[31] *Substantive law* creates, defines, and delimits rights, duties, and obligations. *Procedural law*, in contrast, prescribes the processes by which those substantive rights and obligations are enforced by courts or by other public agencies.

For example, suppose you are seriously injured by a reckless driver. The substantive law determines your right to redress—whether you can obtain damages for your hospital costs, for the pain and suffering you endured, and for the loss of income caused by your hospitalization. The procedural law determines in what court you should file your complaint, what evidence can be admitted, whether you are entitled to a jury trial, and whether you have a right to appeal should the trial court rule against you.

Law/Equity

The distinction between law and equity, which is important in common-law legal systems like that of the United States, dates from the fourteenth century in England.[32] Parties unable to obtain satisfaction in the royal courts, often because of burdensome and inflexible procedural requirements, applied to the king for redress. As petitions for relief outside the normal legal channels increased, the responsibility for deciding on them devolved from the monarch to the Chancellor, the highest administrative official of the realm. Petitions came to be addressed to the Chancellor directly, who would render decisions based on "the equity of the case," that is, based on his own sense of the justice of the claim.

By the eighteenth century, the process of considering petitions for equitable relief had become institutionalized in a Court of Chancery, separate from the regular law courts and presided over by the Chancellor. This court differed from the regular law courts in the flexibility of its procedures, the absence of a jury, and the broad relief it could provide. Over time, however, as volumes of Chancery decisions were published and a system of precedent established, "the rules of law applied by the Court of Chancery [became] as much fixed by decisions and as much formed into technical legal rules as the rules of the Common Law."[33] As the Court of Chancery became more and more judicial in its decisionmaking, equity emerged as an alternative to—and a rival of—the law propounded by the regular law courts. This dual system of courts operated in England, until the late nineteenth century, when the separate courts of equity were abolished. Thus, when the American colonists developed their legal systems, they typically adopted a dual system of courts, as was familiar to them from England. Most American states merged their law and equity courts during the century after independence, although New Jersey retained separate courts of law and of equity until 1947.[34]

The merger of legal institutions did not eliminate equity from the American legal system; it merely placed law and equity powers in the same set of hands. Thus, in interpreting a statute or awarding monetary damages in a civil case, a judge is exercising law powers. However, when a judge provides a remedy other than monetary damages—when the judge, for example, issues an injunction (a legal order to a defendant to stop or start doing something)—she is exercising equity powers. Judicial orders limiting picketing by strikers outside a business or compelling local school districts to bus children to desegregate their schools are contemporary examples of how judges employ their equity powers.[35] These examples show that a judge's equity powers today are primarily exercised in devising remedies for violations of the law.

COMMON MISCONCEPTIONS ABOUT LAW AND COURTS

Misconceptions about law and the courts, just as much as a lack of information, may prevent a full understanding of the role of courts in the United States. Often these misconceptions are half-truths: they capture part, but only part, of the reality of law and courts. Two common misconceptions are: (1) Law is a body of established rules that govern behavior, and (2) Judicial decisions on important policy issues resolve those issues.

Law and Uncertainty

In thinking of "the law", one tends to think in terms of a body of established, authoritative rules. There is considerable truth to this picture. Obviously, most people most of the time understand what the law requires and conform their conduct to its requirements. According to Justice Oliver Wendell Holmes, one of the most famous justices to sit on the United States Supreme Court, this applies to bad men as well as good. For even the bad man, Holmes suggested, craved certainty about the law, so he could predict how far he could go without running afoul of the public authorities.[36]

Nevertheless, as Holmes himself recognized, not all law is clear and certain. Consider, for example, the case of *Lee v. Weisman*.[37] Robert Lee, the principal of a public middle school in Providence, Rhode Island, invited Rabbi Leslie Gutterman to give the invocation and benediction at the school's graduation. In extending the invitation, Lee was following the school district's long-standing practice of having local clergy offer prayers as part of the graduation ceremony. In this instance, however, Daniel Weisman, a parent of one of the graduating students, objected to the invitation. He claimed that the practice of prayers at graduation violated the establishment clause of the First Amendment, which requires a degree of separation between church and state.[38] Four days prior to the graduation, Weisman filed suit in federal district court to prevent the prayers at graduation. Although Weisman's suit came too late to block the prayers at his daughter's graduation, the court agreed with his contention that religious ceremonies at public-school graduations violated the establishment clause. It therefore issued a permanent injunction prohibiting the Providence school district from including religious ceremonies as part of future graduations. The school district appealed the decision, but both the federal court of appeals and the United States Supreme Court upheld the trial court's ruling.

What is striking about *Lee v. Weisman* is the nature of the dispute. Both Lee and Weisman agreed completely regarding the facts of the case. Both acknowledged that the school had invited Rabbi Gutterman to give the invocation and benediction, that inviting clergy to offer prayers at graduation was an established practice in the district, and that students were not obliged to attend the graduation ceremony. What Lee and Weisman disagreed about was whether the practice of having clergy lead prayers at graduation was legally permissible.

More precisely, they disagreed about the meaning of the law (the establishment clause of the First Amendment) and about its application to religious ceremonies at public-school graduations. If the establishment clause's meaning were clear and well-known, there would have been no litigation.

Lee v. Weisman's exclusive focus on legal, rather than factual, questions is by no means exceptional. Often, in cases ranging from the most highly charged constitutional conflicts to the most mundane private disputes, the issue is solely the meaning of the law and how it applies. Many other cases raise issues of fact and of law simultaneously. Yet this picture of litigation aimed at defining the meaning of law is inconsistent with the notion of law as as a set of rules, whose meaning is stable and certain. Indeed, much litigation arises precisely because the law is not certain.

There are several reasons why the law may be uncertain. The language of the law may be vague or general, either by design or because of poor draftsmanship. The aims of those who enacted the law may be unclear. The situation in the case may not have been contemplated by those who enacted the law. And so on.[39] But whatever the reason, judges, when called upon, must "say what the law is."[40] And if the litigation arises because the law is unclear, then judges must choose between the competing understandings of the law and of how it applies that are offered by the attorneys arguing the case. In making this choice, judges are doing more than merely substituting certainty for uncertainty, clarity for obscurity. They are in a very real sense creating the law.

This is not to say, of course, that judges are free to give whatever interpretation they wish to the law, to decide cases however they choose. Judges operate within a set of legal and political constraints. For example, all judges take an oath to decide cases in accordance with the law. Even before their elevation to the bench, they are socialized through years of legal training and experience as to the proper behavior for a judge. Once on the court, they must take account of the expectations of colleagues and lawyers. These factors affect the range of discretion that judges exercise and the sorts of constraints that they feel. Yet ultimately judicial choice is channeled rather than completely eliminated. Because the law may be uncertain or unclear, a judicial commitment to decide cases according to the law does not eliminate the necessity of judicial choice.

Courts, Law, and Public Policy

Courts in the United States often must resolve disputes involving contentious public issues. Indeed, one of the most perceptive observers of American politics, Alexis de Tocqueville, suggested that "there is hardly a political question in the United States which does not sooner or later turn into a judicial one."[41] This transformation of political issues into legal disputes furnishes judges with the opportunity to influence the course of public policy. And judges have sometimes been more than willing to seize the opportunities presented to them.

Because courts regularly decide cases that involve important policy issues, it might seem that they are in a position to dominate policymaking in the United States. Indeed, some commentators have made that very claim.[42] For, after all, by "saying what the law is" on a wide range of issues, don't courts set policy for the nation?

This view, however, rests on an misconception of the role that courts play in policymaking.[43] Judicial rulings do not necessarily determine public policy. Rather, the relationship between judicial decisions and public policy is quite complex. *Regents of the University of California* v. *Bakke*, the U.S. Supreme Court's first ruling on affirmative action, reveals some of these complexities.[44]

Ten years after graduating from the University of Minnesota with a degree in engineering, Allan Bakke decided to become a physician.[45] He applied to the medical school of the University of California at Davis in 1973 and again in 1974, but on both occasions he was denied admission. At that time the University had a special-admissions program, under which sixteen seats in the entering class were reserved for minority students. This quota system was not established to remedy prior discrimination by the medical school—there was no evidence that the school had discriminated—but to redress societal discrimination against minority-group members. Bakke, who was white, did not qualify for admission under the program. His undergraduate grades and his score on the Medical College Admission Test, however, were substantially higher than those of most students accepted under the special-admissions program. Bakke believed that he was the victim of "reverse discrimination" and sued the university in state court, claiming that his constitutional rights had been violated.

When the United States Supreme Court heard Bakke's case on appeal, the justices split sharply. Four justices voted to strike down the University's affirmative-action program, insisting that racial preferences in admissions were illegal. But four other justices voted to uphold the University's program and deny Bakke admission. Justice Lewis Powell cast the decisive vote. Powell agreed that the University had violated Bakke's rights by establishing a racial quota and denying him admission on that basis. Yet Powell also concluded that the Constitution did not bar affirmative-action admissions programs, as long as there were no fixed quotas, even if race figured in the admissions decisions.

When the Supreme Court announced its decision in *Bakke,* the case was viewed as a landmark ruling. And in one sense it was. For the ruling did more than compel the University of California to admit Allan Bakke to its medical school and to abandon its system of quotas for the admission of minority-group members. It also established national policy on affirmative action in college admissions. Thus, other universities which had instituted similar quota programs were likewise obliged to eliminate them in order to comply with the Court's ruling.

Nevertheless, *Bakke* did not resolve the issue of affirmative action. Opponents of affirmative action might hail the invalidation of the University of California's quota system and call upon other universities to abandon their race-conscious admissions programs. But proponents of affirmative action could reply that the Court permitted the use of race as a factor in admissions decisions and urge universities to adopt more aggressive programs of affirmative action consistent with the Court's ruling.[46] Thus, instead of being converted by the Court's ruling, both opponents and proponents of affirmative action used it to buttress their own positions.

Bakke also did not affect the incidence of affirmative-action admissions programs. Despite Allan Bakke's successful challenge to the affirmative action program at the University of California, colleges and universities actually expanded their programs of affirmative action in admissions in the decade after *Bakke.* The University of California at Davis itself introduced a new affirmative-action admissions program.[47] Instead of establishing public policy, the Court's landmark ruling turned out to be merely one skirmish in an ongoing policy debate. The issue of affirmative action was no closer to resolution after *Bakke* than it had been before the Court's decision.

In this respect, *Bakke* was hardly unique. Although judicial rulings may establish legal obligations, those affected by a ruling may refuse to comply with it. For example, a decade after the Supreme Court in *Brown* v. *Board of Education* ordered the elimination of dual (racially segregated) school systems, less than two percent of black children in the South were attending integrated schools.[48] Rather than endorsing judicial rulings, public officials may ignore them, attack them, or attempt to overturn them. A case in point is President George Bush's vigorous support for a constitutional amendment to override the Supreme Court's ruling that the First Amendment protected the burning of the American flag.[49] Groups too may reject judicial rulings and organize to oppose them in other political arenas. The most visible example of this during the 1970s and 1980s was the right-to-life movement, which was formed in direct response to the Supreme Court's ruling in *Roe* v. *Wade* which announced a constitutional right to obtain an abortion.[50] Indeed, the controversy engendered by the Supreme Court's abortion rulings suggests that judicial rulings may at times aggravate, rather than resolve, policy disputes.

Taken together, these examples indicate that although courts often announce rulings on policy issues, they are not in a position to dictate public policy. Rather, whether judicial rulings accomplish their objectives often depends upon—among other things—the political support that they generate and the opposition they encounter.[51] Courts do not operate outside the political process; like other institutions, they are enmeshed in it.

CONCLUSIONS

This chapter has examined law and the American legal system from both legal and political perspectives. From a legal perspective, probably the most important point to note about the American legal system is that it is a common-law legal system. As a common-law system, it shares many features with the legal systems of Great Britain and its other former colonies. From a political perspective, the distinctive aspect of the American legal system is the courts' involvement in policymaking. This involvement stems from the courts' responsibility to say what the law is, even in cases that have political ramifications. Thus, while courts in America do not dominate policymaking, their responsibilities nonetheless involve them in the political process.

This chapter has also briefly examined the character of law. From a legal perspective, what is most striking are the diverse types of law that courts interpret. As we have seen, in order to make sense of this diversity, scholars and attorneys have categorized law in various ways: public law/private law, criminal law/civil law, law/equity, and so on. From a political perspective, what is most important is the degree of uncertainty in the law. This uncertainty in the law provides the basis for disputes and hence for litigation. It also creates opportunities for judicial discretion in interpreting the law and in deciding cases. The range of discretion that judges exercise—and the uses that they make of it—will be an ongoing theme of this volume. Our concern in the next section of this book, however, is with the structure of American legal institutions and with the judges, lawyers, and litigants who are involved with them.

NOTES

1. Data on the size of the American legal profession and its growth in relation to the population of the United States are found in Richard L. Abel, *American Lawyers* (New York: Oxford

University Press, 1989), p. 280, Table 22. In 1991, 43,286 students graduated from law schools accredited by the American Bar Association, according to *The Official Guide to U.S. Law Schools* (Newtown, Pa.: Law School Admissions Council, 1992), p. 34.

2. Reliable comprehensive data on court cases are difficult to obtain. Our estimate of case filings is based on *State Court Caseload Statistics: Annual Report 1990* (Williamsburg, Va.: National Center for State Courts, 1992), pp. 4 and 51, and on the *Annual Report of the Director of the Administrative Office of the United States Courts, 1990* (Washington, D.C.: Government Printing Office, 1990), p. 2 and p. 103, Table A-1.

3. On prayer at public school graduations, see *Lee* v. *Weisman,* 60 LW 4723 (1992); on prison conditions, see *Hudson* v. *McMillan,* 60 LW 4151 (1992); on radioactive waste disposal, see *New York* v. *United States,* 60 LW 4723 (1992); and on the relocation of sports franchises, see City of *Oakland* v. *Oakland Raiders,* 193 Cal. Rptr. 673 (Supp. Ct. 1982), and *Los Angeles Memorial Coliseum Commission* v. *National Football League,* 727 F.2d 1381 (9th Cir. 1984).

4. The United States Supreme Court recognized a broad right for women to terminate their pregnancies in the companion cases of *Roe* v. *Wade,* 410 U.S. 113 (1973), and *Doe* v. *Bolton,* 410 U.S. 479 (1973). Subsequent rulings have substantially narrowed that right—see, for example, *Webster* v. *Reproductive Health Services,* 109 S.Ct. 3040 (1989), and *Planned Parenthood of Southeastern Pennsylvania* v. *Casey,* 60 LW 4795 (1992). The Supreme Court's most important ruling on racial discrimination is *Brown* v. *Board of Education,* 347 U.S. 483 (1954). The Court's rulings on abortion and racial discrimination are discussed in detail in Chapter 10.

5. John Grisham, *The Firm* (New York: Doubleday, 1991), and Scott Turow, *Presumed Innocent* (New York: Farrar, Straus, Giroux, 1987).

6. See the discussion in Mary Ann Glendon, *Rights Talk; The Impoverishment of Political Discourse* (New York: Maxwell Macmillan, 1991).

7. In June, 1989, the Gallup polling organization asked 1235 interviewees: "How much confidence do you have in the ability of the courts to convict and properly sentence criminals?" Fifty-nine percent of the interviewees responded "not very much" and another fourteen percent indicated "none." Both these data represent increases from interviewees' responses to the same questions in 1985. See *The Gallup Report* 285 (June 1989), p. 27.

8. In September and October, 1986, the Louis Harris polling organization asked 2008 interviewees if they agreed or disagreed with the following statement about the civil justice system: "The overall cost of the system to society is reasonable." Fifty-four percent of respondents disagreed with the statement, and another nine percent answered "not sure." These data are reported in *Public Attitudes Toward the Civil Justice System and Tort Law Reform* (New York: Louis Harris and Associates, 1987), p. 20, Table 2-1.

9. The text of President Bush's acceptance speech is found in *New York Times,* August 21, 1992, p. 14.

10. For differing interpretations of these reform proposals, see Deborah R. Hensler, "Taking Aim at the American Legal System: The Council on Competitiveness's Agenda for Legal Reform," *Judicature* 75 (February-March 1992): 244-250; and Gregory B. Butler and Brian D. Miller,

"Fiddling While Rome Burns: A Response to Professor Hensler," *Judicature* 75 (February-March 1982): 251-254.

11. See, for example, Christine B. Harrington, *Shadow Justice; The Ideology and Institutionalization of Alternatives to Court* (Westport, Conn.: Greenwood Press, 1985); Marc Galanter, "Reading the Landscape of Disputes: What We Know and Don't Know (and Think We Know) about Our Allegedly Contentious and Litigious Society," *UCLA Law Review* 31 (1983): 4-71; and Stephen Daniels, "The Question of Jury Competence and the Politics of Civil Justice Reform: Symbols, Rhetoric, and Agenda-Building," *Law and Contemporary Problems* 52 (Autumn 1989): 269-310.

12. Major works analyzing contemporary legal systems include Konrad Zweigert and Hein Kotz, *Introduction to Comparative Law,* 2nd revised edition (Oxford: Clarendon Press, 1987), and Rene David and John Brierly, *Major Legal Systems of the World Today,* 2nd edition (London: Stevens & Sons, 1978).

13. See Yosiyuki Noda, *Introduction to Japanese Law,* trans. and ed. by Anthony H. Angelo (Tokyo: University of Tokyo Press, 1976).

14. This account of the development of the common law in England relies primarily upon Theodore F. T. Plucknett, *A Concise History of the Common Law,* 5th edition (Boston: Little, Brown, 1956), and Geoffrey R. Y. Radcliffe and Geoffrey N. Cross, *English Legal System,* 6th edition, edited by Geoffrey J. Hand and David J. Bently (London: Butterworths, 1977).

15. Plucknett, *History of the Common Law,* p. 104.

16. William Blackstone, *Commentaries on the Law of England,* vol. I (Chicago: University of Chicago Press, 1979), p. 63.

17. Blackstone, *Commentaries,* p. 69.

18. Plucknett, *History of the Common Law,* p. 342.

19. Roscoe Pound, *The Spirit of the Common Law* (Francestown, N.H.: Marshall Jones Co., 1921), p. 1.

20. William E. Nelson, *Americanization of the Common Law: The Impact of Legal Change on Massachusetts Society, 1760-1830* (Cambridge: Harvard University Press, 1975).

21. Morton J. Horwitz, *The Transformation of American Law, 1780-1860* (Cambridge: Harvard University Press, 1977).

22. Our account of the rediscovery of Roman law relies upon Zweigert and Kotz, *Introduction to Comparative Law,* pp. 76-86; David and Brierly, *Major Legal Systems of the World Today,* pp. 33-59; and Alan Watson, *The Making of the Civil Law* (Cambridge: Harvard University Press, 1981), Chapters 1-3.

23. Our account of the creation of the Napoleonic Code and its consequences derives from Zweigert and Kotz, *Introduction to Comparative Law,* pp. 82-122, and Watson, *The Making of the Civil Law,* Chapters 8-9.

24. Our analysis here follows that of Zweigert and Kotz, *Introduction to Comparative Law*, Chapter 20.

25. Thomas Mackay Cooper, "The Common Law and the Civil Law—A Scot's View," *Harvard Law Review* 63 (January 1950), pp. 470-471.

26. John H. Merryman, *The Civil Law Tradition* (Stanford, Calif.: Stanford University Press, 1969), p. 100.

27. United States Constitution, Article VI, section 2.

28. For a recent listing of federal and state statutes invalidated by the United States Supreme Court, see *The Constitution of the United States of America; Analysis and Interpretation* (Washington, D.C.: Government Printing Office, 1987), pp. 1883-1912 (acts of Congress) and 1913-2114 (state laws), and the supplements updating the volume.

29. This account of administrative law relies chiefly upon E. Allan Farnsworth, *An Introduction to the Legal System of the United States*, 2nd edition (London: Oceana Publications, 1983), pp. 134-138.

30. Our definitions of criminal and civil law are derived from *Black's Law Dictionary; Centennial Edition*, 6th ed. (St. Paul: West, 1990). For detailed discussion of the distinction between criminal and civil law, see Farnsworth, *Introduction to the Legal System of the United States*, pp. 148-152.

31. Our discussion here follows that of Edgar Bodenheimer, John Bilyeu Oakley, and Jean C. Love, *An Introduction to the Anglo-American Legal System* (St. Paul, Minn.: West Publishing Co., 1980), pp. 10-11, and Farnsworth, *Introduction to the Legal System of the United States*, pp. 84-85.

32. Our account of the development of equity relies on Gary L. McDowell, *Equity and the Constitution* (Chicago: University of Chicago Press, 1982), Chapter 1; David and Brierly, *Major Legal Systems of the World Today*, pp. 300-306; and Zweigert and Kotz, *Introduction to Comparative Law*, pp. 194-198.

33. Zweigert and Kotz, *Introduction to Comparative Law*, p. 195.

34. For discussion of the development of the courts in New Jersey, see G. Alan Tarr and Mary Cornelia Aldis Porter, *State Supreme Courts in State and Nation* (New Haven: Yale University Press, 1988), pp. 186-191.

35. See Gary L. McDowell, *Equity and the Constitution: The Supreme Court, Equitable Relief, and Public Policy*, especially Chapter 1.

36. Oliver Wendell Holmes, "The Path of the Law," *Harvard Law Review* 10 (1897), quoted in Walter F. Murphy and C. Herman Pritchett, eds., *Courts, Judges, and Politics*, 2nd ed. (New York: Random House, 1974), p. 21.

37. *Lee* v. *Weisman*, 60 L.W. 4723 (1992).

38. The establishment clause states: "Congress shall make no law respecting an establishment of religion." Originally a limitation only on the national government, the establishment clause was

incorporated (made applicable to state and local governments) through the due process clause of the Fourteenth Amendment, in *Everson* v. *Board of Education*, 330 U.S. 1 (1947).

39. This topic is covered in greater detail in Chapter 9.

40. The reference to the judicial responsibility to "say what the law is" is drawn from *Marbury* v. *Madison*, 5 U.S. (1 Cranch) 137, 173 (1803).

41. Alexis de Tocqueville, *Democracy in America*, ed. J. P. Mayer (Garden City, N.Y.: Doubleday, 1969), p. 270.

42. See, for example, Nathan Glazer, "Towards an Imperial Judiciary?" *The Public Interest* 41 (Fall 1975): 104-123.

43. See Stuart A. Scheingold, *The Politics of Rights: Lawyers, Public Policy, and Political Change* (New Haven: Yale University Press, 1974); Charles A. Johnson and Bradley C. Canon, *Judicial Policies: Implementation and Impact* (Washington, D.C.: Congressional Quarterly Press, 1984); and Gerald N. Rosenberg, *The Hollow Hope; Can Courts Bring About Social Change?* (Chicago: University of Chicago Press, 1991).

44. *Regents of the University of California* v. *Bakke*, 438 U.S. 265 (1978).

45. For background on the *Bakke* case, see Allan P. Sindler, *Bakke, DeFunis, and Minority Admissions: The Quest for Equal Opportunity* (New York: Longman, 1978), and Bernard Schwartz, *Behind Bakke: Affirmative Action and the Supreme Court* (New York: New York University Press, 1988).

46. Reactions to the *Bakke* ruling are reported in Schwartz, *Behind Bakke*, and in Ron Simmons, *Affirmative Action; Conflict and Change in Higher Education After Bakke* (Cambridge: Schenckman Publishing Co., 1982).

47. For data on the use of affirmative action in admissions, see Simmons, *Affirmative Action*, Appendix I.

48. *Brown* v. *Board of Education*, 347 U.S. 483 (1954). The figures on the response to *Brown* are drawn from Rosenberg, *The Hollow Hope*, p. 50, Table 2.1. For further discussion of the response to *Brown*, see Chapter 10.

49. *Texas* v. *Johnson*, 491 U.S. 397 (1989).

50. *Roe* v. *Wade*, 410 U.S. 113 (1973). For a detailed discussion of the response to *Roe*, see Chapter 10.

51. This point is emphasized in Rosenberg, *The Hollow Hope*, Chapter 1, and documented in the case studies throughout that volume.

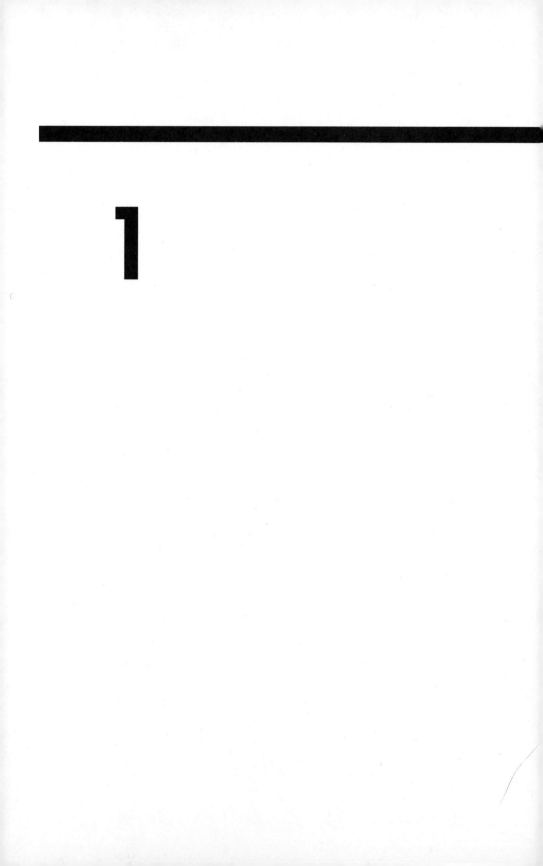

1

STRUCTURES AND PARTICIPANTS IN THE JUDICIAL PROCESS

2

THE FEDERAL
AND STATE
COURT SYSTEMS

On its face, the case seemed routine. Although Clarence Earl Gideon was not a professional criminal, at age fifty-seven he had a history of run-ins with the law and had four times been convicted of minor felonies and imprisoned. Thus, when he was charged with breaking into a poolroom in Bay Harbor, Florida with intent to commit petty larceny, it seemed like merely another episode in Gideon's rather unsuccessful criminal career.[1]

Gideon was tried before a six-member jury in one of Florida's circuit (trial) courts in August, 1961. At the outset of the trial, Gideon requested that a lawyer be appointed to defend him, because he was too poor to hire one himself. But the judge refused Gideon's request, maintaining that neither Florida law nor the United States Constitution required that an attorney be provided. The trial thus commenced with Gideon representing himself.

One prosecution witness testified that he had seen Gideon leaving the poolroom carrying a pint of wine at 5:30 A.M. on the morning of the break-in. The eyewitness also claimed that, looking into the poolroom, he could see that someone had removed the front of the cigarette machine and emptied its money box. The operator of the poolroom confirmed that a window had been smashed and the cigarette machine and the jukebox broken into. Gideon's cross-examination of the witnesses was unfocused and ineffectual, and he offered no explanation for why he was outside the poolroom in the early morning. The jury quickly convicted Gideon, and three weeks later Judge Robert McCrary sentenced him to five years in prison.

This, however, did not end the case. Writing from his prison cell, Gideon petitioned the Florida Supreme Court for a writ of habeas corpus, a legal order freeing him on the ground that he was illegally imprisoned. The Florida justices denied Gideon's petition, rejecting his claim that the United States Constitution guaranteed him a right to an attorney at trial. Gideon then appealed the Florida Supreme Court's decision to the United States Supreme Court, requesting that the Court agree to review his case.

The Supreme Court annually receives hundreds of petitions from prisoners claiming that their trials were unfair and that they should be released. Thus, Gideon's petition—four pages painstakingly printed in pencil on lined paper— was hardly unique. Most of these petitions lack substantial legal merit and are dismissed by the Court. In this instance, however, the justices granted Gideon's petition in order to consider whether the Constitution requires states to provide a defense attorney to poor defendants in criminal cases. After receiving legal briefs and hearing oral argument from Florida's Assistant Attorney General and from Abe Fortas, a prominent Washington attorney appointed by the Court to represent Gideon, the justices unanimously ruled in Gideon's favor. Overruling a twenty-year-old precedent, *Betts* v. *Brady* (1942), the Court concluded that the Sixth Amendment, which was made applicable to the states by the Fourteenth Amendment, required that the states provide counsel for indigent defendants in felony cases.[2]

The Supreme Court's decision in *Gideon v. Wainwright*[3] overturned Gideon's conviction, but it did not decide his fate. The state of Florida appointed an attorney to represent Gideon and proceeded to retry him for the break-in. Having an attorney at trial made all the difference for Gideon. Gideon's lawyer deftly undermined the credibility of the prosecution's eyewitness, and after an hour's deliberation, the jury returned a verdict of not guilty.

The story of Clarence Gideon illustrates several basic aspects of the structure and operation of courts in the United States:

A dual court system: Under American federalism each of the fifty states operates its own judicial system. So too does the federal government. Although the state and federal judicial systems are separate, federal and state courts can both rule on the same case. *Gideon* v. *Wainwright,* for example, began in a Florida state court, was appealed to the United States Supreme Court, and eventually was returned to a Florida trial court for resolution.

Gideon's case, however, is atypical. The vast majority of cases remain in the judicial system in which they are initiated. Indeed, this might well have happened in Gideon's case. Had he not appealed the Florida Supreme Court's ruling, his case would have been resolved within the state judicial system; and if the United States Supreme Court had refused to review that ruling, the Florida court's decision would have been final.

Separate courts performing distinct functions: Gideon's case was considered by two different types of courts, each of which played a distinct role in the resolution of the case. The Florida Circuit Court served as the trial court, hearing evidence from witnesses about the facts of the case, deciding whether Gideon was innocent or guilty, and imposing sentence following his conviction. When Gideon appealed his conviction to the Florida Supreme Court and then to the U.S. Supreme Court, the issue changed, and so too did the function of the courts. For these appellate courts (courts that review the rulings of lower courts), the concern was less Gideon's factual guilt or innocence and more the legal correctness of the procedures under which Gideon was convicted. Thus, when the Florida Supreme Court concluded that the trial judge had acted properly in refusing to appoint a lawyer to defend Gideon, it upheld his conviction. When the U.S. Supreme Court ruled that the judge had erred and that Gideon was entitled to a lawyer, it did not decide his guilt or innocence. Rather, it sent the case back for a new trial at which Gideon's right to counsel was honored.

Hierarchies of courts: Not only are there various types of courts but those courts are hierarchically arranged. This means that cases follow a set path when they move from one court to another, proceeding step by step from the lowest court up the various rungs of the judicial ladder. In *Gideon,* for example, the case began in a Florida trial court, moved to the highest court in the state, and then to the nation's highest court, the United States Supreme Court. In addition, the hierarchical arrangement of courts reflects the authority exercised by some courts over others. Lower courts are legally obliged to abide by the rulings of higher courts. Thus, once the Supreme Court had ruled in *Gideon* that states must furnish an attorney to indigent defendants, the Florida court retrying Gideon had to comply with the ruling and appoint a lawyer to defend him.

Multiple bodies of law: Just as both the state and federal governments have their own court systems, so too each has its own body of law. It might seem logical therefore for state courts to decide cases involving state law and federal courts cases involving federal law. In actuality, however, the rules governing the jurisdiction of American courts—that is, the types of cases a court is authorized to decide—are not that simple. For one thing, a single case might involve more than one body of law. Gideon, for example, was convicted of violating a Florida criminal statute in a court established by the constitution and laws of Florida. However, he claimed that the United States Constitution guaranteed him the right to an attorney. Thus, the Florida courts in Gideon's case had to consider both state law (the criminal statute) and federal law (the constitutional rights guaranteed to defendants in state court).

Having highlighted some of the intricacies of the structure and operation of American courts, we now turn to a more detailed treatment of those courts, beginning with the federal judicial system.

THE FEDERAL COURT SYSTEM

Structure

Although Article III of the Federal Constitution establishes only the United States Supreme Court, it authorizes "such inferior Courts as the Congress may from time to time ordain and establish."[4] The courts that Congress creates under Article III of the Constitution are known as constitutional courts (or Article III courts), and those it creates under Article I are known as legislative courts (or Article I courts). Constitutional courts handle the bulk of federal litigation. The independence of their judges is secured by constitutional guarantees that the judges serve during "good behavior" and that their salaries cannot be reduced while they remain in office.[5] By contrast, legislative courts may have administrative and quasi-legislative responsibilities, as well as judicial duties. Congressional statutes determine how long judges on legislative courts shall serve and whether their salaries can be reduced. Because they do not have the Article III guarantees of judicial independence, the Supreme Court ruled in 1982 that judges on legislative courts cannot be assigned the same duties and jurisdiction as judges on constitutional courts.[6] In fact, legislative courts usually have quite specialized jurisdictions—current legislative courts include, for example, the U.S. Court of Military Appeals and the Court of International Trade. Thus Table 2.1, which lists specialized federal courts, includes several legislative courts.

Figure 2.1 outlines the organization of the federal judicial system. Despite the multiplicity of courts, the structure of the federal judicial system is really quite simple—basically, a three-tiered structure. The most important federal courts are the constitutional courts: the district courts, the courts of appeals, and the United States Supreme Court. The district courts serve as the primary trial courts of the federal judicial system. Most federal cases originate in the district courts and are resolved by those courts. However, dissatisfied litigants may appeal the district courts' rulings to the courts of appeals, the main first-level appellate courts. The United States Supreme Court is the sole second-level appellate court, the court of last resort. It hears some appeals from the courts of appeals, from various specialized federal courts, and—when questions of federal law are involved—from state supreme courts. In some cases, it may also hear appeals directly from federal district courts. Whereas the district courts and the

TABLE 2-1 SPECIALIZED FEDERAL COURTS				
Court	**Date Established**	**Level of Court**	**Status of Judges**	**Constitutional Basis**	**Jurisdiction**
Tax Court	1942[a]	Trial	Permanent	Article I	Federal taxes
Claims Court	1982[b]	Trial	Permanent	Article I	Claims against the Federal Government for violations of the law, of contracts, of patents, or of copyrights
Court of Military Appeals	1950	Appellate	Permanent	Article I	Criminal appeals from courts martial
Court of International Trade	1980[c]	Trial	Permanent	Article III	Suits against or by the Federal Government under tariff laws
Court of Appeals for the Federal Circuit	1982	Appellate	Permanent	Article III	Patents, trademarks, foreign trade, suits against the Federal Government
Temporary Emergency Court of Appeals	1971	Appellate	Borrowed	—	Economic stabilization and energy laws
Special Court on Regional Rail Reorganization	1973	Trial	Borrowed	—	Railroad reorganization
Foreign Intelligence Surveillance Court	1978	Trial	Borrowed	—	Warrants for foreign intelligence surveillance
Foreign Intelligence Surveillance Court of Review	1978	Appellate	Borrowed	—	Warrants for foreign intelligence surveillance
Court of Veterans Appeals	1988	Appellate	Permanent	Article I	Appeals from the Board of Veterans Appeals, relating to veterans' benefits

SOURCE: Lawrence Baum, *American Courts; Process and Policy.* Second Edition. Copyright (c) 1990 by Houghton Mifflin Company. Page 37, Table 2.2. Adapted with permission.

KEY: a - established as an independent agency in the executive branch in 1924, became the Tax Court of the United States in 1942, and assumed its current name in 1969

b - successor to the United States Court of Claims, established in 1855

c - originally established as the Board of U. S. General Appraisers in 1890, named the U. S. Customs Court in 1926, integrated into the federal court structure in 1956, and given its present name in 1980

FIGURE 2-1   THE FEDERAL COURT SYSTEM

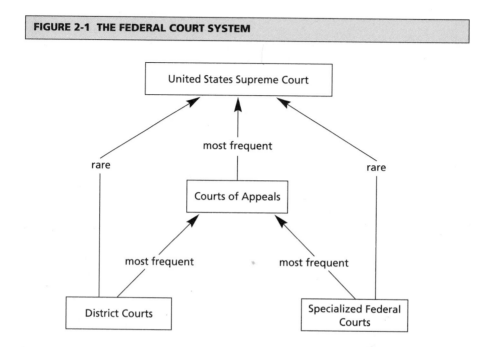

courts of appeals must decide all cases that are properly brought before them, the Supreme Court has broad discretion in choosing what cases it will hear.

The Development of the Federal Judicial System[7]

The Creation of the Federal Judicial System

Political conflict over the structure of the federal judicial system has erupted periodically throughout American history. The conflict began at the Constitutional Convention of 1787. Although the delegates agreed that a national judiciary should be established, they disagreed sharply over its structure and organization. Some delegates wanted only a single federal court, a supreme court, which would review state court decisions on matters of federal concern. Other delegates, among them James Madison, distrusted state courts and insisted that federal trial courts should also be instituted. Rather than resolving the conflict, the delegates in effect postponed it. Article III created the U.S. Supreme Court but left the creation of additional courts to Congress.

As its first order of business, Congress enacted the Judiciary Act of 1789, establishing the nation's judicial system. Atop the structure was a Supreme

Court of six justices. The Act also provided for two tiers of federal trial courts. The thirteen district courts were each staffed with a single district judge. Although the number of districts and judges has of course increased, this set of federal trial courts, organized along geographic lines that do not overlap state boundaries, has survived to the present day. Less familiar is the second set of trial courts created in 1789, the three circuit courts. These courts had no judges of their own. They operated in three-judge panels consisting—at least at the outset—of the district court judge for the district and two Supreme Court justices who "rode circuit" to hear cases.

From the very beginning these circuit courts posed problems. The roads and means of transportation in the new nation were primitive, and the justices found themselves riding circuit almost constantly. As early as 1792, they complained to Congress, arguing that it was "too burdensome" for them "to pass the greater part of their days on the road, and at inns, and at a distance from their families."[8] Advocates of state power, however, opposed the creation of circuit-court judges, fearing that increasing the number of federal judges would permit more cases to be routed to federal courts. When Congress finally did create circuit judges in 1801, the partisan fashion in which it proceeded virtually guaranteed that the reform would not last. After having lost the election of 1800, President John Adams and the lame-duck Federalists who controlled Congress pushed through legislation that abolished circuit riding and created judgeships for each circuit. Adams then proceeded to appoint Federalists to all the new positions. Incoming president Thomas Jefferson and his Democratic-Republican Party were outraged, and in 1802 Congress—now controlled by Jefferson's party—abolished the new judgeships and reinstituted circuit riding.[9]

The Nineteenth and Twentieth Centuries

Throughout most of the nineteenth century, the basic structure of the federal judicial system remained unchanged. In 1891 Congress added a new set of courts, the circuit courts of appeals, in order to expand the capacity of the federal courts to hear appeals and to relieve caseload pressures on the Supreme Court. These courts, now simply called the courts of appeals, remain a vital component of the federal judicial system. In 1911 Congress completed the basic structure of the modern federal judicial system by abolishing the circuit courts and transferring their responsibilities for conducting trials to the district courts.

Since 1911, two important changes have occurred in the structure of the federal judicial system. First, Congress has accommodated the growth in federal courts' caseloads "by increasing the number of geographic units into which the system is divided."[10] Thus in 1980 Congress created a new court of appeals by dividing the overburdened Fifth Circuit in two, with the old Fifth Circuit becoming the new Fifth and Eleventh Circuits.[11] Congress has also created new district courts as conditions have warranted.

Second, Congress has added various specialized legislative courts to the federal judicial system. Although the first specialized federal court, the United States Court of Claims, was established in 1855, most of these courts were created relatively recently. Some of these specialized courts resolve cases arising under particular statutes. For example, the United States Tax Court, originally part of the Internal Revenue Service, was established as an independent court in 1969 and charged with deciding taxpayer challenges to income tax assessments. Other specialized courts deal with cases in a specific area of the law. The U.S. Court of Military Appeals (1950) hears appeals from court martial convictions, and, as its name suggests, the Foreign Intelligence Surveillance Court (1978) oversees the issuance of warrants to use electronic surveillance to acquire "foreign" intelligence within the United States.

Congress has thus far rejected proposals for more fundamental structural changes. One controversial proposal, introduced in the 1970s and periodically revived, is for a national court of appeals, which would be positioned between the Supreme Court and the existing courts of appeals. According to its proponents, who include such luminaries as Chief Justice William Rehnquist and his predecessor Warren Burger, such a court is needed to help the Supreme Court with its work.[12] The new court would take over screening petitions for Supreme Court review and would resolve conflicting interpretations of federal law by the various appeals courts. However, several former justices—among them, Justice Arthur Goldberg and Justice William Brennan—have objected that screening cases is the way the Court determines its agenda.[13] Delegating this function to another court, they argued, would undermine the Court's ability to set its own course and, thus, diminish its role within the American governmental system. One wonders, for example, whether Clarence Gideon's petition would have been accepted by the national court of appeals.

Whatever the merits of the opposing views, the controversy over a national court of appeals underscores two more general points about the reform of the federal judicial system. First, even when problems have been obvious, Congress has tended to act slowly and to prefer marginal adjustments rather than fundamental reforms. Second, Congress's reluctance to act has reflected a recognition that proposals designed to increase efficiency can, as the opponents of the National Court of Appeals pointed out, have unforeseen effects on the operation and decisions of the federal courts.

Federal Jurisdiction

The Law of Federal Jurisdiction

For a court to decide a case, the case must fall within its jurisdiction, that is, the range of cases that it is empowered to rule on by constitutional provision or by statute.   Article III of the United States Constitution sets the outer reaches of the federal judicial power by specifying the types of cases that federal courts may be empowered to hear.[14]   Table 2-2 describes the scope of the federal judicial power and explains why those types of cases were given to the federal courts.

Within these boundaries, the Constitution generally leaves it to Congress to define the jurisdiction of the various federal courts. Congress is not obliged to vest the full federal judicial power in the federal courts.[15] Thus, congressional legislation largely determines the actual division of responsibility between federal and state courts and among federal courts.

TABLE 2-2 THE FEDERAL JUDICIAL POWER

Article III of the U.S. Constitution defines the federal judicial power. Underlying the specific grants of power are four basic purposes:

1. Vindicating the authority of the federal government
    a. Cases arising under the laws of the United States
    b. Cases arising under the United States Constitution
    c. Cases in which the federal government is a party

2. Maintaining the exclusive control of the federal government over foreign relations
    a. Admiralty and maritime cases
    b. Cases arising under treaties
    c. Cases affecting ambassadors or other representatives of foreign countries
    d. Cases between states, or the citizens thereof, and foreign states, citizens, or subjects

3. Umpiring interstate disputes
    a. Controversies between two or more states
    b. Controversies between a state and the citizen of another state

4. Protecting out-of-state litigants from the possible bias of local tribunals
    a. Controversies between citizens of different states

SOURCE: Adapted from Paul M. Bator, Paul J. Mishkin, David L. Shapiro, and Herbert Wechsler, *The Federal Courts and the Federal System,* 2nd ed. (Mineola, N.Y.: Foundation Press, 1973).

The bases for exercising federal jurisdiction are diverse and complex. The subject matter of a case, the identity of the parties to a case, or the citizenship of those parties all may provide the basis for federal courts to hear the case. For example, a job applicant may sue an employer for discrimination in federal court (a) if the statute securing the right against employment discrimination is a federal statute, or (b) if the employer is the federal government or one of its agencies, or (c) if the employer and the job applicant are citizens of different states. If the job applicant sues in a state court, and the employer and job applicant are citizens of different states, the employer can have the case transferred to a federal district court on the basis of diversity of citizenship.

Although the federal judicial power is extensive, it hardly extends to all possible cases. When a person is charged with violating a state criminal statute, the case is heard in state court. Most criminal statutes—for example, those involving theft, armed robbery, and rape—are state statutes, and most criminal prosecutions occur in state court. State courts also have exclusive jurisdiction when a civil case involves only state law and the parties to the case are each citizens of a single state. Since the vast majority of civil cases have that character, they likewise are heard in state courts.

Congress has not required that all cases arising under the federal judicial power be heard in federal court. Instead, it has allowed state courts to decide some of these cases by generally granting concurrent, rather than exclusive, jurisdiction to federal courts. What this means is that, with a few exceptions like criminal cases based on federal statutes, cases that could be filed in federal court can be initiated in state courts as well. Lawyers, thus, can choose to file a case in the court where they believe they have the best chance of winning or where they expect the highest awards should they win. Throughout the nation's history, Congress has also limited the jurisdiction of federal courts. One example is federal jurisdiction over "diversity-of-citizenship" cases. Although the Constitution permits federal courts to be assigned all cases involving a suit by a citizen of one state against the citizen of another state, Congress has restricted federal courts to those cases in which a sizable amount is involved. As a result of legislation enacted by Congress in 1988, federal courts can hear "diversity" cases only when at least $50,000 is at stake.

The Politics of Federal Jurisdiction[16]

Federalism and Federal Jurisdiction

Although federal jurisdiction might seem merely a technical concern, it has generated intense, if episodic, political conflict for over two centuries. During the nation's first century, the conflict over federal jurisdiction centered largely on questions of federalism. Nationalists in Congress sought to enlarge federal jurisdiction, while champions of states' rights attempted to maintain the prerogatives of state courts, assuming those courts would reflect a more localistic perspective.

The Judiciary Act of 1789 was a partial victory for both the nationalists and the states' rights advocates. Congress created lower federal courts, as the nationalists wished. However, it severely limited their jurisdiction. Federal district courts were vested with jurisdiction only over admiralty cases and petty crimes—those for which punishment could not exceed six months in jail, a fine of $100, or thirty stripes of whipping. Federal circuit courts, the main trial courts, could hear diversity-of-citizenship cases (where more than $500 was at stake), major criminal cases arising under federal law, and appeals from the district courts in admiralty cases. But neither district nor circuit courts were given jurisdiction over all cases arising under federal law ("federal question" cases). Thus, many of these "federal question" cases were heard in state courts. Not until 1875 were federal trial courts awarded this "federal question" jurisdiction.

The appellate jurisdiction of the Supreme Court was likewise circumscribed under the Judiciary Act of 1789. The Court could not review federal court rulings in criminal cases. Moreover, it could review state rulings involving federal constitutional claims only if the state judges rejected the constitutional claim and upheld the challenged state law. Underlying this latter limitation was the assumption that, whereas state judges might be prone to favor state law against federal claims, they would be unlikely to expand federal restrictions on the governing power of the states.

The strength of states' rights forces was also manifest in a controversy that erupted just four years after the passage of the Judiciary Act of 1789. In *Chisholm* v. *Georgia*[17] the Supreme Court ruled that the executor of the estate of a South Carolina citizen could sue the State of Georgia in federal court to recover payment for war supplies that were sold to the state during the American Revolution. The Court's decision was a faithful reading of Article III of the Constitution, which authorized federal courts to hear disputes "between a state and citizens of another state." However, states rights' advocates were outraged, detecting a threat to state sovereignty in the Court's ruling. The lower house of the Georgia legislature responded by passing a bill to punish by hanging without benefit of clergy any person aiding in the enforcement of the *Chisholm* decision.[18] A more lasting response was the adoption of the Eleventh Amendment, which prohibited the federal courts from hearing suits against a state by a citizen of another state or of a foreign country.[19]

The Impact of the Civil War

Following the Civil War, the issue of federal jurisdiction reemerged, but this time a nationalist perspective prevailed. Congress suspected, with good reason, that state courts—especially in the Southern states—might be unwilling to vindicate the rights of the newly freed slaves. To ensure that those rights were protected, it expanded the jurisdiction of the federal courts. The Habeas Corpus Act of 1867 enabled all persons in custody "in violation of the constitution, or of any treaty or law of the United States" to seek redress in federal court. This in effect authorized federal courts to oversee state courts in criminal cases to ensure that defendants were not imprisoned in violation of federal law. The Judiciary Act of 1875 conferred on the federal courts jurisdiction in all cases involving questions of federal law and in all diversity cases where more than $500 was at stake. This ensured that those who believed their federal rights had been infringed could get a hearing before a federal judge.

Congress versus the Courts

Since the late nineteenth century, changes in federal jurisdiction have reflected either congressional dissatisfaction with judicial decisions or a concern to relieve the caseload pressures on the federal courts. An example of the former is a law enacted in 1914, which empowered the Supreme Court to review all state rulings that relied on federal law. Congress's action was in response to *Ives* v. *South Buffalo Railway*[20], in which New York's supreme court ruled that the state's workmen's compensation act (the first in the nation) violated the federal constitution. Because most members of Congress favored such legislation and believed it constitutional, they wanted the Supreme Court to be able to overturn excessive constraints placed on state legislatures by state courts. The congressional enactment ensured that state courts could not restrict state power on federal constitutional grounds more than was authorized by the Supreme Court. More recently, during the 1970s and 1980s, Senator Jesse Helms of North Carolina and other conservative members of Congress—distressed by the Supreme Court's rulings on such matters as abortion, school prayer, and school busing—proposed legislation to restrict the power of federal courts to rule in cases involving those issues.[21] Underlying these bills was the hope that state courts, which would hear the cases if the federal courts could not, would decide cases involving these issues differently than had the federal courts. However, none of the bills that the conservatives introduced was enacted.

Caseloads and Federal Jurisdiction

The concern about caseload pressures on the federal courts emerged following Congress's expansion of the federal courts' jurisdiction in 1875. Congress's action created a demand for court services that those courts were ill-equipped to handle.   Data on pending cases in the circuit and district courts illustrate the heavy caseloads in those courts.   In 1873 federal trial courts had 29,013 pending cases.   Following the expansion of federal jurisdiction in 1875, however, the number of pending cases jumped to 38,045 by 1880 and to 54,194 by 1890. Similar caseload problems plagued the Supreme Court: its docket rose from 636 cases in 1870 to 1212 in 1880 to an astronomical 1816 cases in 1890.[22]

Congress has attempted to alleviate the caseload pressures on the Supreme Court by reducing its mandatory jurisdiction, that is, those cases it is legally obliged to hear.   Until 1925 the Court had relatively little control over what cases it decided, because Congress had awarded litigants a right of appeal to the Supreme Court. The Judges' Bill of 1925—so named because it was drafted by Chief Justice William Howard Taft and supported by the other justices—dramatically altered the Court's jurisdiction by giving the justices broad discretion in choosing their cases. This reform temporarily relieved case pressures. Since 1925, as caseloads have again mounted, Congress has incrementally eliminated more and more of the Supreme Court's mandatory jurisdiction.   In 1988 Congress gave the Court almost total discretion in setting its agenda. (The proposal for a national court of appeals, discussed earlier (pp. 29), represents another attempt to alleviate the caseload pressures on the Court.)

The contraction of the Supreme Court's mandatory jurisdiction, although prompted by caseload concerns, has also affected how the Court views its responsibilities. Relieving the Court of relatively unimportant cases has allowed it to focus its attention on those cases that are crucial to the development of federal law.   The justices now deliberately choose the cases they hear with that function in mind.   Thus the reform of the Court's jurisdiction has produced effects probably never contemplated by its proponents.

As we have seen, Congress has sought to ease caseload pressures on federal district and appeals courts by increasing the number of courts and judges.   Some scholars and jurists—most notably Chief Justice William Rehnquist—have proposed reducing the caseloads of federal district and appeals courts by eliminating their diversity-of-citizenship jurisdiction.[23]   These reformers insist that state courts today treat residents and non-residents even-handedly.   Thus, the original justification for the diversity jurisdiction (avoiding possible bias against non-residents in state courts) no longer exists. Certainly shifting diversity cases to state courts would have an effect on caseloads: in 1988 diversity-of-citizenship cases accounted for over 28% of all civil cases filed in federal district courts.[24] Opposing this change have been the American Bar Association and various trial lawyers' organizations, who argue that federal courts do a better job of dispensing justice than do state courts.[25]   Thus far, these groups have successfully blocked efforts to curtail federal jurisdiction over diversity cases.

Although both proponents and opponents of this reform may be sincerely concerned about the just and efficient operation of the federal judicial system, this is not all that is involved. Because of the different procedural rules in federal and state courts, attorneys find that their clients may have a better chance of presenting their case or winning it in one forum rather than in another.[26] The fact that some litigants seek to have their cases heard in federal court and others in state court indicates a perception that where a case is heard makes a difference. Finally, the transfer of diversity cases to state courts will increase the caseloads of those courts.[27] Thus we see once again that reforms designed to promote efficiency may have other effects as well.

THE FEDERAL COURTS TODAY

The District Courts

Most federal cases begin (and end) in the district courts, the primary trial courts of the federal judicial system. To hear these cases, Congress has established ninety-four district courts, staffed by 649 judges (as of January, 1993), serving the fifty states, the District of Columbia, and some U.S. territories. As Figure 2-2 indicates, every state has at least one district court, and no district extends beyond the borders of a single state. Larger or more populous states are divided into more than one district, with three states—California, New York, and Texas—each having four district courts.

Every district court has at least two judges. The number of judges assigned to a district court, however, depends on its caseload and thus varies considerably from district to district. The Southern District of New York, which includes Manhattan and the Bronx, is currently the nation's largest with 27 district judges. By federal law, reapportionment cases and voting rights cases must be heard by three-judge panels, comprised of two district court judges and one appeals court judge. But the vast majority of cases in district courts are tried before a single judge. District courts can therefore hear several cases simultaneously at courthouses located throughout the district.

The Cases

District courts exercise no discretion over the cases they confront. Any litigant who satisfies the jurisdictional requirements and follows proper legal procedures can initiate a case in federal district court. However, a federal district court cannot address a legal issue unless a litigant brings it before the court in a bona fide

FIGURE 2-2 FEDERAL DISTRICT COURTS AND COURTS OF APPEALS

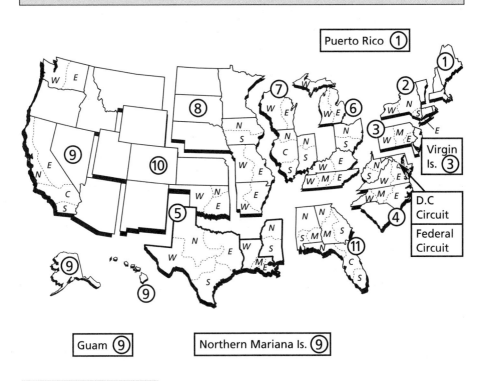

SOURCE: This figure is adapted from Russell Wheeler and Cynthia Harrison, *Creating the Federal Judicial System* (Washington, D.C.: Federal Judicial Center, 1989), Figure 4. The letters and boundaries within states refer to federal court districts with states (W=West, C=Central, etc.). The circled numbers refer to federal appellate circuits.

case. Thus, the business of the district courts is determined solely by litigant demand.

Over the past few decades, the filings in federal district courts have risen sharply: from 87,421 cases in 1960 to 279,524 cases in 1989.[28] Within the past few years, however, overall filings have declined slightly. A decline in civil filings from a high of 273,670 in 1985 to 233,529 in 1989 has more than offset a continuing rise in criminal cases.[29]

Congressional legislation and executive-branch actions affect the number and types of cases brought before the district courts. In 1960, for example, only

306 civil rights cases were filed in district courts. During the 1960s, Congress adopted major civil rights laws, such as the Civil Rights Act of 1964, the Voting Rights Act of 1965, and the Fair Housing Act of 1968. These laws encouraged victims of discrimination to seek redress in the federal courts, and the number of civil rights cases rose accordingly. In 1989, for example, there were 24,174 civil rights cases, accounting for over 10% of all civil cases filed in district courts.[30]

A similar pattern can be seen in criminal cases. During the 1980s, concern mounted about the influx of cocaine and other illegal drugs into the United States, and President Ronald Reagan announced a "war on drugs" to deal with the problem. By devoting more funds and personnel to the interdiction of drugs and to the enforcement of drug laws, the federal government increased its number of drug arrests and thus the number of drug cases coming before the district courts. In the course of the decade, the criminal workload of the district courts increased 50 percent, but drug cases increased over 270 percent and now constitute more than one quarter of the criminal cases in district courts.[31]

Court Operations

In hearing these cases, the district courts may operate as we have come to expect from television and novels. In criminal trials the judge presides, while the prosecutor and defense attorney call witnesses and introduce other evidence designed to prove either the guilt or innocence of the defendant. In trials in civil cases, it is the legal rights or obligations of the plaintiff and defendant that are at issue, but the process is much the same. If it is a jury trial—and just under half of the trials in district courts are—the judge instructs the jury about the law following the presentation of evidence and the attorneys' closing arguments, and the jury decides the case. If there is no jury, the judge decides the case and, when the case has a broader legal significance, may write a judicial opinion explaining the reasons for the decision.

More frequently, however, cases follow a quite different pattern. Most criminal cases in federal district courts are resolved by guilty pleas, and most civil cases by a settlement between the parties following pre-trial negotiations. In such circumstances, of course, no jury is selected, no witnesses called, and no formal courtroom sessions are held except to ratify the decision reached by the parties in the case.

The Courts of Appeals

The courts of appeals are the first-level appellate courts of the federal judicial system. As Figure 2-2 indicates, these courts are organized regionally, with most "circuits" made up of three or more states. Thus, the Fifth Circuit includes Texas, Louisiana, and Mississippi, and the Seventh Circuit includes Illinois, Indiana, and Wisconsin. The sole exception is the Court of Appeals for the District of Columbia, which reviews large numbers of appeals from administrative agencies and serves as a sort of state supreme court for the District of Columbia.[32] The boundaries of most circuits were established long ago, and as population shifts have occurred, some courts of appeals have experienced disproportionate increases in their caseloads. Congress has responded by adding judges to overburdened circuits, and as a result the number of judges varies considerably among the courts of appeals. The First Circuit, which includes Maine, Vermont, New Hampshire, Massachusetts, and—surprisingly—Puerto Rico has the fewest appeals-court judges (6). The Ninth Circuit, which includes Alaska, Washington, Oregon, California, Nevada, Idaho, and Montana, has the most (28).

The Cases

Every litigant in federal court has a right to one appeal. As a result, courts of appeals primarily engage in error correction, overseeing the work of the district courts in cases that are of interest only to the immediate parties.[33] More than three-quarters of their cases come to courts of appeals from district courts within their circuits, with the remainder coming from certain federal administrative agencies and from some specialized courts, such as the Tax Court. The mix of cases varies from circuit to circuit. The Court of Appeals for the Second Circuit, for example, considers large numbers of banking cases because New York City, the hub of the nation's banking, is within its jurisdiction. And because so many federal administrative agencies are located in the District of Columbia, about half the caseload of its court of appeals involves challenges to orders issued by those agencies.[34]

Like the district courts, the courts of appeals have experienced an enormous increase in their caseloads in recent years.[35] Indeed, the figures for the two courts are connected, since an increase in district court rulings means an increase in the number of potential appeals. In 1982, the courts of appeals heard 27,946 cases, but by 1989 the figure had jumped to 39,734.[36] Much of this change reflects the increase in criminal cases currently being heard in district courts and the greater willingness of defendants, particularly in drug cases, to appeal their convictions.[37] From 1988 to 1989, for example, appeals in criminal cases rose over 33 percent, whereas appeals in civil cases rose less than 2 percent.[38] Still, civil cases make up almost 80 percent of the caseload of courts of appeals, which is hardly surprising, given the composition of the caseloads of federal district courts.

Intercourt Relations

After a court of appeals decides a case, a dissatisfied litigant might appeal to the Supreme Court. As Figure 2-3 reveals, however, most litigants accept the appeals court ruling as final, and the Supreme Court generally refuses to hear most appeals. As a result, the courts of appeals have the final say in over 99 percent of the cases they decide.

Over time, a rough division of labor has developed between the courts of appeals and the Supreme Court. As the Supreme Court has become more involved in resolving constitutional disputes, it has in effect ceded primary responsibility for the interpretation of federal statutes and for the supervision of administrative agencies to the courts of appeals.[39] This, however, poses the danger that a court of appeals in one circuit might interpret a statute differently from a court of appeals in another circuit. This would mean that different interpretations of the same law would be authoritative in various regions of the country. What prevents this threat to the uniformity of federal law from posing a serious problem is the tendency of courts of appeals to consider the rulings of sister courts—even if those rulings are not authoritative, they may well be persuasive. When differences in interpretation do emerge, the Supreme Court can also step in to resolve the conflict. In fact, the rules of the Supreme Court list conflict between the circuits as one of the criteria for deciding to hear cases.[40]

Court Operations

The courts of appeals hear over 95 percent of their cases in three-judge panels, deciding cases by majority vote. This means that several cases can be heard simultaneously by different three-judge panels, often sitting in various cities throughout the circuit. In some cases the judges decide on the basis of the written record from the lower court and the legal briefs submitted by the attorneys on each side. Particularly in important cases, however, counsel for each side may present oral argument as well. When the judges have reached a decision in a case, they may announce their decision in a brief order or in a longer written opinion.

Because judges bring different perspectives to the law, the decision an appeals court renders may depend on the composition of the panel that hears the case.[41] In the past, some chief judges were accused of "stacking" the panels to achieve the results they favored.[42] Today, extraordinary efforts are made to prevent this. Judges are rotated so that the same judges do not sit together constantly. The Eleventh Circuit, for example, uses a computer-generated random matrix to set the composition of every panel a year in advance. In addition, each circuit has

FIGURE 2-3 SUPREME COURT REVIEW OF COURT OF APPEALS CASES, 1945-1989

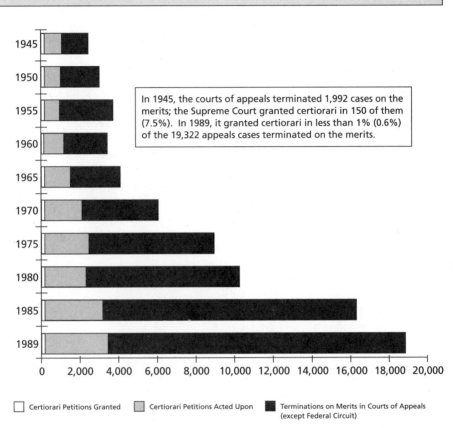

In 1945, the courts of appeals terminated 1,992 cases on the merits; the Supreme Court granted certiorari in 150 of them (7.5%). In 1989, it granted certiorari in less than 1% (0.6%) of the 19,322 appeals cases terminated on the merits.

Certiorari Petitions Granted   Certiorari Petitions Acted Upon   Terminations on Merits in Courts of Appeals (except Federal Circuit)

SOURCE: Cynthia Harrison and Russell Wheeler, *The Federal Appellate Judiciary in the Twenty-First Century* (Washington D.C.: Federal Judicial Center, 1989), p. 260, Figure 8.

developed mechanisms for ensuring randomness in the assignment of cases to panels.[43]

Federal statutes also permit courts of appeals to hear cases *en banc,* that is, with the court's entire membership hearing the case together. Courts of appeals use this procedure to resolve intracircuit conflicts, when different panels within a circuit have reached conflicting results in similar cases. They also may sit *en banc* to decide particularly important cases. Each circuit has discretion to determine when an *en banc* panel is warranted.

The United States Supreme Court

The United States Supreme Court sits at the apex of the federal judicial system. It hears appeals from the federal courts of appeals, from state supreme courts, and—occasionally—from federal district courts or from the Court of Military Appeals. The Constitution also assigns the Supreme Court a very limited original jurisdiction (cases it hears as a trial court), but this rarely involves more than one or two cases per year. Altogether, over 4000 cases are appealed to the Supreme Court each year, and the Court typically accepts less than 5 percent for review. In choosing the cases it will hear, the Court exercises almost total discretion. Because virtually all cases coming to the Court have already been tried and received appellate review, the justices are less concerned with correcting lower-court errors than with establishing legal principles or resolving disputes that have broad national implications. In recent years this has led the Court to focus primarily on constitutional questions—during its 1991-1992 term, for example, over 50 percent of the cases it decided raised constitutional issues.[44]

We shall discuss the operations of the Supreme Court in greater detail in Chapter 5.

STATE COURTS

Justice William Brennan, who served on the New Jersey Supreme Court prior to his elevation to the U.S. Supreme Court, once observed that "the composite work of the courts in the fifty states probably has greater significance [than that of the U.S. Supreme Court] in measuring how well America attains the ideal of equal justice for all."[45] This is true in part because of the sheer volume of cases that state courts decide annually. The trial courts of California, for example, decided over fifteen million cases in 1990, more than fifty times the number decided by federal district courts during the same year.[46] Thus, for most Americans, their personal experience with courts—and the ideas they develop about the fairness of the nation's courts—usually involve state courts.

In addition, the decisions that state courts render have a more direct and immediate impact on the daily lives of ordinary citizens than do most rulings of federal courts. The vast majority of criminal cases are state cases, arising under state criminal laws. Familial matters (divorce, child custody, and adoption) and landlord-tenant relations are regulated by state law and addressed in state court. So too are traffic violations, creditor-debtor disputes, most personal injury suits, and most commercial transactions. These types of issues not only arise in state courts but are ultimately settled by them. Although some state judicial decisions are subject to review by the federal courts, most fall outside the federal judicial power—for example, they resolve disputes under state law between citizens of the same state. Even when the U.S. Supreme Court in theory might review state rulings, the sheer number of state cases means that only a miniscule percentage actually receive federal judicial scrutiny.[47] Thus, state courts render the final and determinative decision in the vast majority of cases they consider, including most cases that announce major policy initiatives.

The Structure of State Court Systems

State court systems share certain basic organizational features (see Figure 2-4):[48]

Supreme court: Forty-eight states vest ultimate appellate authority in a single court, usually designated as the supreme court. (The sole exceptions, Oklahoma and Texas, each have established a Court of Criminal Appeals, which is the court of last resort in criminal cases, and a Supreme Court, which has the final responsibility for appeals in civil cases.) A state supreme court is responsible for the development of state law, and its decisions serve as authoritative precedent within the state court system. Its jurisdiction is defined by the state constitution and/or state statutes. Usually it does not enjoy the nearly total discretion over the cases it hears that the U.S. Supreme Court does. The mandatory jurisdiction of the Washington Supreme Court, for example, includes certain criminal, administrative agency, juvenile, and lawyer-discipline cases. Not surprisingly, given the more extensive mandatory jurisdiction, most state supreme courts decide more cases per year than does the United States Supreme Court.[49]

Intermediate court of appeals: Thirty-nine states have also created intermediate courts of appeals, that is, first-level appellate courts below the state supreme court.[50] These courts generally focus on error correction: they review decisions of trial courts to ensure that judges did not make errors in procedure or in the interpretation of the law that would warrant reversal of their decisions. Because all litigants under American law are entitled to one appeal, these courts—like the federal courts of appeals—exercise no discretion over the appeals they hear. If the appeal is properly filed, they must review the lower court's decision. Decisions of an intermediate court of appeals typically can be appealed to the state supreme court, though that court may have some control over what decisions it reviews. In practice, intermediate courts of appeals render the final decision in most cases that come before them.

Intermediate courts of appeals were initially established in populous states to alleviate caseload pressures on state supreme courts, but in recent years many other states have also created intermediate courts of appeals. There is wide variation in the structure and operation of these courts. Some sparsely populated states—for example, Alaska—have a single court that hears appeals *en banc* (that is, with all

FIGURE 2-4 THE BASIC STRUCTURE OF STATE COURT SYSTEMS

SUPREME COURT

The state's court of last resort for appeals in civil and criminal cases: a state may have a single supreme court (48 states) or separate courts for civil and for criminal appeals (Oklahoma and Texas)

Name of Court: Supreme Court (46 states). Court of Appeals (Maryland, New York). Supreme Judicial Court (Maine, Massachusetts). Court of Criminal Appeals (Okahoma, Texas).

Number of justices: varies from state to state: 3 justices (Oklahoma's Court of Criminal Appeals), 5 justices (18 states), 7 justices (26 states), and 9 justices (6 states)

INTERMEDIATE COURT OF APPEALS

The state's main appellate court, handling routine appeals and subject to review in some cases by the state supreme court (39 states)

Name of court: varies from state to state; most frequent is Court of Appeals (28 states)

Number of judges: ranges from 3 (Alabama, Alaska, Hawaii, Idaho) to 88 (California); 27 states have 10 or more judges

TRIAL COURTS OF GENERAL JURISDICTION

Found in all states, the trial courts for more serious criminal and civil cases; may hear appeals from trial courts of limited jurisdiction

Name of court: varies from state to state; most frequent names are Circuit Court (18 states) and District Court (16 states)

Number of judges: Over 7500 judges

Jurisdiction: On the basis of geography (judicial districts) and subject-matter (cases not delegated to trial courts of limited jursdiction)

TRIAL COURTS OF LIMITED JURISDICTION

Found in all but six states, the trial courts for less serious criminal and civil cases; may also handle preliminary matters, such as arraignments and preliminary examinations, in more serious cases

Number of judges: Over 13,000 judges

Jurisdiction: Usually on the basis of geography (for example, municipal courts) though also may be specialized on the basis of subject-matter (for example, traffic court) or the amount involved (for example, small claims court)

SOURCE: *Book of the States, 1990-1991* (Lexington, Ky.: Council of State Governments, 1990).

the judges sitting on each case). Other states like California and Louisiana have followed the model of the federal courts of appeals, with several courts serving various regions of the state. These courts typically meet in three-judge panels, just like the federal courts of appeals. In contrast, Alabama and Tennessee have created separate courts for appeals in criminal cases and in civil cases.

Trial courts: Six states—Idaho, Illinois, Iowa, Massachusetts, Minnesota, and South Dakota—have a single set of original jurisdiction (trial) courts.[51] Forty-four states, however, operate two sets of trial courts—courts of limited jurisdiction and courts of general jurisdiction. Courts of limited jurisdiction go under a variety of names—municipal court, county court, district court, justice of the peace court, etc. They handle less serious criminal cases and civil cases involving relatively small sums of money. For example, North Carolina's trial courts of limited jurisdiction, known as district courts, decide civil cases involving less than $10,000, domestic relations cases, and criminal cases involving juveniles or misdemeanors.[52] Courts of general jurisdiction, on the other hand, decide more important civil cases and serious criminal cases. In several states they may also hear appeals, often with a new trial (called a trial *de novo*), from courts of limited jurisdiction. (This new trial is necessary because limited jurisdiction courts do not keep a verbatim record of proceedings.)

Despite these basic uniformities, what is most striking about state court systems is their bewildering organizational diversity. No two state court systems are exactly the same. One important source of variation is found in the organization of state trial courts. Although forty-four states divide original jurisdiction between courts of limited jurisdiction and courts of general jurisdiction, most further subdivide it on the basis of geography, subject-matter, or both. Thus Maryland has a separate Orphans' Court, Colorado a Water Court, and New York ten separate sets of trial courts, including special civil and criminal courts for New York City. Figure 2-5, which depicts New York's judicial system, illustrates the complexities that may result.

Another source of variation among state judicial systems involves the assignment of appellate responsibilities. Some states, particularly less populous states such as Hawaii and South Dakota, route all appeals to their supreme courts. Others, as noted earlier, permit their trial courts of general jurisdiction to hear some appeals. Still others have created intermediate courts of appeals to relieve caseload pressures on their supreme courts.

The Development of State Court Systems

Historical factors generally account for the organizational complexity found in state court systems.[53] In creating their court systems, most states designed

FIGURE 2-5 THE COURT SYSTEM OF NEW YORK

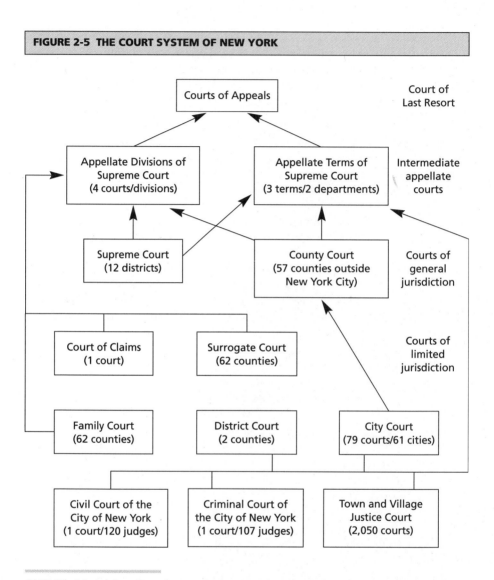

SOURCE: Adapted from Court Statistics Project, *State Court Caseload Statistics: Annual Report 1990*, p. 218. National Center for State Courts in cooperation with the Conference of State Court Administrators, Williamsburg, Va., 1992.

them to serve a relatively sparse and predominantly rural citizenry. Over time, urbanization and population growth produced new demands for court services. In some states constitutional amendments were adopted to modernize the court system, but these amendments themselves frequently were outpaced by subsequent development, requiring further changes. In other states the legislatures responded not by overhauling the existing court structure but by creating additional trial courts to satisfy those demands. Thus, in contrast to the federal court system, whose basic structure was largely established in 1789, many state court systems reflect the continuing pattern of demand and response that occurred in the state. Typically the new state trial courts were added with little consideration of their impact on the overall coherence of the judicial system, and the result was a multiplicity of separate courts reflecting no underlying organizational principle.

Over the past four decades, significant changes have occurred in the structure of state court systems. First, many states have consolidated their trial courts, eliminating various specialized courts and defining more clearly the jurisdictional boundaries among their trial courts.[54] The movement toward trial court consolidation reflects the success of court reformers, who have championed "court unification," claiming that the fragmentation of state trial courts interferes with the efficient and uniform administration of justice (see Box 2-1). Although only

---

BOX 2-1 THE BATTLE OVER COURT UNIFICATION

In a famous speech in 1906, legal scholar Roscoe Pound charged that the American judicial system was plagued by inefficiency and injustice. Pound's address sparked the formation of a reform movement that has campaigned for major changes in state judicial systems. These judicial reformers maintained that some courts within a state were overloaded with work, while others had little to do. Moveover, the complexities of state court systems made justice difficult to obtain. Litigants often did not know in which court to file suits, and procedural requirements varied from court to court, so cases were often dismissed on procedural grounds without consideration of their merits. What was needed, they argued, were fundamental structural and administrative reforms, based on recognized organizational principles such as simplification of structure, hierarchy, and centralization of authority. The reformers' proposals, which together came to be known as "court unification," included:

Court consolidation would simplify the complex and confusing state court systems by establishing a four-tiered judicial system, with a supreme court, an intermediate appellate court, a trial court of general jurisdiction, and a trial court of limited jurisdiction.

Centralized management would mold state courts into a coherent judicial system by creating a hierarchical administrative structure under the direc-

continued on page 52

continued from p. 51

tion of the state chief justice and of the state court administrator selected by the chief justice.

Centralized rulemaking would remove administrative and procedural rule-making authority from the state legislature and/or local courts and vest it exclusively in the state supreme court.

Unitary budgeting would vest the administrative head of the judicial branch with responsibility for preparing and administering a budget encompassing all operating expenses of the court system.

State financing would replace the system of local funding for trial courts by making the state responsible for all aspects of court operations.

What would these proposals accomplish? According to their proponents, simplification of the court system and clear definition of jurisdictional boundaries between levels would make it less likely that litigants would initiate cases in the wrong court. It would also promote greater flexibility, allowing judges to be reassigned to reduce backlogs. Centralization of budgeting and administrative authority would eliminate duplication, promote economies of scale, and allow systemwide planning by experts. In addition to serving those purposes, centralized rulemaking would vest responsibility to ensure uniform rules throughout the state in the state supreme court, the only body possessing the expertise for and interest in the task. It would also prevent local lawyers from using their knowledge of the rules of the local court to gain an unwarranted advantage. Finally, state financing would ensure a rough parity of court services throughout the state and would, arguably, produce more generous funding for the courts.

Spearheading the judicial reform effort have been two major national organizations, the American Judicature Society and the American Bar Association. However, where judicial reform has succeeded, it has done so because state or local groups, such as the state bar association or the League of Women Voters, have endorsed and worked to implement the reform recommendations.

The reformers have met opposition from general-practice and trial lawyers, who are accustomed to working with local courts on a day-to-day basis and who fear that the changes may disrupt their practices. Rural lawyers may also reject change because the problems cited by reformers are less pressing in their local courts. So too may sitting judges and other court personnel, who fear that the reforms may cost them their jobs or at least impose new requirements on them. Finally, ordinary citizens may oppose court unification because of a concern that it will be expensive.

continued on page 53

---

continued from p. 52

Despite such opposition, state judicial reformers have had considerable success getting their proposals adopted, particularly during the 1970s. Almost all the states have consolidated their courts, at least to some extent, and many have centralized administrative authority or assigned rule-making authority to the supreme court. As a result, state judicial systems today often differ dramatically from the state systems of a half-century ago.

SOURCES: G. Alan Tarr, "The Effects of Court Unification on Court Performance: A Preliminary Assessment," *Judicature* 64 (March 1981): 356-368; Larry Berkson and Susan Carbon, *Court Unification: History, Politics, and Implementation* (Washington, D.C.: Government Printing Office, 1978); and Henry R. Glick, "The Politics of State Court Reform," in Philip L. Dubois, ed., *The Politics of Judicial Reform* (Lexington, Mass.: Lexington Books, 1982).

a few states have approached the simplicity of structure advocated by court reformers, several have made major efforts to reduce the number of their courts and to eliminate overlapping jurisdiction among courts. If one compares Virginia's court structure (Figure 2-6), which embodies the reformers' prescriptions, with New York's (depicted in Figure 2-5), the differences are obvious. Despite some researchers' insistence that the alleged benefits of trial court consolidation are unsubstantiated, the success of reformers in some states has fueled similar efforts in other states.[55] If anything, the pace of consolidation appears to have accelerated in recent decades.

Second, as noted above, several states have instituted intermediate courts of appeals in response to increases in the number of appeals filed in state courts. By itself, this structural change has little effect on caseload problems. The number of appeals tends to increase following the establishment of an intermediate court of appeals, and with appeals from that court to the state supreme court, filings in the supreme court may soon approximate earlier levels.[56] When this reform is combined with a limitation on the right to a second appeal, however, it can substantially reduce the caseloads of state supreme courts.[57] Equally important is the effect of the reform on the types of cases coming before the state supreme court and on the role that the court plays in the state. By diverting routine cases to intermediate appellate courts, a state allows its supreme court to devote more attention to cases that raise important policy questions and to assume a position of leadership in the legal development of the state.[58] As we shall see in Chapter 11, some state supreme courts have availed themselves of this opportunity to undertake major initiatives in tort law (involving such matters as products liability and personal injury cases) and in constitutional law.

FIGURE 2-6 THE COURT SYSTEM OF VIRGINIA—A REFORMED COURT SYSTEM

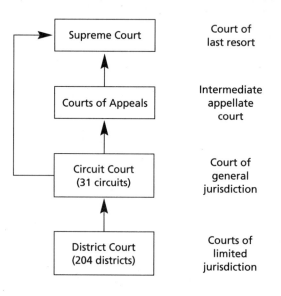

SOURCE: Adapted from Court Statistics Project, *State Court Caseload Statistics: Annual Report 1990,* p. 233. National Center for State Courts in cooperation with the Conference of State Court Administrators, Williamsburg, Va., 1992.

CONCLUSIONS

In choosing federalism, the United States embraced complexity in its governmental structures in general and in its courts in particular. The structure of courts in the United States, however, is complex even in comparison with that in other federal systems. Both the federal government and each state government operate a full complement of trial and appellate courts. Perhaps not surprisingly, the division of responsibility between national and state courts has remained a contentious political issue throughout most of the nation's history.

The structure of both the federal and state courts has changed over time, largely in response to increases in population and in the demand for court services. For the federal courts, the changes have been less dramatic. The Judiciary Act of 1789 created the three-level structure of the federal judicial system that has remained to the present day. During the late nineteenth and early twentieth centuries, however, Congress established an entirely new set of courts, the

courts of appeals, and eliminated the circuit courts. More recently, congressional legislation has granted the U.S. Supreme Court the discretion to set its own
agenda, thus facilitating its transformation into a court that deals primarily with
constitutional issues. Another recent change has been the proliferation of specialized federal courts, though most cases continue to be resolved by the federal
district courts and courts of appeals.

The development of state courts has followed a quite different pattern. For
most of the nation's history, the states responded to demands for court services
by creating new courts, frequently with limited or specialized jurisdictions.
Often these incremental steps provided only temporary relief and were soon followed by renewed demands and further piecemeal responses. These changes
over time produced unduly complex and incoherent court systems that simply
did not function well. Thus, whereas in recent years the number of specialized
federal courts has increased, judicial reformers in the states have urged the elimination of specialized courts and a simplified court structure. Many states have
adopted the reformers' model, in whole or in part, and state court systems now
resemble one another more closely than at any time in the past.

Some reforms—for instance, the creation of the federal courts of appeals—
have undoubtedly produced a more efficient administration of justice. The verdict on others, among them court unification, is less clear. What is clear, however, is that structural and jurisdictional changes can and have had diverse—and
at times unanticipated—effects on the role that courts play in governing. As
burgeoning caseloads prompt renewed calls for reform, wise reformers will keep
in mind the broader effects that their efforts to alleviate caseload pressures might
produce.

NOTES

1. Our description of this landmark case draws upon Anthony Lewis's fascinating account,
Gideon's Trumpet (New York: Vintage, 1964).

2. "Incorporation" is the name given to the process by which the Supreme Court, relying on the
Due Process Clause of the Fourteenth Amendment, has extended federal judicial protection
against state violation of rights. For an overview of how the Court has proceeded, incrementally
applying various guarantees of the Federal Bill of Rights against state governments, see Ronald
Mykkeltvedt, *The Selective Incorporation of the Bill of Rights: Fourteenth Amendment Due Process
and Procedural Rights* (New York: Kennikat, 1982), and Richard C. Cortner, *The Supreme Court
and the Second Bill of Rights* (Madison: University of Wisconsin Press, 1981).

3. *Gideon* v. *Wainwright,* 372 U.S. 335 (1963).

4. U.S. Constitution, Article III, section 1.

5. U.S. Constitution, Article III, section 1.

6. *Northern Pipeline Construction Co.* v. *Marathon Pipeline Co.*, 458 U.S. 50 (1982).

7. Standard accounts of the development of the federal judicial system include Paul M. Bator, Paul J. Mishkin, David L. Shapiro, and Herbert Wechsler, *Hart and Wechsler's The Federal Courts in the Federal System*, 2nd ed. (Mineola, N.Y.: Foundation Press, 1980), and Howard Ball, *Courts and Politics: The Federal Judicial System*, 2nd ed. (Englewood Cliffs, N.J.: Prentice-Hall, 1987).

8. David M. O'Brien, *Storm Center; The Supreme Court in American Politics*, 2d ed. (New York: Norton, 1990), p. 138.

9. The conflict over the "midnight judges" also led to *Marbury* v. *Madison* (1 Cranch 137 [1803]), the Supreme Court's first exercise of judicial review to strike down a federal statute.

10. Richard A. Posner, *The Federal Courts* (Cambridge: Harvard University Press, 1985), p. 25.

11. In referring to a "circuit," we mean the states (and possibly territories) served by a specific court of appeals. Figure 2-2 indicates the circuits for the various courts of appeals.

12. The case for the National Court of Appeals is presented in *Federal Judicial Center Report of the Study Group on the Case Load of the Supreme Court* (Washington, D.C.: Administrative Office of the Courts, 1973).

13. Justice Brennan's argument against the National Court of Appeals is presented in William J. Brennan, "The National Court of Appeals: Another Dissent," *University of Chicago Law Review* (1973): 473-485. A more general critique of the proposal is found in Nathan Lewin, "Helping the Court with Its Work," in Walter F. Murphy and C. Herman Pritchett, eds., *Courts, Judges, and Politics*, 2nd ed. (New York: Random House, 1974), pp. 87-94.

14. The Tenth Amendment to the United States Constitution states: "The powers not delegated to the United States by the Constitution, nor prohibited by it to the States, are reserved to the States respectively, or to the people." This means that the range of cases not falling within the federal judicial power are to be decided by state courts.

15. The Constitution does specify the original jurisdiction of the U.S. Supreme Court—that is, the range of cases in which the Court rules as a trial court. When Congress in the Judiciary Act of 1789 attempted to expand the Court's original jurisdiction, the Supreme Court struck down that section of the act as unconstitutional in *Marbury* v. *Madison* (1 Cranch 137 [1803]).

16. Our account relies on those of Bator et al., *Federal Courts in the Federal System*; Ball, *Courts and Politics*; and Martin H. Redish, *Federal Jurisdiction: Tensions in the Allocation of Judicial Power* (Indianapolis: Michie, 1980).

17. *Chisholm* v. *Georgia*, 2 Dallas 419 (1793).

18. Henry J. Abraham, *The Judicial Process*, 5th ed. (New York: Oxford University Press, 1986), p. 178.

19. Although the Eleventh Amendment prohibits suing a state in federal court, it does not preclude suits against state officials. For example, the "Wainwright" in *Gideon* v. *Wainwright* was the state director of corrections.

20. *Ives* v. *South Buffalo Railway*, 201 N.Y. 271 (1911).

21. For a discussion of these proposals and their possible constitutional bases, see Ralph A. Rossum, *Congressional Control of the Judiciary: The Article Three Option* (Washington, D.C.: Center for Judicial Studies, 1988); and Gary L.McDowell, *Curbing the Courts: The Constitution and the Limits of Judicial Power* (Baton Rouge: Louisiana State University Press, 1988).

22. Felix Frankfurter and James M. Landis, *The Business of the United States Supreme Court* (New York: Macmillan, 1927), p. 60.

23. For a discussion of the proposals for elimination of the federal courts' diversity jurisdiction, see Thomas D. Rowe, Jr., "Abolishing Diversity Jurisdiction: The Silver Lining," *American Bar Association Journal* 66 (January 1988): 177-180, and Harry Phillips, "Diversity Jurisdiction: Problems and a Possible Solution," *University of Toledo Law Review* 14 (Spring 1983): 747-757.

24. These data are drawn from *Annual Report of the Director of the Administrative Office of the United States Courts, 1990* (Washington, D.C.: Government Printing Office, 1990), p. 8, Table 6.

25. For a summary of arguments against the elimination of the federal courts' diversity jurisdiction, see John P. Frank, "An Idea Whose Time Is Still Here," *American Bar Association Journal* 70 (June 1984): 17-18, and Victor E. Flango, "Attorneys' Perspectives on Choice of Forum in Diversity Cases," *Akron Law Review* 25 (Summer 1991): 41-122.

26. Flango, "Attorneys' Perspectives on Choice of Forum."

27. For the effect on state court caseloads of eliminating the federal courts' diversity jurisdiction, see Victor Eugene Flango, "How Would the Abolition of Federal Diversity Jurisdiction Affect State Courts?" *Judicature* 74 (June-July 1990): 35-43.

28. These data are drawn from the 1990 *Annual Report of the Director of the Administrative Office of the United States Courts, 1990*, p.

29. Ibid., p. 7, Table 5, and p. 10, Table 8.

30. Ibid., p. 139, Table C-2A.

31. Ibid., p. 10, Table 8.

32. Thus *State Court Caseload Statistics: Annual Report 1990* on p. 194 depicts the Court of Appeals as the court of last resort for the District of Columbia.

33. See J. Woodford Howard, Jr., *Courts of Appeals in the Federal Judicial System* (Princeton: Princeton University Press, 1981), and Donald R. Songer, "The Circuit Courts of Appeals," in John B. Gates and Charles A. Johnson, eds., *The American Courts; A Critical Assessment* (Washington, D.C.: CQ Press, 1991).

34. *Annual Report of the Director of the Administrative Office of the United States Courts, 1990*, p. 114, Table B-3.

35. For short-term changes, see ibid., p. 3, Table 1. For an historical account of changes, see Lawrence Baum, Sheldon Goldman, and Austin Sarat, "The Evolution of Litigation in the Federal Courts of Appeals, 1895-1975," *Law and Society Review* 16 (1981-1982): 291-309.

36. *Annual Report of the Director of the Administrative Office of the United States Courts, 1990,* p. 3, Table 1.

37. On the greater willingness of defendants in drug cases to appeal their convictions, see ibid., p 42.

38. Ibid., p. 5, Table 3.

39. This is reflected in the composition of the Supreme Court's caseload. In its 1990 term, the Court reviewed the actions of administrative agencies in 16 cases and the interpretation of federal statutes in 36. See "Statistics," *Harvard Law Review* 104 (November 1991): pp. 364-366, Table III.

40. Although Rule 17 lists conflict between the circuits as one criterion for granting review, the Court is not obliged to grant review even when such conflicts exist. See H. W. Perry, Jr., *Deciding to Decide; Agenda Setting in the United States Supreme Court* (Cambridge: Harvard University Press, 1991), pp. 246-252.

41. See Howard, *Courts of Appeals in the Federal Judicial System,* Chapter 7.

42. Ibid., pp. 241-247.

43. Ibid., pp. 232-235.

44. In the Supreme Court's 1990 term, roughly half the cases it decided with full opinion (68 of 137) involved constitutional issues. See "Statistics," *Harvard Law Review* 104 (November 1991), pp. 364-366, Table III.

45. William J. Brennan, Jr., "State Supreme Court Judge Versus United States Supreme Court Justice: A Change in Function and Perspective," *University of Florida Law Review* 19 (1966), p. 236.

46. The data for California's trial courts are taken from the *State Court Caseload Statistics: Annual Report 1990,* p. 109, Table 8. That volume also offers a comparison of federal and state workloads at pp. 42-43, Text Tables I.17 and I.18.

47. State supreme courts issued opinions in over 9700 cases in 1990. See ibid., pp. 102-106, Table 6.

48. Charts depicting the structure of every state court system are found in ibid., pp. 186-237.

49. For data on the caseloads of state supreme courts, see ibid., pp. 70-83, Table 2.

50. Ibid., p. 48, Map II.1.

51. Ibid., p. 8, Map I.1.

52. Ibid., p. 219.

53. This account draws upon Larry Berkson and Susan Carbon, *Court Unification: History, Politics, and Implementation* (Washington, D.C.: National Institute of Law Enforcement and Criminal Justice, 1978); Frank Munger, "Movements for Court Reform: A Preliminary Interpretation," in Philip E. Dubois, *The Politics of Judicial Reform* (Lexington, Mass.: Lexington

Books, 1982); and Henry R. Glick, "The Politics of State-Court Reform," in Dubois, *Politics of Judicial Reform.*

54. See *State Court Caseload Statistics: Annual Report 1990,* pp. 8-9, Maps I.1-I.4.

55. For analyses critical of the reformers' claims, see Carl Baar and Thomas Henderson, "Alternative Models for the Organization of State-Court Systems," in Philip Dubois, ed., *The Analysis of Judicial Reform* (Lexington, Mass.: Lexington Books, 1982); G. Alan Tarr, "The Effects of Court Unification on Court Performance: A Preliminary Assessment," *Judicature* 64 (March 1981): 356-368; and Geoff Gallas, "The Conventional Wisdom of State Court Administration: A Critical Assessment and an Alternative Approach," *Justice System Journal* 2 (Spring 1976): 35-56.

56. Victor Eugene Flango and Nora F. Blair, "Creating an Intermediate Appellate Court: Does It Reduce the Caseload of a State's Highest Court?" *Judicature* 64 (August 1980): 74-84.

57. For examples of this, see Roger D. Groot, "The Effects of an Intermediate Appellate Court on the Supreme Court Work Product: The North Carolina Experience," *Wake Forest Law Review* 7 (1971): 548-572; and John M. Scheb and John M. Scheb II, "Making Intermediate Appellate Courts Final: Assessing Jurisdictional Changes in Florida's Appellate Courts," *Judicature* 67 (May 1984): 474-485.

58. See Paul D. Carrington, Daniel J. Meador, and Maurice Rosenberg, *Justice on Appeal* (St. Paul: West, 1976), p. 150; and Groot, "Effects of an Intermediate Appellate Court."

3 JUDGES

When Justice Lewis Powell announced his retirement in June, 1987, the Reagan White House viewed it as a unique opportunity to influence the future direction of the Supreme Court.[1] The Court was closely divided on several constitutional issues on which the president felt strongly—including affirmative action, abortion, and the rights of defendants—and Justice Powell had often cast the decisive vote. Replacing Powell with a conservative justice could tip the balance on the Court and dramatically shift its orientation. At a press conference six days after Powell's announcement, President Ronald Reagan nominated Robert H. Bork, a member of the Court of Appeals for the District of Columbia, to fill the vacant seat.

The president's three previous nominees for the Supreme Court had all been confirmed, and Bork himself had easily won Senate approval in 1982 when appointed to the court of appeals. However, the Bork nomination pitted a lame-duck Republican president, weakened politically by disclosures of executive-branch wrongdoing, against a Democratically controlled Senate one year before a presidential election. Political observers in Washington expected a bitter battle over confirmation, and they were not disappointed.

Liberals too knew how crucial Powell's successor could be to the future direction of the Supreme Court, and Reagan's nomination of Bork confirmed their worst fears. As a law professor at Yale University, Bork had sharply criticized rulings of the Supreme Court that gave a broad reading to rights claims. After his appointment to the bench, his rulings solidified his reputation as a leading judicial conservative. Senator Ted Kennedy of Massachusetts, who was to lead the fight against Bork, forecasted a catalogue of horrors if the Senate confirmed him:

Robert Bork's America is a land in which women would be forced into back-alley abortions, blacks would sit at segregated lunch counters, rogue police would break down citizens' doors in midnight raids ... and the doors of the Federal courts would be shut on the fingers of millions of citizens for whom the judiciary is often the only protector of the individual rights that are the heart of our democracy.[2]

Although Kennedy's statement exaggerated and distorted Bork's views, as he himself later acknowledged, it did signal the intensity of the opposition to the nomination and the determination of liberals to block it in the Senate.

Senator Joseph Biden of Delaware, chairman of the Senate Judiciary Committee, scheduled the committee hearings for eleven weeks after the nomination, allowing the anti-Bork forces plenty of time to mobilize. Groups such as People for the American Way, the NAACP, and the National Abortion Rights League spearheaded a massive lobbying and media campaign against Bork—seldom, if ever, had a Court nominee generated such intense opposition. In radio and television ads, these groups portrayed Bork as a dangerous radical, outside the legal mainstream. Their claim received a boost when the American Bar Association's Select Committee on the Federal Judiciary split sharply on the nomination, with four members rating Bork "not qualified" for the Court. Pro-Bork forces denounced what they termed the politicization of the selection process but, unsure of what strategy to follow, failed to mount an effective counter-offensive. By the time the committee hearings commenced, public opinion had coalesced against Bork, and the nomination was in serious trouble.

Although scores of witnesses testified for or against Bork, it was his five days of testimony that proved decisive. Under questioning from committee members, Judge Bork repeated his earlier criticism of the Supreme Court's recognition of an unenumerated constitutional right to privacy (the basis for the Court's rulings striking down statutes banning abortion and contraception). However, he did seek to distance himself from positions he had espoused in law review and periodical articles written before he ascended the bench, prompting accusations that he was experiencing a "confirmation conversion." Whatever the truth of the accusation, many senators remained convinced that if elevated to the Court, Bork would seek to reshape constitutional law fundamentally. By a 9-5 vote, with Republican Senator Arlen Specter of Pennsylvania joining all the Democratic members, the Judiciary Committee voted against confirmation.

Faced with an adverse vote in committee, a nominee usually withdraws from consideration. Bork, however, vowed to combat what he termed the "public campaigns of distortions" by carrying the fight to the floor of the Senate. Continuation of the process allowed Bork's supporters to make his case before the full Senate, but it did not change many minds. The Senate rejected the nomination by a 58-42 vote.

The monumental battle over the Bork nomination seemed to exhaust both sides. President Reagan next announced plans to nominate Douglas Ginsburg, a 41-year-old appeals court judge, to fill Justice Powell's seat. But shortly after the announcement, reports surfaced that Ginsburg had smoked marijuana at parties while a faculty member at Harvard Law School. This revelation led some conservatives within the Reagan administration to oppose the nomination, and Ginsburg was forced to withdraw from consideration. With his third nominee, Judge Anthony Kennedy, President Reagan enjoyed better luck. Of all the groups that had opposed Bork, only the National Organization for Women also opposed Kennedy. His testimony before the Judiciary Committee convinced the Senate of his moderation and judicial temperament, and he easily won confirmation.

The conflict over Justice Powell's successor illustrates three important themes that will guide our discussion of judges and of judicial selection:

The political character of judicial selection: Though political conflict over judgeships is rarely as visible and intense as in the Bork nomination, it is never totally absent. Judges in the United States may be appointed or elected, chosen by political officials, by "merit selection," or by popular vote. But no selection system altogether banishes political or ideological considerations. Different selection systems may affect who exercises political influence, but not whether it will be exercised.

The importance of who the judges are: Though they agreed on little else, both proponents and opponents of the Bork nomination assumed that his appointment would affect the Court's decisions. This was not because they feared—or hoped—that Bork would cynically ignore his oath of office and use the position to advance his own policy views. Rather, partisans on both sides recognized that even judges who seek to banish personal predilections and decide in accordance with the law may arrive at quite different conclusions. These differences among judges may occur because judges' views and values inevitably influence their judgment, or because the exercise of judgment necessarily involves an element of discretion, or for a variety of other reasons. But whatever the reason, the possibility that judges may have different perspectives on the same legal question underlines the importance of who judges.

Ambiguity about judicial qualifications: When President Reagan announced his choice for the Supreme Court, he stressed Robert Bork's legal qualifications. However, opponents of the nomination focused on Bork's constitutional views, arguing that they placed him outside the mainstream of American legal thought. Responding to charges that they were politicizing the selection process, the anti-Bork forces responded that the president himself had considered Bork's views before nominating him. Since judicial decisions have important consequences, they contended, senators too should assess how a nominee will decide cases before voting to confirm.

The debate between the pro- and anti-Bork forces reflects a more general ambiguity in Americans' expectations about judges. On the one hand, we want judges to be independent and impartial. On the other hand, we want all officials who exercise power to be responsive to public sentiment and accountable for their actions. Over the course of the nation's history, Americans have alternated between these two perspectives, and changes in the mode of selecting state judges have reflected this alternation. It is to these competing perspectives, and to their effect on judicial selection, that we now turn.

WHAT SORT OF JUDGES DO WE WANT?

Judicial Independence versus Accountability

Basic to our understanding of a fair trial are the notions of judicial impartiality and neutrality, of rulings unaffected by political considerations or by the identity of the litigants. Yet not all legal systems share this expectation. In some legal systems, judges are expected to decide politically sensitive cases so as to further the ends of the regime. Even in systems that proclaim their commitment to "equal justice under law," such as the United States, officials sometimes attempt to influence judicial decisions, and judges sometimes succumb to political pressures.[3] It follows that if judges are to act impartially, they must be freed from pressures to act otherwise. This freedom from external pressures is known as judicial independence.

Historically, the pressures on judges have often involved threats to a judge's salary or position. For example, Americans complained in the Declaration of Independence that King George III had made "judges dependent upon his will alone for the tenure of their offices and the amount and payment of their salaries." To prevent similar pressures on federal judges, Article III of the United States Constitution guarantees that judges "shall hold their Offices during good Behaviour, and shall, at stated Times, receive for their Services a Compensation which shall not be diminished during their Continuance in Office." Although most states do not safeguard judicial independence to quite that extent, they tend to award longer terms of office to judges than to other officials.

The American concern for judicial independence, however, is in tension with another deeply held American value, namely, the accountability of governmental officials. In democratic systems citizens select those who wield power and hold them accountable for its exercise. This ensures that the government's decisions reflect the values and perspectives of the community. Advocates of judicial accountability maintain that because judges, like legislators, make decisions that have broad societal effects, they too should be answerable for their decisions. The Federal Constitution establishes a degree of accountability by providing for the impeachment of judges. Although Thomas Jefferson dismissed this check as a "mere scarecrow," two district court judges have been impeached in recent years.[4] However, the states have gone considerably further. Some fill judgeships by popular election and require judges to run for reelection. Most others limit judges' terms of office and require that they seek reappointment or public approval of their performance in office.

Representativeness

In recent decades some groups have also voiced concern about the representativeness of the judiciary, that is, the extent to which the judiciary reflects—or fails to reflect—the demographic make-up of the populace. Underlying this concern is the belief that a demographically homogeneous judiciary cannot adequately take into account the perspectives and interests of excluded groups.

Demographic considerations have influenced the selection of judges for most of our history: political parties have sought to "balance the ticket" in judicial elections, and presidents and governors have considered religion and ethnicity in appointing judges. Indeed, during the early twentieth century there were identifiable Catholic and Jewish seats on the Supreme Court.[5] However, the recent pressure for a more representative judiciary has become entangled in the larger societal debate over affirmative action. Women's organizations and civil-rights groups, noting the discrepancy between the proportion of group members in the population and their representation on the bench, have called for concerted action to remedy the disparity. Those opposing affirmative action in judicial selection insist that judges function not as representatives but as neutral arbitrers and should be selected on the basis of merit rather than group membership.

The debate over representativeness, like the tension between judicial independence and accountability, reflects the competing views Americans have about judges and judging. We want judges who are impartial, yet we also want them to be mindful of community sentiment. We want a legal system free of racial and gender bias but disagree about whether efforts to achieve demographic representativeness promote or jeopardize equal justice for all. As Box 3-1 suggests, we also differ among ourselves about the attributes and qualities that judges should have. In the sections that follow, we shall examine how the states and the federal government have attempted to balance these conflicting concerns for independence, accountability, and representativeness in their systems of judicial selection.

BOX 3-1   JUDICIAL QUALIFICATIONS—A SAMPLING OF VIEWS

"All persons selected as judges should be of good moral character, emotionally stable and mature, physically able to discharge the duties of office, patient, courteous, and capable of deliberation and decisiveness when required to act on their own reasoned judgment." (American Bar Association)

"Judges ought to be more learned than witty, more reverend than plausible, and more advised than confident." (Francis Bacon, English philosopher)

"The trial judge ought to be neutral, detached, kindly, benign, reasonably learned in the law, firm but fair, wise, knowledgeable about human behavior, and in lesser respects as well, somewhat superhuman." (Judge Marvin Frankel)

"The more relevant things about an appointee are his breadth of vision, his imagination, his capacity for disinterested judgment, his power to discover and to suppress his prejudices." (Justice Felix Frankfurter)

"It is as important to a judge called upon to pass on a question of constitutional law, to have at least a bowing acquaintance with Acton and Maitland, with Thucydides, Gibbon, and Carlyle, with Homer, Dante, Shakespeare and Milton, with Machiavelli, Montaigne and Rabelais, with Plato, Bacon, Hume and Kant, as with the books which have been specifically written on the subject." (Judge Learned Hand)

"In the long run, there is no guarantee of justice except the personality of the judge." (Justice Benjamin Cardozo)

SOURCES: American Bar Association, *Standards Relating to Court Organization* (1990 edition), Section 1.21; Francis Bacon, "Of Judicature," in Michael J. Hawkins, ed., *Bacon's Essays* (London: J. M. Dent & Sons, 1972), p. 162; Marvin Frankel, "The Adversary Judge: The Experience of a Trial Judge," in Mark W. Cannon and David M. O'Brien, eds., *Views from the Bench* (Chatham, N.J.: Chatham House, 1985), p. 47; Felix Frankfurter and Learned Hand quoted in David O'Brien, *Judicial Roulette* (New York: Priority Press, 1988), p. 5; and Benjamin Cardozo, *The Nature of the Judicial Process* (New Haven: Yale University Press, 1921), p. 149.

JUDICIAL SELECTION IN THE STATES

Modes of Judicial Selection

Each state establishes its own mode of judicial selection by constitutional provision or by statute. As Table 3-1 indicates, five methods are currently used in selecting state court judges:

TABLE 3-1 JUDICIAL SELECTION IN THE STATES*

Merit Selection	Appointment by Governor	Election by Legislature	Nonpartisan Election	Partisan Election
Alaska	California (A)	Rhode Island(A)	Arizona (T)	Alabama
Arizona (M)	Maine	South Carolina	California (T)	Arkansas
Colorado	New Hampshire	Virginia	Florida (T)	Illinois
Connecticut	New Jersey		Georgia	Indiana (T)
Delaware	Rhode Island (T)		Idaho	Mississippi
Florida (A)			Kentucky	New York (T)
Hawaii			Louisiana	North Carolina
Iowa			Michigan	Pennsylvania
Kansas			Minnesota (M)	Tennessee (SC, T)
Maryland			Montana	Texas
Massachusetts			Nevada	West Virginia
Missouri (M)			North Dakota	
Nebraska			Ohio	
New Mexico			Oklahoma (M)	
New York (A)			Oregon	
Oklahoma (SC, T)			South Dakota (T)	
South Dakota (A)			Washington	
Tennessee (ICA)			Wisconsin	
Utah				
Vermont				
Wyoming				

* - Listings do not include trial courts of limited jurisdiction. All listings are for initial selection, not for retention or for filling vacancies occurring during a judicial term.

SOURCES: *Book of the States, 1990-91* (Lexington, Kentucky: Council of State Governments, 1990), pp. 210-212, Table 4.4; and Larry Berkson, Scott Beller, and Michele Grimaldi, *Judicial Selection in the United States: A Compendium of Provisions* (Chicago: American Judicature Society, 1981).

Key for symbols following the names of states: A - appellate judges only; ICA - judges of intermediate court of appeals only; M - most judges, but with idiosyncratic variations; SC - supreme court justices only; T - trial-court judges only.

Merit selection: This system—also called the Missouri Plan after the state in which it originated—is designed to remove politics from the selection process. Its key feature is a judicial nominating commission, comprised of lawyers selected by the state bar and of nonlawyers usually appointed by the governor. When a judicial vacancy occurs, the commission nominates three—or in some states, as many as five—qualified persons to fill the position. The governor then selects the judge from that list. After a short period of service on the bench, the judge runs in a uncontested retention election, which allows voters to decide whether or not the judge should remain in office. Twenty-one states currently employ some version of merit selection.

Election by the legislature: In Rhode Island, Virginia, and South Carolina, the legislature elects state judges. This system favors the judicial candidacies of former legislators—a recent survey found that over three-quarters of the supreme court justices in these states had served in the state legislature.[6]

Appointment by the governor: In seven states governors appoint judges; in most, another body—usually the state senate—must confirm the appointees. Judges appointed under this system typically serve for a set term of office. In New Jersey, for example, judges serve for seven years after which, if reappointed by the governor and confirmed by the senate, they hold office until the retirement age of 70. In California judges run in a retention election at the general election after their appointment and serve twelve year terms.

Partisan election: Under this system, now the main mode of selection in eleven states, political parties nominate candidates for judicial office, and they run with party labels in the general election. Once elected, they serve for terms which range from two years for Arkansas's Justice Courts (courts of limited jurisdiction) to fourteen years for New York's trial courts of general jurisdiction. The judges usually must seek reelection in a partisan election, although Illinois and Pennsylvania provide for retention elections for incumbent judges.

Nonpartisan elections: Eighteen states now conduct judicial elections with no party affiliation indicated on the ballot. Typically, the top two candidates in a nonpartisan primary qualify for the general election. In most states judges elected in nonpartisan elections run for reelection in retention elections.

No listing of modes of selection, however, can do justice to the incredible interstate and intrastate diversity one finds. Some states have adopted different modes of selection for judges on various courts. South Dakota, for example, uses merit selection to choose its appellate judges but nonpartisan elections for trial-court judges. In addition, many permit local political authorities to select judges for some trial courts of limited jurisdiction. Some also use a different system for filling interim vacancies (those occurring during a judicial term because of death or resignation) than for the initial selection of judges. This can altogether transform the system of judicial selection in the state. In California, for example, 88 percent of the trial judges were selected initially to fill a vacancy (that is, by gubernatorial appointment) rather than by the "normal" method provided by law, nonpartisan election.[7] Finally, some states that elect their judges have introduced distinctive elements to the process. In Michigan and Ohio, which elect their judges in nonpartisan elections, candidates are nominated in party primaries. In North Carolina, which has instituted partisan election of judges, candidates for the Superior Court bench are nominated in primaries within the district in which they will serve but elected by statewide ballot.

What accounts for the differences among states in how they select their judges? In part, the interstate variation follows a regional pattern. Gubernatorial appointment is most common in the northeast, partisan election in the south, nonpartisan election in the northern tier of states from Michigan to Washington, and merit selection in the rest of the west. Thus shared political values within regions of the country and the tendency to emulate the laws and institutions of neighboring states provide part of the answer.

The interstate diversity also reflects the waves of political reform that have periodically swept the nation.[8] At the time the U.S. Constitution was ratified, all thirteen states selected their judges either by gubernatorial appointment (the system used in the colonies before Independence) or by legislative election. All three states whose legislatures now elect judges have retained that system since the late eighteenth century, and three states in which the governor appoints judges had adopted that system prior to 1800. During the Jacksonian era, many states underwent a democratizing process, removing property-holding requirements for voting and providing for popular election of most governmental officials. This movement, combined with popular distrust of judicial power, fueled efforts to secure greater judicial accountability. By the Civil War 24 of the 34 states had instituted popular (partisan) election of judges, and every new state from Iowa in 1846 to Arizona in 1912 provided for an elective judiciary. Most states which currently elect judges in partisan elections initially adopted this mode of selection during the nineteenth century. During the Progressive Era, when reformers sought to improve government by restricting the influence of partisan politics, several states established nonpartisan elections for judges. Since 1940, when Missouri first adopted it, merit selection has replaced nonpartisan elections as the preferred means to eliminate partisan influences from judicial recruitment and attract highly qualified persons to the bench. Since 1960 eleven states have instituted merit selection. When a state changes its mode of selection, of course, it changes the politics of judicial selection in the state. Let us look at the two main modes of judicial selection—elections and merit selection—and at the politics associated with each.

The Politics of Judicial Elections

Those who favor judicial elections insist that they promote judicial accountability, but critics dispute this contention. They argue that judicial elections are uncompetitive, do not provide the basis for an informed choice by voters, and have little or no effect on judicial behavior in office. Political scientists have conducted numerous studies examining these claims.

Uncompetitive Elections?

Electoral accountability requires that voters be offered a choice between an incumbent and a challenger or between two candidates for office. Yet critics maintain that judicial elections often are uncontested or not seriously contested. Incumbents, who often were elevated to the bench as interim appointees (that is, following the resignation or death of their predecessors), tend to win lopsided victories and remain in office indefinitely.

Studies of nonpartisan elections confirm many of the critics' charges. One researcher found that in states with nonpartisan judicial elections, most state supreme court justices were appointed to fill unexpired terms. Almost half of these justices ran unopposed in their first election, and over 95 percent were elected.[9] Nonpartisan elections for trial courts are even less competitive. "Judges on the major trial courts of Ohio were opposed only 27 percent of the time, those of Michigan 26 percent of the time, and those of California only 7 percent."[10] For incumbent judges who were challenged, close races were rare, and defeat even rarer.

Partisan elections for the state supreme court promote greater competition. Far fewer justices reach the state high court by appointment, appointed justices who run for election are almost always opposed, and one-third of them have been defeated in their first election. Moreover, partisan elections for state supreme court judgeships tend to be highly competitive: in over half the margin of victory has been less than 10 percent.[11] However, this greater competitiveness does not usually extend to partisan elections for the trial court bench. These elections instead follow the pattern for other local elections, which is generally one of domination by a single party. For trial court judges, therefore, nomination by the majority party is tantamount to election, and incumbent judges are rarely defeated unless they lose their party support.

An Uninformed Electorate?

Electoral accountability requires that voters not only have a choice but also the information necessary to determine which candidate has the views or other

qualifications they desire. Critics charge, however, that judicial elections seldom promote informed choice because the campaigns tend to be low-intensity,
low-visibility affairs. Financial constraints and ethical norms prevent candidates
from communicating their views to the public, and voters either make unin-
formed choices or, recognizing their ignorance, refrain from voting in judicial
elections altogether.

Many of these assertions are accurate. Judicial candidates rarely have sufficient funds to publicize their views, and even if they did, legal ethics severely
restrict the issues that candidates can raise.[12] They cannot, like prospective legislators, promise to benefit particular groups or say how they will vote on future
issues. Rather, they can merely pledge to deal impartially with the cases coming
before them. When both candidates make the same pledge, however, voters
have little basis for deciding between them.

Not surprisingly, such issueless campaigns attract little voter interest and
make it difficult to mount a strong challenge to incumbent judges. Often voter
knowledge of candidates is woefully inadequate: a survey of voters in one Texas
election found that fewer than 5 percent could name a candidate for the trial
court of general jurisdiction.[13] Voters deal with this lack of information in various ways. In partisan elections, voters typically take their cues from the party
affiliation of the candidates, and thus the vote for judges tends to reflect the
partisan division in the state.[14] In nonpartisan elections, where voters lack even
that cue, voting patterns tend to be more diffuse, as voters look for something—a familiar name, a newspaper endorsement, or incumbency—to differen-
tiate the candidates. When judicial elections are not concurrent with elections
for other offices, many potential voters do not bother to turn out. When the
judicial elections are concurrent, voters still may ignore the judicial races, particularly in nonpartisan systems. According to one study, 90 percent of voters
going to the polls voted for judicial candidates in contested partisan elections,
but only 70 in contested nonpartisan elections.[15]

Yet not all judicial elections are ill-financed, issueless endorsements of the
incumbent. At times special interests may blatantly try to buy influence on a
court. While an $11 billion lawsuit by Pennzoil against Texaco was pending
before the Texas Supreme Court, the representatives of Texaco made campaign
contributions totalling $72,000 to members of the court, and Pennzoil's
lawyers responded by contributing over $315,000 to the justices.[16] More fre-
quently, allegations of improprieties against a sitting judge may whet media and
voter interest and enable a challenger to upset an incumbent. A case in point
was the successful challenge in 1986 to Frank Celebrezze, the controversial
Democratic chief justice of Ohio.[17] Since his election in 1978, which had
ended the long-standing Republican domination of the Ohio Supreme Court,

Celebrezze had presided over a "quiet revolution" in Ohio law. Rulings of the Celebrezze court facilitated suits against employers, doctors, landlords, manufacturers, and the state and municipalities. The court's decisions earned it the approval of labor and consumer groups but the enmity of business interests, which campaigned for his defeat. However, what galvanized popular opposition to Celebrezze were his abrasive personal style and his penchant for unjudicial behavior. Celebrezze conducted a running feud with the Ohio Bar Association after it rated his brother "not qualified" for a seat on the Ohio Supreme Court, and he repeatedly clashed publicly with the Republican minority on the court. While on the bench, he actively explored a campaign for the governorship, giving speeches and raising campaign funds. After a decision ordering utility companies to pay refunds to customers, he apparently sought to curry favor by sending the refund checks out over his signature. These actions earned him media notoriety, gave his Republican challenger a ready campaign issue—"restoring the dignity of the court"—and directly led to his defeat.

No Predictable Effect on Judicial Behavior?

Critics claim that judicial elections cannot influence judges' decisions because voters have no way of knowing what cases will arise or how judges will resolve them. Furthermore, judges are bound to decide cases in accordance with the law, so elections cannot—and should not—influence their conduct in office. Although (as Chapter 8 will show) judges have some leeway in their interpretation of the law, judges who decided cases on the basis of public opinion or political advantage would be violating their oath of office.

Yet even if voters in judicial elections do not directly affect the outcome of particular cases, this does not mean that their votes have no effect. The prospect of a forthcoming election may induce judges to take account of community sentiments in their decisions. Moreover, voters in judicial elections, like those in congressional elections, can select that candidate whose overall orientation most closely resembles their own. When they do so, they influence the general direction of judicial decisions, even if they do not determine the outcomes in particular cases.

Judicial elections can directly affect judicial decisionmaking only if there are competing candidates and if voters can distinguish between their orientations. In nonpartisan elections, often these conditions are not met. In partisan elections, party labels can serve as indicators of general orientation—Republican candidates are more likely to be conservative and Democratic candidates to be liberal. Studies of voting behavior on state courts by and large confirm that

party affiliation is a fairly good predictor of how judges do decide.[18] Kathleen
Barber has explained why this can happen:

> Direct response to the bidding of a political party is probably rare.... Indirect
> response to needs expressed by groups in the political system with which judges
> have been and may still be identified is more probable. The deepest and possi-
> bly unconscious level of response reflects consonance of the values of judges and
> of parties with which they have been affiliated, values which predispose judges
> both to associate themselves with a given party and to make decisions which
> favor that party.[19]

The Politics of Merit Selection

Merit selection, developed as an alternative to the political selection of judges, is
designed to enhance judicial independence and limit judicial accountability.
Instead of party leaders or voters, a permanent commission composed of
lawyers (selected by the organized bar) and nonlawyers (usually selected by the
governor) nominates prospective candidates. Although governors select judges
under merit selection, their range of choice is limited. In contrast to appointive
systems, in which a governor exercises complete discretion, merit selection
requires the governor to choose the judge from the short list of candidates submitted by the commission. A retention election offers voters an opportunity to
approve or reject the governor's choice, but neither party labels nor competing
candidates appear on the ballot.

Those who originated merit selection expected that, while retention elections
would accommodate demands for popular involvement and serve to remove
judges who had committed gross abuses, they would guarantee long tenure for
most judges.[20] Critics have charged that in practice retention elections eliminate judicial accountability altogether. Several criticisms levelled against judicial
elections in general apply with particular force to retention elections. Many voters do not bother to cast ballots in retention elections.[21] Without electoral
competition, incumbents enjoy an immense advantage. During the 1970s only
33 judges (1.6 percent of those running) were defeated in retention elections.
A five-state study of retention elections from 1964-1984 reported similar
results, noting that the mean affirmative vote for incumbents was 77.2 percent.[22] Often voters lack even rudimentary information about the incumbent
judge—for example, more than half the voters in a Wyoming retention election
admitted that they knew nothing at all about any of the candidates for retention.[23] Because voters in retention elections typically support incumbents unless
they have a basis for opposing them, this lack of information virtually guarantees that judges will be returned to office.

Incumbents have been defeated in retention elections only when confronted by an organized opposition publicizing judicial misconduct. Perhaps the most bitterly fought retention election ever occurred in California in 1986, when conservative forces spent $5 million to unseat Chief Justice Rose Bird and two associate justices of the supreme court (see Box 3-2). In less publicized retention elections, incumbents have tasted defeat only when the legal profession, the press, and/or other groups have campaigned against them. To generate such opposition, judges usually have to have broken the law or grossly violated professional norms. One judge, for example, was unseated after consistently appearing on the bench drunk; another after repeatedly patronizing or insulting female lawyers and witnesses in his courtroom; and a third after using his power to assign cases to ensure that the judges deciding politically sensitive cases would be responsive to the Democratic Party.[24]

Even if merit selection does not guarantee accountability, its proponents maintain that it removes politics from judicial selection. In actuality, however,

---

BOX 3-2 CONFLICT IN CALIFORNIA

Bill Roberts, the leader of one group seeking to unseat Chief Justice Rose Bird, put it bluntly: "There's nothing that's going to save her. She is going to be slam dunked out of business." Retention elections seldom generate such strong feelings. But from the moment Governor Jerry Brown appointed her in 1977 as California's first female chief justice, Rose Bird found herself embroiled in controversy. Although the necessary two members of the Commission on Judicial Appointments voted to confirm her, one member dissented because the forty-year-old secretary of agriculture had no judicial experience. Throughout her tenure as chief justice, Californians remained sharply divided about her qualifications and performance.

In 1978, twenty months after her appointment, Chief Justice Bird narrowly avoided defeat in a retention election. The conservative groups campaigning against Bird argued that she and her fellow justices had unduly expanded the rights of defendants, allowing criminals to escape punishment because of legal technicalities. They also charged that she had purposely withheld publication of a controversial decision until after the election. A state Commission on Judicial Performance, convened at Bird's request, cleared her of the latter charge, but its investigation revealed a court split by conflicts of personality and of judicial philosophy.

After 1978 the California Supreme Court, with Chief Justice Bird in the lead, continued in its liberal course. The court's reliance on the state consti-

continued on p. 75

---

continued from p. 74

tution to expand defendants' rights led California voters to adopt a constitutional amendment, the so-called Victim's Bill of Rights, overturning several of these decisions. When opponents challenged the amendment as a
violation of the Federal Constitution, the California Supreme Court upheld
the measure, but Chief Justice Bird dissented. Even more controversial
were the court's rulings in death penalty cases. After California voters ratified a constitutional amendment to reverse a pre-Bird decision invalidating
the death penalty, the California court overturned the death sentences in
over 90 percent of the capital cases that came before it. Bird herself voted
to strike down the death sentence in every capital punishment case.

Chief Justice Bird's votes in these cases became the major issue in the
retention election of 1986, when conservative groups targeted Bird and
two other justices for defeat. Leading the anti-Bird coalition were Crime
Victims for Court Reform, whose membership included relatives of the victims in thirty murder cases in which the Bird court had overturned convictions, and Californians to Defeat Rose Bird. Prominent politicians, such as
Republican Governor George Deukmejian, also urged voters to reject her.
The anti-Bird forces spent the previously unheard-of sum of $5.5 million in
the campaign, hammering home her opposition to the death penalty with
hard-hitting media ads and mass mailings. In response, Bird unsuccessfully
sought to rally support by raising the banner of judicial independence.
Quite early in the campaign, it became evident that she stood no chance of
victory, and many Democratic politicians distanced themselves, refusing to
support her publicly.

When the votes were counted, California had made political history. Never
before had a California chief justice lost a retention election, but Rose Bird
was defeated by an extraordinary 66-34 percent. Never before had
California voters removed more than one justice at an election, but the
two liberal associate justices running in 1986 also suffered lopsided
defeats. In the short term, the rejection of the incumbent justices gave
Governor Deukmejian the opportunity to appoint three new members of
the California Supreme Court. As a result of those appointments, the
court's orientation has changed dramatically. In the long run, the election
demonstrates that justices who make unpopular decisions can be defeated
if opponents have the organization and finances to mount a major campaign to oust them. Whether California's experience will be repeated in
other states remains to be seen.

SOURCES: This analysis is based on John H. Culver and John T. Wold, "Rose Bird and the Politics of
Judicial Accountability in California," *Judicature* 70 (August-September, 1986): 81-89; and John T. Wold
and John H. Culver, "The Defeat of the California Justices: the Campaign, the Electorate, and the Issue of
Judicial Accountability," *Judicature* 70 (April-May, 1987): 348-355.

merit selection merely transforms the politics of judicial selection.[25] Lawyers are placed on the selection commission because they "have daily opportunities to observe the character and professional qualifications of their fellow lawyers seeking judicial appointment ... and of the judges . . . seeking reappointment."[26] But as Box 3-1 suggests, judicial qualifications are rather nebulous—it is easier to state minimal qualifications than full qualifications—and it is often difficult to determine who possesses the qualifications. Thus, once commission members eliminate obvious incompetents, other factors necessarily come into play. Plaintiffs' attorneys on the commission may favor members of their group, Republicans or Democrats fellow party members, and so on. Although selection of judges solely on the basis of qualifications may be the aim of merit selection, it is not—and cannot be—the full reality.

At one time nonlawyer members of the selection commissions were predominantly white businessmen. However, as a result of efforts to secure greater representativeness, selection commissions now more accurately reflect the states' demographic diversity.[27] Yet, in one sense, the lay commissioners are not representative of the general populace. Appointed by the governor, they tend to reflect his or her political perspective. In fact, one-third have served in a party office, and one-quarter have held some public post.[28] As one observer in Missouri noted: "some of the laymen are more concerned with politics than anything else, and some of them will do whatever the governor wants them to do when it comes to the selection of panels of nominees."[29]

In addition to appointing lay members of the commission, the governor can also influence the commission's deliberations by letting members know whom he or she favors for a vacant judgeship. The pressure on commission members need not be overt to be effective. Once commissioners know whom the governor wants for a position, they are unlikely to omit that person from the list of candidates unless the person is clearly unqualified.[30] As a result, under merit selection governors may exercise almost as much control as they do under a system of gubernatorial appointment.

What Effect Do Judicial Selection Systems Have?

Underlying the debate between proponents of merit systems and advocates of judicial elections is the assumption that the mode of selection affects the decisions judges render. However, this assumption is questionable. Political scientists have conducted several studies comparing the voting patterns and decisions of the judges selected by various methods. Looking at similar cases in various states, they found no significant relationship between the mode of selection and judicial voting behavior.[31] Other studies, focusing on how various classes of litigants (such as corporations, criminal defendants, and state agencies) have fared before judges selected by various methods, likewise concluded that the mode of selection did not affect outcomes.[32] At a minimum, these findings raise questions about the connection between mode of selection and judicial decision-making.

Advocates of merit selection also proclaim that their system produces more qualified judges. Given the difficulty in determining what qualifications are most important, it is impossible to test this claim directly. Scholars have therefore examined the backgrounds and characteristics of judges chosen through various modes of selection, under the assumption that these factors might serve as indicators of judicial quality. Even if they cannot, they do indicate what sorts of people become state judges under various selection systems.

WHO ARE THE STATE JUDGES?

Altogether, there are over 28,000 state judges: 354 supreme court justices, 804 other appellate court judges, 8937 judges in trial courts of general jurisdiction, and 18,563 judges in courts of limited jurisdiction.[33] Because it would be impossible to collect detailed background information on so many judges, scholars have focused their attention on state supreme court justices. Table 3-2 summarizes their findings.

What is most striking about the supreme court justices are the similarities in their backgrounds. Whatever the mode of selection, the justices tend to be white, male, middle-aged, and middle-to-upper class. To some extent this reflects the pool of candidates from which judges are chosen: the legal profession itself is hardly representative of the nation's population either demographically or economically. Usually state supreme court justices are natives of the state in which they serve, have attended law school there, and have been active in state or local politics. Again, this is not surprising. If political considerations cannot be altogether excluded from judicial selection, then prospective judges who develop good contacts within the state and have been politically active will have an advantage. According to one judge, "frequently judgeships become consolation prizes for those who failed in big-time elected politics."[34]

The backgrounds of the justices do vary somewhat from state to state. For example, judges in the west are more likely to be born out of state than their counterparts elsewhere, judges in the south are more likely to be Democrats, and more Catholic and Jewish judges are found in the northeast.[35] Political scientists have concluded that region, rather than different modes of selection, explains almost all the interstate differences. Thus, at least in terms of judicial

TABLE 3-2 CHARACTERISTICS OF STATE SUPREME COURT JUSTICES, 1980-81

Localism

	In-state birth	84.7%
	In-state undergraduate school	70.0
	In-state law school	69.0

Race and gender

	Female	3.1
	African-American	0.6

Religious affiliation

	Protestant	60.2
	Catholic	23.9
	Jewish	11.6
	Other	4.2

Government career experience

	Prosecutor	21.5
	Legislator	20.3
	Previous judicial	62.9
	Other	34.7

Democratic party affiliation   66.7

Type of law practice

	Solo	26.1
	2-4 partners	54.0
	Larger firm	19.9

Average age upon reaching court   53.0

SOURCES: Henry R. Glick and Craig F. Emmert, "Stability and Change: Characteristics of State Supreme Court Judges," *Judicature* 70 (August-September, 1986): 109, Table 2; and Henry R. Glick and Craig F. Emmert, "Selection Systems and Judicial Characteristics: The Recruitment of State Supreme Court Judges," *Judicature* 70 (December-January, 1987): 232, Table 1.

backgrounds, merit selection does not produce judges who differ significantly from those selected by other means.

The demographics of state courts have also changed over time. Table 3-2 documents the small number of women and African-Americans on state high courts in 1980. However, these figures represent a significant increase over the 1960s, when there were only three female and no black justices. The change is continuing: a more recent study found 23 women, 9 African-Americans, and 2 Asians serving on state supreme courts.[36] In 1991 Governor Rudy Perpich appointed Judge Sandra Gardebring to the Minnesota Supreme Court, thereby making it the first state supreme court to have a female majority.

One can expect these changes to continue and perhaps accelerate. Civil rights groups have challenged systems of judicial selection that allegedly exclude racial minorities from judicial positions (see Box 3-3). If these legal challenges succeed, their effect could be substantial. Even if they fail, as previously excluded groups comprise a larger proportion of the legal profession and become more influential politically, their greater numbers and influence will be reflected in the composition of the state bench.

THE SELECTION OF FEDERAL JUDGES

Article II of the Constitution grants the President the power to appoint federal judges, including Supreme Court justices, with the advice and consent of the Senate. In the view of the founders, this system of shared responsibility had several advantages. As Alexander Hamilton argued in Federalist No. 76, appointment of judges by a single person secured better judgment, imparted a greater sense of responsibility for the choice, and ensured there would be "fewer personal attachments to gratify" in selecting judges. Senatorial confirmation of appointees served as "an excellent check upon a spirit of favoritism in the President" and, more generally, encouraged the President to appoint only highly qualified persons.[37]

The reality of federal judicial selection is more complex than the constitutional text suggests. The respective influence of the President and the Senate on selection differs depending upon the level of court, upon the importance the President attaches to judicial appointments, and upon whether a single party controls both the presidency and the Senate. In selecting lower-court judges, members of the Senate often play the initiating role. When a justice of the Supreme Court is appointed, the President usually is actively involved. Yet, as the hearings on Judge Bork (1989) and Justice Clarence Thomas (1991) show, members of the Senate can assume an adversarial stance and conduct their own detailed investigation of the nominee's qualifications and constitutional views. Within the executive branch, the officials involved in selecting candidates vary according to the level of court and the wishes of the President. Moreover, the criteria used in selecting judges vary from administration to administration.

What does not change from administration to administration is the political character of the process. As a rule, presidents appoint judges who are politically active members of their own party. Merit certainly plays a role in the appointment of federal judges, but competence is a minimum requirement. In choos-

BOX 3-3 LITIGATING FOR A REPRESENTATIVE JUDICIARY

Although African-Americans and Hispanic-Americans comprise over 18 percent of the nation's population, recent figures indicate that only about 5 percent of state judges are members of those groups. Some civil rights groups have charged that this disparity results from racial discrimination in state judicial elections. No state, of course, bans minority-group members from running for judgeships or voting in judicial elections. However, several states do use at-large elections or multi-judge districts. Civil rights groups argue that these districting practices dilute the voting strength of minority groups by placing them in large districts in which they are a numerical minority. Given the prevalence of voting along racial lines, creation of large districts effectively precludes members of minority groups from electing the candidates they favor. As a result, few minority-group members serve on state courts.

Civil rights groups have challenged the use of at-large elections and multi-member districts in several southern states under the Voting Rights Act of 1965. Originally this act prohibited states with a history of racial discrimination in voting from changing their voting laws without the approval of federal authorities, who presumably would ensure that the change was not discriminatory. Direct challenges to existing laws were also possible. In 1982, after the Supreme Court had ruled that litigants had to prove that state laws were designed to discriminate, Congress amended the Voting Rights Act to permit challenges based on the laws' discriminatory effect. This has provided the basis for the legal challenges to at-large judicial elections and multi-member districts.

Aside from affirming that the Voting Rights Act applies to judicial elections, even though judges do not really represent the views of those who vote for them, the Supreme Court has not addressed the challenges to state judicial districting. Several federal district courts and courts of appeals, however, have entertained such suits. In Mississippi in 1988, a federal district court found that the state's at-large judicial elections violated the Voting Rights Act, divided various judicial districts into single-member subdistricts, and ordered those sub-districts to hold primaries and general elections. In the election that followed the redistricting, two black judges were elected, the first ever in the state. Challenges also succeeded in Texas and Louisiana, but failed in Illinois. More litigation is in the pipeline, and it appears that several states will have to redesign their systems of electing judges to create districts in which minority-group judges have a realistic possibility of election.

SOURCES: Judith Haydel, "Section 2 of the Voting Rights Act of 1965: A Challenge to State Judicial Election Systems;" "The Voting Rights Act and Judicial Elections: An Update on Current Litigation;" Robert McDuff, "The Voting Rights Act and Judicial Elections Litigation: The Plaintiffs' Perspective;" and Ronald E. Weber, "The Voting Rights Act and Judicial Elections Litigation: The Defendant States' Perspective," all of which appeared in *Judicature* 73 (August-September, 1989): 68-86; and Barbara Luck Graham, "Judicial Recruitment and Racial Diversity on State Courts: An Overview," *Judicature* 74 (June-July, 1990): 28-34.

ing among qualified candidates, political considerations necessarily tip the balance.

The Size of the Federal Judiciary

Of course, for the President to appoint a judge, there must be a vacant judgeship. Vacancies can occur because of the death, the retirement, or—in rare cases—the impeachment of a judge. Most federal judges regard their service on the bench as the capstone of their legal careers, and relatively few leave the bench before required to do so by age or failing health. In 1986, 40 district court judges appointed prior to 1969 were still on the bench.[38]

Vacancies can also occur when Congress creates new judgeships. Although the Supreme Court has had nine justices since 1869, caseload pressures have forced Congress to increase the number of district court and appeals court judges. Since 1970, their number has more than doubled: as of July, 1991, there are 649 district court judges and 167 appeals court judges. Adding large numbers of positions at one time can drastically alter the composition of the federal bench, and so political factors may affect Congress's timing in creating new judgeships. During the 1970s the Democratically controlled Congress delayed adding judgeships until there was a Democratic president to appoint the judges. After the election of Jimmy Carter in 1976, it passed the Omnibus Judgeship Act of 1978, creating 152 new positions. But there are limits to this. The press of judicial business forced Democrats in Congress to expand the federal judiciary during President Ronald Reagan's term of office. This action, together with with normal attrition on the federal courts, gave Reagan the opportunity to appoint 290 district court judges and 78 court of appeals judges—almost half of the federal judiciary and more than any other American president.

The Selection of District Court and Appeals Court Judges

Since at least the 1840s, the selection of district court judges has reversed the constitutional prescription and lodged the primary power in the Senate. More precisely, under the system that developed during the mid-nineteenth century, power rests in the hands of the senators from the President's party in the state in which a judge is to serve. If these senators invoke *senatorial courtesy*, indicating their opposition to a nominee, the Senate will almost always reject the President's choice. This does not mean that the Senate frequently rejects nominees; it does not. Rather, the prospect of defeat in the Senate creates a powerful incentive for presidents—or, more accurately, for the officials in the Justice Department to whom the President has delegated the responsibility—to confer with the appropriate senators before selecting nominees. Usually senators have their own candidate, or list of candidates, for the vacant seat, and the President typically endorses the senators' recommendation. This means that candidates for judgeships will campaign to win the support of the senators. Some senators may dislike the process—according to one, "all you get out of that mess is hundreds of enemies and one ingrate"—but most recognize it as an important opportunity to distribute patronage.[39] Presidents have usually viewed the system as an opportunity to trade judgeships for senatorial support on other matters. Attorney General Robert Kennedy exaggerated only slightly when he described the process: "Basically, it's senatorial appointment with the advice and consent of the Senate."[40]

Senatorial courtesy influences what sorts of people are appointed to the district courts. Because these judgeships serve as political patronage for senators, the vast majority of appointees are affiliated with the Senator's (and the President's) political party. Over the last hundred years, roughly 95 percent of all district court judges have been members of the appointing president's party.[41] In addition, district court judges usually have "earned" their positions by active party service prior to their appointment. From the point of view of prospective judges, this establishes a clear career path. As one judge put it, "if I wanted that appointment, [I knew] I had better get back into politics—which I did."[42] Because state party contacts are particularly important in securing support, this political activity typically involves state or local, rather than national, politics. The judges therefore tend to share the political perspectives dominant in the state. This has at times posed a problem, as illustrated by the reluctance of some southern district court judges to enforce the Supreme Court's school desegregation decisions in the 1950s and 1960s.[43]

In selecting judges for courts of appeals, the President's power is enhanced and that of the Senate somewhat diminished. Because of the importance of the positions, the attorney general and other high-ranking officials in the Justice Department participate in identifying and screening potential nominees. Occasionally the President himself may be involved. Because each appeals court encompasses more than one state, no state's senators can control its membership. Nonetheless, a modified form of senatorial courtesy has developed, extending to the specific seats on the court that have been informally earmarked for each state in the circuit. Still, this extra leverage for the state's senators is balanced by the greater presidential interest in these appointments, resulting in a need for negotiation and compromise.

The appeals court judges selected through this process in many ways resemble their counterparts on the district courts—indeed, a sizable minority serve on district courts before being promoted to the court of appeals. Most of the judges were politically active members of the President's party before their appointment, and many had held or run for public office. A perfect example is former Attorney General Griffin Bell, who served on the Fifth Circuit before resigning to head the Justice Department. In addition to his legal credentials, Bell noted that he had other qualifications for the court of appeals:

> I managed John F. Kennedy's presidential campaign in Georgia. Two of my oldest and closest friends were the two senators from Georgia. And I was the campaign manager and special, unpaid counsel for the governor.[44]

Finally, because positions on the courts of appeals are avidly sought, those who are selected usually have campaigned actively (though discreetly) for the position, lining up a coalition of supporters when a vacancy occurred. One judge candidly stated: "Anybody who thinks judicial office seeks the man is mistaken. There's not a man on the court who didn't do what he thought needed to be done."[45]

A final unofficial participant in the process of selecting federal judges is the American Bar Association, through its Standing Committee on Federal Judiciary. Since the Eisenhower administration (1953-1961), presidents have submitted the names of judicial nominees to the committee for an evaluation of their professional qualifications. After conducting an investigation, the committee rates nominees. Some presidents—for example, Richard Nixon—pledged not to nominate anyone who received an unfavorable rating. Others—for example, John Kennedy—refused to give the committee a veto over nominations and appointed some persons who had received a "not qualified" rating. During the Reagan administration, the ABA committee came under fire from both the political right and the political left. Conservatives claimed that liberals on the ABA committee were allowing their political disagreement with the Reagan administration to color their evaluations of its nominees. Meanwhile, liberals charged that the committee was approving unqualified nominees rather than risk a confrontation with the Reagan administration. The election of President Bush defused the controversy over the ABA's role.

Selection of Lower-Court Judges Under Carter, Reagan, and Bush

In contrast to most previous presidents, Jimmy Carter and Ronald Reagan made concerted efforts to advance their political agendas through the appointment of district court and appeals court judges. In so doing, they altered the traditional politics of judicial selection. President George Bush followed the leads of both Reagan and Carter in his appointments.

Judicial Selection Under Carter

President Carter assumed office committed to using affirmative action to increase the demographic representativeness of the federal judiciary by appointing African-Americans, women, and other minorities. As he stated: "If I didn't have to get Senate confirmation of appointees, I could tell you flatly that 12 percent of my appointees would be Black and 3 percent would be Spanish-speaking and 40 percent would be women and so forth."[46] To identify qualified candidates for appeals courts who might have been overlooked under the traditional selection system, President Carter established circuit nominating commissions and included women and minority group members on them. Although he did not directly challenge senatorial prerogatives in naming candidates for seats on district courts, he urged senators to establish their own nominating commissions. Several did so, and Democratic senators who did not were nonetheless made aware of the president's affirmative action goals.

Tables 3-3 and 3-4 document the success of President Carter's efforts: he named more women and African-Americans to the federal bench than had all of his predecessors put together. Moreover, his attempt to "open up" judicial selection apparently did not undermine the quality of the federal judiciary. The American Bar Association rated over 50 percent of his district court appointees and 75 percent of his appeals court appointees exceptionally well qualified or well qualified, ratings comparable to those received by the nominees of preceding presidents. Yet in seeking to elevate qualified minority candidates to the federal bench, Carter followed the established practice of seeking out politically active party members. Over 90 percent of the judges he appointed were Democrats and over 63 percent were political activists prior to appointment.

Judicial Selection Under Reagan

President Reagan was concerned less with the demographics of his nominees than with their legal and political views. Early in his administration, he announced that he would only appoint judges who embraced the philosophy of judicial restraint, that is, who would defer to the popularly elected branches of government and give a presumption of constitutionality to governmental actions. To accomplish this, Reagan devised what one participant called "the most thorough and comprehensive system for recruiting and screening federal judicial candidates of any administration ever."[47] In place of the nominating commissions, he established the Office of Legal Policy, which scrutinized the backgrounds of prospective nominees and conducted rigorous daylong interviews with them. Candidates whose views meshed with the Reagan administration's were put forward, but candidates who failed what critics called an "ideo-

TABLE 3-3 CHARACTERISTICS OF FEDERAL DISTRICT COURT JUDGES			
	Bush	**Reagan**	**Carter**
Occupation			
Politics/govt.	10.8%	12.8%	4.4%
Judiciary	41.9	37.2	44.6
Gender			
Male	80.4	91.7	85.6
Female	19.6	8.3	14.4
Ethnicity or race			
White	89.2	92.4	78.7
African-American	6.8	2.1	13.9
Hispanic	4.0	4.8	6.9
Asian	——	0.7	0.5
A.B.A. ratings			
EWQ/WQ	57.4	54.1	50.9
Qualified	42.6	45.9	47.5
Not qualified	——	——	1.5
Party affiliation			
Democratic	5.4	4.8	92.6
Republican	88.5	93.1	4.4
Independent	6.1	2.1	2.9
Past party activism	60.8	58.6	60.9
Net worth at appointment			
Under $200,000	10.1	17.6	35.8
$200,000-499,000	31.1	37.8	41.2
$500,000-999,999	26.4	27.1	18.9
$1+ million	32.4	23.1	4.0
Total number of appointees	148	290	202
Average age at nomination	48.1	48.7	49.7

SOURCE: Adapted from Sheldon Goldman, "Bush's Judicial Legacy: The Final Imprint," *Judicature* 76 (April-May, 1993), p. 287, Table 2. Reprinted from *Judicature*, the journal of the American Judicature Society.

KEY: EWQ/WQ = Exceptionally well qualified or well qualified

TABLE 3-4 CHARACTERISTICS OF FEDERAL APPEALS COURT JUDGES

	Bush	Reagan	Carter
Occupation			
Politics/govt.	10.8%	6.4%	5.4%
Judiciary	59.9	55.1	46.4
Gender			
Male	81.1	94.9	80.4
Female	18.9	5.1	19.6
Ethnicity or race			
White	89.2	97.4	78.6
African-American	5.4	1.3	16.1
Hispanic	5.4	1.3	3.6
Asian	——	——	1.8
A.B.A. ratings			
EWQ/WQ	64.9	59.0	75.0
Qualified	35.1	41.0	25.0
Party Affiliation			
Democratic	5.4	——	82.1
Republican	89.2	97.4	7.1
Independent/other	5.4	2.6	10.7
Past party activism	70.3	69.2	73.2
Net worth at appointment			
Under $200,00	5.4	15.6	33.3
$200,00-499,999	29.7	32.5	38.5
$500,00-999,999	21.6	33.8	17.9
$1+ million	43.2	18.2	10.3
Total number of appointees	37	78	56
Average age at nomination	48.7	50.0	51.9

SOURCE: Adapted from Sheldon Goldman, "Bush's Judicial Legacy: The Final Imprint," *Judicature* 76 (April-May, 1993), p. 293. Table 4. Reprinted from *Judicature,* the journal of the American Judicature Society.

KEY: EWQ/WQ = Exceptionally well qualified or well qualified logical litmus test" were not. As a result, far more than in previous administrations, President Reagan's nominees reflected a consistent legal and political perspective.

The President's efforts to appoint judicial conservatives ran into some opposition from liberal and moderate Republican senators, whose choices for district court judgeships did not always coincide with the president's. When the White House requested that Republican senators submit the names of at least three candidates for vacant judgeships within their state, some senators refused to comply. The outcomes of these conflicts were mixed. In some instances the President refused to nominate candidates he perceived as too liberal; in other instances, particularly when President Reagan needed the senator's vote on other issues, he was willing to compromise. Nonetheless, Reagan's success in getting judicial candidates he favored, like Carter's, indicates that presidents who feel strongly about lower-court judgeships can have a real impact, even in an area which the Senate has traditionally dominated.

There is some evidence that President Reagan's attempt to realign the federal courts succeeded. Scholars have found that Reagan's appointees were only half as likely as Carter's to support the claims of defendants in criminal cases or of plaintiffs with civil liberties claims.[48] Reagan's appointees were also far more likely to rule against abortion-rights claims than were federal judges appointed by previous presidents, including Republican presidents.[49] Another study revealed that district court judges appointed by Reagan rendered liberal decisions in only 36 percent of the cases before them, the most conservative record of any group of judges appointed since 1912.[50] These data underscore the important effects that a president can have on the lower federal courts.

Judicial Selection Under Bush

Congressional legislation expanding the federal judiciary, together with normal attrition, permitted President Bush to have a significant impact on the lower federal courts. During his administration, he appointed almost 200 federal judges, making the federal judiciary about 75% Republican. Not since the days of Franklin Roosevelt has there been such a partisan preponderance on the federal courts.[51]

President Bush's nominees for the lower federal courts did not face intense opposition in the Senate, perhaps because of their excellent ABA ratings. Yet in certain respects his approach to judicial selection resembled Reagan's. Like Reagan, he sought to guarantee presidential influence over nominations by asking senators for several nominees for each vacancy. He also continued the practice of screening the views of prospective nominees with an eye to judicial restraint. Finally, he chose nominees who in many ways resembled those of his predecessor. Bush's nominees were for the most part young, white Republicans, often with prior judicial experience. However, while Bush (like Reagan before him) found few African-American Republicans to appoint to the bench, he appointed a higher percentage of women to the lower federal bench than any previous president, including Carter.

THE SELECTION OF SUPREME COURT JUSTICES

When Justice William Brennan retired in 1990, he had served over a third of a century on the Supreme Court. Appointed by President Dwight Eisenhower in 1956, only two years after the Court's historic ruling in *Brown* v. *Board of Education*[52], Brennan remained on the bench through the turmoil of the 1960s, through the Watergate scandal of the 1970s, and through the Reagan Revolution of the 1980s. Altogether he participated in the decision of almost 5000 cases, and his opinions defined the Court's positions on freedom of religion, flag burning, libel, political patronage systems, and the exclusion of illegally seized evidence.[53] For the last two decades of his service, he was the acknowledged leader of the liberal wing of the Court, sometimes in the majority but more recently in dissent. Justice Harry Blackmun summed up Brennan's career upon his retirement: "By any measure, Justice Brennan must be regarded as one of the great names among those who have served on the Supreme Court of the United States."[54] President Eisenhower's assessment was less laudatory. Asked if he had made any mistakes during his presidency, Eisenhower reputedly replied, "Yes, two, and they [Justice Brennan and Chief Justice Warren] are both sitting on the Supreme Court."[55]

Criteria for Selection

Justice Brennan's career, spanning eight presidencies, shows that Supreme Court appointments can influence the course of the nation, for better or worse, long after a president's term has ended. Not surprisingly, then, presidents tend to take an active part in the selection of Supreme Court justices. Those selected characteristically have had distinguished public careers—they include a dozen members of Congress, numerous Cabinet officers, and even an ex-President— and possess outstanding legal credentials. Many of the justices have served as judges at some time prior to selection, though this is not a requirement, and several outstanding justices had no judicial experience. Beyond these minimal qualifications, presidents have weighed a variety of factors in making their

TABLE 3-5 JUSTICES OF THE U. S. SUPREME COURT, 1993

	Born	Home State	Position Prior to Appointment	Prior judicial experience	Party affiliation	Year appointed	Appointing president
William Rehnquist*	1924	Arizona	Associate Justice Assistant Attorney General	No	Republican	1986 (CJ) 1972 (AJ)	Reagan Nixon
Harry Blackmun	1908	Minnesota	U.S.Court of Appeals	Yes	Republican	1970	Nixon
John Stevens	1920	Illinois	U.S.Court of Appeals	Yes	Republican	1975	Ford
Sandra Day O'Connor	1930	Arizona	State appeals court	Yes	Republican	1981	Reagan
Antonin Scalia	1936	New Jersey	U.S. Court of Appeals	Yes	Republican	1986	Reagan
Anthony Kennedy	1936	California	U.S. Court of Appeals	Yes	Republican	1988	Reagan
David Souter	1939	New Hampshire	U.S. Court of Appeals	Yes	Republican	1990	Bush
Clarence Thomas	1948	Georgia	U.S.Court of Appeals	Yes	Republican	1991	Bush
Ruth Bader Ginsburg	1933	New York	U.S. Court of Appeals	Yes	Democrat	1993	Clinton

* - William Rehnquist was appointed as Associate Justice by Richard Nixon and then elevated to Chief Justice by Ronald Reagan.

SOURCES: Ralph A. Rossum and G. Alan Tarr, *American Constitutional Law*, 3rd ed. (New York: St. Martin's Press, 1991), and Henry J. Abraham, *Justices and Presidents*, 3rd ed. (New York: Oxford University Press, 1991).

appointments, with the importance of various factors changing over time and from president to president.[56]

Party Affiliation

Presidents have drawn over 90 percent of all nominees from the ranks of their own party. If a president does cross party lines, he usually anticipates some political advantage from doing so. Thus when Republican President Eisenhower appointed Justice Brennan, a New Jersey Democrat and a Catholic, he viewed the appointment as a way of appealing to potential cross-over voters during an election year and of portraying his administration as nonpolitical and bipartisan.[57] Presidents typically choose only members of the opposition party with whom they feel ideologically compatible. This is exemplified in President Richard Nixon's selection of Justice Lewis Powell, a conservative Democrat from Virginia, for the Supreme Court.

Region

Well into the twentieth century, region played an important part in appointments to the Supreme Court. Initially, having representation from the various sections of the country bolstered the legitimacy of the Court and of the national government. From the founding through 1971, except during Reconstruction, there was a Southern seat on the Court and, until the 1930s, a New England seat as well. Today the concern for regional balance has largely disappeared. For example, President Reagan appointed Arizona Judge Sandra Day O'Connor to the Court, even though Justice William Rehnquist was also an Arizonan.

Demographic Characteristics

If region has declined in importance, demographic characteristics have increased. During the early twentieth century, the concern was with religious representation, with identifiable Catholic and Jewish seats on the Court. By the late twentieth century, however, race and gender were major concerns. In 1967 President Lyndon Johnson appointed Justice Thurgood Marshall, the first African-American to serve on the Court; and when Marshall retired in 1991, President George Bush took into consideration the concern for black representation on the Court in naming Justice Clarence Thomas as Marshall's replacement. In 1980, while campaigning for the presidency, Ronald Reagan pledged to appoint a woman to the Court, and he fulfilled that promise a year later in naming Justice Sandra Day O'Connor. William Clinton also made a woman his first appointee to the court. Ethnicity too is important. Justice Antonin Scalia, appointed by President Reagan in 1986, is the first Italian-American on the Court, and one expects that in the future there will be efforts to ensure representation for Hispanics and for Asian-Americans.

Legal-Political Compatibility

Presidents want justices on the Supreme Court who share their views on constitutional issues. Usually they are concerned less with a potential justice's overall jurisprudential approach than with his or her position on certain salient legal issues. Thus President Franklin Roosevelt appointed judges who shared his broad view of the national government's power to regulate the economy and who would uphold the New Deal programs he had championed. President Richard Nixon, concerned about the Court's expansion of the rights of defendants, sought to select "strict constructionist" justices who would "strengthen the peace forces as against the criminal forces of the land."[58] President Reagan sought proponents of "judicial restraint" who might reverse the Supreme Court's decisions on abortion, voluntary prayer in the schools, and the rights of defendants.

Obstacles to Presidential Influence

Presidents do not always succeed in influencing the Court's orientation by their appointments. As President Harry Truman ruefully observed, "packing the Supreme Court simply can't be done ... I've tried and it won't work."[59] Once appointed, the justice may not behave on the Court as the president expected. For example, after Theodore Roosevelt appointed Oliver Wendell Holmes to the Court, he wrote opinions in several antitrust cases that so enraged Roosevelt that he complained: "I could carve out of a banana a Judge with more backbone than that!"[60] President Richard Nixon must have felt betrayed when Chief Justice Warren Burger ruled against his claim of executive privilege in *United States* v. *Nixon,* and President Reagan was doubtless disappointed that Chief Justice William Rehnquist rejected a challenge to the appointment of independent counsels to investigate presidential subordinates.[61] In addition, presidents often do not anticipate changes over time in the issues confronting the Court and therefore do not probe a nominee's views on those issues. Thus although President Nixon appointed Justice Harry Blackmun to the Court, expecting that he would take a conservative position on the rights of defendants, Blackmun is best known for his opinion in *Roe* v. *Wade* (1973), announcing that the Constitution safeguarded a woman's right to choose to have an abortion.[62] Indeed, in the years since that decision,

Blackmun has frequently aligned himself with the liberal wing of the Court. In sum, from the perspective of the justice, things may look different than they did prior to appointment. Judicial independence allows justices to shed their partisanship and change their views. When this happens, there is nothing the appointing president can do. As legal scholar Alexander Bickel summed it up, "You shoot an arrow into a far-distant future when you appoint a Justice and not the man himself can tell you what he will think about some of the problems he will face."[63]

Yet one should not overstate the matter. When justices are appointed, they already have established legal views, and only rarely do those views change dramatically once they are on the Court. Moreover, presidents can minimize "mistakes" by canvassing the views of potential nominees prior to appointment. For example, President Reagan appointed several potential nominees to appellate judgeships to get some indication of their judicial philosophy and abilities. With the exception of Chief Justice Rehnquist, already serving as an associate justice, and Justice O'Connor, all of Reagan's Supreme Court nominees had "auditioned" on a court of appeals. Prior to appointing Justice O'Connor, Reagan thoroughly investigated her constitutional views. He dispatched an aide to Arizona for a day of interviews with her and with others knowledgeable about her background and her views. She then was questioned in Washington by the Attorney General, by three senior White House staffers, and by the President himself. Only after this painstaking examination did the President appoint her to the Court. The current orientation of the Supreme Court demonstrates the success of President Reagan's efforts to create a conservative Court.

The Senate can also frustrate presidential efforts to "pack" the Court by refusing to confirm a president's nominee. It has not often done so: only 12 Supreme Court nominees have been rejected, while 16 other nominations were either withdrawn from consideration or indefinitely postponed because of opposition in the Senate.[64] Since 1968, however, the Senate has refused to confirm six of sixteen nominees. Moreover, the controversy over the nomination of Clarence Thomas illustrates that Senate questioning of nominees can be grueling, even when they are ultimately confirmed. The recent spate of rejections can be attributed in part to perceived problems with particular nominees ethical problems (Fortas, Haynsworth, Ginsburg), perceived lack of competence (Carswell), and/or allegedly extreme views (Bork). However, the Senate's willingness to deny the President his choice also depends upon interbranch relations. The Senate is more likely to reject a nominee if the Senate and the presidency are controlled by different parties and/or if the President has been politically weakened by scandal, unpopular policies, or a forthcoming presidential election. With Democratic control of the White House and the

Senate, President Clinton's initial nominee for the Supreme Court received easy confirmation.

WHAT DO JUDGES DO?

From Advocate to Arbitrer

Upon assuming office, new judges immediately confront daunting responsibilities. Often they feel themselves unprepared and isolated. In civil-law countries, such as France, a judge attends a specialized school and follows a separate career path from lawyers (see Box 3-4). In contrast, in the United States, prospective judges receive no special preparation. They attend law school like other lawyers and then typically pursue a career in either government or private practice. Once selected for the bench, however, they are expected to shed their identities as advocates and partisans and become impartial arbitrers. Not surprisingly, many new judges encounter problems.[65]

First of all, new judges are frequently unfamiliar with much of the law that they must apply. This may seem strange, since judges are chosen from the ranks of attorneys. However, the lawyers elevated to the bench often had specialized legal practices. They focused on criminal law or, more likely, on civil law; they were plaintiffs' lawyers, defense attorneys, or prosecutors; they were patent attorneys, environmental lawyers, or tax specialists. Judges, in contrast, are generalists—they have jurisdiction over a wide range of conflicts, and most judges must accept whatever cases come before them. Trial judges may preside over a murder case one day and a products liability suit the next. In order to undertake these diverse responsibilities, they must become knowledgeable in areas of law that they may not have studied since law school.

Second, new judges must change their basic orientation. Lawyers are accustomed to acting as advocates, taking a position and arguing it. However, "the essence of the judicial role, active or passive, is impartiality and detachment, both felt and exhibited."[66] Thus as Justice Charles Russell of the Virginia Supreme Court put it, "your skills [as an advocate] are so diametrically opposed to those demanded of a judge that you've got to do a frightful gear shift."[67]

Third, prior to their selection, judges tend to be actively involved in politics—indeed, political involvement is often a prerequisite for selection. Except in systems with partisan elections, however, judges are expected to avoid partisanship not only in their decisions but also in their behavior off the bench. Many states forbid judges from engaging in any sort of political activity—from endorsing

BOX 3-4 FRENCH JUDGES

In France, as in other civil law systems, judges are *not* selected from the ranks of practicing attorneys. Prospective judges receive an education designed to prepare them for their professional responsibilities and upon graduation immediately commence their judicial careers.

To become a judge, one must first graduate from a university law school. Except for a few minor exceptions, law graduates opting for a judicial career must take the examination for admission to the Ecole Nationale de la Magistrature (National Judicial College) before their twenty-eighth birthday. The exam is highly competitive: in 1988 over 1300 applicants took the exam, but only 186 (77 men and 109 women) were admitted. Those admitted to the Ecole Nationale not only receive professional training in the law and in the responsibilities of a judge in a civil law system but also serve a probationary period before graduating.

Upon graduation, the new judges are initially assigned to one of the criminal or civil courts at the lower end of the judicial hierarchy. Because most French courts, including trial courts, sit as multi-judge courts, the new graduate has the advantage of working with more experienced colleagues. From their initial assignments, judges may, over time, be promoted to higher and more important posts within the French judicial system. Advancement in the system depends both on seniority and on the "notations" a judge receives from senior judges and from supervisors. The French judiciary is a career service: judges cannot be removed from office except for a gross abuse of their positions.

The closest American analogy to the French system of selection, training, and promotion is the civil service system. Like the civil service, the French system is designed to create a set of professionals pursuing careers in a specialized field. Like the civil service, the French system also eliminates political considerations and personal favoritism in the selection phase through competitive examinations. The promotion process, however, may pose a threat to judicial independence because those determining promotions may reward loyalty and conformism and penalize independence. One factor that reduces these pressures on judges toward conformity is the collegial character of most French courts. Because of the practice of announcing decisions without indicating who authored an opinion or whether there were any dissents, all judicial decisions are rendered in the name of the court as a whole, and no individual judge must take responsibility for a decision. Nonetheless, judicial independence remains a fundamental issue in civil law systems.

SOURCES: Henry W. Ehrmann, *Comparative Legal Cultures* (Englewood Cliffs, N.J.: Prentice-Hall, 1976); John H. Merryman, *The Civil Law Tradition* (Stanford: Stanford University Press, 1969); John Bell, "Principles and Methods of Judicial Selection in France," *Southern California Law Review* 61 (September 1983): 1757-1794; and Jacqueline Lucienne Lafon, "The Judicial Career in France: Theory and Practice Under the French Republic," *Judicature* 75 (August-September, 1991): 97-106 candidates to speaking at political meetings to making political contributions. Some judges take this insulation from politics very seriously indeed: Justice John Marshall Harlan even refused to vote during his service on the U.S. Supreme Court. Others seek to reconcile, often unsuccessfully, their political concerns and their judicial role. Justice Abraham Fortas, for example, was sharply criticized for continuing as an adviser to President Lyndon Johnson even after his appointment to the Supreme Court.[68] For many judges the transition from politically engaged lawyer to what Justice Felix Frankfurter referred to as "judicial monk" is a difficult one.

Related to this is a more general isolation that accompanies elevation to the bench. Becoming a judge affects one's social life: lawyers with whom one associated prior to selection are reluctant to socialize for fear of being seen as currying favor. Beyond that, trial judges find themselves moving from the collegial context of a law firm to presiding alone over a court, forced to make momentous decisions without the opportunity to confer with others. New judges feel this pressure particularly in sentencing. As one judge put it, "This is the hardest part of being a judge. You see so many pathetic people and you're never sure of what is a right or fair sentence."[69]

How do judges cope with these problems? Many avail themselves of formal judicial training. The Federal Judicial Center conducts seminars for newly appointed judges and continuing education courses for their more senior colleagues. State trial judges may take courses at the National Judicial College, and appellate judges at the Institute for Judicial Administration. In addition, new judges try to emulate successful colleagues—as one judge put it, "judges learn through role models."[70] Finally, they may seek the counsel of veteran judges to ease the transition from advocate to arbitrer.

The Work of the Trial Judge

If asked, many people would probably say that trial-court judges preside over jury trials. Scholars have discovered, however, that a trial judge's responsibilities are more diverse than conventional wisdom suggests. In a nationwide survey, over 3000 judges in courts of general jurisdiction described the tasks they most commonly performed in the course of a day.[71] The results of this survey are summarized in Table 3-6.

The survey revealed that jury trials are the most time-consuming of judicial activities: those judges who reported conducting jury trials on their most common workday indicated that they spent almost five hours a day on them. However, less than one-half of the judges reported presiding at a jury trial on

TABLE 3-6 THE WORKDAY OF THE TRIAL JUDGE

Tasks	Percentage of judges reporting the task on their most common workday
Courtroom work	
Conducting jury trials	44.3%
Conducting nonjury trials	44.5
Non-trial work	52.0
Waiting time	42.4
Negotiations	
Case-related discussions with attorneys	47.5
Socializing with attorneys	38.9
Settlement discussions	32.0
Plea negotiations	18.9
Legal work	
Reading case files	70.1
Keeping up with the law	68.1
Preparing/writing decisions, judgments, orders	56.2
Administrative work	71.2

SOURCE: Adapted with the permission of The Free Press, a Division of Macmillan, Inc. from AMERICAN TRIAL JUDGES: Their Work Style and Performance, by John Paul Ryan, Allan Ashman, Bruce D. Sales, and Sandra Shane-DuBow. Copyright © 1980 by The American Judicature Society. Page 29, Figure 2—2.

their most common workday. Likewise, less than one-half reported presiding over non-jury trials. But on a typical day more than one-half reported being involved in non-trial courtroom work. This work may involve ruling on pre-trial motions, such as whether evidence was illegally seized and should be excluded from trial. Judges may also preside over the resolution of cases without trial, through guilty pleas in criminal cases or through default judgments in civil cases. Finally, judges may sentence those convicted in criminal cases.

Much of the trial judge's work, however, takes place outside the courtroom. As Chapters 5 and 6 will show, most cases are resolved by some sort of negotiated settlement, and judges promote settlement either by urging negotiations between the parties in a case or by actively participating in them. Although some judges believe it inappropriate to get involved in plea negotiations in criminal cases, many others discuss with prosecutors and defense counsel the evidence in a case, the charges to which a defendant will plead guilty, and the sentence he or she will receive. Judges also meet with opposing counsel in civil cases in order to encourage the two sides to settle before trial. Effective partici-pation in these case negotiations depends not on judges' legal expertise but on other interpersonal skills. It thus underscores the range of talents a successful judge needs.

Judges foster settlements in civil cases and negotiated pleas in criminal cases because settlements expedite the flow of cases: it is less time-consuming to settle a case than to try it. Many of a judge's administrative responsibilities are also associated with managing the flow of cases. Judges must schedule the cases on their dockets, keep up-to-date with the cases assigned to them, and keep track of case files and materials. In addition, a judge may be responsible for hiring law clerks and other court personnel. In trial courts with several judges, usually a senior judge is designated as chief judge and assumes administrative responsi-bilities for the court on a full-time basis.

Finally, trial judges must keep abreast of the legal work associated with their position. Unlike appellate judges, trial judges do not issue written opinions in most cases they decide, so their writing responsibilities are not onerous. However, whether judges are to be involved in negotiations or in trying a case, they must read the files in all the cases assigned to them. In addition, they must inform themselves about pertinent legal developments, such as appellate court decisions that affect their work. Taken altogether, the responsibilities of the trial judge are daunting indeed.

The Work of the Appellate Judge

Appellate courts are multi-judge courts whose job it is to review the legal cor-rectness of lower-court rulings in cases that are appealed to them. The appellate court announces its rulings in judicial opinions that explain the legal bases of its decisions. Because the responsibilities of trial and appellate courts differ, so too do the jobs of trial and appellate judges. Frank Coffin, formerly Chief Judge of the U. S. Court of Appeals for the First Circuit, has identified the various steps in his cycle of work as an appellate judge (see Table 3-7), and his experience is likely quite typical.

Several differences between the work of an appellate judge and that of a trial judge are immediately apparent. First, appellate judges conduct their work in rel-ative isolation from the outside world. Trial judges continually come into contact with members of the general public, who serve as parties, witnesses, or jurors.

TABLE 3-7 THE WORK CYCLE OF THE APPELLATE JUDGE

Although the list may differ in some details from judge to judge, this list identifies the main stages in appellate decisionmaking.

1. I read (or scan) briefs alone, usually at night.
2. I talk over each case with my clerks, one of whom has given particular attention to it. I make notes of our colloquy.
3. I listen to oral argument in court and ask a few questions.
4. I confer with my fellow judges late in the day after the argument.
5. I research, discuss, and draft an opinion in chambers or discuss, edit, and redraft the first draft of a clerk.
6. I circulate my draft to my colleagues and respond to their suggestions; when they circulate their drafts, I propose changes to which they respond.

SOURCE: Reprinted from *On Appeal; Courts, Lawyering and Judging*, by Frank M. Coffin, by permission of W.W. Norton & Company, Inc. Copyright (c) 1994 by W.W. Norton & Company, Inc.

They also regularly interact with attorneys, both within the courtroom and in conferences and other negotiations outside it. Over a period of time they get to know the "regulars" in their court quite well and tend to socialize with them during the course of the workday. In contrast, appellate judges have no direct contact with the parties or witnesses in the cases they hear, and their communications with lawyers are formal, occurring solely through the submission of legal briefs and through oral argument in court. Because the appellate court draws cases from a much larger geographic area than the trial court, appellate judges are unlikely to develop close ties with the attorneys who argue before them.

Second, appellate judges' isolation from the outside world is mitigated by their interaction with other appellate judges and court personnel. Whereas trial courts operate within severe time constraints in processing cases, the pace of work on appellate courts promotes deliberation. Often the chambers of an appellate judge works like an autonomous little "law firm," conducting legal research, discussing cases, and preparing opinions. Judges also discuss cases with colleagues after they are argued, and participate in the continuing interchange necessary to produce decisions that reflect truly collaborative deliberations. The trial judge may be the ruler of his or her courtroom, but the appellate judge acts as part of a team.

Third, in contrast with a trial court, an appellate court issues written opinions in most of the cases it decides. As a result, a large proportion of an appellate judge's time is spent either researching and writing judicial opinions or responding to the draft opinions of colleagues. Typically, the response to a colleague's opinion itself takes the form of a memorandum selectively accepting some aspects of the opinion and constructively critiquing other aspects. When a judge perceives problems with an argument in a colleague's opinion, collegiality demands that the judge offer an alternative line of argument or a different formulation. Such a detailed critique usually cannot be conveyed orally, and thus much of the communication among the judges on a case is written. In many instances this interchange enables the court to devise an opinion which all the judges can join. Failing that, the exchange of views may narrow the differences among the judges. Because so much hinges on the opinions issuing from the court, appellate judges need to be good writers.

Finally, in reviewing the rulings of trial courts, appellate judges continually confront complex and difficult legal questions. Resolving these questions tests both the judges' knowledge of the law and their analytic capacities. Because they must decide whether the trial court's actions are consistent with authoritative legal precedent, they must continually update themselves on recent legal developments. Yet often the pertinent precedents offer guidance without altogether resolving an issue. In such circumstances, the appellate judge must analyze the issue in the light of logic, precedent, policy, concern for the parties, and a host of other factors, guided by professional norms and the traditions of the law. They then must provide a persuasive justification for the conclusions they reach. These responsibilities can challenge even the most talented and conscientious appellate judge.

CONCLUSIONS

This chapter has revealed important differences in the responsibilities of trial court judges and appellate judges. Yet what distinguishes these judges is less important than what unites them: all of these judges play an important role in governance. Their decisions help define the law that governs in state and nation. Moreover, their rulings reflect—at least to some extent—the legal perspectives of the judges who render them. Not surprisingly, then, both the criteria for selecting judges and the processes by which they are selected have aroused controversy throughout American history.

Some have argued that the independence of judges should be safeguarded, so that judges can render decisions unaffected by partisan concerns or external pressures. Advocates of this position have championed modes of selection that minimize the influence of political parties, such as merit selection and nonpartisan elections. They also have promoted extended terms of office for judges—where possible, tenure during good behavior—and have opposed competitive elections for the retention of judges. To some extent their efforts have succeeded, as indicated by the rapid spread of merit selection in the states over the last few decades.

However, other commentators on judicial selection have argued that judges—like other officials whose decisions have political consequences—should be accountable to, perhaps even responsive to, the populace. Proponents of this position have usually promoted partisan judicial elections or the appointment of judges by the executive. Despite the spread of merit selection, there seems to be a resurgence of efforts to hold judges accountable for their views and their judicial decisions. This can be seen in the defeat of Chief Justice Rose Bird and her fellow justices, whose rulings in criminal-justice cases angered many Californians. It is also evident in the Senate's rejection of Judge Robert Bork and in its close scrutiny of the charges against Justice Clarence Thomas.

Finally, still other commentators have insisted that the state and federal bench should reflect the demographic diversity of the nation. Supporters of a demographically representative judiciary have persuaded the courts that the Voting Rights Act applies to judicial elections and have had some success challenging selection systems that seemed to disadvantage minority-group candidates. Even Presidents Reagan and Bush, who announced their opposition to affirmative action, considered demographics in their appointments—witness, for example, the appointments of Sandra Day O'Connor and Clarence Thomas. It remains to be seen what priority President Clinton places on ensuring a demographically representative judiciary.

Yet even as one recognizes the importance of who judges, one must also recognize that judges alone do not determine the political role played by courts. Judges can address the issues that are brought before them, and thus they depend upon lawyers and their clients for their agenda. It is to these equally important actors in the judicial process that we now turn.

NOTES

1. This discussion of the Bork nomination relies on Robert H. Bork, *The Tempting of America* (New York: Free Press, 1990); Ethan Bronner, *Battle for Justice* (New York: W. W. Norton, 1989); and Patrick B. McGuigan and Dawn M. Weyrich, *Ninth Justice: The Fight for Bork* (Washington: Free Congress Research and Education Foundation, 1990).

2. Quoted in Bronner, *Battle for Justice,* p. 98.

3. For an example of political pressures being visited upon judges and their reactions to those pressures, see Jack Peltason, *Fifty-Eight Lonely Men* (New York: Harcourt, Brace and World, 1961).

4. Quoted in David O'Brien, *Judicial Roulette* (New York: Priority Press, 1988), p. 16. Altogether, only seven federal judges have been impeached and convicted. For discussion of judicial impeachments, see "Impeaching Federal Judges: Where Are We and Where Are We Going?" *Judicature* 72 (1989): 359-365.

5. For discussion of the Jewish and Catholic seats, as well as of other demographic factors affecting presidential appointment of Supreme Court justices, see Henry Abraham, *Justices and Presidents*, 2d ed. (New York: Oxford University Press, 1985), pp. 62-64, and Barbara A. Perry, *A "Representative" Supreme Court?* (Westport, Conn.: Greenwood Press, 1991).

6. Henry R. Glick and Craig F. Emmert, "Selection Systems and Judicial Characteristics: The Recruitment of State Supreme Court Justices," *Judicature* 70 (December-January 1987): 232.

7. John Paul Ryan, Allan Ashman, Bruce D. Sales, and Sandra Shane-Dubow, *American Trial Judges* (New York: Free Press, 1980), p. 122. According to one scholar, less than 40% of the justices in states with partisan elections were originally appointed to the supreme court, while in states with nonpartisan elections, roughly two out of every three justices reached the supreme court by appointment. See Philip L. Dubois, *From Ballot to Bench* (Austin: University of Texas Press, 1980), pp. 246-247.

8. Dubois, *From Ballot to Bench*, pp. 1-3.

9. Ibid., Ch. 3. These figures only pertain to judicial elections outside the South.

10. Lawrence Baum, *American Courts*, 2d ed. (Boston: Houghton Mifflin, 1990), p. 102.

11. The discussion of accountability in judicial elections relies on Dubois, *From Ballot to Bench*, Chs. 1-2. The figures on patterns of competition in state judicial elections are computed from data presented in Table 3, p. 50.

12. Philip L. Dubois, "Penny for Your Thoughts? Campaign Spending in California Trial Elections, 1976-1982," *Western Political Quarterly* 38 (June 1986).

13. R. Neal McKnight, Roger Schaefer, and Charles A. Johnson, "Choosing Judges: Do the Voters Know What They're Doing?" *Judicature* 62 (August 1978): 94-99.

14. Dubois, *From Ballot to Bench*, Chapter 3.

15. Ibid., Chapter 2, and Philip Dubois, "Voter Turnout in State Judicial Elections: An Analysis of the Tail of the Electoral Kite," *Journal of Politics* 41 (August 1979): 865-88.

16. James J. Alfini and Terrence J. Brooks, "Ethical Constraints on Judicial Election Campaigns: A Review and Critique of Canon 7," *Kentucky Law Journal* 77 (1988-89), p. 671; and more generally, Donald W. Jackson and James W. Riddlesperger, Jr., "Money and Politics in Judicial Elections: The 1988 Election of the Chief Justice of the Texas Supreme Court," *Judicature* 74 (December-January, 1991): 184-189.

17. This account relies on G. Alan Tarr and Mary Cornelia Aldis Porter, *State Supreme Courts in Nation and State* (New Haven: Yale University Press, 1988), Chapter 5.

18. Relevant studies include: Dubois, *From Ballot to Bench*, Chapters 5-7; David Adamany, "The Party Variable in Judges' Voting: Conceptual Notes and a Case Study," *American Political Science Review* 63 (March, 1969): 57-73; Burton M. Atkins and Henry R. Glick, "Formal Judicial Recruitment and State Supreme Court Decisions," *American Politics Quarterly* 2 (October 1974): 427-449; Edward N. Beiser and Jonathan J. Silberman, "The Political Party Variable: Workmen's Compensation Cases in the New York Court of Appeals," *Polity* 3 (Summer, 1971): 521-531; Malcolm M. Feeley, "Another Look at the 'Party Variable' in Judicial Decision-Making: An Analysis of the Michigan Supreme Court," *Polity* 4 (Fall 1971): 91-104; and Stuart S. Nagel, "Political Party Affiliation and Judges' Decisions," *American Political Science Review* 55 (December, 1961): 843-850. For further discussion of this issue, see Chapter 8.

19. Kathleen L. Barber, "Partisan Values in the Lower Courts: Reapportionment in Ohio and Michigan," *Case Western Reserve Law Review* 20 (February, 1969), p. 403.

20. Susan B. Carbon, "Judicial Retention Elections: Are They Serving Their Intended Purpose?" *Judicature* 64 (November, 1980), p. 220.

21. William K. Hall and Larry T. Aspin, "What Twenty Years of Judicial Retention Elections Have Told Us," *Judicature* 70 (April-May, 1987): 347.

22. Ibid., pp. 343—346.

23. Kenyon N. Griffin and Michael J. Horan, "Patterns of Judicial Behavior in Judicial Retention Elections for Supreme Court Justices in Wyoming," *Judicature* 67 (August 1983), p. 72.

24. Carbon, "Retention Elections," p. 226.

25. The classic account of the politics of merit selection is Richard A. Watson and Rondal G. Downing, *The Politics of the Bench and the Bar: Judicial Selection Under the Missouri Non-Partisan Court Plan* (New York: John Wiley & Sons, 1969).

26. Quoted in Martin A. Levin, *Urban Politics and the Criminal Courts* (Chicago: University of Chicago Press, 1977), p. 13.

27. Hall and Aspin, "What Twenty Years of Judicial Retention Elections Have Told Us," pp. 344-345.

28. Ibid., p. 332.

29. Quoted in Watson and Downing, *Politics of Bench and Bar*, p. 186.

30. Baum, *American Courts*, p. 110.

31. Atkins and Glick, "Formal Judicial Recruitment and State Supreme Court Decisions."

32. Dubois, *From Ballot to Bench*, Chapters 5-7.

33. *Book of the States, 1990-91* (Lexington, Ky.: Council of State Governments, 1990), p. 200.

34. Richard Neeley, *Why Courts Don't Work* (New York: McGraw-Hill, 1983), pp. 41-42.

35. Henry R. Glick and Craig F. Emmert, "Selection Systems and Judicial Characteristics: The Recruitment of State Supreme Court Judges," *Judicature* 70 (December-January, 1987), p. 233, Table 2; and Craig F. Emmert and Henry R. Glick, "The Selection of State Supreme Court Justices," *American Politics Quarterly* 16 (October, 1988): 445-465.

36. Fund for Modern Courts, *The Success of Women and Minorities in Achieving Judicial Office: The Selection Process* (New York: Fund for Modern Courts, 1985).

37. Alexander Hamilton, James Madison, and John Jay, *The Federalist Papers*, ed. by Clinton Rossiter (New York: New American Library, 1961), p. 456.

38. O'Brien, *Judicial Roulette*, p. 25, Table 1.4.

39. Neeley, *Why Courts Don't Work*, p. 37.

40. Quoted in O'Brien, *Judicial Roulette*, p. 33.

41. These data are drawn from O'Brien, *Judicial Roulette*, p. 35 (updated to 1992).

42. Joseph Samuel Perry, "How I Got to Be a Federal Judge," in Walter F. Murphy and C. Herman Pritchett, eds., *Courts, Judges, and Politics*, 2nd ed. (New York: Random House, 1974), p. 169.

43. See Peltason, *Fifty-Eight Lonely Men.*

44. Quoted in J. Woodford Howard, Jr., *Courts of Appeals in the Federal Judicial System* (Princeton, N.J.: Princeton University Press, 1981), p. 93.

45. Quoted in ibid., p. 101.

46. Quoted in O'Brien, *Judicial Roulette*, p. 58.

47. Ibid., p. 61.

48. C. K. Rowland, "The Federal District Courts," in John B. Gates and Charles A. Johnson, eds., *The American Courts: A Critical Assessment* (Washington, D.C.: CQ Press, 1991), p. 70; and Ronald Stidham and Ronald Carp, "Judges, Presidents, and Policy Choices: Exploring the Linkage," *Social Science Quarterly* 68 (1987): 395-407.

49. Steve Alumbaugh and C. K. Rowland, "The Links Between Platform-Based Appointment Criteria and Trial Judges' Abortion Judgments," *Judicature* 74 (October-November, 1990): 153-162.

50. Robert A. Carp and Ronald Stidham, *Judicial Process in America* (Washington, D.C.: CQ Press, 1990), pp. 236-238.

51. The discussion of President Bush's appointments relies on Sheldon Goldman, "Bush's Judicial Legacy: The Final Imprint," *Judicature* 76 (April-May, 1993): 282-297.

52. *Brown* v. *Board of Education*, 347 U.S. 483 (1954).

53. On freedom of religion, see *Sherbert* v. *Verner*, 374 U.S. 398 (1963), and *Edwards* v. *Aguillard*, 482 U.S. 578 (1987); on flag-burning, see *Texas* v. *Johnson*, 491 U.S. 397 (1989); on libel, see *New York Times* v. *Sullivan*, 376 U.S. 254 (1964); on political patronage, see *Rutan* v. *Republican Party of Illinois*, 110 S.Ct. 2729 (1990); and on exclusion of illegally seized evidence, see *Mapp* v. *Ohio*, 367 U.S. 643 (1961).

54. Harry A. Blackmun, "A Tribute to Mr. Justice Brennan," *Harvard Civil Rights Civil Liberties Law Review* 26 (Winter 1991), p. 1.

55. Quoted in Abraham, *Justices and Presidents*, p. 263.

56. This list of factors is derived from David O'Brien, *Storm Center*, 2d ed. (New York: W. W. Norton, 1990), Chapter 2.

57. Abraham, *Justices and Presidents*, pp. 262-263.

58. Quoted in ibid., p. 70.

59. Quoted in ibid., p. 69.

60. Quoted in ibid., p. 69.

61. *United States* v. *Nixon*, 418 U.S. 683 (1974), and *Morrison* v. *Olson*, 487 U.S. 108 (1988).

62. *Roe* v. *Wade*, 410 U.S. 113 (1973).

63. Quoted in Abraham, *Justices and Presidents*, p. 70.

64. O'Brien, *Judicial Roulette*, p. 67, Table 4-1.

65. The analysis in this section relies on "On Becoming a Judge: Socialization to the Judicial Role," *Judicature* 69 (October-November 1985): 139-146, and Robert Carp and Russell Wheeler, "Sink or Swim: The Socialization of a Federal District Judge," *Journal of Public Law* 21 (1972): 359-394.

66. "On Becoming a Judge," p. 140.

67. Quoted in ibid., p. 141.

68. For discussion of Fortas's activities and the criticism they engendered, see Bruce A. Murphy, *Fortas: The Rise and Ruin of a Supreme Court Justice* (New York: William Morrow, 1988), and Laura Kalman, *Abe Fortas: A Biography* (New Haven: Yale University Press, 1990).

69. Quoted in Carp and Wheeler, "Socialization of a Federal District Judge," p. 373; cf. Donald Dale Jackson, *Judges* (New York: Atheneum, 1974), Chapter 10.

70. Quoted in "On Becoming a Judge," p. 141.

71. Ryan, *American Trial Judges*, pp. 150-51.

4 LAWYERS

This is a tale of two lawyers, who pursued very different legal careers before serving together on the United States Supreme Court.[1] Lewis Powell was born in 1907 to a wealthy, "old line" family in southern Virginia—the original Powell landed at Jamestown in 1607. As an undergraduate, Lewis Powell excelled at Washington and Lee College, graduating first in his class. Two years later he received his law degree from the same school. After a year at Harvard Law School, where he received a master's degree in 1932, Powell joined one of the most prestigious law firms in Richmond, Virginia. He rose to the rank of senior partner in the firm, which had over 100 lawyers by the time he was appointed to the Court. In his thirty-five years of private practice, he represented a long roster of important corporate clients, such as the Baltimore and Ohio Railroad, the Prudential Insurance Company, and the Virginia Electric and Power Company. He also served on the board of directors of eleven major companies.

Powell's national stature led to his election as president of the American Bar Association (ABA) in 1964 and as president of the American College of Trial Lawyers in 1968. Like many lawyers, he was also involved in community affairs. As president of the Richmond School Board, Powell guided the desegregation of the city's schools in the 1950s. He also served as president of the state board of education in the late 1960s. In 1971 President Richard Nixon appointed him to the Supreme Court, and after both the ABA and the Virginia chapter of the National Association for the Advancement of Colored People (NAACP) enthusiastically endorsed him, the Senate confirmed him by an 89-1 vote.

Thurgood Marshall, probably the most important American lawyer of the twentieth century, came from considerably less prosperous circumstances. The great-grandson of a slave, Marshall was born in 1908, a year later than Powell, in Baltimore, Maryland. His parents, a club steward and an elementary school teacher, stressed education; his mother sold her engagement ring to help pay his college expenses. Marshall repaid this confidence by excelling in his studies at Lincoln University and then at Howard University Law School, where he graduated first in his class. Following graduation, Marshall enlisted in the efforts of the NAACP to combat racial discrimination through litigation. For more than twenty years as head of the NAACP Legal Defense Fund, he instituted or managed literally hundreds of cases challenging discriminatory laws dealing with voting, housing, education, and public accommodations. Several times he successfully pursued these challenges to the Supreme Court. His most important victory came in 1954 in *Brown* v. *Board of Education,* when he persuaded the Supreme Court to invalidate racial discrimination in public education.

Marshall's formidable skills as an advocate were not limited to his service with the NAACP. Four years after his elevation to the United States Court of Appeals by President John Kennedy, President Lyndon Johnson appointed him solicitor general, the government's chief advocate before the Supreme Court. As the nation's first African-American solicitor general, he won several important civil rights victories, including a Supreme Court ruling upholding the constitutionality of the 1965 Voting Rights Act. By the time President Johnson appointed him to the Supreme Court in 1967, Marshall had argued 32 cases before that court and won 29 of them.

The careers of Thurgood Marshall and Lewis Powell illustrate several important points about lawyers and the legal profession:

Diverse legal practices: Prior to their appointment to the Supreme Court, Marshall and Powell pursued altogether different legal practices. They differed in the types of clients they served, the sorts of issues they addressed, the amount of time they spent in court, and the ends they sought to achieve. Their careers demonstrate that lawyers may employ their talents in a wide variety of contexts for quite different clients and ends. They may become litigators, like Marshall, pursuing their clients' interests in the clash of courtroom conflict. Many lawyers—including prosecutors, criminal defense attorneys, and lawyers in personal injury cases—are regularly involved in trial or appellate litigation. Alternatively, like Powell, they may serve primarily as legal counsellors, negotiating contracts or other legal agreements or seeking by their advice to prevent legal disputes from arising. In fact, most lawyers spend little or no time in court.

One could easily multiply examples of the sorts of careers a lawyer might pursue—high-powered lawyer/lobbyist; solo practitioner serving the legal needs of average citizens; in-house counsel to a corporation; investigator for a government agency; and so on. This diversity of career choices underscores both the myriad uses to which legal skills can be put and the fact that most activities in our society have aspects that demand legal expertise. It also shows that most lawyers specialize to some extent in the sort of law they practice and in the types of clients they represent.

The ends of lawyering: In his legal practice Lewis Powell—like most lawyers—served as the "delegate" of his clients, that is, he sought to advance the aims and interests of his clients, as they defined them, within the confines of the law. In contrast, Thurgood Marshall served more as the "trustee" for his clients: he sought to advance the interests of his African-American clients by promoting political goals that those clients—and other African-Americans— could be assumed to share. Thus, Marshall's choice of cases and the way he framed legal issues were determined by how those choices would serve long-term political goals.[2]

Each of these relationships between lawyer and client poses dilemmas. "Delegate" attorneys may face a conflict between the interests of their clients and the demands of justice or the good of the society. This conflict is clearest perhaps when an attorney defends a guilty client in a criminal case, though it is not confined to the criminal law. On the other hand, "trustee" attorneys may confront situations in which the pursuit of their political goals seems to conflict with the immediate interests of their clients. In such circumstances they must determine how to advance the interests of particular clients without compromising those political goals.

The law as a public profession: Law is considered a "public profession" because the practice of law affects the public life of the nation. Obviously, this is true when lawyers serve as judges, as Marshall and Powell did. It is equally true when lawyers pursue careers in politics or in public service. But even without holding public office, lawyers have important effects on law and on public policy. They may, like Marshall, deliberately design their legal practices to advance political ends. Or they may influence public affairs less directly, as did Powell, through their involvement in national organizations such as the American Bar Association or through their representation of large economic enterprises. Whatever the avenue, however, lawyers affect the public life of the nation because of the expertise they possess and the uses to which they put that expertise.

Americans recognize the political importance of the legal profession, but this does not mean that they are reconciled to it. Rather, Americans tend to be ambivalent about lawyers, the skills they employ, and the power they exercise. Thus a 1973 Harris Poll found that a smaller proportion of Americans had faith in lawyers than in garbage collectors.[3] This ambivalence is captured in the quotations collected in Box 4-1. Let us look more closely at the causes and consequences of American attitudes toward lawyers and the legal profession.

BOX 4-1 PERSPECTIVES ON LAWYERS

"Woe unto you, lawyers! for ye lade men with burdens grievous to be borne, and ye yourselves touch not the burdens with one of your fingers." (Luke 11:46)

"Underneath, most lawyers are boy scouts." (Geoffrey Hazard, Yale Law School professor)

"Lawyer: One skilled in circumvention of the law." (Ambrose Bierce, American writer and humorist)

"The zealous defense attorney is the last bastion of liberty, the final barrier between an overreaching government and its citizens." (Alan Dershowitz, famous defense attorney)

"Lawyers are plants that will grow in any soil that is cultivated by the hands of others; and when once they have taken root they will extinguish every other vegetable that grows around them . . . . They are here what the clergy were in past centuries . . . A reformation equally useful is now wanted." (St. John Crevecoeur, 18th century writer)

"The first thing we do, let's kill all the lawyers." (William Shakespeare)

SOURCES: The King James *Bible*; Geoffrey Hazard, "Reflections on Four Studies of the Legal Profession," *Law and Society* 48 (1965), quoted in David Mellinkoff, *The Conscience of a Lawyer* (St. Paul: West, 1973), p. 9; Ambrose Bierce, *The Devil's Dictionary* (Cleveland: World Publishing, 1911), p. 187; Alan Dershowitz, *The Best Defense* (New York: Random House, 1982), p. 415; St. John Crevecoeur, *Letters from an American Farmer* (1782), quoted in Lawrence Friedman, *History of American Law*, 2d ed. (New York: Simon & Schuster, 1985), p. 304; and William Shakespeare, *Henry VI, Part 2*, act 4, scene 2, line 74.

THE TROUBLE WITH LAWYERS

From Clarence Darrow to Thurgood Marshall, lawyers have been celebrated for seeking justice for their clients and for promoting just but unpopular causes. Yet the specialized knowledge that enables lawyers to crusade for justice may be put to other uses as well. Lawyers may use their legal expertise to advance their own interests. Critics often accuse lawyers of dishonesty or of generating business by creating disputes where none existed.

Major breaches of professional ethics can presumably be handled through the disciplinary procedures of the bar association or through disbarment by a court, although some critics question how vigorous the legal profession has been in weeding out dishonest or incompetent attorneys. More serious is the complaint that lawyers are "hired guns," who have no compunction about using their skills in the service of reprehensible people and immoral purposes. This charge reflects in part a concern about the distorting effects of wealth on the legal process. Legal expertise is a form of power, and the wealthy can afford more and better legal representation than can the average citizen. More generally, however, the charge reflects a perception that most lawyers are unconcerned about justice. Criminal lawyers seek the acquittal of defendants accused of violent crimes, even when they believe the defendants committed the crimes. Attorneys for defendants in personal-injury suits assist their clients in seeking to reduce or escape altogether their legal liability for the injuries they caused. If the actions of clients are immoral, it is argued, lawyers should not promote or defend them. When lawyers do so, they are viewed as participating in the immorality.

It should be obvious that such criticism is at least somewhat inconsistent with the praise of fearless defense attorneys—are only the innocent entitled to an effective legal defense? What underlies this criticism of the legal profession is a concern about how effective the American adversary system is in achieving justice. For, within this adversary system, lawyers who vigorously defend reprehensible clients are acting properly. As the American Bar Association has put it, "the duty of a lawyer to his client and to the legal system are the same: to represent his client zealously within the bounds of the law."[4] (For the quite different responsibilities of a lawyer in an inquisitorial system, see Box 4-2.) Obviously, the partisan advocacy of an attorney in an adversarial system does not by itself guarantee just outcomes. However, the attorney presenting his client's case is only one element in the process. Another lawyer will present evidence and arguments for the other side in the case, a judge will serve as umpire of the dispute, and a judge or jury will reach a decision by weighing the arguments and evidence presented. The assumption is that a partisan presentation by each side will ensure that all relevant facts and legal arguments are brought forward and evaluated, thereby promoting a well-informed decision. Most members of the American legal profession believe strongly in the adversary system.

Does the adversary system guarantee justice? Obviously not; there are undoubtedly instances in which the innocent are convicted or, perhaps more frequently, the guilty go free. The real question is whether it works better than other legal systems. The answer to this question is far from clear. Neither those nations that employ the adversarial system nor those that utilize the inquisitorial system seem inclined to change, as they presumably would if the alternative

BOX 4-2 LAWYERS AND TRIALS UNDER AN INQUISITORIAL SYSTEM

To those familiar, from television or real life, with the aggressive trial advocacy of American attorneys, a trial in an inquisitorial system will seem quite odd. In an adversarial system the opposing lawyers formulate the issues and largely control the development of the trial by calling their own witnesses, examining them, and vigorously cross-examining the witnesses called by the other side. The judge's role is largely to act as umpire in the battle between the opposing sides.

In contrast, in an inquisitorial system the role of the judge is expanded and that of the lawyers reduced. The presiding judge at trial is actively involved in the search for justice. Although the lawyers for each side may nominate witnesses to be called, the judge determines whether they shall testify and whether additional witnesses, including expert witnesses, are also questioned. The witnesses themselves are questioned by the presiding judge, not by the attorneys, although an attorney may pose additional questions after the judge has concluded his or her questioning. (In practice attorneys rarely ask further questions, since too many questions might imply that the presiding judge had not done a good job, hardly a wise thing to suggest.) The lawyers cannot even prepare and rehearse their witnesses before they appear, as is common practice in the United States. Such preparation of witnesses is viewed as inconsistent with the search for justice. In Germany, for example, the rules of legal ethics expressly forbid attorneys from coaching witnesses and even discourage them from contacting witnesses at all prior to trial.

This is not to say that lawyers in an inquisitorial system play no role. They submit written pleadings on behalf of their clients and may, in civil cases, prepare amended pleadings as the case progresses. They also make closing arguments at trial, though the fact that these arguments are addressed to a panel of judges rather than to a jury presumably limits the effectiveness of rhetorical flourishes. Such flourishes are unlikely anyway, since they are inconsistent with the responsibility of the lawyer under an inquisitorial system. In an adversarial system the duty of attorneys during litigation is, according to the American Bar Association, to "represent their clients zealously within the confines of the law." In an inquisitorial system, in contrast, the lawyer is—according to the German code of legal ethics—an "independent organ in the administration of justice." Thus the American attorney's concern is for his or her client, the German attorney's for justice.

Whatever their inclinations, American lawyers recognize that a whole-hearted commitment to their clients is necessary to prevail at trial and that success at trial leads to greater status and (presumably) higher fees. Inquisitorial systems, however, have largely eliminated that inducement to vigorous advocacy. In Germany, for example, the legal fees for various

continued on p. 111

> *continued from p. 110*
>
> types of cases are established by law. Whether one wins or loses, devotes countless hours to case preparation or not, one receives the same fee. Thus inquisitorial systems not only discourage excessive zeal in advocacy but also remove the material incentives to engage in it.
>
> Does this all mean that an inquisitorial, judge-centered system is superior to an adversarial, lawyer-centered one? On that question there is no consensus. The inquisitorial system places considerable faith in the wisdom and fairness of the presiding judge. Americans are less likely to rely so heavily on the good faith and good judgment of a single individual. It may be that different legal systems work well for different societies.

SOURCES: John Langbein, "The German Advantage in Civil Procedure," *University of Chicago Law Review* 52 (1985): 823-66; David Luban, *Lawyers and Justice* (Princeton, N.J.: Princeton University Press, 1988); and John Merryman, *The Civil Law Tradition* (Stanford, Calif.: Stanford University Press, 1969).

system were demonstrably superior. Yet, unless the United States abandons the adversary system—and there is no real prospect that it will—lawyers will continue (quite properly) to act as advocates for morally dubious clients and enterprises.

THE LEGAL PROFESSION

Becoming a Lawyer

Today in the United States the steps necessary to become a lawyer are quite straightforward. First, a student must earn an undergraduate degree. During the undergraduate's senior year, or in the summer immediately preceding it, the prospective law student takes the Law School Admission Test (LSAT), which is designed to measure her ability to succeed in law school. (To simplify matters, we ignore here the increasing number of applicants who have entered the work force for a period prior to applying to law school.) Law schools use the score on this test, together with undergraduate grades, recommendations, and other factors in deciding whom to admit. Law school itself involves three years of intensive legal studies, four or five years if one enrolls in a part-time evening program. Upon graduation from law school, one must still pass the bar examination for the state in which one wishes to practice law. This test, which lasts several days, examines the prospective lawyer's knowledge of the law of the state. Most jurisdictions also include a multistate component, which poses more general legal questions. Because so much rides on passing the bar exam, recent graduates of law school characteristically enroll in bar-preparation (cram) courses before taking the exam. Nationally, about 70 percent of those taking a bar exam pass it, though success rates vary dramatically from state to state. (Some states—most notably, California and Florida—have sought to limit the number of attorneys practicing within their borders by creating very difficult bar exams.) Those who fail the bar exam are permitted to retake it, and roughly 90 percent eventually do pass. If one passes the bar exam and survives the character check made by the state bar, one is admitted to legal practice.

Legal Education Abroad

In other countries the path to becoming a lawyer is quite different. In France, for example, students study law without first obtaining a bachelor's degree. Great Britain has a bifurcated legal profession (see Box 4-3), with the primary courtroom attorneys (barristers) receiving their training at the Inns of Court rather than at university law schools. In Germany students must serve a period of apprenticeship following their formal legal education before becoming full-fledged lawyers. Even in the United States, the process of becoming a lawyer has changed dramatically over time.

The Transformation of Legal Education in the United States

Until the twentieth century, most American lawyers never attended law school. Very few law schools existed—in 1860 there were only 22 nationwide—and those schools enrolled relatively few students. Harvard Law School averaged only nine students a year from 1817-1829, its first twelve years of operation.[5] Thus, prior to 1900 most lawyers received their legal education by clerking in the office of a practicing attorney, reading law books and assisting the lawyer, often by taking on the drudge work of the practice. The quality of the preparation this apprenticeship provided varied enormously, but even poor preparation rarely prevented one from practicing law. Legal requirements tended to be lax—in 1879 only 15 of 38 states required formal training prior to practicing law—and bar examinations, typically conducted orally by local judges, were perfunctory at best. Gustave Koerner, who began his practice in Illinois in the 1830s, described his exam as lasting only half an hour, in which a few desultory questions were asked, after which everyone adjourned for rum toddies.[6]

The latter part of the nineteenth century witnessed the emergence of the modern law school and, with it, a movement toward formalized legal education. The central figure in these changes was Christopher Columbus Langdell, who served as dean of Harvard Law School from 1870 to 1895.[7] Langdell conceived of law as a science, consisting of a certain number of principles or doc-

BOX 4-3 THE LEGAL PROFESSION IN GREAT BRITAIN

Venture into a British courtroom, and you might be surprised to discover the prosecutor and defense attorney dressed in flowing robes and wearing powdered wigs. However, their attire is not all that distinguishes British attorneys from their American counterparts. Upon admission to the bar, American lawyers can undertake all the functions associated with legal practice. Such is not the case in Great Britain. From at least the fourteenth century, the British have had a bifurcated legal profession, with those practicing law divided into barristers and solicitors. The members of these groups receive different legal training and perform distinct functions in the British legal system.

Most legal business is taken care of by solicitors. (There are currently about 46,000 solicitors in Great Britain, serving a population of over 57 million.) The solicitor has traditionally been a law office practitioner, advising clients on legal, business, and personal matters. Thus solicitors' responsibilities may run the gamut from matrimonial matters and divorce, to the drawing up of wills, to the drafting of business contracts, to the attempt to secure redress from debtors. By law, solicitors also hold a monopoly on the conveying of property (the transfer of land from one person to another), which for most solicitors is a major source of income. In addition, solicitors can appear as advocates in minor legal disputes that are resolved in limited jurisdiction courts, such as magistrates' courts or county courts.

At times, however, a client beset by more serious legal problems may require the services of a barrister as well. Note the "as well", for in all cases a client is obliged first to seek legal advice from a solicitor. If the solicitor believes that the problem will involve litigation in a general jurisdiction court or appellate court, the solicitor then selects a barrister and "briefs" him or her on the case. The barrister then argues the case in court.

As this description suggests, barristers are an elite group, who specialize in trial and appellate advocacy. The elite character of the group is reinforced by its size: there are only about 5,500 barristers altogether in Great Britain. Within the ranks of barristers there is a further division between Queen's (or King's) counsel and junior counsel. The former, also known as "silks" because of the material of their robes, comprise roughly ten percent of all barristers. They are chosen by the Lord Chancellor, the nation's highest legal official, for their legal ability and their reputation. The Queen's counsel not only argue the most important cases, sometimes assisted by junior counsel, but also form the pool from which British judges are selected.

continued on p. 114

continued from p. 113
Under this system a litigant in an important case may have three lawyers (the solicitor, the Queen's counsel arguing the case, and the junior counsel assisting in the argument). Aside from tradition, is there any reason to retain this rather cumbersome and expensive division of the legal profession? According to advocates of the current system, the fusion of the legal profession would not necessarily produce economy, because in a difficult case a lawyer might still wish to bring in a specialized advocate with expert knowledge in the field. Moreover, systems with an undivided legal profession, such as the United States, are hardly models of efficiency or economy. In addition, the selection of the barrister by the solicitor rather than by the client serves to create a distance between barrister and client, which enables the barrister to provide more dispassionate advice. Finally, under the "cab rank" principle that requires barristers to take any brief sent to them, the system ensures that even the most brutal or politically unpopular defendant will obtain legal representation.

These arguments persuaded a Royal Commission in 1979 to recommend that the division of the legal profession be perpetuated. It thus seems unlikely that Great Britain will eliminate the distinction between barristers

SOURCES: Mary Ann Glendon, Michael W. Gordon, and Christopher Osakwe, *Comparative Legal Traditions in a Nutshell* (St. Paul: West, 1982); Gavin Drewry, *Law, Justice and Politics* (London: Longman, 1975); and Timothy Harper, "Bye bye Barrister; the End of Britain's Two-Tiered Bar?" *American Bar Association Journal* 76 (March 1990): 58-62.

trines that could be applied to "the ever-tangled skein of human affairs."[8] The way to discover these principles, he believed, was by studying appellate court opinions. Several innovations in legal education followed from these assumptions. If law is a science, then legal study belongs in an academic setting rather than in a law office; law school, not apprenticeship, is the way to produce qualified lawyers. The teachers at such schools should be selected on the basis of their knowledge of those principles, rather than their experience in the law. Langdell therefore hired full-time law professors rather than relying on practicing lawyers who taught part-time. These instructors should introduce students to the important appellate decisions elaborating those principles, and to facilitate this process, pertinent cases were for the first time collected in casebooks. Finally, instead of merely lecturing, instructors should develop students' skill in analyzing cases and identifying legal principles. Thus, the standard mode of instruction became Socratic questioning, with the instructor calling on students to answer probing questions about the cases they had read. The contemporary flavor of these innovations testifies to the success of Langdell's efforts. Although his innovations were controversial initially, all law schools today employ faculties of full-time academics who use the case method and Socratic questioning.

The spread of Langdell's innovations coincided with enormous growth in the number of law schools and law students. Between 1889 and 1909, the number of law school doubled, while the number of law students quadrupled.[9] The expansion occurred particularly in urban centers, where part-time schools—often with lax admissions standards—flourished by providing opportunities for recent immigrants and other working people to pursue a professional career. During the first third of the twentieth century, however, bar associations and the American Association of Law Schools campaigned to raise admissions standards for law school, both to upgrade the quality of the legal profession and to reduce competition within it. The lure of accreditation by the American Bar Association, often backed by state requirements that candidates for the bar graduate from an accredited law school, combined with the Great Depression of the 1930s to raise standards and eliminate many of the part-time schools, which could not meet the ABA's demands. Among the casualties were three of the nation's four black law schools. Portia Law School, founded in 1908 to serve an all-female student body, abandoned its special mission and became the New England School of Law.[10]

Since World War II, legal education has expanded considerably. From 1947-1987, the number of ABA-approved law schools jumped from 109 to 170, and many schools have also increased the size of their student bodies.[11] This proliferation of law schools has not made access to the legal profession easier. Over the past thirty years, the demand for legal education has outpaced the supply, which has allowed law schools to become increasingly selective in admissions. As late as 1960, Harvard Law School admitted half of all applicants.[12] Today, elite law schools are incredibly selective—Yale Law School in 1990 admitted only 373 of 5638 applicants—and the ratio of applications to admissions even at less prestigious institutions has increased dramatically.[13] To assess the effects of these developments, let us consider the characteristics of the legal profession in America today.

A Portrait of the Legal Profession

Size

The United States today has more lawyers and more lawyers per capita than any other country.[14] In part, the proliferation of lawyers can be attributed to the nation's economic development, because economic activity tends to generate business for lawyers.[15] But economic activity alone cannot explain the growth of the American legal profession. For one thing, other advanced industrialized nations get along with far fewer lawyers. Japan, for example, currently has only

15,000 private attorneys—less than are graduated by American law schools in a single year—serving a population of 123 million.[16] In addition, whereas the nation's economic growth has been fairly steady, Figure 4-1 reveals that the size of the legal profession has fluctuated, alternating between periods of dramatic growth and periods of stability. Nor can the increasing number of lawyers be attributed merely to the burgeoning legal demands of an increasing population; for the growth of the legal profession has not paralleled population growth. The late nineteenth and early twentieth centuries saw a substantial increase in the number of lawyers. Yet from 1940 to 1965, the size of the legal profession remained relatively stable, at least in relation to population. In recent decades, the production of new lawyers has shot up at an unprecedented pace. In 1990, for example, 35,520 students graduated from law schools in the United States, and 129,698 were pursuing legal studies.[17]

FIGURE 4-1 THE GROWTH OF THE LEGAL PROFESSION AND U.S. POPULATION

SOURCE: Terrence C. Halliday, "Six Score Years and Ten: Demographic Transitions in the American Legal Profession," *Law & Society Review* 20 (1986): p. 56, Figure 1. Reprinted by permission of the Law and Society Association.

Composition

Changes have occurred not only in the number of lawyers but also in the composition of the legal profession. One obvious effect of recent trends has been a decline in the median age of those practicing law. This generational change may affect the political perspective of the legal profession, as expressed by the American Bar Association and other legal institutions. Also, with a smaller proportion of the profession closer to retirement age, future increases in the number of attorneys are unlikely to be offset by retirements or deaths within the profession.

The recent influx of lawyers also reflects the collapse of many barriers to admission for previously excluded groups. The largest increase has been in the number of female attorneys. Until the 1870s there were no women lawyers. Many states did not allow women to practice law, and the U.S. Supreme Court ruled that the exclusion of women did not violate their constitutional rights.[18] By 1910, however, only Arkansas and Georgia persisted in excluding women. Law schools also discriminated, either by denying women admission—Harvard Law School did not admit women until 1950, and Washington and Lee Law School until 1972[19]—or by capping female enrollments. The combination of overt discrimination and cultural and social barriers reduced women's presence in law school—the class of 1968 at the University of Virginia Law School included only three women[20]—and in the legal profession. As of 1970, women comprised less than five percent of the legal profession.[21]

Since that time, a revolution has occurred. As Table 4-1 documents, between 1967 and 1983, the enrollment of women in ABA-approved law schools increased 1650 percent: women today comprise about 40 percent of law-school students.[22] (Indeed, the number of white males enrolled in law schools has remained constant for the past two decades, even as the schools' enrollments have skyrocketed.) Roughly 15 percent of American lawyers today are women, and this percentage will increase as current and prospective female law students enter the profession.[23]

Less dramatic gains have been registered by members of racial and ethnic minorities. African-Americans suffered systematic discrimination in the legal profession, as elsewhere, well into the twentieth century. For instance, when the American Bar Association discovered in 1914 that it had inadvertently admitted three blacks, it "persuaded" them to resign and refused thereafter to admit blacks until 1943.[24] Howard University Law School, established in 1868, ensured that African-Americans were not completely excluded from legal education, but segregation remained a formidable barrier for prospective black

TABLE 4-1 WOMEN IN THE LEGAL PROFESSION

Year	Number of Female Lawyers	Percentage of Profession
1870	5	.01%
1900	1,010	.9
1930	3,385	2.2
1960	7,434	3.5
1970	13,000	4.7
1975	26,471	6.6
1980	43,918	8.1
1984	83,072	12.8

* These data are selected from among several sets of figures in the Abel volume.

SOURCE: Adapted from *American Lawyers* by Richard L. Abel. Copyright (c) 1989 by Oxford Press, Inc. Reprinted by Permission. Page 284, Table 26.

lawyers until the 1960s. As of 1970, African-Americans made up only 1.3 percent of the legal profession.

Since that time, law schools have made concerted efforts to attract qualified minority-group members. To some extent they have succeeded: enrollments of minority students in ABA-approved law schools rose from 4.3% in 1969-70 to 10.4% in 1985-86.[25] However, the rate of increase for minority students has lagged behind that for women, and in recent years the pace has slowed. Moreover, the schools' use of affirmative action programs to recruit minority students has provoked controversy in an era of intense competition for admissions. Despite the elimination of overt bars to admission, members of minority groups continue to face social, economic, and educational disadvantages that keep them a rather small percentage of the American legal profession.

The Organization of the Legal Profession

The oldest and most important national legal organization is the American Bar Association (ABA). Membership in the ABA is voluntary, not compulsory, and less than half the nation's lawyers join. High-status lawyers and members of large law firms are disproportionately represented in its ranks. The ABA exercises no direct authority over lawyers or over the state bar associations that do regulate the legal profession. Nonetheless, as the recognized voice of the legal profession, the ABA does exert considerable influence.

As Chapter 3 described, the ABA's Standing Committee on Federal Judiciary evaluates the qualifications of prospective federal judges, and nominees who receive an "unqualified" rating from the committee are unlikely to be confirmed. The ABA may also take formal positions on legal or political issues and lobby on behalf of those positions. Given the diversity of the legal profession and concern about alienating segments of its membership, the ABA has usually avoided taking positions on controversial political issues. But on issues that directly affect the legal profession, such as lawyer advertising and government-funded legal services for the poor, it has been more outspoken. In addition, the ABA commissions studies and issues reports that may influence political debate or the behavior of lawyers. The association's Model Code of Judicial Conduct is a prime example. Finally, the ABA supervises legal education through its power to accredit—or not accredit—law schools.

Because the states control admission to the legal profession, state bar associations are also important. Although membership in some state bar associations is voluntary, over thirty states have an "integrated bar." This means that all persons admitted to the bar in the state must belong to the state bar association. These state bar associations generally have less political influence than the ABA. They tend to be more concerned with admission to the legal profession in the state, continuing education of the state's lawyers, and disciplining attorneys guilty of illegal or unprofessional conduct than with political lobbying.

PRACTICING LAW

An Overview of Legal Practice

Major changes have occurred not only in the size and demographics of the legal profession but also in the types of legal practice. During the settlement of the American West, when frontier areas were sparsely populated, judges rode circuit to hold court in various locations, and lawyers often accompanied them, providing representation for those who had awaited the judge's arrival to settle their disputes. As a commentator of the era described it, "[t]he lawyer would, perhaps, scarcely alight from his horse when he would be surrounded by two or three clients requiring his services."[26] Wherever a community grew up, a lawyer would also settle and set up his office, handling whatever legal business came his way. Because the nation's population was dispersed, so was its lawyer population. Thus the typical nineteenth century lawyer was a non-specialized solo practitioner, serving a wide diversity of clients and legal needs.[27]

By the late twentieth century, the non-specialized solo practitioner has become the exception, not the rule. Indeed, the percentage of the legal profession engaged in the private practice of law has declined dramatically, from 83 percent in 1948 to 68 percent in 1980.[28] As Figure 4-2 reveals, many lawyers are now employed by various levels of government or by private industry. Even among private practitioners, less than half currently have solo practices, and almost 15 percent work in firms with more than twenty lawyers (see Table 4-2). Far more than in the past, then, lawyers are employees rather than autonomous professionals. Instead of being geographically dispersed, over 88 percent of American lawyers today are concentrated in metropolitan areas.[29] Let us examine several types of law practice now found in the United States.

FIGURE 4-2 TYPES OF EMPLOYMENT FOR LAWYERS

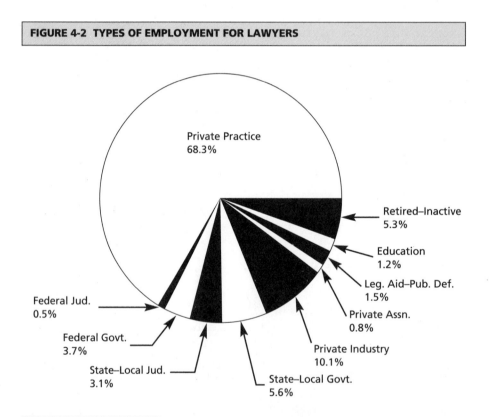

SOURCE: Barbara Curran, *The Lawyer Statistical Report* (Chicago: American Bar Foundation, 1985), p. 12, Figure 5.

TABLE 4-2 PRIVATE PRACTITIONERS AND THEIR PRACTICE SETTING (1980)		
Practice Setting	**Number**	**Percent of Private Practitioners**
Solo practice	179,923	48.6%
2-lawyer firm	32,509	8.8
3-lawyer firm	22,635	6.1
4-lawyer firm	16,233	4.4
5-lawyer firm	11,574	3.1
6-10 lawyer firm	33,377	9.0
11-20 lawyer firm	24,130	6.5
21-50 lawyer firm	22,529	6.1
50+ lawyer firm	27,200	7.3
Total	370,111	100.0

SOURCE: Barbara A. Curran, "American Lawyers in the 1980s: A Profession in Transition," *Law & Society Review* 20 (1986), p. 28, Table 5. Reprinted by permission of the Law and Society Association.

Types of Legal Practice

The Elite Law Firm

Imagine defending IBM against an antitrust suit with over $300 million at stake, or helping the Chrysler Corporation negotiate for federal guarantees for loans to avoid bankruptcy, or fighting to stave off a hostile takeover of Kennecott Copper, or guiding the first stock issue of Genentech, a major genetics engineering company, that would generate $35 million in working capital.[30] The high stakes, the powerful clients, and the intense pressures and rich rewards that accompany representing them all define the world of the elite law firm.

As Table 4-3 suggests, these large, elite firms primarily represent the nation's major economic institutions, such as corporations, banks, insurance companies, and other powerful financial enterprises.[31] A large number of these firms have their home office in New York, though many have expanded in recent years, establishing branch offices in major cities in the United States and overseas. Baker & McKenzie, the nation's largest firm, in 1987 employed 297 lawyers in the United States but another 649 in offices in twenty-four other countries.[32] The size of successful firms has increased substantially in recent years, in part through acquisition of other law firms. A case in point is Finley Kumble which, founded in 1968 with only nine attorneys, had expanded to 684 attorneys less than two decades later.[33]

TABLE 4-3 ELITE LAW FIRMS

Name	Location	Size	Date Founded	Key Clients	Notes
Cravath, Swaine & Moore	New York	213	1819	IBM, CBS Chemical Bank	The archetype of elite corporate firms
Davis Polk & Wardwell	New York	230	1849	ITT, LTV Morgan Guaranty	Long known as the top "white shoe" firm
Debevoise & Plimpton	New York	154	1931	Chrysler, Prudential	A relative new comer; strong in corporate
Donovan Leisure Newton & Irvine	New York	185	1929	Mobil, Westinghouse	Litigation strength, firm's standing threatened by Kodak
Kirkland & Ellis	Chicago	290	1908	Standard Oil (Indiana)	Awesome reputation in litigation
Milbank, Tweed Hadley & McCloy	New York	211	1860	Chase Manhattan, the Rockefellers	Pre-eminent in trusts and estates
Pillsbury, Madison & Sutro	San Francisco	245	1865	Standard Oil (California)	The established West Coast firm
Shearman & Sterling	New York	341	1860	Citibank, United Technologies	The ultimate banking firm
Simpson Thacher & Bartlett	New York	211	1884	Manufacturers Hanover, Gulf & Western	On the rise; strong banking and corporate
Sullivan & Cromwell	New York	215	1897	Exxon, General Foods, GE	The quintessential business practice

SOURCE: James B. Stewart, *The Partners* (New York: Simon and Schuster, 1983), Appendix 1. Copyright © 1983 by James Stewart. Reprinted by permission of Simon & Schuster, Inc.

Within these large firms, a clear hierarchy exists. Atop the hierarchy are the senior partners, who manage the firm and determine the division of profits at year's end. They are followed in descending order by junior partners, permanent associates who remain with the firm after being bypassed for partner, and associates. The most important distinction is that between partner and associate. The elite firms recruit the most promising graduates (top grades, membership on the law review) from the nation's most prestigious law schools with starting salaries of over $75,000 a year. As associates, these young attorneys work under the direction of a partner, gradually advancing from apprenticeship to increased autonomy. The work can be demanding—70 to 80 hour weeks are not uncommon—and the pressure enormous. Associates know that only about a quarter of them will receive partnership offers.

What these large firms claim to offer their clients is the perfection of the legal craft, a combination of legal talent and specialized expertise which ensures that "no stone is left unturned, no matter how seemingly insignificant, and with virtually no regard for time or money."[34] This dedication and legal expertise is expensive, of course. Elite firms may bill their clients up to $300 an hour for the time of a senior partner and over $100 an hour for the work of an associate. But these figures purchase an extraordinary devotion: during the Kennecott takeover fight "the lawyers at Sullivan & Cromwell didn't have a day off from Thanksgiving 1980 to the end of January 1981, including holidays."[35] When legal disputes involve millions of dollars, companies are quite willing to pay premium prices for top-flight legal work.

Solo Practice

At the opposite end of the spectrum from the large law firm is the solo practitioner. The solo practitioner epitomizes the idea of the independent professional and thus occupies an honored place in the mythology of the legal profession. Certainly the prospect of being one's own boss and choosing one's own clients attracts some attorneys to solo practice. There may also be social or other barriers that prevent a lawyer from pursuing other sorts of law practice. A 1962 study found that "the individual practitioner of law in Chicago is a self-made man who came up the hard way from poor, immigrant surroundings" by attending the local law school, usually at night.[36] When neither his social background nor the quality of his legal education recommended him to major law firms, he became a solo practitioner.

The number of solo practitioners has declined sharply in recent years, particularly in urban areas, as attorneys have gravitated toward large law firms or toward employment with corporations. A contributing factor has been the tendency of corporations and other businesses to deal with their legal problems in-house or to take them to law firms with specialized expertise rather than to solo practitioners. As a result, solo practitioners are often "confined to those residual matters (and clients) that the large firms have not pre-empted."[37]   Thus solo practitioners primarily serve the legal needs of middle-class and blue-collar clients.   According to a recent study of Chicago lawyers, their legal concerns generally involve personal business matters (general litigation, personal real estate, personal tax, and probate) and personal plight concerns (criminal defense, divorce, general family practice, and personal injury claims).[38]

Even in dealing with these problems, solo practitioners face increased competition today. Taking advantage of Supreme Court rulings that have removed restrictions on advertising by lawyers, legal entrepreneurs have developed "legal clinics" that seek to provide routine legal services at low prices by serving a large clientele.[39]   Hyatt Legal Services, now among the largest firms in the country, and Jacoby & Myers are among the best known of these clinics, but they are hardly isolated examples. Whereas in 1974 there were eight clinics in the United States, by 1984 there were over a thousand. Solo practitioners have found it difficult to compete with the clinics' ability to attract clients through advertising and low prices.

Corporate Counsel

In 1980 10 percent of lawyers worked in private industry, frequently in firms involved in finance, insurance, real estate, communications, or manufacturing. Major corporations are most likely to employ lawyers and maintain large legal departments. About 30 percent of all in-house counsel work for Fortune 500 companies, with General Electric employing over 400 attorneys and Exxon over 200 in their law departments. Although one report noted a slight decline in the percentage of lawyers working for corporations during the 1970s (the actual number increased), other reports suggest that the trend in recent decades is toward increased use of in-house counsel.[40]

In part, the growth in corporate law offices represents an attempt by major companies to reduce legal costs by relying less heavily on elite law firms. By using in-house counsel, some companies have halved their legal costs. In part, too, it reflects a recognition that, in the words of one board chairman, "the most active companies now require—or are best served by—the constant availability of counsel who is informed on a day to day basis of the company's activities and directions."[41] Most often the corporate counsel is engaged in preventive law, ensuring that legal problems do not arise. When large corporations do litigate, they still tend to rely on outside counsel.

From the perspective of the attorney, there are both advantages and disadvantages in working in-house. On the one hand, house counsel are not their own boss and earn less than does a partner in a top law firm, especially since most house counsel reach their highest positions after twelve to fifteen years with a corporation. On the other hand, corporate employment offers job security and a more than comfortable income—a 1986 survey reported that the average income of chief general counsel was $174,000.[42] Moreover, as Catherine Rein, corporate general counsel for The Continental Group, has observed, by working for a single client, you see "the long-term effects of [your] legal advice, become part of a team, and can take continuing pride in your contribution."[43]

Government Attorney

About 10 percent of American attorneys are now employed by federal, state, or local governments (excluding judges, who comprise 4 percent of the legal profession).[44] More than three-fifths of these attorneys work for state and local governments, with the largest number involved in criminal justice as prosecutors or public defenders (attorneys employed by the government to represent defendants who cannot afford a private attorney). Almost 40 percent of government attorneys work for the federal government. Large contingents of federal attorneys are found in the Department of Justice, which handles federal civil cases and criminal prosecutions, and in the Internal Revenue Service. However, as Table 4-4 indicates, attorneys occupy positions in a wide array of departments and agencies.

This diversity of positions reflects the diverse responsibilities of government attorneys. Government attorneys dominate the practice of criminal law: government prosecutors conduct all criminal prosecutions, and public defenders represent the vast majority of defendants. Government attorneys are also involved in civil litigation. They may initiate civil suits on behalf of federal, state, or municipal governments or their subunits. They also defend the government and its various departments against suits by private parties. In addition, through the Legal Services Corporation the federal government and states supply attorneys to represent the poor in certain civil cases. Still other government attorneys work outside the courtroom. Their responsibilities may include drafting legislation or administrative regulations, administering government departments and programs, lobbying on behalf of the department before Congress, or helping governmental agencies to avoid legal problems. We shall discuss the responsibilities of various government attorneys in detail later in this chapter and in Chapters 5 and 6.

Women and minority attorneys, perhaps concerned about discrimination in the private sector, have disproportionately chosen careers in government service.[45] However, government employment offers advantages for all attorneys, particularly early in their careers. Lawyers in the public sector find a degree of job security and avoid the intense competition and job pressures char-

TABLE 4-4 EMPLOYMENT OF LAWYERS BY THE FEDERAL GOVERNMENT (1980)

Department or Agency	Percent of Federal Lawyers (N=20,132)	Cumulative Percent (N=20,132)
Department of Justice	17.9	17.9
Internal Revenue Service	9.4	27.3
Department of Defense and armed services	8.4	35.7
Department of Health and Human Services	6.5	42.2
National Labor Relations Board	4.8	47.0
Congress	4.5	51.4
Veterans Administration	3.5	54.9
Department of Energy	3.1	58.0
Securities and Exchange Relations	3.0	61.0
Federal Trade Commission	3.0	64.0
Department of Labor	2.9	66.9
Department of Commerce	2.7	69.6
Department of Housing and Urban Development	2.3	71.9
Department of the Treasury	2.2	74.1
Department of the Interior	2.0	76.1
Department of State	2.0	78.0
Environmental Protection Agency	1.8	79.8
Department of Transportation	1.7	81.5
Interstate Commerce Commission	1.6	83.1
Federal Communications Commission	1.5	84.6
Department of Agriculture	1.2	85.9
Equal Employment Opportunity Commission	1.1	87.0
Small Business Administration	1.1	88.1
All other departments and agencies	11.9	100.0

SOURCE: Barbara Curran, "American Lawyers in the 1980s: A Profession in Transition," *Law & Society Review* 20 (1986): p. 35, Table 13. Reprinted by permission of the Law and Society Association.

acteristic of large law firms. While salaries hardly match those in large firms, they are respectable, particularly for more junior attorneys. In addition, young attorneys may be given significant responsibilities in government earlier than in a large law firm. (Of course, this may have its downside as well. As one public defender described it, after only a day or two of orientation he was told: "We're all attorneys and you handle the case any way you want to handle it, at your complete discretion. Just right on, brother, and good luck."[46]) Nonetheless, government employment can offer young attorneys a chance to gain valuable experience early in their careers.

Not surprisingly, then, many attorneys use government service for that purpose, moving into corporate work or private practice after a period in the public sector. Although this migration to the private sector creates openings for newly minted attorneys, that is not its only effect. Attorneys who have worked for a government often find their experience and expertise in demand by private employers or clients and end up representing the very groups they sought to regulate while in government service. As one lawyer put it, when asked whether he felt any remorse about his shift in position: "I have no qualms about changing sides. Will I be comfortable representing [business] in front of the [agency]? I can hardly wait! Certainly there are two sides to every story."[47]

The Divided Legal Profession

Our discussion thus far has emphasized the diversity of clients lawyers represent, the range of legal issues they address, and the varied contexts in which they practice law. In their study of the legal profession in Chicago, however, John Heinz and Edward Laumann found a fundamental division underlying this diversity.[48] According to these authors, the American legal profession is divided into "two hemispheres," between those who represent large organizations (primarily corporations) and those who represent individuals. As they observe:

> Lawyers who serve major corporations and other large organizations differ systematically from those who work for individuals and small businesses whether we look at the social origins of the lawyers, the prestige of the law schools they attended, their careers histories and mobility, their social or political values, their networks of friends and professional associations, or several other social variables.... [T]his fundamental difference in the nature of the client served appears to be the principal factor that structures the social differentiation of the profession.[49]

Even if, as Heinz and Laumann contend, no other profession is as divided, what difference does that make? The authors suggest that this bifurcation has at least two adverse effects. First, because the interests and perspectives of its members diverge so sharply, the legal profession cannot speak with one voice on the issues that affect it. Second, it sends a troubling message about the orientation of the legal profession. All Americans are aware that inequalities of wealth and power exist in their society. The bifurcation of the legal profession—with the most notable members of the legal profession serving the needs of corporate

America and a less prestigious group serving private persons—seems to reinforce those inequalities. Thus, in the final section of this chapter, we turn to the availability of adequate legal services for the general public.

ACCESS TO LEGAL SERVICES

The Nebraska Constitution provides that "[a]ll courts shall be open, and every person, for any injury done him in his lands, goods, person, or reputation, shall have a remedy by due course of law."[50] This guarantee, repeated in similar language in several other state constitutions, reflects a commitment to the principle that all persons should have access to the courts for settling disputes and redressing injuries. Although litigants have the right to represent themselves, effective presentation of their claims almost always requires the services of an attorney. So do many other commonplace activities, from the drawing up of contracts, to the closing on a purchase of a house, to the adoption of a child or the probating of a will. Yet purchasing the services of an attorney to resolve even routine legal problems can be expensive. According to a 1984 survey, lawyers in the United States on average charged almost $90 per hour for their services.[51] Concern about costs thus may deter poor or middle-class people from consulting an attorney, even when they need legal assistance.

Government, the legal profession, and private groups have attempted to ensure that all members of the society obtain the legal assistance they require. Let us look at the character and success of those efforts.

Criminal Justice

The Sixth Amendment to the United States Constitution guarantees to every defendant the right "to have the Assistance of Counsel for his defense." This guarantee permits those accused of crime to hire counsel but, on its face, it does not oblige the government to provide an attorney to indigent defendants. However, if the government fails to provide legal assistance, this creates an unequal system of justice. It may also interfere with the operation of the adversary system. Well-to-do defendants will hire counsel, thus assuring a rough balance of legal expertise between prosecution and defense. But indigent defendants, unable to afford an attorney, will be forced to defend themselves, despite their lack of familiarity with the law and with courtroom procedures. As our discussion of *Gideon* v. *Wainwright* in Chapter 2 suggested, such defendants are unlikely to mount a strong defense, even when they are innocent. Since the effectiveness of the adversary system depends on a vigorous presentation of both sides in a case, the imbalance of legal expertise between prosecution and defense increases the possibility that innocent people will be convicted.

Recognizing this, the United States Supreme Court in 1938 ruled that criminal defendants in federal courts had a constitutional right to representation by counsel, even if they could not afford to pay a lawyer.[52] Several states also recognized a right to counsel for indigent defendants as a matter of state law—Wisconsin did so as early as 1859.[53] However, the most important step toward securing equal justice for indigent defendants was *Gideon* v. *Wainwright* (1963), which extended the right to counsel to all felony defendants in state courts, where the bulk of criminal prosecutions take place.[54] In subsequent cases the Supreme Court extended the logic of *Gideon* to guarantee legal representation for defendants in juvenile courts and for all defendants facing the possibility of imprisonment if convicted.[55] In addition, recognizing that earlier stages of the criminal justice process, such as police interrogations and line-ups, may determine the outcome of a case, the Court extended the right to counsel to those earlier stages as well.[56]

The states had two options in responding to their obligation to provide counsel for indigent defendants: they could establish offices of government-employed defense attorneys (public defenders) or could pay private attorneys to represent defendants. The latter approach has not worked well. The rates that governments have paid have not been high enough to attract many good lawyers. If all attorneys in a jurisdiction are obliged to take a turn at criminal defense, defendants may well receive perfunctory representation by lawyers who have little familiarity with the criminal law. Many jurisdictions, therefore, have chosen to employ public defenders to handle criminal defense.

Providing representation has not only improved the lot of indigent defendants but also increased the fairness of the criminal justice system. Nonetheless, some critics have charged that public-defender offices are chronically underfunded and understaffed, so public defenders lack the time to provide their clients with an adequate defense. Other critics have complained that public defenders have used liberal Supreme Court rulings to manipulate the criminal justice system and secure the release of guilty defendants. Whatever their validity, these allegations underscore the crucial role that public defenders play today. Public defenders provide legal representation for more than two-thirds of criminal defendants. We shall examine the work of public defenders more closely in Chapter 6.

Civil Law

Although the United States Constitution requires government to provide legal assistance for indigent defendants accused of crime, it does not guarantee legal assistance in civil cases. Yet from time to time most people do require the services of a lawyer. They may need legal representation to file suit—for damages when they have been injured, for divorce when a marriage fails, or for various other reasons. They may also find themselves as respondents in a civil suit. Or they may need legal advice or assistance in dealing with a business matter, such as the purchase of property or the drafting of a contract, or with a personal matter, such as an adoption.

Nonetheless, many people either find it difficult to obtain legal services or do not seek them out because of concern about costs, an inability to locate a lawyer, or a lack of knowledge about the legal implications of the problems they confront. Government, the legal profession, and private groups have pioneered various approaches to ensuring the availability of legal services. Let us examine the nature and success of several approaches.

Legal Aid

Although there is no constitutional right to counsel in civil cases, government or private groups may provide attorneys for those who cannot afford one. The federal government's first involvement with legal aid for the poor grew out of the Freedman's Bureau during Reconstruction, when the Bureau retained private attorneys to represent poor blacks in civil and criminal cases.[57] During the late nineteenth century, several private legal aid societies were formed. Illustrative of these societies were Der Deutsche Rechtsschutz Verein, established by New York City's German Society to protect recent German immigrants, and "The Protective Agency for Women and Children," created by the Women's Club of Chicago to combat the "seductions and debaucheries of young girls under guise of proferred employment."[58] By 1919 legal aid societies were in operation in forty-one cities, and the number grew in succeeding decades. Despite this, the private legal aid societies lacked the resources to serve adequately the legal needs of the poor.

The federal government's more recent involvement in legal aid grew out of the "War on Poverty" launched by President Lyndon Johnson. The Legal Services Program (LSP), established in 1965, encouraged the formation of local legal aid agencies to serve the poor through grants that covered the costs of their operations. These local agencies retained considerable discretion in deciding how best to serve the needs of their clientele. Some local LSP agencies emphasized solving the legal problems of individual clients, following the approach of legal aid societies in the past, although their greater resources permitted them to serve more poor people and take more cases to court. Other local agencies placed greater emphasis on law reform, challenging laws and policies that they believed disadvantaged the poor. Such challenges, usually referred to as "impact cases," typically entailed more time and effort than the resolution of individual disputes and often involved appellate litigation. Not surprisingly, these law-reform efforts were controversial—conservative critics charged that they reduced the number of clients served, created the odd phenomenon of one part of government suing another, and permitted left-wing lawyers to politicize the Legal Services Program by pursuing their own political agendas under the guise of helping the poor. (The next section of this chapter addresses this concern as one aspect of the perplexing issue of client vs. lawyer control of litigation.)

The political controversy over the Legal Services Program led Congress to reconstitute it as the Legal Services Corporation (LSC) in 1974, and it continues in this form to the present day. The LSC functions as a non-profit corporation, providing funds by grant or contract to legal service programs in all fifty states, with the majority going to 284 basic field offices. Like its predecessor, the LSC has become mired in political controversy. President Ronald Reagan sought to abolish the LSC, but Congress refused to go along. However, appropriations for the Legal Services Corporation were slashed, and the president named outspoken critics of the LSC to its board of directors.

Whatever the deficiencies of the Legal Services Corporation, the government's involvement in legal aid has substantially increased the poor's access to legal assistance.[59] During 1987, for example, almost 1.4 million cases were closed by negotiated settlement, litigation, referral to another agency, or other means. The most common legal problems handled by legal-aid lawyers involve family issues, such as divorce, child support, spouse abuse, and custody and visitation rights. About 19 percent of LSC cases concern housing matters, such as landlord and tenant disputes. Another 18 percent involve disputes with government agencies about claims for benefits under government programs including Aid to Families with Dependent Children (AFDC), disability benefits, food stamps, and unemployment compensation. Other areas in which LSC lawyers have been active include consumer/finance issues, employment problems, health matters, and questions of individual rights.

Legal Clinics

Legal clinics are high-volume private law firms that seek to provide routine legal services for large numbers of clients at low cost. Their number increased dramatically during the 1970s—whereas in 1974 there were only eight law clinics, by 1980 there were about 800.[60] The growth of legal clinics was stimulated by Supreme Court rulings that opened the door to aggressive price competition within the legal profession. In *Bates* v. *State Bar of Arizona* (1977), the Supreme Court ruled that the First Amendment protected the right of lawyers to advertise their prices for legal services, and in *Goldfarb* v. *Virginia State Bar* (1975), it struck down minimum fee schedules established by bar associations as a violation of federal antitrust laws.[61] These rulings freed legal entrepreneurs to seek to attract clients by price advertising, claiming to provide legal services more cheaply than their competitors can.

In part, legal clinics can charge lower rates because of economies of scale. Although they frequently locate branch offices in neighborhoods or malls for the convenience of their clients, legal clinics are among the largest law firms in the United States. One well-known clinic, Hyatt Legal Services, in 1985 had 550 lawyers in 174 offices in 17 states. Even more important, these clinics cut personnel costs by relying on paralegals rather than lawyers for routine tasks and by employing standard forms for common legal procedures. Many clinics have prospered by focusing on such problems as divorces, wills, personal bankruptcy, and preparation of tax returns.

Legal clinics have primarily attracted middle-class and working-class clients. While they have introduced competition into the provision of legal services. it is unclear whether they have increased the availability of lawyers to those who would not otherwise use their services. It may be that legal clinics have merely displaced traditional firms, redistributing business within the legal profession.

Lifting the Lawyers' Monopoly

Like the members of other professions, lawyers have sought to establish a state-enforced monopoly over the provision of their professional services and to prevent non-lawyers from providing legal services. To a large extent their efforts have succeeded. Laws in various states mandate that only lawyers may provide legal advice, draft wills, transfer property titles, and represent persons before administrative agencies.

Such laws help maintain the high cost of legal services by restricting competition to those who have law degrees. The legal profession has justified the restrictions as necessary to protect the public, arguing that only attorneys have the expertise to provide competent legal assistance. However, critics charge that the restrictions serve the interests of the legal profession rather than those of the general public. Legal clinics' intensive use of paralegals for tasks traditionally undertaken by lawyers does suggest that trained non-lawyers can perform some of the tasks currently undertaken by lawyers. The chairman of the Legal Services Corporation under President Reagan went considerably further, suggesting that the LSC could be abolished if legal restrictions on the unauthorized practice of law were lifted.

Some jurisdictions have responded to criticisms of the legal monopoly. California, for example, adopted a form for wills simple enough to allow most persons to draft their own. Meanwhile, groups and commercial concerns have begun to publish forms and other materials designed to enable laypersons to conduct real estate transactions, probate estates, and handle their own no-fault divorces. While self-help materials may reduce legal costs for those who use them, they can be used only for simple and routine legal matters. Furthermore, while reducing the monopoly position of lawyers may reduce legal costs, it is not clear whether it actually increases access to legal services.

Contingent Fees

Potential litigants may fail to consult a lawyer because they fear that the damages they are awarded may not cover the legal fees and court costs associated with their cases. To remove this disincentive to pursue legal claims, the American legal system has developed the contingent fee, which displaces the financial risk from the client to the lawyer. Under a contingent-fee arrangement, the attorney bears the costs of the litigation and receives an agreed-upon percentage (often one-third) of the award or settlement in the case. If the lawyer's efforts net the client a large award, the lawyer shares in the good fortune. However, if the client receives nothing, neither does the attorney. Thus a contingent-fee arrangement makes sense for a lawyer only when the prospect of a substantial fee outweighs the risk of no fee at all. This occurs most often in personal-injury cases, where clients are suing because of injuries sustained in an accident or as the result of defects in a product they purchased. In such cases the question frequently is not whether the plaintiff will obtain damages but rather the size of the award or settlement.

Contingent fees are highly controversial.[62] Critics charge that they encourage frivolous suits because plaintiffs bear no financial risk. They also claim that contingent fees may create a conflict between the interests of the attorney and the client. An attorney operating under a contingent-fee arrangement may be tempted to settle a case, thereby obtaining some reward for his efforts, rather than take it to trial and risk losing both the case and his fee. Furthermore, contingent fees allow attorneys to receive extremely high fees for relatively little work, when they negotiate large settlements in straightforward personal-injury cases.

Proponents argue that most criticism of contingent fees is self-interested, coming from attorneys who represent insurance companies, corporations, and other defendants in personal-injury cases rather than from plaintiffs in personal-injury cases. More substantively, they insist that without contingent fees average citizens would often not bring cases, even when they had suffered real injuries. They also deny that lawyers receive unduly high contingent fees. Such claims, they maintain, rely on a few atypical cases and ignore the risk that attorneys bear under contingent-fee arrangements.

Although no jurisdiction has outlawed contingent fees, some have sought to regulate them. The New Jersey Supreme Court, for example, has established a graduated scale of maximum permissible contingent fees, with attorneys receiving no more than 10 percent of any award over $100,000.

Group Legal Services

Group-legal-services (GLS) plans are a form of legal insurance, under which group members pay a premium that entitles them to various legal services. GLS plans resemble medical insurance plans and, like them, vary in how they provide services. Open-panel plans are like Blue Cross/Blue Shield, in that GLS members can seek legal services from a wide range of lawyers. A closed-panel plan is more like an HMO: members "can consult only lawyers (sometimes a single firm) who belong to the plan and have agreed to accept a schedule of fees, generally below the market rate."[63]

Such prepaid plans developed early in the twentieth century, when the Physicians' Defense Company and automobile clubs began to offer legal services or coverage of legal fees for subscribing members. But opposition from the American Bar Association limited experimentation with group legal services until the 1970s. Promoting the renewed interest in group legal plans were a series of Supreme Court rulings during the 1960s that held that restrictions could not be placed on group efforts to ensure legal representation for their members.[64] Thus, associations could offer prepaid legal plans to their members, and unions could seek coverage for their members in collective bargaining. By 1987 roughly 17 million employees belonged to group plans negotiated by their unions. Yet whether group plans will continue to expand is unclear: fewer workers belong to unions today than in the past, and group legal plans remain a low-priority fringe benefit for most workers.

Pro Bono Work

The ABA's Model Rules of Professional Conduct suggest that attorneys have an obligation to perform "pro bono" work, that is, to undertake legal work without compensation for the economically disadvantaged or for charitable causes. (The term "pro bono" comes from the Latin "pro bono publico," for the public good.) However, this professional obligation is self-enforced, and most lawyers actually engage in little or no "pro bono" work. A survey of 224 lawyers in large firms in Chicago found that they gave an average of 15 hours a year to pro bono activities, while a 1985 ABA survey concluded that 30 percent of all lawyers devoted less than 25 hours a year to pro bono work.[65]

Some jurisdictions and local bar associations have begun to require attorneys to devote a minimum number of hours to pro bono work. Such pro bono requirements are controversial; some attorneys have even argued that they violate the Thirteenth Amendment ban on involuntary servitude. Even where mandatory pro bono exists, it imposes only minimal burdens (about two cases a year), and attorneys can buy out of their obligations. Thus a knowledgeable commentator has concluded: "Although pro bono activities undoubtedly help the particular recipients and ease the consciences of lawyers, they do relatively little to fulfill the promise of equal justice...."[66]

LAWYERS AND CLIENTS

In an adversary system lawyers are expected to represent the interests of their clients. Attorneys who fail to do so risk serious penalties. Those who provide inadequate or incompetent assistance can be sued for malpractice; and those who are dishonest, who—for example—make use of or steal money entrusted to them, are subject not only to criminal prosecution but also to discipline by the state bar association. In serious cases a lawyer may be disbarred, that is, prohibited from practicing law again.

Yet for attorneys who are neither incompetent nor dishonest, the perplexing issue remains: how *does* one serve the interests of one's client? The answer to this question is inevitably tied up with the question of the proper relationship between lawyer and client. Historically, this relationship has resembled the traditional relationship between doctors and patients or between other professionals and their clients.[67] The client seeks the counsel of the professional and puts the matter in his or her hands, relying on the professional's expertise and judgment. Thus, the professional has full autonomy in deciding how best to advance the client's interests. The assumption is that the interests of both parties are best served by this arrangement.

In recent years, however, this model of professional dominance has come under attack. In medicine this is reflected in the development of the notion of informed consent: physicians should explain the various options available to patients and proceed with a course of treatment only after receiving their consent. In law too, the idea of a more collaborative relationship between lawyer and client has gained currency. Proponents of this more cooperative approach suggest that clients should consider together with their lawyers such matters as

> whether to sue at all, the ground rules of the lawyer's and client's mutual contact, the lawyer's fee, the preparation of the case, the best time to sue, whether to seek a jury trial or special trial preference, various issues of settlement strategy, and the preparation for examination before trial.[68]

However, as the relationship between professional and client becomes more collaborative, defining the responsibilities of each becomes more difficult.

The appropriate relationship between lawyer and client is particularly difficult to determine in political litigation, where the aim is not merely to vindicate the interests of a single person but also to establish a legal principle of benefit to a larger group. Political litigation poses fundamental questions: who is the lawyer's client and whose interests should be given priority? *Brown* v. *Board of Education*, the famous school desegregation case, illustrates this. Thurgood Marshall and the NAACP's Legal Defense Fund had undertaken a protracted campaign to overturn laws mandating segregation in schools and other public facilities. As part of the campaign they actively sought out clients willing to serve as vehicles for challenging discriminatory laws. In *Brown*, which represented the culmination of this struggle, the NAACP recruited Oliver Brown, whose daughter attended a segregated school in Topeka, Kansas, to serve as plaintiff. The decision to litigate, the selection of plaintiffs, the choice of when and where to sue, and the decision as to how to frame the legal issues all remained in the hands of Thurgood Marshall and his associates.

As this account suggests, the relationship between lawyers and clients is far different in political litigation than in ordinary litigation. Lawyers in political litigation may actively seek out clients to act as parties to a suit, rather than merely providing a service to those who consult them. Moreover, the lawyers' willingness to initiate suit or file an appeal, as well as the strategy pursued in the course of the litigation, will depend upon how such action will advance the interests of the group, not those of the individual litigant. As long as the "client" understands and accepts this, as is usually the case when a group pursues a litigation strategy, no problem arises.

However, it may happen that the remedy desired by the lawyer in political litigation may diverge from that preferred by clients. In the aftermath of *Brown*, for example, a gap at times developed between the belief of civil rights lawyers in the importance of school integration and the desire of clients—parents and children—for educational improvement, whether in a segregated or an integrated setting. Similarly, in mental health litigation, some lawyers sought to establish a "right to treatment", whereas most residents in institutions preferred a "least restrictive alternative" suit that would release them from the institution to a community-based mental health facility.[69]   Or the choice may be between pressing for a legal ruling that could conceivably benefit a large number of persons or accepting a settlement beneficial to one's client, as when the government agency being sued offers a settlement that will satisfy the client's particular concern without establishing a binding precedent.   In circumstances such as these, lawyers may well wonder how they should balance competing interests and whose interests should be given the greatest weight.

The appropriate relationship between lawyer and client is even more complicated when the lawyer engaged in law-reform litigation is affiliated with a legal-services agency funded by the Legal Services Corporation. Critics charge that legal-services lawyers in "impact cases" dominate the relationship with their clients.   Instead of advancing clients' interests as they define them, the lawyers "use their clients as mere instruments for enacting their own political agendas."[70]   Furthermore, if legal-services lawyers claim to be serving a group beyond the individual client, exactly what is that group? If it is the poor in general, on what basis can the lawyer claim to represent their interests, and who gave the lawyer authority to speak for them? Moreover, since LSC lawyers work for the government, how can they justify pursuing policies in political litigation, such as increased welfare benefits or siting public housing in middle-class neighborhoods, that diverge from the policies endorsed by the government? In sum, critics contend that the law-reform activities of legal-services lawyers go beyond even the traditional relationship between lawyer and client, because the lawyer expects clients to defer not only to his expertise regarding how to serve their interests but also to his view of what those interests are.

Because of these concerns, many LSC attorneys rarely engage in political litigation, preferring to serve the day-to-day legal problems of individual clients.[71]   Other LSC attorneys, however, dismiss the benefits obtained through such legal work as "band-aids" and insist that real advances for the poor come through political litigation.[72]   These lawyers claim that the close ties they maintain with community groups keep them informed about the interests of their real clients, the poor of the community. Thus, they deny that they are unilaterally imposing their views on their clients.   Even when they seek out plaintiffs to pursue issues or aggregate individual complaints into broad-based legal attacks on the practices or policies of a government agency, they insist that it is the community's interests they are seeking to advance. The concern voiced about lawyer domination of poor clients, they argue, is insincere; those voicing the concern are really distressed by the success of the aggressive tactics employed by LSC attorneys.

THE TRANSFORMATION OF THE AMERICAN LEGAL PROFESSION

This chapter has shown that the American legal profession today differs from its counterparts in other countries in its training, its size, and the ways it organizes itself and delivers legal services. However, the contrast with other countries is no sharper than the contrast with the American past.

The transformation of American legal education is a case in point. To become a lawyer in the United States today, a college graduate must survive an increasingly selective admissions process for law school and complete three years of rigorous academic training. Every element of that description represents a change from the past. The current emphasis on academic studies in a university setting marks a departure from the nation's first century, when apprenticeship was the most common form of legal training. Until well into the twentieth century, graduation from college was not a requirement for law school—indeed, some law schools accepted students who did not even have high-school diplomas—and some graduated students after as little as a single year of study. Only recently has admission to law school become fiercely competitive.

A transformation has also occurred in the composition and size of the American legal profession. Initially, the practice of law was largely confined to a relatively small group of native-born white males. But in the late nineteenth century, new groups—women, racial minorities, and immigrants—began to seek admission to the legal profession. Despite legal and social barriers, these groups had gained a tenuous foothold by the early twentieth century. Only within the last three decades, however, have women and racial minorities become a sizable presence within the American legal community. Indeed, the dramatic expansion of the American legal profession in large part reflects the opening of the profession to previously excluded or marginalized groups.

Finally, a transformation has occurred in the practice of law and the delivery of legal services in the United States. For most of the nation's history, the typical lawyer was a solo practitioner or a partner in a very small firm. But three developments during the second half of the twentieth century have altered the practice of law. First, the number of large law firms has increased dramatically, as have the size of those firms, with the largest firms employing hundreds of attorneys in branch offices throughout the nation and abroad. Second, corporations and governments at all levels now hire far more lawyers than in the past. As a result, attorneys today increasingly are employees rather than autonomous professionals.

Third, governmental officials and the legal profession have recognized that segments of the American public cannot normally afford the legal services they

need. This has led to establishment of government programs designed to provide legal aid, such as public defender programs and the Legal Services
Corporation. It has also led the legal profession to introduce innovations
designed to attract new clients by making legal services more affordable. These
innovations extend to the way legal services are delivered, such as legal clinics,
and to how they are paid for, such as the contingent fee and prepaid legal services. How successful these efforts to increase the accessibility of legal services
have been, and to what extent they have given reality to the goal of equal justice
for all, remains a matter of dispute.

NOTES

1. Background information on the two justices was obtained from Henry J. Abraham, *Justices and Presidents*, 3rd ed. (New York: Oxford University Press, 1992); *Guide to the U.S. Supreme Court* (Washington, D.C.: Congressional Quarterly Press, 1979); and Leon Friedman, ed., *The Justices of the United States Supreme Court*, vols. IV & V (New York: Chelsea House, 1969, 1978).

2. The distinction between attorneys as "delegates" and as "trustees" is drawn from Susan E. Lawrence, *The Poor in Court* (Princeton: Princeton University Press, 1990), Chapter 1.

3. Cited in Richard L. Abel, *American Lawyers* (New York: Oxford University Press, 1989), p. 163.

4. American Bar Association Code, EC 7-19, quoted in David Luban, *Lawyers and Justice* (Princeton: Princeton University Press, 1988), p. 51.

5. Robert Stevens, *Law School* (Chapel Hill: University of North Carolina Press, 1983), Chapter 1.

6. Lawrence M. Friedman, *A History of American Law*, 2d ed. (New York: Simon and Schuster, 1985), p. 317.

7. The discussion of Langdell and the impact of his efforts relies on Stevens, *Law School*, Chapters 3-4.

8. Quoted in ibid., p. 52.

9. Abel, *American Lawyers*, p. 41.

10. Stevens, *Law School*, Chapter 11.

11. Ibid., Chapter 12, and Abel, *American Lawyers*, p. 56.

12. Abel, *American Lawyers*, p. 59.

13. The data on admissions standards at Yale Law School and more generally are drawn from *The Official Guide to U.S. Law Schools* (Newtown, PA: Law School Admissions Service, 1991), p. 412 and *passim*.

14. For data on the size of the American legal profession, see Terrence C. Halliday, "Six Score Years and Ten: Demographic Transitions in the American Legal Profession," *Law & Society Review* 20 (1986), p. 62, Table 1.

15. The relationship between economic activity and the size of the legal profession is explored in ibid., pp. 65-70.

16. Data on the Japanese legal profession are found in Masanobu Kato, "The Role of Law and Lawyers in Japan and the United States," *Brigham Young University Law Review* 1987 (1987): 627-698.

17. Data on law-school graduates and populations are drawn from *The Official Guide to U.S. Law Schools*, p. 36.

18. *Bradwell* v. *Illinois*, 83 U.S. 130 (1873). For more general treatments of the barriers confronting women, see Karen Berger Morello, *The Invisible Bar: The Woman Lawyer in America 1638 to the Present* (New York: Random House, 1986), and Cynthia Fuchs Epstein, *Women in Law* (New York: Basic Books, 1981).

19. Abel, *American Lawyers*, p. 90.

20. Nancy L. Buc, "As Washington Lawyer: Using Government Experience in Private Practice," in Emily Couric, ed., *Women Lawyers; Perspectives on Success* (New York: Harcourt Brace Jovanovich, 1984), p. 50.

21. Epstein, *Women in Law*, p. 4.

22. Abel, *American Lawyers*, p. 91.

23. Ibid., p. 284, Table 26.

24. Ibid., p. 100.

25. Ibid., pp. 99-108.

26. John Dean Caton, *Early Bench and Bar of Illinois* (1893), p. 51, quoted in Friedman, *History of American Law*, p. 309.

27. See Friedman, *History of American Law*, Chapter VIII.

28. Data are drawn from Barbara A. Curran, "American Lawyers in the 1980s: A Profession in Transition," *Law & Society Review* 20 (1986): 27, and Abel, *American Lawyers*, p. 178.

29. Barbara A. Curran, Katherine J. Rosich, Clara N. Carson, and Mark C. Puccetti, *The Lawyer Statistical Report: A Statistical Profile of the U.S. Legal Profession in the 1980s* (Chicago: American Bar Foundation, 1985), p. 243.

30. These examples are drawn from actual cases discussed in James B. Stewart, *The Partners* (New York: Simon and Schuster, 1983).

31. Paul Wice, *Judges and Lawyers; The Human Side of Justice* (New York: Harper Collins, 1991), p. 73; for a more general overview of the structure and operations of large law firms, see pp. 79-90.

32. Abel, *American Lawyers*, p. 189.

33. Ibid., p. 184.

34. Stewart, *The Partners*, p. 14.

35. Ibid., p. 281.

36. Jerome E. Carlin, *Lawyers on Their Own* (New Brunswick: Rutgers University Press, 1962), p. 1.

37. Ibid., p. 17.

38. John P. Heinz and Edward O. Laumann, *Chicago Lawyers; The Social Structure of the Bar* (New York: Russell Sage Foundation and American Bar Association, 1982), p. 65, Table 3-1.

39. Relevant judicial rulings include *Bates* v. *State Bar of Arizona*, 433 U.S. 350 (1977) and *Shapero* v. *Kentucky Bar Association*, 486 U.S. 466 (1988). For a discussion of the development and effects of legal clinics, see Abel, *American Lawyers*, pp. 106-07.

40. Data are drawn from Curran, "American Lawyers in the 1980s," pp. 19-21, and Abel, *American Lawyers*, pp. 167-170.

41. Quoted in Eve Spangler, *Lawyers for Hire* (New Haven: Yale University Press, 1986), p. 71.

42. Abel, *American Lawyers*, p. 171.

43. Catherine A. Rein, "As Corporate General Counsel: Hierarchies with Few Women at Top," in Emily Couric, ed., *Women Lawyers*, p. 125.

44. These data are drawn from Curran, *The Lawyer Statistical Report*, pp. 16-18.

45. This discussion of the advantages of government employment for attorneys relies on Wice, *Judges and Lawyers*, p. 78.

46. Quoted in Milton Heumann, *Plea Bargaining* (Chicago: University of Chicago Press, 1977), p. 55.

47. Quoted in Spangler, *Lawyers for Hire*, p. 112.

48. Heinz and Laumann, *Chicago Lawyers*.

49. Ibid., pp. 319-320.

50. Nebraska Constitution, Article I, section 13.

51. "What Price Legal Advice? $88.52 an Hour," *USA Today*, August 6, 1984, p. 4D, cited in Lawrence Baum, *American Courts* (Boston: Houghton Mifflin, 1990), p. 84.

52. *Johnson* v. *Zerbst*, 304 U.S. 458 (1938).

53. *Carpenter* v. *Dane*, 9 Wis. 249 (1859).

54. *Gideon* v. *Wainwright*, 372 U.S. 335 (1963).

55. Representative cases include *In re Gault,* 387 U.S. 1 (1967), and *Argersinger* v. *Hamlin,* 407 U.S. 25 (1972).

56. These cases include *Escobedo* v. *Illinois,* 378 U.S. 478 (1964) and *Miranda* v. *Arizona,* 384 U.S. 436 (1966).

57. Our account of the development of legal aid for the poor, including the Legal Services Program and the Legal Services Corporation, relies primarily on Lawrence, *The Poor in Court;* Mark Kessler, *Legal Services for the Poor* (Westport, Conn.: Greenwood Press, 1987); and Douglas J. Besharov, ed., *Legal Services for the Poor* (Washington, D.C.: AEI Press, 1990).

58. Lawrence, *The Poor in Court,* p. 18.

59. These data are drawn from Besharov, *Legal Services for the Poor,* p. 32, Table 9.

60. This discussion is based on Abel, *American Lawyers,* p. 138, and Wice, *Judges and Lawyers,* pp. 75-76.

61. *Bates* v. *State Bar of Arizona,* 433 U.S. 350 (1977), and *Goldfarb* v. *Virginia State Bar,* 421 U.S. 773 (1975).

62. The critique of contingent fees is drawn from Wice, *Judges and Lawyers,* pp. 125-26.

63. Abel, *American Lawyers,* p. 136. More generally, the discussion of group legal services relies on Lillian Deitch and David Weinstein, *Prepaid Legal Services* (Lexington, MA: Lexington Books, 1976).

64. Pertinent cases include: *NAACP* v. *Button,* 371 U.S. 415 (1963); *Brotherhood of Railroad Trainmen* v. *Virginia ex rel. Virginia State Bar,* 377 U.S. 1 (1964); *United Mine Workers, District 12* v. *Illinois State Bar Association,* 389 U.S. 217 (1967); and *United Transportation* v. *State Bar of Michigan,* 401 U.S. 576 (1971).

65. Cited in Abel, *American Lawyers,* p. 130.

66. Ibid., p. 130.

67. See Douglas E. Rosenthal, *Lawyers and Clients: Who's in Charge?* (New York: Russell Sage, 1974), especially Chapters 1 and 6.

68. Susan M. Olson, *Clients and Lawyers* (Westport, Conn.: Greenwood Press, 1984), pp. 28-29.

69. These examples were suggested in ibid., pp. 29-30.

70. Luban, *Lawyers and Justice,* p. 303. This is a summary of the critique, not an expression of Luban's views.

71. A discussion of the different orientations of LSC lawyers is found in Kessler, *Legal Services for the Poor.*

72. The defense of political litigation by LSC lawyers is elegantly presented by Luban, *Lawyers and Justice,* Chapters 14-16.

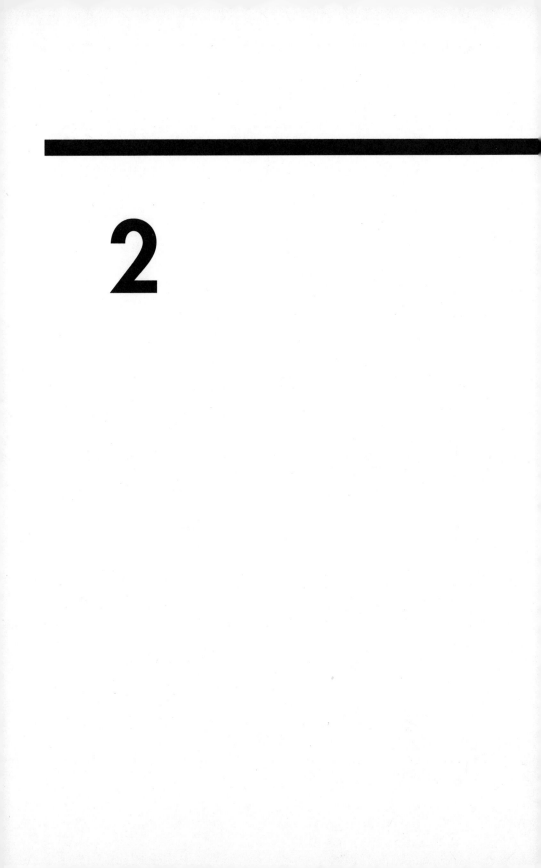

2

JUDICIAL PROCESS AND JUDICIAL DECISIONMAKING

CHAPTER

5 TRIALS AND APPEALS

In March 1982, fifteen months after Sunny von Bulow had lapsed into an irreversible coma, twelve jurors in a Rhode Island Superior Court found her husband, Klaus von Bulow, guilty of attempted murder.[1] The sensational nine-week trial had attracted reporters from all over the country, from *The New York Times* to *The National Enquirer*. And why not? The case had all the elements of a good story. The victim, who had been found lying unconscious in the marble bathroom of her Newport mansion, was a utilities heiress. Her aristocratic Danish husband stood to inherit an estate worth millions if she died—and if he was found not guilty. But her children from a previous marriage, who also had an interest in the estate, had launched the initial investigation into the case, convinced that their stepfather was guilty. In the words of the prosecutor:

> This case has everything. It has money, sex, drugs; it has Newport, New York, and Europe; it has nobility; it has maids, a butler, a gardener. ...This case is where the little man has a chance to glimpse inside and see how the rich live.[2]

The prosecution's theory of the case was simple: although Klaus von Bulow did not love his wife, he did love her money and the lifestyle it afforded him. He also loved his mistress, soap opera star Alexandra Isles, who had threatened to leave him if he did not divorce Sunny. Rather than choose between money and mistress, Klaus decided to have them both by murdering Sunny but making it appear that she had died of natural causes. To do this, the prosecution contended, he surreptitiously injected her with insulin, thereby inducing what he expected to be a fatal coma.

The prosecution introduced physical evidence to support its theory—most importantly, an insulin-encrusted needle allegedly found in a black bag belonging to Klaus von Bulow. It also brought forward an expert witness who stated that Sunny's coma had been induced by an insulin injection. Sunny's maid testified that Klaus owned the black bag and that she had seen needles and insulin in it in the past. Finally, Alexandra Isles admitted that she had threatened to leave Klaus unless he obtained a divorce.

The defense attorneys decided against having Klaus von Bulow take the stand in his own defense. Instead they relied on the testimony of Joy O'Neill, a self-described confidante of Sunny's, who claimed that Sunny gave herself insulin shots. However, on cross-examination the prosecution undermined O'Neill's credibility and with it the defense case. After six days of deliberations, the jury returned a guilty verdict.

After sentencing von Bulow to thirty years in prison, the trial judge commented: "The Trial of Klaus von Bulow is over. The Trial of the Trial Judge is about to begin."[3] And so it was as, proclaiming his innocence, Klaus von Bulow appealed his conviction to the Rhode Island Supreme Court. Newly hired to represent him on appeal was Alan Dershowitz, a Harvard professor and prominent defense attorney. Although appellate courts focus on legal rather than factual questions, Dershowitz was convinced that the Rhode Island court would not overturn von Bulow's conviction unless the justices had some indication that his client was innocent. He therefore framed his argument about errors in the trial proceedings in such a way as to raise doubts about von Bulow's guilt. Whether or not this approach was necessary, it did succeed; the Rhode Island Supreme Court reversed the trial court's decision. Citing the prosecution's failure to make certain potentially relevant documents available to the defense and the police's seizure and testing of pills without a warrant, the justices awarded von Bulow a new trial.

The state of Rhode Island again prosecuted von Bulow for attempted murder, but a different defense strategy produced a different result in the second trial. The documents withheld at the first trial revealed that when questioned early in the investigation, the maid had never mentioned having seen insulin and a syringe in von Bulow's bag. Under intense defense questioning, she retracted her testimony from the first trial about the insulin. The defense also brought forward expert witnesses who countered the prosecution's claim that Sunny's coma had resulted from an insulin injection. In June 1985, the jury found Klaus von Bulow innocent of all charges.

Although this spectacular case is hardly typical of criminal cases, or even of criminal trials, it illustrates several aspects of the roles and operations of trial and appellate courts:

Different courts, different functions. Dershowitz's decision to emphasize doubts about von Bulow's guilt in the appeal was a bold but risky maneuver.

For it is the job of trial courts, not appellate courts, to establish the facts and to decide on guilt or innocence in criminal cases and on liability or non-liability in civil cases. The job of appellate courts is to review whether trial courts have observed proper legal procedures in trying and deciding cases. If the appellate court finds, as it did in the von Bulow case, that procedural irregularities have prevented a fair trial, it can remand the case for new proceedings in which those irregularities are eliminated. This second trial will seek anew to establish the facts and to determine guilt or innocence, liability or non-liability.

Cases and Trials. Most criminal cases, unlike the von Bulow case, are resolved without a trial, usually by the defendant pleading guilty following plea negotiations between the defense attorney and the prosecutor. (Most civil cases are likewise settled prior to trial.) Yet trials have an importance that far exceeds their number. As the von Bulow case illustrates, the more serious the charge, the more likely a criminal case is to go to trial. Defendants charged with serious offenses may be willing to take their chances with a jury because they fear the severe punishment a guilty plea would bring, and prosecutors may refuse to plea bargain because public opinion supports severe punishment for those who commit serious crimes.

In addition, both criminal and civil trials have an effect on those cases resolved without trial. Trials provide a baseline, a point of reference for resolving cases without trial. In plea bargaining the negotiations of prosecutor and defense attorney are influenced by the punishment an offender would likely receive if the case went to trial. In civil cases the willingness of the plaintiff and the defendant to settle often depends on their perception of how they would fare if the case went to trial. Thus even when cases are settled without trial, the negotiations take place in the shadow of the law.[4]

Lawyers' Tactics. Under our adversarial system of justice, trial courts rely on the parties in the case to uncover relevant physical evidence (anything from documents and reports to, in the von Bulow case, a syringe and insulin) and to bring forward witnesses to testify about what happened. As the von Bulow trials reveal, this reliance allows the attorneys for each side to structure the presentation of evidence to advance their clients' interests. They can enlist expert witnesses to support their clients' version of the facts—as we have seen, in the second von Bulow trial the defense called its own experts to counter the medical testimony of the prosecutor's experts. Attorneys can also cross-examine the witnesses called by the other side, and the two von Bulow trials underscore the importance of cross-examination. During the first trial, the prosecutor undermined the defense case by destroying the credibility of its main witness on cross-examination. During the second trial, sharp questioning by defense attorneys caused the maid to change her story. Finally, defense attorneys can decide whether or not their clients should testify in a criminal case.

AN OVERVIEW OF THE CHAPTER

In this chapter we analyze trials and appeals in the United States. Our examination of trials highlights how the trial is structured to ensure accurate fact-finding while safeguarding the rights of the parties at trial. It also describes the tactics that attorneys use to advance their clients' interests during the course of a trial. In doing so, it reveals a possible tension between the legal system's concern for impartial decisionmaking and the quest for partisan advantage implicit in the adversary system.

This tension reappears in our discussion of the American jury. Because jurors control the fate of their clients, attorneys will employ every device to persuade them, regardless of the evidence. We will therefore investigate the extent to which juries do consider factors other than the law and the evidence presented at trial in reaching their verdicts. We shall also consider whether recent changes in the structure and operation of the jury, such as reducing the size of the jury and partially eliminating the requirement of unanimous verdicts, have affected jury deliberations and verdicts. Finally, we shall show how the operation of the jury raises the question whether justice is served by tempering the rule of law with community views of substantive justice.

The last topic of this chapter is the operation of appellate courts. In describing how appellate courts review trial-court rulings, we shall initially highlight the operations of the United States Supreme Court, the most visible and most important of the nation's appellate courts. We shall then consider how the decisionmaking process in other appellate courts both resembles and diverges from that in the Supreme Court. This inquiry will provide some insight into the various ways in which judicial systems can be organized to promote justice.

TRIALS

Disputes and Fact-Finding

A trial is a proceeding for resolving a dispute in accordance with law. More precisely, a trial serves to ascertain the facts about a situation, apply the law to that set of facts, and thereby reach a conclusion about guilt or innocence (in a criminal case) or about liability or non-liability (in a civil case). The disputes to be resolved at trial may involve disputes about the facts in a case, disputes about the applicable law and how it applies, or disputes involving questions of both fact and law:

Disputes about the facts: In some cases the disputing parties agree about the interpretation and application of the law but offer differing versions of the facts. A criminal assault case, for example, may turn entirely on the identity of the assailant or a robbery case on the defendant's claim that the victim actually owed him the money he took. Similarly, civil suits may focus on such questions as whether it was the defendant company's drug that produced the plaintiff's medical problems or whether an employee had been refused a promotion because of her race or gender.

Disputes about the law: In some cases both parties agree on the relevant facts but disagree on the application of the law to those facts. In a criminal case, for example, the prosecution and defense may agree that a police search uncovered evidence of wrongdoing but disagree about whether the search was legal. In civil cases too, the facts may be undisputed but not the legal standards. For example, is a person legally liable for injuries he inadvertently caused? Did an administrative agency have the legal authority to issue the regulations it did?

Mixed disputes involving both facts and law: In some cases the questions of fact and law are intertwined. For example, when a defendant claims to have shot the victim in self-defense, the outcome of the case depends on the facts surrounding the shooting and on the legal definition of self-defense. Similarly, when a plaintiff sues for sexual harassment, the judge or jury must decide what the defendant did and whether those actions meet the legal definition of sexual harassment.

Although trial courts decide both questions of fact and questions of law, their primary task is gathering the evidence necessary to resolve disputes. Indeed, their success in fact-finding is crucial to the administration of justice. If a trial court misinterprets or misapplies the law, its error can be corrected on appeal. But if the trial court does not uncover all the relevant facts, there is no mechanism for introducing new testimony on appeal. Moreover, because they did not hear the witnesses, appellate courts are very reluctant to reverse a trial-court ruling, even if they suspect the trial judge may have misinterpreted the facts of the case.

Thus, if justice is to prevail, trial courts must uncover all evidence pertinent to the cases they are deciding and correctly evaluate that evidence. To ensure that all pertinent evidence is introduced at trial, the American legal system relies on the adversary system, assuming that each side will bring forward all the evidence and legal arguments that support its position. The adversary system also serves to ensure the reliability of the evidence that is introduced by permitting each side to challenge the testimony of witnesses during cross-examination. Further safeguarding the reliability of testimony and physical evidence at trial is the law of evidence, which prescribes what evidence can be admitted, who can present the evidence, and how the evidence should be introduced.

The Diversity of Trials

Most people form their picture of trials from a few highly publicized cases or from courtroom dramas depicted on television or in books. Yet such trials are exceptional. Most trials do not involve weeks of testimony, dramatic revelations from the witness stand, or a barrage of motions and objections by the attorneys. Rather, they are brief and at times perfunctory proceedings.

One study of criminal trials in the late nineteenth century found that most defendants were tried "in slapdash and routine ways, in trials that lasted a few hours or a few minutes at best."[5] Because criminal defendants today are guaranteed legal representation at trial, they are better able to mount a defense than were their counterparts a century ago. Still, unless the charges against a defendant are very serious or unless the defendant demands a jury trial, most contemporary criminal trials do not last long either. In Philadelphia, for example, felony trials conducted without a jury averaged less than an hour.[6] Most trials in civil cases are also short, particularly when the amount at stake is small. In the Los Angeles Small Claims Court, for example, the average trial in contested cases lasted only 8.9 minutes, with the shortest trial taking only one minute.[7]

Not all trials, however, are abbreviated affairs, in which procedural safeguards such as trial by jury are waived and various stages of the process compressed or eliminated. Let us therefore look more closely at the legal safeguards available to defendants and at the various stages of a "full-dress" trial.

Rights at Trial

The Fifth and Fourteenth Amendments to the United States Constitution guarantee that neither the federal government nor the state governments may deprive any person of life, liberty, or property without due process of law. Yet exactly what process is "due" at trial, what procedures are constitutional, is difficult to determine. Justice Felix Frankfurter has described the problem:

> "Due Process", unlike some legal rules is not a technical conception with a fixed content unrelated to time, place, and circumstances. Expressing as it does in its ultimate analysis respect enforced by law for the feeling of just treatment...[and] representing a profound attitude of fairness between man and man, and more particularly between the individual and government, due process is compounded

of history, reason, the past course of decisions, and stout confidence in the strength of the democratic faith that we profess.[8]

To give substance to this general guarantee of procedural fairness, therefore, judges have looked to the rights established by the federal and state constitutions, by statutes, by judicial precedents, and by the common law. Among these rights are:

Trial by jury: Trial by jury allows ordinary citizens to participate in the administration of justice and thus acts as a barrier against governmental tyranny. The U.S. Constitution secures the right to trial by jury in federal criminal cases and in federal civil cases in which more than $20 is at stake.[9] In 1968 the Supreme Court ruled that defendants in state courts also have a federal constitutional right to a jury trial in most *criminal* cases.[10] Various state constitutions and state statutes also recognize a right to trial by jury.

Speedy and public trial: The Sixth Amendment to the U.S. Constitution, together with analogous state provisions, secures to defendants in criminal cases the right to a speedy and public trial. The Constitution prohibits secret trials on the assumption that public scrutiny of the administration of justice protects against governmental abuse of its prosecutorial power and promotes judicial impartiality. State and federal guarantees of a speedy trial ensure that the government cannot charge people with crimes and, by delaying their trials, either keep them in jail or prevent them from proving their innocence. The Speedy Trial Act of 1974 requires that defendants in federal court be brought to trial no more than one hundred days after they are charged with a crime.

Right to counsel: Originally this right, protected by the Sixth Amendment to the U.S. Constitution, was understood to ensure only that those accused of crime could employ and bring to trial an attorney of their own choosing. But over time it became clear that, in the words of Justice Hugo Black, "any person hauled into court, who is too poor to hire a lawyer, cannot be assured a fair trial unless counsel is provided for him."[11] Thus, beginning in the nineteenth century, several states undertook to furnish counsel to indigent defendants. In *Johnson* v. *Zerbst* (1938), the U.S. Supreme Court followed their lead, ruling that the right to counsel included appointment of counsel for indigent defendants in all federal criminal proceedings. In *Gideon* v. *Wainwright* (1963), it further extended this protection to indigent defendants being tried in state courts.[12] But the Constitution does not oblige federal or state governments to provide attorneys to indigent plaintiffs in civil cases.[13]

Securing and confronting witnesses: The adversary system of justice works on the principle that truth will emerge from the clash of partisan presentations by the parties in a case. Each party is expected to bring forth all the evidence and arguments that support its position. The prosecution can secure the evidence it needs through its power to *subpoena* witnesses, that is, to require them to appear under threat of legal punishment. To equalize matters, the Sixth Amendment gives to defendants in criminal cases this same power to compel witnesses to appear. The adversary system also assumes that each party will seek to discredit the evidence and arguments of the opposing party, and so the Sixth Amendment also guarantees the accused the right to confront and question the witnesses against them. However, the Supreme Court has narrowed the right to confront witnesses, permitting children to testify about sexual abuse they suffered without having the defendant present before them.[14]

The burden of proof: In both criminal and civil cases, the burden of proof rests on the party that initiated the proceeding. However, the standard of proof depends on the type of case. For a conviction in a criminal case, the prosecution must prove guilt "beyond a reasonable doubt."[15] Thus, defendants in criminal cases need not prove their innocence; they need merely raise doubts about their guilt. This high threshold of persuasion reflects the belief that it is better to risk letting the guilty go free than to risk convicting the innocent. In civil cases, a lower standard of proof—proof by a preponderance of the evidence—suffices. This standard is satisfied when the balance of probabilities favors the plaintiff or the defendant in the case.

In a criminal trial the prosecution must meet its burden of proof at trial without relying on the assistance of the defendant. Thus the Fifth Amendment, together with analogous state guarantees, forbids compelling witnesses to testify against themselves. Indeed, the prosecution cannot even comment on the defendant's failure to testify, and jurors are cautioned not to draw any inferences from the fact that the defendant did not take the stand.[16]

The Trial Process

Although procedures vary slightly from state to state, a full-scale trial tends to follow certain set steps (see Box 5-1). These steps are basically the same in both civil and criminal litigation. To avoid complicating our discussion, we shall refer to the party initiating the litigation as the prosecutor. But what is said applies to the plaintiff in a civil case as well.

Bench Trial or Jury Trial?

The initial step is the decision whether to choose a jury trial, in which a group of ordinary citizens renders the verdict, or a bench trial, in which a judge conducts the trial without a jury and renders the verdict. In criminal cases in which jury trial is an option, the choice is left to the defendant. In civil cases for which

---

BOX 5-1 THE STAGES OF A TRIAL

1. Choice of a Jury Trial or Bench Trial

2. Jury Selection*

3. Opening Statement of the Prosecutor**

4. Opening Statement of the Defendant's Attorney

5. Presentation of the Prosecution's Case**

6. Presentation of the Defendant's Case

7. Rebuttal Witnesses

8. Closing Argument for the Prosecution**

9. Closing Argument for the Defendant

10. Closing Argument in Response for the Prosecution**

11. Judge's Instructions to the Jury*

12. Deliberations by the Judge (Bench Trial) or the Jury

13. Announcement of the Verdict

KEY: Stages marked with an asterisk (*) occur only in jury trials. Stages marked with two asterisks (**) involve the prosecutor in a criminal trial but the plaintiff's attorney in a civil trial.

jury trial is available, normally both the plaintiff and the defendant must agree to waive a jury trial.

More jury trials are conducted in the United States than in any other country. Still, not all defendants are entitled to a trial by jury. There is no federal constitutional right to a jury trial, for example, in criminal cases involving petty offenses (though state law may provide for one).[17] Thus drunk drivers in five states—Louisiana, Mississippi, Nevada, New Jersey, and New Mexico—are not entitled to a jury trial unless they face jail terms of more than six months.[18] Nor are jury trials available in all civil cases. Most states, for example, mandate bench trials for family matters such as divorces or child custody disputes.

Litigants choose between a jury trial and a bench trial on the assumption that who decides the case will affect its outcome. (We shall analyze the evidence on differences between jury verdicts and bench verdicts below.) Thus, those accused of particularly heinous crimes may waive their right to a jury trial, assuming a judge will be less influenced by emotional factors than will a jury. Conversely, if defendants believe the community will be reluctant to apply the law to them, as in the case of a "mercy killing," they may well opt for a jury trial. Finally, individuals suing corporations or other large organizations may insist on a jury trial, expecting that jurors will identify with them and sympathize with their plight.

Jury Selection

If a jury trial is chosen, the next step is jury selection. Long before the trial, the jurisdiction will have compiled a master jury list (also called a "wheel"), designed to include all potential jurors within its borders. Most jurisdictions create their master jury list from voter rolls, sometimes supplemented by other lists, such as local census lists or lists of taxpayers or of those holding driver's licenses.

From the master jury list, the jury commissioners or court clerks randomly select enough names to comprise a venire (jury pool). Those persons who are selected receive questionnaires designed to determine their eligibility for jury service. Some persons—aliens, those who do not meet local residency requirements, those who cannot read or speak English, and those previously convicted of felonies—are disqualified by statute from serving on juries. Others enjoy statutory exemptions because their occupations are vital (elected officials, physicians, and members of the military), because they might exert too much influence on jury deliberations (lawyers and police officers), or because they may have an occupational prejudice on the question of guilt or innocence (police officers and clergy). Finally, some potential jurors are excused because jury service would impose an undue hardship on them. Most states excuse all persons who request to be excused, assuming their reluctance to serve will make them poor jurors. Citizens who are not excused receive a summons ordering them to appear at the courthouse on a specified day. The court clerk's office then randomly selects groups of prospective jurors from the venire and directs them to courtrooms where they might be needed.

Jurors and alternates are selected for trial through a process called the voir dire (usually translated as "to speak the truth"). During voir dire prospective jurors are questioned to determine if they can decide the case fairly and impartially. Based on their answers, the prosecution or the defense can challenge prospective jurors "for cause," claiming that they are biased about the defendant, the prosecution, or the case. Among the factors that might justify a challenge for cause are personal relationships between the juror and a litigant, pre-conceptions about the case or the parties to it, or prejudice against a particular racial, ethnic, or religious group, where applicable to the case. If the judge rules that cause has been shown, the challenged juror is excused. There is no limit on the number of jurors that can be challenged for cause, and in highly publicized cases the process of jury selection can be quite drawn-out. In the "Hillside Strangler" murder trial in Los Angeles, for example, voir dire and jury selection took 49 court days.[19]

Attorneys may also remove a limited number of prospective jurors through peremptory challenges. In exercising peremptory challenges, attorneys need not specify their reasons nor gain the judge's approval for removing a juror. Thus peremptory challenges enable each side to eliminate prospective jurors whom they suspect of being prejudiced or unsympathetic, even if the jurors have not displayed any overt prejudice that would justify a challenge for cause. There are, however, legal limitations on the prosecution's use of peremptory challenges: the United States Supreme Court has ruled that the race-based exclusion of jurors through peremptory challenges violates the U.S. Constitution.[20] The number of peremptory challenges to be exercised is established by statute and varies from jurisdiction to jurisdiction and according to the seriousness of the charges. Arkansas, for example, permits the prosecution ten peremptory chal-lenges and the defense twelve in capital cases but only six and eight in other felony cases and three apiece in misdemeanor cases.[21]

The mechanics of the voir dire likewise vary from jurisdiction to jurisdiction. In some states the judge alone questions prospective jurors, in others attorneys may pose supplemental questions, and in still others the attorneys conduct all questioning of prospective jurors.[22] Even within court systems, practices may vary. Although by statute federal judges have sole control over voir dire, one study found that a bare majority of judges questioned jurors by themselves, while almost one-third permitted attorneys to ask supplemental questions, and 13 percent let attorneys conduct all questioning of prospective jurors.[23]

Because the composition of the jury may be crucial to their success at trial, most trial lawyers believe that they should conduct voir dire questioning.[24] Doing so enables them to probe for the information they need to exercise their challenges wisely. In addition, conducting voir dire gives them an opportunity to influence the jury and lay the foundation for the case they plan to present. While their aim is obviously to empanel a jury favorable to their client, lawyers argue that an impartial jury will emerge from this competition for advantage.

In recent years attorneys in some cases have enlisted social scientists in the effort to select jurors favorable to their side. The first use of scientific jury selection, during the conspiracy trial of Daniel Berrigan and other anti-war activists in 1972, exemplifies the approach generally used.[25]   Researchers sympathetic to the defendants conducted a telephone survey of the area in which the trial was to take place, asking questions about the issues in the upcoming trial and obtaining demographic information from respondents. From this they developed demographic profiles of the kinds of persons likely to be hostile or sympathetic to the defendants.   Defense attorneys carefully questioned prospective jurors with unfavorable demographic profiles and used their peremptory challenges to eliminate those not excused for cause. Whatever the success of this selection process, Berrigan and his fellow defendants were acquitted of all charges.

Since the Berrigan conspiracy trial, scientific selection methods have been refined and employed in numerous other trials.   Despite the claims of their proponents, there is no conclusive evidence that these new jury selection techniques produce a more favorable jury than could be obtained through the informed judgment of an experienced attorney. Should these methods be proven more effective, their use would raise an ethical question: is it legitimate to use selection techniques that give an "unfair advantage" to one party, that is, the one that can afford to use them?

Opening Statements

Before any evidence is presented, the attorney for the party that initiated the litigation—the prosecution in criminal cases or the plaintiff in civil cases—presents an opening statement to the jury or, in bench trials, to the judge. This opening statement provides a preview of the prosecution's case, identifying the issues and describing the evidence that the prosecutor intends to offer. It thus serves as a road map for jurors to guide them through the trial. The defense usually follows with its opening statement, raising questions about the prosecution's evidence and promising contradictory evidence. On occasion, a defense attorney may postpone her opening statement until after the presentation of the prosecution's case.

By law, opening statements are supposed to be bare outlines of the substance of the evidence, free of argumentation or appeals to emotion. Yet many trial lawyers believe that opening statements can make or break a case. These statements, they note, provide attorneys their first opportunity to establish a rapport with the jury, and the impression attorneys make with their opening statements may predispose jurors toward the prosecution or defense position, even before testimony is presented.[26] Thus attorneys must view the opening statement as an opportunity to persuade. However, given the strictures on persuasive appeals, the trick is to "prepar[e] a persuasive opening statement that appears to be devoid of persuasive appeal."[27]

Presentation of the Prosecution's (Plaintiff's) Case

Each party in a trial offers its evidence in turn, with the party that initiated the litigation (and therefore must prove its case) presenting its witnesses and physical evidence first. The questioning of each witness typically occurs in three stages. During direct examination, the prosecutor elicits testimony as to facts needed to prove the prosecution's case. The defense attorney may then cross-examine prosecution witnesses, attempting to discredit their testimony or undermine their credibility. Finally, the prosecutor may ask additional questions of its witnesses during re-direct examination. These questions may undo damage resulting from an effective cross-examination.

Considerable planning goes into the presentation of the prosecution's case. First, prosecutors must identify the facts that they must prove to win the case and, by interviewing prospective witnesses, determine who will testify to those facts. Usually prosecutors seek more than one witness for each important fact, because multiple witnesses can corroborate each other's testimony. Next, prosecutors prepare their witnesses to testify by going over what the witness will say. Although they cannot dictate the substance of witnesses' testimony, experienced prosecutors never ask a question on direct examination without knowing beforehand the answer they will receive. They may also coach the witnesses on how to present their stories effectively and on what questions to expect during cross-examination. Finally, prosecutors must determine in what order to present their witnesses in order to make a clear and persuasive case. As one manual for trial lawyers puts it:

> A trial to a jury should be viewed as a drama, with the jury the audience, the judge the critic (who delivers his reviews during, not after, each scene), and the witnesses the actors. The trial lawyer is the director, producer, and narrator. To reach your audience, you must view each element of the trial for its potential impact on the jury.[28]

In presenting its case, the prosecution—like the defense—is governed by rules of evidence, which prescribe what evidence can be presented and how it can be presented. These rules serve to promote reliable fact-finding by only admitting evidence which is trustworthy and relevant. For example, the rules of evidence generally exclude hearsay evidence, testimony a witness provides based not on personal knowledge but on what another person has said, because there is no way to test its trustworthiness through cross-examination. They also exclude testimony about a victim's sexual history in rape trials, because it has no bearing on whether the crime was committed and may prejudice the jury's consideration of the case. Yet many rules of evidence are not as clear as these examples, and the prosecution and defense may differ on whether some testimony or physical evidence is admissible. When either objects to the admission of a piece of evidence, the judge must apply the law of evidence in ruling on the objection. If the defense unsuccessfully objects to the admission of some evidence, which is then used to secure a conviction, it may appeal the judge's interpretation of the law of evidence. Similarly, the prosecution may appeal the exclusion of evidence it deems vital to its case.

Presentation of the Defendant's Case

Once the prosecution has completed the presentation of its case, the defense may introduce its own evidence. In a criminal case, where the prosecution must prove guilt beyond a reasonable doubt, the defense need not prove its own version of the facts. It need merely create reasonable doubts about the prosecution's version. Skillful defense attorneys will already have begun to sow such doubts during their cross-examination of the prosecution's witnesses and will continue to do so by offering physical evidence and/or testimony of their own.

The most difficult question defense attorneys face is whether to permit the defendant to testify. On the one hand, jurors are naturally curious about the defendant's version of events, and a convincing assertion of innocence by the defendant may lead to acquittal. Moreover, despite warnings by the judge that no inferences should be drawn from a defendant's failure to testify, jurors may well expect a defendant to take the stand if he or she is innocent, so failure to testify could hurt the defendant's chances. On the other hand, a defendant who testifies is subject to cross-examination by the prosecutor, who may expose difficulties with the defendant's story. In addition, the prosecutor can impeach the defendant's credibility by introducing evidence of his past criminal record. Thus the defense attorney must judge whether jurors will view the defendant as a truthful witness with a believable story.[29]

In civil cases, where the plaintiff need merely prove its case by a preponderance of the evidence, the defense must offer a version of the facts at least equally as convincing as the plaintiff's account. Therefore, although the process of offering testimony and other evidence is the same in civil cases as in criminal cases, the greater burden on the defense usually requires presentation of a more elaborate case for the defense.

After the defense presents its case, the prosecution may call rebuttal witnesses to attempt to discredit the testimony of defense witnesses or to impeach their credibility by giving evidence as to their disreputable character. The testimony of rebuttal witnesses concludes the presentation of evidence at trial.

Closing Arguments

As the name implies, closing arguments provide the attorneys their last chance to sway the jury. An effective closing argument "pulls together the disparate threads of evidence and weaves them into a coherent and compelling whole" leading to a favorable verdict.[30] Even though rhetorical flourishes and emotional appeals alone are unlikely to win a case, closing arguments offer a unique opportunity for eloquent advocacy, and the most effective attorneys can turn a closing argument into a rhetorical tour de force. Yet there are limits here as well, and the use of prejudicial material can result in the verdict being overturned on appeal.

In presenting its closing argument, the prosecution explains the issues in the case, summarizes the facts as it understands them, and explains why the testimony it presented is more reliable than the conflicting testimony offered by the defense. If the jurors are persuaded by this interpretation of what transpired at trial, conviction becomes the obvious and inevitable verdict. In its closing argument, of course, the defense attorney portrays the evidence quite differently, arguing either that the prosecution failed to meet its burden of proof or that the defense's version of events is more persuasive. The party bearing the burden of proof, the prosecution in criminal cases or the plaintiff in civil cases, is allowed to make the final argument to the jury.

Jury Instructions

In a bench trial the judge decides both questions of fact and questions of law. However, a jury trial involves a division of labor, with the jury responsible for deciding questions of fact and the judge responsible for determining the law to be applied. Thus after closing arguments, the judge instructs the jury as to the law in the case, to guide it in its deliberations. The judge's instructions are written explanations of the law, which the judge reads to the jury in open court. Often the instructions are technical and detailed, and some judges therefore allow the jurors to take a copy of the instructions with them to the jury room.

Instructions to the jury include explanations of general matters such as the responsibilities of the jury, the evidence it may consider, and the burden of proof to be met in the case. In criminal cases they also include detailed explanations of the specific legal standards a defendant is charged with violating and of any legal defenses the defendant may have advanced, as they apply to the facts of the case. Thus in a homicide case the instructions might clarify such matters as the distinction between first-degree and second-degree murder, the concept of premeditation, and the legal meaning of self-defense. Finally, the judge instructs the jury about the possible verdicts it might render.

Judges do not draw up these instructions all by themselves. Rather, they rely on the attorneys for the parties to draw up instructions that they wish presented to the jury. (The attorneys themselves tend to rely on volumes containing "model jury instructions," which they then tailor to the facts of the case.) From the alternative versions of instructions submitted by the attorneys on each legal issue in the case, the judge selects the ones that seem most appropriate, modifying them if necessary. An attorney whose version is rejected may base an appeal on that rejection, arguing that the jury was misinformed about the law in the case.

After the judge has instructed the jury, it retires to discuss the case. Once the jury completes its deliberations, it communicates its decision to the judge, who announces the verdict. Because the jury is such an important part of the American legal system, it deserves detailed consideration.

THE JURY IN THE UNITED STATES

The Changing Jury

Although the American jury has its roots in the English jury, which originated prior to the Norman conquest in 1066, it differs from its early counterpart in several respects. For one thing, juries in England initially were comprised of local residents who had personal knowledge of the dispute at trial. Only gradually did the modern notion develop that the jurors should be disinterested citizens who decided cases solely on the basis of evidence presented at trial. It was also not uncommon in England for judges or political authorities to pressure a jury to reach the verdict they desired. A particularly egregious example occurred in the trial of William Penn in 1670 for unlawful assembly and breach of the peace. When the jurors found that Penn was not guilty of the charges, the judge refused to accept their verdict and sent them back to deliberate some more. After two-and-a-half days of deliberation without food, water, or chamberpot, the jury still would not convict Penn; so the angry judge fined each of the jurors and kept them in jail until they could pay their fines. This outrageous conduct produced a backlash and effectively ended the practice of coercing juries to reach "correct" verdicts.[31]

A more recent change has involved the scope of the jury's responsibilities. Currently in jury trials the judge determines the law and instructs the jury about it, while the jury determines the facts and applies the law to those facts. This division of labor, however, only developed in the nineteenth century. Before that, the jury could determine both the facts and the law. Although the judge instructed jurors about the law, they remained free to ignore the judge's instructions and render verdicts based upon their own consciences or their own independent interpretation of the law.[32] Such "jury nullification" undercut unpopular laws by allowing groups of ordinary citizens to decide what laws would be enforced. In the decades preceding independence, for example, juries in the American colonies effectively nullified seditious libel laws (outlawing criticism of the English government) by consistently refusing to convict those charged with violating the laws.

Although the province of the jury diminished when judges were assigned the responsibility to determine what the law is, this change has not altogether eliminated jury nullification. Community sentiment still may play a part in jury verdicts. During the 1920s juries often refused to convict ordinary citizens who had run afoul of the Prohibition laws. And throughout the first half of the twentieth century, segregated juries in the South frequently acquitted whites accused of violence against blacks. Yet in refusing to convict those guilty of violating the criminal law, contemporary jurors exceed their legal authority, and the recognition of their legal obligation to apply the law may lead jurors to do so even when they disagree with the law.

We have already discussed the greatest change in the American jury during the twentieth century, namely, the creation of more representative juries through the inclusion of previously excluded groups, such as African-Americans, Hispanics, and women. Important changes have also occurred in the size and decision rules of juries, and it is to these we now turn.

Jury Size and Jury Decisionmaking

Quite early in the history of the Anglo-American jury, it was established that juries would include twelve members and would reach their verdicts by unanimous vote. If after deliberation the jurors could not agree on a verdict, the judge would rule that the jury was "hung" and dismiss it. If the jury "hung" in a criminal trial, the accused, having been neither convicted nor acquitted, could be tried again for the same offense. (Often, however, the prosecution would decline to reinstitute charges after having failed to win a conviction in the first trial.)

During the twentieth century several states sought to reduce the costs of trials and promote efficiency by reducing the size of juries and experimenting with non-unanimous verdicts. When disappointed litigants challenged these experiments as unconstitutional, the Supreme Court for the most part backed the states. In *Williams* v. *Florida* (1970) the Court ruled that a jury of twelve was not required in state criminal or civil trials, although in 1978 it established a minimum size of six members in state criminal trials.[33]   In two cases decided in 1972, *Johnson* v. *Louisiana* and *Apodaca* v. *Oregon,* the Court also upheld the use of non-unanimous (9-3) verdicts in criminal cases, although seven years later it held that a six-member jury could convict a defendant only by unanimous vote.[34]   These rulings have encouraged previously reluctant states to modify their jury systems. Currently twenty-two states use juries of less than twelve to try civil cases, and twenty-four use them to try misdemeanors. However, forty-three states continue to employ twelve-member juries in felony cases.[35]

Critics of the changes in jury size and decision rules have argued that they affect jury deliberations and the outcome of cases. A six-member jury is likely to be less diverse, and therefore less representative of the community, than a twelve-member jury. Furthermore, decreasing the size of the jury reduces the likelihood of hung juries, because a single juror is unlikely to hold out against group sentiment and is less likely to find allies on a six-member jury. Also, when non-unanimous verdicts are permitted, the majority on a jury need not persuade holdouts that the verdict is correct. This not only means that non-unanimous juries are less likely to hang. It also means that they are less likely to listen carefully to the holdouts' perspectives on the case. Finally, critics argue that non-unanimous juries convict defendants who are not guilty "beyond a reasonable doubt," citing the reluctance of some jurors to convict as conclusive evidence that a reasonable doubt exists.

To some extent empirical studies have confirmed these criticisms. They have shown that permitting non-unanimous verdicts reduces the frequency of hung juries in criminal (but not in civil) cases. They also have found that twelve-member juries and those deciding unanimously tend to deliberate longer before reaching their verdicts, which may suggest a more thorough consideration of the evidence. Finally, they have discovered that the variety of viewpoints tends to be greater on twelve-member juries and that jurors holding minority viewpoints are more likely to participate actively in discussions and more likely to be listened to on unanimous, rather than majority-rule, juries.[36]

Evaluating the Jury

As Box 5-2 indicates, there is considerable controversy about whether the jury serves the cause of justice. In England, the birthplace of the modern jury,

BOX 5-2   EVALUATING THE JURY

"The jury trial at best is the apotheosis of the amateur. Why should anyone think that 12 persons brought in from the street, selected in various ways, for their lack of general ability, should have any special capacity for deciding controversies between persons?" (Erwin Griswold, law professor and attorney)

"[T]rial by jury is more than an instrument of justice and more than one wheel of the constitution: it is the lamp that shows that freedom lives." (Lord Justice Devlin, English judge)

"[W]hile the jury can contribute nothing of value so far as the law is concerned, it has infinite capacity for mischief, for twelve men can easily misunderstand more law in a minute than the judge can explain in an hour." (Jerome Frank, legal scholar and judge)

"Although jurors are extraordinarily right in their conclusion, it is usually based upon common sense 'instincts' about right and wrong, and not on sophisticated evaluations of complicated testimony.... Because Judges, sometimes, consciously reject this laymen's approach of who is right or wrong and restrict themselves to the precise legal weights, they come out wrong more often than the juries." (Louis Nizer, defense attorney)

"I submit that the jury is the worst possible enemy of [the] ideal of the 'supremacy of law.' For 'jury-made law' is, par excellence, capricious and arbitrary, yielding the maximum in the way of lack of uniformity and unknowability." (Jerome Frank)

"The jury...represents an impressive way of building discretion, equity, and flexibility into a legal system. Not the least of its advantages is that the jury, relieved of the burdens of creating precedent, can bend the law without breaking it." (Harry Kalven and Hans Zeisel, legal scholars)

"Jurymen seldom convict a person they like, or acquit one that they dislike. The main work of a trial lawyer is to make a jury like his client, or, at least to feel sympathy for him; facts regarding the crime are relatively unimportant." (Clarence Darrow, famous defense attorney)

"The jury contributes most powerfully to form the judgment, and to increase the natural intelligence of a people; and this is, in my opinion, its greatest advantage. It may be regarded as a gratuitous public school ever open, in which every juror learns to exercise his rights.... I think that the practical intelligence and political good sense of the Americans are mainly attributable to the long use which they have made of the jury in civil causes." (Alexis de Tocqueville, French commentator on America)

SOURCES: Erwin Griswold, "1962-1963 Harvard Law School Dean's Report," pp. 5-6, quoted in Harry Kalven, Jr., and Hans Zeisel, *The American Jury* (Boston: Little Brown, 1966), p. 5; Patrick Devlin, *Trial by Jury* (London: Stevens, 1956) p. 164; *Skidmore v. Baltimore & Ohio Railroad*, 167 F.2d 54 (2d Cir. 1948); Louis Nizer, *My Life in Court* (New York: Jove, 1978), p. 359; Jerome Frank, *Courts on Trial; Myth and Reality in American Justice* (Princeton, N.J.: Princeton University Press, 1949), p. 132; Kalven and Zeisel, *The American Jury*, p. 498; Clarence Darrow, quoted in Valerie P. Hans and Neil Vidmar, *Judging the Jury* (New York: Plenum Press, 1986), p. 131; Alexis de Tocqueville, *Democracy in America*, ed. Richard D. Heffner (New York: New American Library, 1956), p. 128.

jury trials have virtually disappeared in civil cases and declined in criminal cases. In the United States, jury trials have likewise declined, particularly in civil cases. Indeed, an appellate court ruled in one civil case that the issues were so complex that a trial by jury would constitute a denial of due process.[37] Underlying this ruling is the belief that ordinary citizens lack the capacity to comprehend highly technical evidence and apply complicated legal standards so as to render decisions in accordance with law. As Box 5-2 indicates, many opponents of the jury system believe that this criticism is equally applicable to jury decisionmaking in ordinary cases. According to these critics, bench trials are preferable to jury trials because judges are better able to understand and evaluate evidence, more knowledgeable about the law, less affected by prejudice and emotion, and therefore more likely to render law-based decisions.

Do juries in fact misunderstand or ignore the law and reach legally indefensible decisions based on prejudice or emotion? The most thorough investigation of this question is *The American Jury*, which compared jury verdicts in over 3500 criminal trials and in over 4000 civil trials with the verdicts that the trial judges would have rendered.[38] This study found that jury decisionmaking was not arbitrary. In over three-fourths of both the criminal trials and the civil trials, the jury and the judge agreed on the verdict, suggesting that the jury reached the legally required result. Moreover, in most cases in which trial judges disagreed with jury verdicts, they viewed those disagreements as arising not from jury caprice or incompetence but primarily from different evaluations of the evidence or the defendant. In only nine percent of the cases did the trial judge maintain that the jury's verdict was without legal merit. Subsequent studies have corroborated the conclusion of *The American Jury* that jurors generally follow the law and evidence in reaching their verdicts.[39]

Yet if the decisions of judges and juries generally coincide, doesn't it make sense to dispense with jury trials, which may be costly and time-consuming, and allow a judge to decide all cases? According to advocates of jury trials, the costs of eliminating trial by jury far outweigh the benefits (see Box 5-2). The jury is valuable, they insist, because it provides one of the few opportunities

Americans have to participate directly in government. In addition, analysis of those instances in which the judge and jury disagree suggests that the jury brings a distinctive perspective to the administration of justice. In civil cases, according to *The American Jury,* juries do not consistently favor either the plaintiff or the defendant. However, in criminal cases juries are more likely to rule in favor of defendants, acquitting them or hanging when the judge would have convicted, or convicting the defendant of a lesser charge. This greater lenience in some instances reflected a willingness to give the benefit of the doubt to defendants without a criminal record and in some instances a rigorous interpretation of the standard "beyond a reasonable doubt." Jury nullification also played a role: jurors sometimes refused to convict when they disagreed with the law or when they believed that defendants had already suffered enough for their wrongdoing.[40]

According to its advocates, these findings demonstrate the value of the jury as a mechanism for bringing community sentiment to bear and correcting the harshness of the law when it would lead to unjust results. Put differently, the value of the jury lies in its political role. To its critics however, these findings confirm that the jury system is at odds with the rule of law and that it substitutes community prejudices for the even-handed administration of justice. One's verdict on the jury thus largely depends on whether one views the infusion of community values into the administration of justice as a positive or a negative phenomenon.

APPEALS

The Appellate Process

In the United States, after trial courts render their decisions, dissatisfied litigants are entitled to one appeal. Less than 10 percent of state trial-court decisions and roughly 13 percent of federal district court rulings are appealed.[41] The appellate court's main job is error correction, that is, ensuring that the law was correctly interpreted and applied at trial. After a first-level appellate court (such as a federal court of appeals or a state intermediate court of appeals) rules on their cases, litigants may appeal those decisions as well. However, the second-level appellate court typically has some discretion over whether it will hear the case. For cases that fall within the jurisdiction of the federal courts, the final resort for litigants is the United States Supreme Court. For cases that do not, the final appeal is to the state's supreme court.

Appellate courts differ among themselves in terms of:

(1) Agenda-setting: to what extent do legal guidelines determine what cases a court must decide, and to what extent does the court exercise discretion in deciding what cases to hear?

(2) Information-gathering: how does the court secure the information it needs about the facts of the case, about the applicable law, and about the likely consequences of its decisions?

(3) Decisionmaking: what is the process by which the members of the court resolve their differences and reach decisions?

(4) Promulgating decisions: how does the court convey its decisions to the litigants and to the general public?

Rather than considering in detail how all appellate courts deal with these matters, we shall focus on the operations of the nation's most important appellate court, the United States Supreme Court, and then briefly compare that court with other appellate courts in the United States.

The United States Supreme Court

Agenda-setting

The Cases

Each year the Supreme Court receives about 4500 petitions for review, the vast majority appealing rulings of either federal courts of appeals or of state supreme courts. Litigants who cannot afford the costs of an appeal (like Clarence Gideon whose case was discussed in Chapter 2) can file their petitions *in forma pauperis* (literally, in the manner of a pauper), and the Court will waive fees and other costs. The Court annually accepts about 150 cases—less than 5 percent of the cases appealed to it—for oral argument and decision. Over the course of the twentieth century, Congress has gradually expanded the justices' control over their agenda, so that today the justices exercise virtually total discretion in deciding which appeals to hear and which to reject.

Of course, like other courts, the Supreme Court operates within legal constraints. It can only rule on cases that fall within its jurisdiction. In addition, the justices cannot address an issue unless a litigant brings it before them. Thus the pool of cases from which the justices select is outside their direct control. Still, it is easy to overestimate the influence of these considerations.

For one thing, as Alexis de Tocqueville observed over 160 years ago, "there is hardly a political question in the United States which does not sooner or later turn into a judicial one."[42] This means that, as a matter of course, the justices will have the opportunity to address most of the important political issues of the day. From a different angle, it also means that the cases appealed to the Court will tend to reflect the political concerns of the era. In the 1980s, for example, the Court confronted such controversial political issues as drug testing, abortion, and affirmative action. Indeed, groups may seek to shape the political agenda of their era by bringing their concerns before the Court. This is illustrated by the NAACP's campaign against racial segregation from the 1930s to the 1950s, by the efforts of Legal Services lawyers to establish new rights for the poor in the late 1960s and the 1970s, and by the attempt by right-to-life groups to overturn the Court's abortion rulings during the 1980s and 1990s.

By their decisions, the justices may also influence the pool of cases brought before them. An extreme example occurred in the Supreme Court's flag-salute cases. In 1940 the Court had ruled that states could require public-school students to salute the American flag, notwithstanding their religious objections to the practice. Two years later, however, three members of the Court majority used the occasion of an unrelated case to admit that they had erred and to repudiate their votes. This admission, together with personnel changes on the Court, invited new litigation, and the Court overruled its earlier flag-salute decision only three years after it was rendered.[43]

Generally, the Court's influence on the types of cases appealed to it is less direct. If the justices reveal a willingness to entertain a type of claim, then litigants are encouraged to bring cases raising such claims to the Court. During the 1960s the Court's receptivity to the rights claims of criminal defendants prompted a proliferation of claims by those seeking to overturn their convictions. More recently, after the Court indicated in 1989 that it would reconsider its position on abortion, several cases were initiated to provide a vehicle for the Court to overrule *Roe* v. *Wade*.[44] Conversely, if the Court consistently rejects certain types of legal claims, litigants will be reluctant to bring such claims before the Court. Thus the Court's tendency to read defendants' rights narrowly during the 1980s discouraged some defendants from appealing their cases to the Court.

Finally, at times the Court purposely announces rulings that leave important questions unresolved. In such circumstances the justices can expect litigants to raise those questions in the lower courts and to appeal adverse rulings to the Supreme Court. Thus the Court will have the opportunity to address those unresolved questions at a later date, with their judgment illuminated by the opinions of the lower-court judges who already had confronted them. A prime example involves police interrogations. In *Escobedo* v. *Illinois* (1964), the Court ruled that police could not deny an accused person access to his attorney during a police interrogation.[45] But the ruling in *Escobedo* did not indicate whether the accused had to request an attorney, whether the police could delay granting access to one, or whether they had to provide one for indigent persons. Over a period of eighteen months, 150 cases raising *Escobedo*-type issues were appealed to the Court.[46] In 1966 the Court resolved most of those issues with its decision in *Miranda* v. *Arizona*, which outlined the warnings that had to be given prior to police interrogations.[47]

The Process of Case Selection

The process by which the justices select cases for review is well-established. The party appealing the lower court's decision petitions the Court for a writ of certiorari (from the Latin, "made more certain"), asking that the Court hear the case. The various justices, in conjunction with their law clerks (see Box 5-3), review the petitions, and individually determine what cases they believe merit consideration. The Chief Justice prepares and circulates a "discuss list," which includes the cases he believes warrant collective consideration, and other justices may add cases to the list. Unless a justice requests that a petition be discussed in conference, it is automatically denied. Over 70 percent of all petitions for certiorari are thereby disposed of prior to conference.

Collective consideration of the petitions on the discuss list begins at the three-to-four-day conference held prior to the beginning of the Court's term in October. During this conference, which like all the Court's conferences is attended only by the justices themselves, they screen the large number of petitions for certiorari that have accumulated over the previous summer. In their 1989 pre-term conference, the Court granted review in 24 cases, disposed of 3 more without opinion, and denied review in 988 cases.[48] At the weekly Friday conferences held throughout the Court's term, the justices continue their screening of petitions. If four justices vote to hear a case—the so-called Rule of Four—it is accepted for review and scheduled for oral argument. If fewer than four justices favor review, the petition for certiorari is denied, and the decision of the lower court stands.

Criteria for Case Selection

It is difficult to tell what factors influence the justices' decisions to grant or deny review, because the justices neither publish nor explain their votes. The Court's own Rule 10, "Considerations Governing Review on Certiorari," offers some guidance (see Box 5-4), but the justices can grant review when the listed factors are absent or deny review even when they are present. To some extent

BOX 5-3 LAW CLERKS

Imagine being only a couple years out of law school and yet drafting judicial opinions for the United States Supreme Court. Farfetched as this may sound, drafting opinions would likely be one of your responsibilities if you were one of the elite group of young lawyers chosen annually to serve as law clerks for the justices of the Supreme Court. This does not mean, of course, that the clerks determine how the Court decides—as Chief Justice William Rehnquist has emphasized, they are not "legal Rasputins," manipulating the justices to advance their own legal or policy goals. Yet working under the close supervision of the justice who selected them, these law clerks play a crucial role in the operations of the Supreme Court.

The first justice to hire a law clerk was Justice Horace Gray, who had initiated the practice while a member of the Supreme Judicial Court of Massachusetts and brought his clerk with him when appointed to the Supreme Court in 1882. Gray's successor on the Court, Oliver Wendell Holmes, continued the practice, and gradually other justices followed their lead. Today each justice chooses four clerks each year to assist him with his work. These clerks are truly a select group. Typically, they include the top graduates of major law schools—for a long time, Harvard and Yale dominated, but in recent years other law schools have contributed their share. Usually the clerks come to the Court with the experience of a year's clerkship for another judge, usually on a court of appeals. However, the justices are free to employ their own criteria in selecting their clerks, and some have been partial to clerks from their own region or law school. For example, Justice William O. Douglas, a native of Washington, characteristically chose Westerners as his clerks.

Since the clerks are to assist the justices, each justice determines the tasks his clerks will perform. Justice Gray, for example, asked his clerk's advice in picking out a ring when he became engaged at age 60, and Justice Hugo Black required his clerks to play tennis with him. However, almost all clerks share certain common tasks. The clerks assist their justice first of all in reviewing the petitions for certiorari, drafting memos that detail the issues and legal arguments in each case and recommend whether certiorari should be granted. Or if their justice belongs to the "cert pool"—and six do—the clerks prepare memos on their assigned cases which are then circulated to all the justices participating in the pool. The limited data we have suggest that the justices usually go along with their clerks' recommendations, perhaps because those recommendations take into account the perspectives of the justice to whom they are addressed. Justice John Paul Stevens has underscored the importance of the clerks' work in screening petitions for review, noting: "I don't even look at the papers in over 80 percent of the cases that are filed."

continued on p. 172

continued from p. 171

Clerks also participate in preparing opinions, though the justices differ in the responsibilities they assign their clerks. All clerks conduct legal research for their justices. Some do little actual writing—one of Justice Felix Frankfurter's clerks said that the justice wrote the opinion, and he wrote the footnotes. Most justices, however, allow their clerks to prepare rough drafts, along lines dictated by the justice. The justice will then revise the draft before circulating it to other members of the Court, and their comments will lead to further revisions. The opinion that is eventually published may bear little resemblance to the draft the clerk prepared. Finally, some clerks serve as "sounding boards" for their justices, providing them with opportunities to discuss the issues in the cases they are deciding. Justice Lewis Powell, for example, reputedly chose clerks whose views were more liberal than his own in order to ensure that he confronted the arguments against his own conservative proclivities. Although justices could conceivably be swayed by the arguments of their clerks, this probably does not happen often. For one thing, with their political experience the justices are used to working with a staff without being dominated by it. For another, the clerks themselves are transients—with rare exceptions, they serve for only a single year.

SOURCES: David O'Brien, *Storm Center*, 2nd ed. (New York: W. W. Norton, 1990); William Rehnquist, *The Supreme Court* (New York: Morrow, 1987); *Guide to the U.S. Supreme Court* (Washington, D.C.: Congressional Quarterly Press, 1979); and David Crump, "Law Clerks: Their Roles and Relationships with Their Judges," *Judicature* 69 (December-January, 1986): 236-240.

the criteria used in voting on certiorari petitions may be idiosyncratic, varying from justice to justice and even from case to case. Thus Chief Justice Earl Warren asserted that the standards governing the justices' determinations "cannot be captured in any rule or guideline that would be meaningful."[49] Nonetheless, some general observations are possible.

First of all, the Court accepts cases that involve political disputes of national import. Thus during the Korean War, it ruled on the constitutionality of President Truman's seizure and operation of the nation's steel mills.[50] And during the Watergate scandal of the early 1970s, it reviewed a challenge to President Nixon's claim that he could withhold incriminating tape recordings from a special prosecutor.[51] However, the Court tends to avoid becoming embroiled in political disputes that it feels it cannot resolve—for example, it refused to hear several challenges to the constitutionality of the Vietnam War.[52] Moreover, it may postpone consideration of sensitive issues to avoid losing public support. Thus after the Court had angered many white Southerners by inval-

BOX 5-4 RULE 10: CONSIDERATIONS GOVERNING REVIEW ON CERTIORARI

1. A review on writ of certiorari is not a matter of right, but of judicial discretion, and will be granted only when there are special and important reasons therefor. The following, while neither controlling nor fully measuring the Court's discretion, indicate the character of reasons that will be considered:

(a) When a federal court of appeals has rendered a decision in conflict with the decision of another federal court of appeals on the same matter....

(b) When a state court of last resort has decided a federal question in a way in conflict with the decision of another state court of last resort or of a federal court of appeals.

(c) When a state court of last resort or a federal court of appeals has decided an important question of federal law which has not, but should be, settled by this Court, or has decided a federal question in a way in conflict with applicable decisions of this Court.

2. The same general considerations outlined above will control in respect of petitions for writs of certiorari to review judgments of the Court of Claims, of the Court of Customs and Patent Appeals, and of any other court whose judgments are reviewable by law on writ of certiorari.

idating state laws mandating racial segregation in public schools, it refused for over a decade to consider challenges to state laws banning racial intermarriage.[53]

Some political scientists have suggested that the Court's decisions on whether to grant certiorari can be predicted on the basis of certain "cues" that trigger review.[54] Underlying this theory is the assumption that, faced with a deluge of petitions for review, the justices and their clerks develop shortcuts to identify meritorious cases. In recent years the most important cue seems to be whether the federal government is a party to the case and is seeking review. Other relevant cues include conflict between a lower court decision and a Supreme Court precedent, conflict between circuits on a matter of federal law, and the presence of a civil liberties issue. When several of these cues are present in a single case, the likelihood of Supreme Court review increases. Although this research accounts for patterns in the Court's agenda-setting, it cannot explain the Court's decision to hear or not hear a particular case. Moreover, the theory must be continually updated because the cues that are important change over time in response to changes in the membership and orientation of the Court.

Other scholars have concluded that the justices' votes on certiorari reflect their views on constitutional policy.[55] That is, justices vote to hear cases when they expect that doing so will advance their constitutional views and to deny certiorari when that will best advance their views. Two considerations are involved here: the justice's perception of whether the lower court decided the case correctly, and his or her perception of how the Supreme Court is likely to rule on the case. Thus, justices may vote for review when they disagree with a lower court's ruling in order to "correct" the perceived error and establish precedent that reorients lower-court decisions. But justices may vote against granting certiorari despite disagreeing with a lower-court's ruling, if they believe that the Court will affirm the lower court. As one justice explained, the concern in such circumstances is damage control: "I might think the Nebraska Supreme Court made a horrible decision, but I wouldn't want to take the case, for if we take the case and affirm it, then it would become a precedent."[56]

Interviews with the justices suggest, however, that legal considerations—conflicts among the circuits, the *legal* importance of the issue—also figure heavily in the justices' votes on certiorari.[57] In sum, it appears that the legal or political importance of the issue, the lower courts' rulings on the issue, the parties to the case, and the justices' own policy views all figure into the decision to grant or deny certiorari.

Information-gathering

In order to decide a case, the Supreme Court needs information about the facts of the case, the applicable law, and the likely consequences of its decision. Under our adversary system, the justices look to the litigants in the case for much of this information. The attorneys for each party file legal briefs and then argue the case orally before the justices. Other groups interested in the outcome of the case may, with the Court's permission, also submit legal briefs—called a *micus curiae* (literally, friend of the court) briefs. Finally, the justices can rely on the record of proceedings and the opinions of the lower courts.

Legal Briefs

Legal briefs are first and foremost partisan documents, designed to persuade the Court to rule in favor of one's client or position. This persuasion takes the form of marshalling and interpreting pertinent legal materials (precedents, statutes, constitutional provisions) and factual information in a manner favorable to one's client and one's position.

For *amicus curiae* briefs as well as for those submitted by the litigants, the goal is to gain a favorable ruling. Yet typically those who file *amicus* briefs are interested primarily in the constitutional issue raised by the case rather than in the fate of the particular litigants. Some organizations file amicus briefs out of concern for the effects the Court's decision might have on them or on their members. Twenty-seven states, for example, submitted a brief in *Miranda* v. *Arizona* urging the Court not to get involved in setting standards for police interrogations. For other groups the concern is primarily ideological. Thus the American Civil Liberties Union, a group committed to a broad interpretation of constitutional rights, also filed a brief in *Miranda* urging the Court to extend the rights of the accused.[58]

Oral Argument

During oral argument the attorneys for each party have their final opportunity to influence the Court's ruling. Early in the nation's history, when the Court's docket was less crowded, the oral argument in a case could extend over several days, and the flowery oratory of the attorneys attracted large audiences. Daniel Webster is actually reputed to have moved those in the court to tears as he concluded his argument in *Dartmouth College* v. *Woodward*.[59] As the demands on the Court's time have increased, it gradually cut back on the time available to each party for oral argument. Since 1970 the Court has limited arguments to thirty minutes for each side, except in those rare circumstances where the importance and complexity of a case justified additional time.

Lawyers soon discover that oral argument is not an opportunity to make a set speech. The justices pepper the attorneys with questions, testing the soundness of the legal positions they are advancing. These questions frequently force attorneys to confront weaknesses in their arguments or to clarify the implications of the positions they are urging on the Court. For an ill-prepared attorney, the half-hour may seem a lifetime. Yet if oral argument can be a harrowing experience, and it can, it also provides a unique opportunity. As Chief Justice William Rehnquist has observed, "it is the only time before conference discussion of the case later in the week when all of the judges are expected to sit on the bench and concentrate on one particular case."[60]

Does oral argument make a difference? Most justices agree that it does. According to Justice Antonin Scalia, "things can be put in perspective during oral argument in a way that they can't in a written brief."[61] For in responding to the justices' questions, attorneys can correct misunderstandings, demonstrate unappreciated strengths in their positions, and remove obstacles to the justices voting for their clients. Indeed, Justice John Marshall Harlan concluded that oral argument "may in many cases make the difference between winning and losing, no matter how good the briefs are."[62]

Decisionmaking

During the Court's term, the justices meet in conference twice a week to consider the cases that have been argued. Only the justices are present at these conferences. On Wednesday afternoons, the justices discuss and vote on the four cases argued the previous Monday, and on Fridays the justices consider the cases argued on Tuesday and Wednesday. The chief justice begins the discussion of each case by summarizing the facts and legal arguments and offering his own views on how it should be decided. The senior associate justice then explains his views, and the remaining justices follow in order of seniority. By the time their turns arrive, the most junior justices may have little new to offer other than their votes. When all the justices have spoken, the chief justice tabulates the justices' votes and announces the Court's tentative decision.

These deliberations have little of the sharp give-and-take characteristic of legislative debate. In fact, according to Chief Justice Rehnquist, there is surprisingly little interplay among the justices at conference.[63]   In part, this reflects the format for discussion: allowing each justice to express his or her views without interruption is hardly conducive to lively debate. In part, too, the justices may shy away from face-to-face attacks on the positions of fellow justices because of personal friendships that transcend philosophic differences or because of the need to maintain cordial relations with colleagues with whom one will serve for a long time. (The justices do, however, attack the views of other members of the Court, at times quite harshly, in the opinions they write.)

Also, in contrast with legislators, the justices have only limited means to influence the votes of fellow justices. Judicial ethics prevent them from offering to trade votes in order to gain support on issues of importance to them. And, given judicial independence, justices cannot bring outside pressures to bear on their colleagues. Thus, their main source of influence is the quality of the arguments that they can marshall. If the chief justice is also the intellectual leader of the Court, his power to frame the issues—and thereby direct the course of debate—can give him some advantage. Thus, according to Justice Felix Frankfurter, Chief Justice Charles Evans Hughes "radiated authority," and the other justices did not venture an opinion after the chief justice had spoken unless they were very sure they knew what they were talking about.[64] An associate justice too may exhibit the intellectual acuity and force of personality necessary to assume a leadership role on the Court. Still, it is difficult to present a fully developed argument on complex legal issues orally, and it is certainly difficult to follow such an argument. Thus intellectual leadership on the Court is likely to manifest itself more in written opinions than in debate during conference.

Once the Court has reached its tentative decision on a case—and the vote in conference is tentative, since justices can change their minds up to the time that the decision is announced—a justice is assigned to write the opinion of the Court. If the chief justice has voted with the majority, he assigns the opinion of the Court to himself or to another member of the majority coalition. When the case is a momentous one, the chief justice typically assigns himself the opinion, as Chief Justice Warren did in *Brown* v. *Board of Education* and as Chief Justice Burger did in *United States* v. *Nixon.* If the chief justice is in dissent, the senior associate justice aligned with the majority assigns the opinion of the Court. Other justices, of course, remain free to write concurring or dissenting opinions.

Writing opinions is a long and difficult process. Most justices permit their clerks to draft the initial version of opinions, along lines specified by the justice. Once the justice has made whatever changes seem appropriate, the draft opinion is circulated among the justices. Other justices may also circulate concurring and dissenting opinions at this time, seeking support for their views. The justices carefully scrutinize the opinions that are circulated and often return them with requests for changes, sometimes making such changes a condition for joining the opinion. Particularly crucial are the negotiations over the opinion of the Court, since the justice assigned the opinion must craft an opinion that can gain the support of five justices. Often an opinion goes through several drafts before it is accepted—Justice William Brennan once circulated ten versions of an opinion before it became the opinion of the Court.[65] Yet sometimes deep-seated divisions may prevent a majority of justices from coalescing behind a single opinion. In *Webster* v. *Reproductive Health Services,* for example, a majority of five justices upheld various state restrictions on abortions, but Justices Antonin Scalia and Sandra Day O'Connor refused to join Chief Justice Rehnquist's opinion and filed separate concurring opinions. When no opinion expresses the perspective of the Court, it complicate the efforts of lower-court judges to determine the exact meaning of the Court's ruling.

The opinion-writing phase provides an opportunity for further consideration of cases, and justices may change their votes after reading the draft opinions. Indeed, on several occasions justices assigned to write the opinion of the Court have reported back that additional research had led them to change their votes. On a closely divided court, defection by a single justice can produce a new majority and, with it, a different decision. According to one study of a ten-year period, the justices' final votes differed from those in conference nine percent of the time. However, in most instances the changes merely served to increase the size of the Court majority, as justices refrained from dissenting, rather than to create a new majority.[66]

Even if no votes change, the opinion-writing phase is crucial. The Court's decisions have a dual aspect: they resolve particular disputes, and they announce legal standards to be applied in future cases. Often the grounds upon which the Court decides, or the breadth of the legal principles it announces, are as important as the vote itself. In *Miranda* v. *Arizona,* for example, the Court not only overturned Miranda's conviction but also used the case to establish standards governing all future police interrogations. By framing the opinion in this way, the Court ensured that its decision would have a broad effect. In contrast, in *Webster* v. *Reproductive Health Services* the justices upheld state restrictions on abortion but decided on narrow grounds so as to avoid directly overruling *Roe* v. *Wade.* which established a constitutional right to abortion. By leaving open the question of whether *Roe* remained a viable precedent, the Court encouraged further litigation on the issue.

Promulgating Decisions

A term of the Court follows a predictable pattern. Oral argument commences immediately, on the first Monday in October, but because preparing opinions is time-consuming, the Court does not begin announcing decisions immediately. Early in the term, it follows the traditional practice of announcing its decisions on Mondays ("decision Mondays"). However, as the term rushes toward its conclusion, the increasing number of decided cases leads the Court to announce its decisions on other days as well. By the conclusion of the Court's term in late June or early July, the Court will have decided and written opinions in over 150 cases.

The Court jealously guards the secrecy of its decisions. Once the opinions in a case are written, they go to the printshop in the basement of the Court, which prepares copies for transmission to reporters and the general public. In the printshop each copy of an opinion is numbered to prevent any from being removed from the premises. "Leaks" are extremely rare; reporters at the Court are not even informed ahead of time what decisions the justices will announce that day.

The Court announces its decisions in open court. Usually the justice who wrote the opinion of the Court announces the decision, and justices who filed concurring or dissenting opinions may also state their views. When several decisions are handed down on the same day, the justices delivering the opinions of the Court do so in reverse order of seniority. In the past, justices used to read their full opinions from the bench, but time pressures have eliminated that practice. Still, justices may occasionally read portions of their opinions or offer extemporaneous remarks about a case. Thus, dissenting in one contentious case, Justice James McReynolds hit the bench with his fist, exclaiming: "The Constitution is gone!"[67]

While the justices are announcing the Court's decisions, the Court's press office releases copies of the opinions to reporters. Most members of the general public will get their notions of the Court's rulings from the news stories filed by these reporters. However, published versions of the Court's opinions are available from a variety of sources. The official source for the Court's rulings is United States Reports, bound volumes containing all the Court's opinions and other actions. Private companies also publish the Court's decisions, seeking to attract readers by providing fast service or commentary on the decisions.

Other Appellate Courts

Agenda-setting

The U.S. Supreme Court's power to decide what cases it will hear distinguishes it from most other appellate courts. First-level appellate courts, such as federal courts of appeals and state intermediate appellate courts, have no control over their dockets. Because all litigants are entitled to one appeal, these first-level appellate courts must hear whatever cases are brought before them. Most second-level appellate courts, such as state supreme courts, also have only limited control over their dockets. Most states by either statute or constitutional provision mandate that their supreme courts hear certain types of appeals. States with the death penalty, for instance, generally require their supreme courts to review convictions in all cases in which the defendant is sentenced to death. Beyond that, the states vary enormously in the mandatory jurisdiction they assign to their supreme courts. These constitutional or statutory mandates usually increase the caseloads of state supreme courts—most hear far more cases per year than the U.S. Supreme Court does—and may burden them with cases of little legal importance.

Information-gathering

As we have seen, the U.S. Supreme Court obtains information for its decision-making from the briefs of the parties in the case, from *amicus curiae* briefs, and from oral argument. But *amicus curiae* briefs are not often filed in cases before other appellate courts. For what attracts groups to a case is its broad legal significance, and many appeals before other appellate courts raise issues of interest solely to the parties. Other appellate courts also rely less heavily on oral argument—indeed, some dispense with it altogether or reserve it for complex or important cases. As a result, these appellate courts decide most appeals on the basis of the briefs of the parties and the lower-court record.

Decisionmaking

Because all appellate courts are multi-member courts, appellate decisionmaking necessarily has a group dimension. The process of decisionmaking on many appellate courts resembles that on the U.S. Supreme Court. That is, the judges meet in conference, and the writing of the opinion of the court is assigned to a member of the majority coalition following the vote in conference. However, a few state appellate courts rotate opinion assignments, so that a judge is assigned the opinion in a case even before it is argued. Under this system the judge assigned the opinion tends to be far more knowledgeable about the case than his or her colleagues, and they therefore tend to defer to the assigned judge's view of how it should be decided.

When cases merely resolve disputes between the contending parties and have no broader legal significance, some appellate courts do not issue opinions but merely announce their decisions. In cases in which opinions are published, those opinions usually are shorter than the opinions authored by Supreme Court justices. Judges on other appellate courts also tend to file fewer concurring or dissenting opinions. Federal courts of appeals decide most cases in three-judge panels, and in part because of this, dissenting opinions are filed in less than 10 percent of their decisions. Most state supreme courts report dissents in less than a quarter of the cases they decide, but dissent levels vary considerably from court to court. On some courts—perhaps because of a tradition of unanimity, or a homogeneity in the court's membership, or the routine character of the cases they decide—dissent is rare. Thus the Alabama Supreme Court until recently had dissents filed in only about 5 percent of its cases. On other courts—for example, the Ohio Supreme Court—dissent is an established tradition, occurring in roughly half the cases.[68]

Promulgating Decisions

Few decisions of state appellate courts and lower federal courts attract the sort of public attention that is given to Supreme Court rulings. Indeed, some are of such minimal interest even to the legal profession that the court merely announces its decision without writing an opinion in the case.

When a federal court of appeals decides a case with opinion, the opinion can be found in the Federal Reporter series. Many states publish important state appellate rulings in their own state reporter series. Other states rely on the privately published National Reporter series, which groups the decisions of state appellate courts in regional reporters. The Southeastern Reporter, for example, includes state appellate rulings from West Virginia, Virginia, North Carolina, South Carolina, and Georgia.

BEYOND TRIALS AND APPEALS

This chapter has examined the conduct of trials and the review of trial-court rulings by appellate courts. Important as these processes are, they comprise only a small portion of the activities of American courts. Appellate courts can review lower-court rulings only if litigants appeal those rulings, and most litigants do not appeal. Trial courts can conduct trials only when there is an ongoing dispute between two parties. Yet in criminal cases most defendants plead guilty prior to trial, and in the vast majority of civil cases the parties settle rather than going to trial. Thus a complete understanding of court operations requires looking beyond the formal processes of trial and appeal. This is the project of the next two chapters.

NOTES

1. This account of the Von Bulow case relies on Alan M. Dershowitz, *Reversal of Fortune* (New York: Random House, 1986), and William Wright, *The Von Bulow Affair* (New York: Delacorte, 1983).

2. Quoted in Dershowitz, *Reversal of Fortune*, p. xvii.

3. Quoted in Wright, *The Von Bulow Affair*, p. 354.

4. Robert Mnookin and Lewis Kornhauser, "Bargaining in the Shadow of the Law: The Case of Divorce," *Yale Law Journal* 88 (1979): 950-997.

5. Lawrence M. Friedman, *A History of American Law*, 2d ed. (New York: Simon & Schuster, 1985), p. 576.

6. Stephen J. Schulhofer, "Is Plea Bargaining Inevitable?" *Harvard Law Review* 97 (March 1984), p. 1096.

7. Barbara Yngvesson and Patricia Hennessey, "Small Claims, Complex Disputes: A Review of the Small Claims Literature," *Law and Society Review* 9 (Winter 1975): 219-274.

8. *Joint Anti-Fascist Refugee Committee* v. *McGrath*, 341 U.S. 123, 162 (1951).

9. United States Constitution, Article III, Section 2, Paragraph 3, and Sixth Amendment (criminal trials); Seventh Amendment (civil trials).

10. *Duncan* v. *Louisiana*, 391 U.S. 145 (1968); *Baldwin* v. *New York*, 399 U.S. 66 (1970).

11. *Gideon* v. *Wainwright*, 372 U.S. 335, 348 (1963).

12. Supreme Court rulings extending the right to counsel in criminal cases are *Johnson* v. *Zerbst*, 304 U.S. 458 (1938); *Gideon* v. *Wainwright*, 372 U.S. 335 (1963); and *Argersinger* v. *Hamlin*, 407 U.S. 25 (1972). The details of the *Gideon* case are presented in Chapter 2. Among state rulings extending the right to counsel under state law are *Carpenter* v. *Dane*, 9 Wis. 249 (1859) and *Cogdill* v. *State*, 246 S.W.2d 5 (Tenn. 1951).

13. *Lassiter* v. *Department of Social Services of Durham, N.C.*, 452 U.S. 18 (1981).

14. *Maryland* v. *Craig*, 110 S.Ct. 3157 (1990).

15. *In re Winship*, 397 U.S. 358 (1970).

16. *Griffin* v. *California*, 380 U.S. 609 (1965).

17. *Baldwin* v. *New York*, 399 U.S. 66 (1970).

18. *Blanton* v. *City of North Las Vegas*, 489 U.S. 538 (1989).

19. Jon M. Van Dyke, *Jury Selection Procedures* (Cambridge: Ballinger Publishing Co., 1977), p. 180.

20. *Batson* v. *Kentucky*, 476 U.S. 79 (1986), and *Powers* v. *Ohio*, 111 S.Ct. 1364 (1991).

21. Van Dyke, *Jury Selection Procedures*, Appendix D, p. 282.

22. Ibid., Appendix D, pp. 282-284.

23. *The Jury System in the Federal Courts* (Works of the Committee on the Operation of the Jury System of the Judicial Conference of the United States, 1966-73) (St. Paul: West Publishing Co., 1974), p. 174.

24. This analysis derives from Gordon Bermant and John Shapard, "The Voir Dire Examination, Juror Challenges, and Adversary Advocacy," in Bruce D. Sales, ed., *The Trial Process* (New York: Plenum Press, 1981), and Valerie P. Hans and Neil Vidmar, *Judging the Jury* (New York: Plenum Press, 1986), Chapter 5.

25. See Hans and Vidmar, *Judging the Jury*, Chapter 6.

26. Maxwell M. Blecher and Robert M. Lindquist, "Opening Statements," in William A. Masterson, ed., *Civil Trial Practice: Strategies and Techniques* (New York: Practising Law Institute, 1986), p. 115. See also E. Allen Lind and Gina Y. Ke, "Opening and Closing Statements," in Saul M. Kassin and Lawrence S. Wrightsman, eds., *The Psychology of Evidence and Trial Procedure* (Beverly Hills: Sage Publications, 1985), pp. 232-233.

27. Lind and Ke, "Opening and Closing Statements," p. 234.

28. Jerold S. Solovy and Robert L. Byman, "Direct Examination," in Masterson, *Civil Trial Practice*, p. 134.

29. David W. Neubauer, *Judicial Process; Law, Courts, and Politics in the United States* (Pacific Grove, Cal.: Brooks/Cole Publishing Co., 1991), pp. 318-320.

30. Paul A. Renne, "Final Argument," in Masterson, *Civil Trial Practice*, p. 293.

31. Valerie P. Hans and Neil Vidmar, *Judging the Jury* (New York: Plenum Press, 1986), pp. 21-22, and Paula DiPerna, *Juries on Trial* (New York, Dembner Books, 1984), p. 28.

32. Gary J. Jacobsohn, "Citizen Participation in Policy-Making: The Role of the Jury," *Journal of Politics* 39 (February 1977): 73-96, and Hans and Vidmar, *Judging the Jury*, pp. 31-37.

33. *Williams* v. *Florida*, 390 U.S. 78 (1970); *Ballew* v. *Georgia*, 435 U.S. 223 (1978). In federal courts twelve-member juries are required in criminal cases and no less than six-member juries in civil cases. See *Thompson* v. *Utah*, 170 U.S. 343 (1898), and *Colegrove* v. *Battin*, 413 U.S. 149 (1973).

34. *Johnson* v. *Louisiana*, 406 U.S. 356 (1972); *Apodaca* v. *Oregon*, 406 U.S. 404 (1972); *Burch* v. *Louisiana*, 441 U.S. 130 (1979). Under rules for federal courts established by the Supreme Court, all verdicts in federal cases must be unanimous.

35. DiPerna, *Juries on Trial*, pp. 70-71.

36. Major social science studies of the effects of jury size and decision rules, many of them quite critical of the Supreme Court's rulings, include: Michael J. Saks, *Jury Verdicts* (Lexington, Mass.: Lexington Books, 1977); Reid Hastie, Steven D. Penrod, and Nancy Pennington, *Inside the Jury* (Cambridge: Harvard University Press, 1983); Hans Zeisel, "...And Then There Were None: The Diminution of the Federal Jury," *University of Chicago Law Review* 38 (1971): 710-724; Hans Zeisel and Shari Diamond, "Convincing Empirical Evidence on the Six Member Jury," *University of Chicago Law Review* 41 (1974): 281-295; Robert Roper, "Jury Size: Impact on Verdict's Correctness," *American Politics Quarterly* 7 (1979): 438-452; and C. Nemeth, "Interactions Between Jurors as a Function of Majority vs. Unanimity Decision Rules," *Journal of Applied Social Psychology* 7 (1977): 38-56.

37. *In re Japanese Products Antitrust Litigation*, 631 F.2d 1069, 1084 (3d Cir. 1980). For analyses of jury performance in complex litigation, see Arthur. D. Austin, *Complex Litigation Confronts the Jury System: A Case Study* (Frederick, Md.: University Publications of America, 1984); Molly Selvin and Larry Picus, *The Debate over Jury Performance; Observations from a Recent Asbestos Case* (Santa Monica, Calif.: Rand Corporation, 1987); and Peter Sperlich, "The Case for Preserving Trial by Jury in Complex Litigation," *Judicature* 65 (March-April 1982): 395-419.

38. Harry Kalven, Jr., and Hans Zeisel, *The American Jury* (Boston: Little Brown, 1966).

39. This research is discussed in Hans and Vidmar, *Judging the Jury*, Chapters 8-10.

40. Kalven and Zeisel, *The American Jury*, Chapters 5-6 and 18-22.

41. The percentage of rulings by federal district courts that are appealed to federal courts of appeals is computed from *Annual Report of the Director of the Administrative Office of the United States Courts 1990*, pp. 2-7, esp. Tables 2, 3, and 5. The percentage of state trial-court rulings that are appealed is drawn from *State Court Caseload Statistics: Annual Report 1990* (Williamsburg, VA.: National Center for State Courts, 1992), p. 11, Text Table I.4, and p. 53, Text Table II.1.

42. Alexis DeTocqueville, *Democracy in America*, ed. J. P. Mayer (Garden City, N.Y.: Doubleday, 1969), p. 270.

43. The compulsory flag salute was upheld in *Minersville School District* v. *Gobitis*, 310 U.S. 586 (1940). Justices Black, Douglas, and Murphy repudiated their *Gobitis* votes in *Jones* v. *Opelika*, 316 U.S. 584 (1942). The Court overruled *Gobitis* in *West Virginia State Board of Education* v. *Barnette*, 319 U.S. 624 (1943).

44. The Supreme Court recognized that the right to privacy encompassed the right to terminate a pregnancy in *Roe* v. *Wade*, 410 U.S. 113 (1973). However, the Court narrowed *Roe* and raised questions about its continued viability in *Webster* v. *Reproductive Health Services*, 109 S.Ct. 3040 (1989), and *Planned Parenthood of Southeastern Pennsylvania* v. *Casey*, 60 LW 4795 (1992).

45. *Escobedo* v. *Illinois*, 378 U.S. 478 (1964).

46. Liva Baker, *Miranda: Crime, Law and Politics* (New York: Atheneum, 1983), p. 98.

47. *Miranda* v. *Arizona*, 384 U.S. 436 (1966).

48. These data are drawn from 58 U. S. Law Week 3181 (October 3, 1989).

49. "Retired Chief Justice Warren Attacks . . . Freund Study Group's Composition and Proposal," *American Bar Association Journal* 59 (July 1973), p. 728.

50. *Youngstown Sheet & Tube Company* v. *Sawyer*, 343 U.S. 579 (1952).

51. *United States* v. *Nixon*, 418 U.S. 683 (1974).

52. See, for example, *Katz* v. *Tyler*, 386 U.S. 942 (1967), and *Sarnoff* v. *Schultz*, 409 U.S. 929 (1971).

53. The Court finally struck down state laws forbidding racial intermarriage in 1967, thirteen years after its decision in *Brown* v. *Board of Education*, 347 U.S. 483 (1954). The case striking down such laws was the aptly named *Loving* v. *Virginia*, 388 U.S. 1 (1967).

54. The original attempt to apply cue theory to the Court's certiorari decisions was Joseph Tanenhaus, Marvin Schick, M. Muraskin, and D. Rosen, "The Supreme Court's Certiorari Jurisdiction: Cue Theory," in S. Sidney Ulmer, ed., *Courts, Law, and Judicial Processes* (New York: Free Press, 1981). Refinements of the theory were proposed in S. Sidney Ulmer, "The Supreme Court's Certiorari Decisions: Conflict as a Predictive Variable," *American Political Science Review* 78 (December, 1984): 901-911; Donald R. Songer, "Concern for Policy Outputs as a Cue for Supreme Court Decisions on Certiorari," *Journal of Politics* 41 (November 1979): 1185-1194; and Stewart Teger and Donald Kosinski, "The Cue Theory of Supreme Court Certiorari Jurisdiction: A Reconsideration," *Journal of Politics* 42 (August 1980): 834-846.

55. For discussions of strategic voting on certiorari, see Lawrence Baum, "Policy Goals in Judicial Gatekeeping: A Proximity Model of Discretionary Jurisdiction," *American Journal of Politics* 21 (1977): 13-33; Walter Murphy, *Elements of Judicial Strategy* (Chicago: University of Chicago Press, 1964); and S. Sidney Ulmer, "The Decision to Grant Certiorari as an Indicator to 'Decision on the Merits,'" *Polity* 4 (1972): 429-447.

56. Quoted in H. W. Perry, Jr., *Deciding to Decide; Agenda Setting in the United States Supreme Court* (Cambridge: Harvard University Press, 1991), p. 200.

57. Ibid., Chapters 6-8.

58. Baker, *Miranda: Crime, Law and Politics*, pp. 108-109.

59. David M. O'Brien, *Storm Center; The Supreme Court in American Politics*, 2nd ed. (New York: W. W. Norton, 1990), pp. 269-270, discussing *Dartmouth College* v. *Woodward,* 4 Wheat. 518 (1819).

60. William H. Rehnquist, *The Supreme Court* (New York: William Morrow, 1987), p. 277.

61. Quoted in O'Brien, *Storm Center*, p. 273.

62. Quoted in Anthony Lewis, *Gideon's Trumpet* (New York: Random House, 1964), p. 162, n. 23.

63. Rehnquist, *The Supreme Court*, p. 290.

64. Ibid., p. 292.

65. O'Brien, *Storm Center*, p. 295.

66. Saul Brenner, "Fluidity on the United States Supreme Court: A Reexamination," *American Journal of Political Science* 24 (August 1980): 526-535.

67. Quoted in O'Brien, *Storm Center*, p. 328.

68. For discussion of dissent rates on federal courts of appeals, see Richard J. Richardson and Kenneth N. Vines, *The Politics of Federal Courts* (Boston: Little Brown, 1970), p. 135. For dissent rates on the Alabama and Ohio supreme courts, see G. Alan Tarr and Mary Cornelia Aldis Porter, *State Supreme Courts in State and Nation* (New Haven: Yale University Press, 1988), p. 106, n. 111, and p. 139, n. 23. For an overview of dissent on state supreme courts, see Henry R. Glick and Robert W. Pruet, Jr., "Dissent in State Supreme Courts: Patterns and Correlates of Conflict," in Sheldon Goldman and Charles M. Lamb, eds., *Judicial Conflict and Consensus: Behavioral Studies of American Appellate Courts* (Lexington, Ky.: University of Kentucky Press, 1986).

6 CRIMINAL JUSTICE AND THE COURTS

The scene, a hall outside a Detroit courtroom; a defendant and his attorney deep in conversation; the subject, whether to plead guilty or go to trial:

DEF[ENSE] COUNSEL: We've got a problem. It looks like the prosecutor has a pretty good case—there are the people in the store and the customer's paycheck found in your wallet. Judge Singleton will probably find you guilty if we go without a jury. Of course, nobody ever knows what a jury will do, but my feeling is they'll probably convict you in a case like this.

[DEFENDANT]: One of those dudes can't say for sure it was me robbed the place.

DEF. COUNSEL: I know, I know. Look, the other two can. And you were in the neighborhood and had that paycheck. What do you think a jury will do?

[DEFENDANT]: Well, what can I do?

DEF. COUNSEL: I'll give it to you straight. If we go to trial, it will be on the armed robbery. You'll probably be convicted, and the law says the judge has got to give you some time. Knowing Singleton, if the jury convicts you, he won't hesitate to give you time either. You can plead guilty to the other charge—assault with intent to rob while being armed.

[DEFENDANT]: What would I get then?

DEF. COUNSEL: Well, if you plead, it will be a conviction. You *could* get probation, but you might still get some time. I really don't know what he'll give you.

[DEFENDANT]: Damn! What should I do, man?

DEF. COUNSEL: Look, I'm just your attorney. You have to decide. I guess if I were in your shoes, I'd take the plea.

[DEFENDANT]: Yeah. Yeah. OK.

After pleading guilty, the defendant was sentenced to from three to five years in prison.[1]

This conversation between defendant and counsel illustrates a basic aspect of criminal justice in the United States: most of those accused of crime plead guilty instead of going to trial. Although the frequency of guilty pleas varies from jurisdiction to jurisdiction, it is estimated that defendants plead guilty in over eighty percent of felony cases (those involving serious crimes) and in an even larger percentage of misdemeanor cases.

In examining the process of criminal justice, therefore, this chapter focuses primarily on those cases that do not go to trial. Initially, we identify the major actors in the process of criminal justice. Next we survey the process by which cases proceed from arrest to guilty plea, looking in detail at key aspects of the process. We then address the process of plea negotiations (or plea bargaining) that frequently precedes guilty pleas. Finally, we examine the policy debates over the exclusionary rule, the insanity defense, and the sentencing of criminals.

PROSECUTORS AND DEFENSE ATTORNEYS

Prosecutors

The prosecutor—also known in some jurisdictions as the district attorney, the state's attorney, or (for federal prosecutors) the United States attorney—is the community's chief law enforcement official. Typically, prosecutors in the states are elected locally and have a political base that enables them to operate independently of the state's attorney general. (Federal prosecutors are appointed by the president with the advice and consent of the Senate.) In some rural jurisdictions, prosecutors serve part-time while maintaining a private practice. In urban areas, however, the prosecutor occupies a full-time position and usually has a staff of assistant prosecutors to help deal with the heavy workload of criminal cases (see Box 6-1). For example, the district attorney's office in Dallas employs over 170 attorneys.[2]   Many of these assistant prosecutors are recent law-school graduates seeking litigation experience before moving on to other positions, so turnover in the prosecutor's office is continuous.

BOX 6-1   THE PROSECUTOR'S BLUES

Novelist Tom Wolfe has sketched the work of the assistant prosecutor in harshly unromantic terms:

One thing Kramer had learned within two weeks as an assistant D.A. in the Bronx was that 95 percent of the defendants who got as far as the indictment stage, perhaps 98 percent, were truly guilty. The caseload was so overwhelming, you didn't waste time trying to bring the marginal cases forward, unless the press was on your back. They hauled in guilt by the ton, those blue-and-orange vans out there on Walton Avenue. But the poor bastards behind the wire mesh barely deserved the term *criminal,* if by criminal you had in mind the romantic notion of someone who has a goal and seeks to achieve it through some desperate way outside the law. No, they were simpleminded incompetents, most of them, and they did unbelievably stupid, vile things.

SOURCE: Excerpt from THE BONFIRE OF THE VANITIES, by Tom Wolfe. Copyright © 1987 by Tom Wolfe. Reprinted by permission of Farrar, Straus and Giroux, Inc. Page 105.

Prosecutors are the most powerful officials in the criminal courts because of the broad discretion they exercise. In most jurisdictions, they screen felony arrests to determine if charges should be filed and, if so, what charges. If they decide not to file charges, the suspects are released. At later stages of the criminal process, they may decide whether or not to seek a grand jury indictment, whether to drop or reduce the charges they initially filed, and whether or not to plea bargain with defendants.

In exercising this discretion, the assistant prosecutors are guided by the policies and expectations of the prosecutor who heads the office. Usually, however, prosecutors accord the attorneys under them considerable leeway in conducting cases, as long as they safeguard the prosecutor's reputation by maintaining a high conviction rate. This emphasis on convictions affects how the assistant prosecutors view cases. Often "they prefer dismissing charges to subjecting themselves to possible criticism for 'losing'."[3]

Defense Attorneys

The Sixth Amendment and analogous state constitutional provisions guarantee defendants the right to counsel. As a result of the Supreme Court's decision in *Gideon* v. *Wainwright* (see Chapter 2), states are required to furnish counsel to indigent defendants in felony cases.[4] A subsequent Supreme Court ruling, *Argersinger* v. *Hamlin* (1972), extended this right to counsel to all cases in which the defendant could be sentenced to jail or prison. Some states have gone even further, providing counsel to all indigents charged with misdemeanors.[5] Prior to these initiatives, many indigent defendants were not represented by counsel, which placed them at a severe disadvantage. The requirement that counsel be provided to indigent defendants has revolutionized criminal justice in the United States.

Because most defendants are indigent, they cannot afford a private attorney, and thus relatively few lawyers specialize in criminal law. States and localities have devised three systems to provide representation for indigent defendants:[6]

Public defender programs: Fifteen states and many localities, particularly in urban areas, operate public defender programs, employing attorneys whose sole responsibility is to represent indigent defendants. Many of these attorneys, like their counterparts in the prosecutor's office, are recent law-school graduates who do not remain in the public defender's office for their entire careers. Although their skills as advocates have sometimes been questioned—one inmate, when asked if he had a lawyer at his trial, replied: "No, I had a public defender"—there is little evidence that public defenders provide less effective representation than other defense attorneys do.[7]

Assigned counsel systems: Assigned counsel systems operate in almost two-thirds of all counties but are particularly prevalent in counties with fewer than 50,000 residents. Under an assigned counsel system, a court appoints private attorneys from a list of available lawyers to represent indigent defendants. In some jurisdictions, this service is considered a professional obligation, and the attorney is not paid. In others the lawyer receives a reduced fee. Although this system disperses the responsibility of defending the poor among all practicing attorneys, the defendant runs the risk of being represented by a lawyer who has neither expertise nor experience in criminal law.[8]

Contract systems: In recent years some communities have experimented with contract systems, either as an alternative to other systems or as a supplement to public defender offices. Under a contract system, the government awards defender services contracts to individual attorneys or private law firms, which agree to provide representation for a specified dollar amount.

THE PROCESS OF CRIMINAL JUSTICE

Figure 6-1 illustrates the sequence of events in the criminal justice system from the commission of a felony to the final disposition of a case. Until the initial

FIGURE 6-1 SERIOUS CRIMES AND CRIMINAL JUSTICE

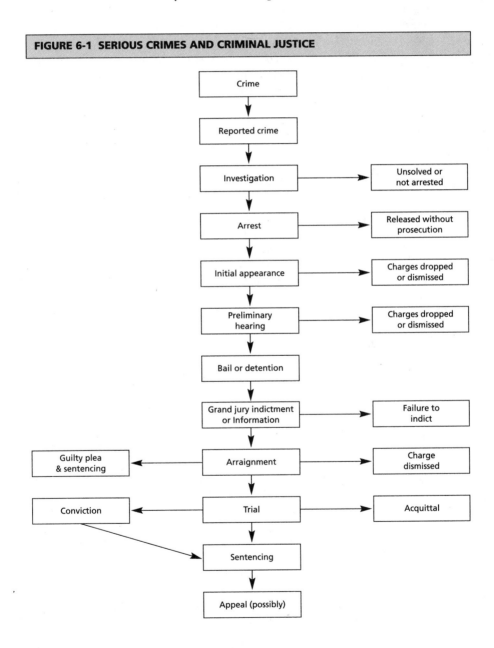

SOURCE: Adapted from *The Challenge of Crime in a Free Society* (Washington, D.C.: President's Commission on Law Enforcement and Administration of Justice, 1967).

appearance in court, the process is similar for misdemeanors. However, unlike those accused of felonies, most defendants in misdemeanor cases plead guilty at their initial appearance in court. Some do so because they are guilty of the offenses with which they are charged. But another factor may also be involved. The costs of making bail and paying an attorney, as well as the prospect of docked wages and possible loss of a job because of days spent in court or in jail awaiting trial, may deter defendants from contesting their innocence, especially when the penalties for conviction (usually a fine and/or probation) are not severe. As Malcolm Feeley has observed: "The time, effort, money, and opportunities lost as a direct result of being caught up in the system can quickly come to outweigh the penalty that issues from adjudication and sentence." Or more succinctly, "the process is the punishment."[9]

For those accused of felonies, however, the potential penalty upon conviction may be severe (see Box 6-2). Thus defendants may be less willing to admit their guilt—the more serious the charges, the more likely a trial—or willing to admit it only in exchange for some concession from the prosecution. As a result, the processing of felony cases is more drawn-out and complex.

Our analysis will focus on four key aspects of this process: the commission of the crime and the arrest, the prosecutor's charging decision, the setting of (or denial of) bail, and the official accusation of the accused in felony cases through indictment by a grand jury or other procedures.

Crime and Arrest

Most crimes are never solved, and their perpetrators never arrested or punished. What accounts for this striking fact? For one thing, most crimes are not reported to the police. Survey data suggest that the level of crime is three times as high as reported by the Federal Bureau of Investigation's Uniform Crime Reports (UCR), which are based on crime statistics submitted by police departments nationwide. Some victims of crime are simply not in a position to report offenses to the police—a drug purchaser, for example, can hardly complain of being cheated by a dealer. Other victims may not report crimes because they either distrust the police or, as in the case of some rape victims, wish to avoid the unpleasantness of a police investigation and testimony at trial. Some victims of crime also are in a continuing relationship with an offender—incidents of domestic violence provide one example—and they either may be too intimidated to report offenses or may wish to deal with the

---

BOX 6-2   CRIME IN THE UNITED STATES

Level and type of crime:

From 1981 to 1990, the level of crime in the United States—as measured by the FBI's Uniform Crime Reports—increased by 78 percent.

Property crimes outnumber violent crimes about 9 to 1.

Crime surveys suggest that only about one-third of all crimes are reported to the police.

Victims of crime:

Younger people are more likely than the elderly to be victims of crime. Young males are most likely to be victims of violent crime, and elderly women the least likely.

African-Americans are more likely than whites or members of other racial groups to be victims of crime in general and violent crime in particular.

In a sizable minority of confrontational crimes (e.g., rape, robbery, assault), the victim knows the offender.

Offenders and the criminal law:

Police "clear" by arrest only 21 percent of all reported crime on the FBI's Uniform Crime Reports Index.

Most cases that are prosecuted result in a conviction either by a plea of guilty or following a trial (73 percent of jury trials result in convictions in felony cases).

71 percent of all offenders convicted of felonies are sentenced to serve time in prison or in jail.

The prison population of the United States increased over 52 percent from 1985 to 1990.

SOURCES: *Report to the Nation on Crime and Justice,* 2nd ed. (Washington, D.C.: U.S. Department of Justice, Bureau of Justice Statistics, 1988); *Sourcebook of Criminal Justice Statistics* (Washington, D.C.: Government Printing Office, various years).

problem privately. Some crimes too, such as minor thefts, are viewed by victims as "not important enough to report." And finally, some crimes, such as illegal gambling or teenagers' drinking, do not have an identifiable victim and so often go unreported.[10]

Even when crimes are reported to the police, in most instances their perpetrators are never arrested. According to recent data, police "cleared" by arrest only 21 percent of all UCR felonies.[11] However, clearance rates differ dramatically from offense to offense. The highest clearance rates for reported crimes are for victimless crimes—typically the discovery (report) of the crime and the arrest are made simultaneously by a police officer.[12] Arrest rates tend to be higher for violent crimes such as aggravated assault and rape, in which the victim may be able to identify the assailant, than for crimes against property, such as larceny, auto theft, and burglary, which may occur without the presence of the victim.[13] Most arrests depend not on investigative work by the police but on immediate or almost immediate apprehension of a suspect. According to one study, 56 percent of felony arrests took place either at the scene of the crime or nearby, with another 24 percent occurring because the victim was able to identify the offender.[14]

Charges and Dismissals

"In the real world," political scientist James Q. Wilson has observed, "an arrest rarely ends anything."[15] Figure 6-2, which depicts what happens after arrest, confirms this. In none of the four cities were as many as one-third of those arrested in felony cases convicted of felonies. Prosecutors dismissed over half the cases or downgraded them to misdemeanors and sent them to a trial court of limited jurisdiction. Often the cases sent to the lower court were subsequently dismissed there. Thus although most cases that were prosecuted resulted in convictions, large numbers of cases were not prosecuted. What accounts for this attrition?

The most important factor leading assistant prosecutors to dismiss cases is the absence of evidence sufficient to prove guilt beyond a reasonable doubt.[16] Potential witnesses may be reluctant to testify or may lack credibility, perhaps because they have criminal records or a drug or alcohol dependency. Complainants may also withdraw their complaints, especially if they had a prior relationship with the accused and have reconciled their differences with him. This occurs most often in intra-family disputes. Even if there is sufficient evidence to convict, prosecutors may dismiss potentially convictable cases when they believe that prosecution will not serve the cause of justice. For example, a prosecutor may not file charges against a person arrested for a minor felony to avoid giving a first offender a criminal record.[17] Such an exercise of prosecutorial discretion has the same effect as an acquittal.

If the prosecutor files charges, the defendant is brought to court for his or her *initial appearance,* usually before a judge in a court of limited jurisdiction.

FIGURE 6-2 HOW CRIMINAL CASES ARE PROCESSED

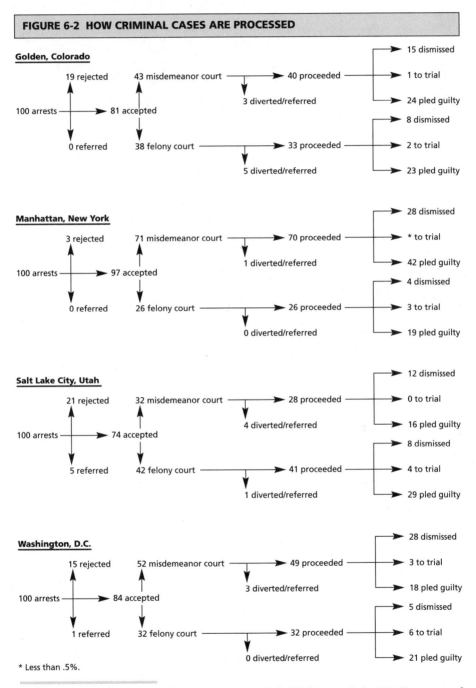

* Less than .5%.

SOURCE: *Report to the Nation on Crime and Justice,* 2nd ed. (Washington, D.C.: U.S. Department of Justice, Bureau of Justice Statistics, 1988), p. 71.

At this stage most defendants accused of ordinance violations and minor misdemeanors plead guilty. The judge informs those accused of more serious crimes
of the charges against them, advises them of their constitutional rights, and
appoints an attorney for defendants who are indigent. She also determines
whether defendants will be released from custody pending trial and schedules
the defendant's next appearance in court.

Bail and Pretrial Release

As befits a system in which the accused is presumed innocent until proven
guilty, most defendants are eligible for release prior to trial. Typically, those
accused must post bail as a guarantee that they will return for trial and other
court proceedings. In medieval times the accused was bailed to a third party,
who was tried in place of the accused if he or she failed to appear for trial.
Today, bail involves posting a monetary bond with the court that is forfeited if
the accused fails to appear.

Usually the bail required depends upon the seriousness of the charges against
defendants and their prior criminal record—the more serious the charges and
the more extensive the record, the higher the bail. However, as long as they do
not violate the Eighth Amendment's ban on "excessive bail," judges have considerable discretion in setting bail. Some states have sought to eliminate undue
leniency or harshness in setting bail by establishing a fixed schedule that specifies the bail for various offenses. However, critics have claimed that this substi-
tution of a "going rate" prevents judges from responding to the circumstances
in individual cases.

In some jurisdictions, defendants are required to post the full amount of bail
with the court. In others defendants rely on bail bondsmen, who sign a promis-
sory note to the court for the bail and charge defendants a non-refundable fee
for their service (usually 10 percent of the bail). Both of these systems—the
only ones in operation until bail reforms began in the 1960s—place particular
burdens on indigent defendants, who may be unable to raise the money or
afford the bondsman's fee. A study of twenty cities during the early 1960s
found that more than half of all defendants remained in jail, often for months,
awaiting trial.[18]

Reformers attacked this incarceration as "punishment before trial." They
claimed that it cost indigent defendants their jobs, undermined family relationships, and made it more difficult for defendants to mount an effective defense.[19]
They sought to sever the connection between indigency and pretrial confine-

ment by limiting the role of bail bondsmen and by developing alternatives to monetary bail. Their reforms included:[20]

Deposit bail: Defendants secure their release by depositing a percentage of the full bail with the court, rather than with a bondsman, and recover the full amount deposited when they appear for trial.

Unsecured bail: When bail is set, defendants are released without paying any money to the court, but they are liable for the full amount if they fail to appear for trial.

Release on recognizance: Defendants with strong ties to the community, who are therefore unlikely to flee prosecution, are released on the promise that they will appear in court.

Conditional release: Defendants are released subject to certain non-monetary conditions, such as that they will seek treatment or check in with court officials periodically.

The widespread adoption of these alternative release options during the 1960s and 1970s had dramatic effects. A study of 20 cities found that the release rate rose from 48 percent of all defendants in 1962 to 67 percent in 1971, and a more recent study of eight communities found a release rate of 85 percent.[21] Despite the liberalization of pretrial release, few defendants—less than 4 percent, according to one study—try to flee or otherwise fail to appear in order to avoid conviction.[22]

However, as the number of defendants released prior to trial rose, so did concern that the release of some defendants might pose a threat to the community. Research offers some support for this concern. The eight-community study of pretrial release mentioned earlier found that 16 percent of all released defendants were rearrested prior to trial and that 30 percent of those rearrested were rearrested more than once.[23] Most states have responded to this concern by requiring judges to consider community safety, as well as the likelihood of appearance at trial, in deciding on pretrial release.[24] Critics have charged that there is no reliable basis for predicting future criminal behavior and that therefore some offenders will be unnecessarily confined awaiting trial while dangerous ones will be released.[25] In practice, the implementation of these "preventive detention" enactments has been haphazard, so it is difficult to determine how effective they really have been.[26]

Preliminary Hearings and Grand Juries

To protect against governmental abuse of its prosecutorial power, defendants in the United States cannot be tried for a felony until the case against them has been reviewed by someone other than a law enforcement official. During this process of formal accusation, the prosecutor must demonstrate that there is probable cause to believe that a crime has been committed and that the accused has committed the crime. In most states, this process of formal accusation occurs during a preliminary hearing conducted before a lower-court judge.

In federal courts and in some state courts, however, the process of formal accusation takes a different form. The Fifth Amendment to the United States Constitution requires that felony prosecutions in federal court be initiated by an indictment by a grand jury, that is, by a determination by an independent body of citizens that there is sufficient evidence to go to trial. Eighteen states likewise mandate that indictment by a grand jury precede all felony prosecutions, and six more require indictments in capital cases.[27] In these states, thus, the defendant at the preliminary hearing is bound over to a grand jury for indictment.

The Grand Jury

The grand jury differs from the trial (petit) jury in several respects:[28]

Membership and length of service: Although the grand jury, like the trial jury, is composed of ordinary citizens, its size varies from as few as six members (in Indiana) to as many as twenty-three (for federal grand juries). Moreover, whereas trial jurors sit on a single case, grand jurors are empaneled for a set term (frequently three months) and during that period the prosecutor brings a large number of cases before them for review.

Function: Grand juries, unlike petit juries, do not determine the guilt or innocence of defendants. Rather, they serve investigative and/or accusatory functions. In some states grand juries investigate issues of official corruption and organized crime. But in most states, their primary responsibility is to determine whether there is sufficient evidence to indict defendants.

Standard for decision: In most states trial juries in serious criminal cases states can only convict defendants by a unanimous vote. However, grand juries indict defendants by a plurality vote—from a simple majority to a two-thirds vote, depending on the law of the state. Moreover, the standard that grand juries use in deciding whether to indict is "probable cause" rather than the more stringent standard of "beyond a reasonable doubt."

Mode of operation: Unlike trials, grand jury hearings are conducted in secret, in part to protect the reputations of those persons against whom there is insufficient evidence for an indictment. Most states relax the rules of evidence that operate at trial: for example, in a grand jury hearing prosecutors may introduce hearsay evidence or illegally seized evidence that would be inadmissible at trial. Also in most states witnesses do not have a right to have counsel with them during grand jury proceedings.

If a grand jury concludes that there is sufficient evidence to proceed to trial, it votes an indictment or "true bill". If not, it votes "no true bill", and the case is dismissed. This requirement of grand jury indictment prior to prosecution serves, according to the United States Supreme Court, as "a primary security for the innocent against hasty, malicious, and oppressive prosecution."[29] In practice, however, prosecutors seldom find it difficult to secure a grand jury indictment. One study, for example, found that federal grand juries over the course of a year voted over 17,000 indictments but voted no true bill in less than 70 cases.[30] Even when a grand jury refuses to indict, it may be following the direction of the prosecutor, who was obliged to bring a politically sensitive case before the grand jury but did not want to prosecute. Small wonder, then, that one judge concluded that most grand juries would "indict a ham sandwich" if the prosecutor asked them to.[31]

The Preliminary Hearing

As an alternative to indictment by a grand jury, some states permit the prosecutor to present evidence at the preliminary hearing that the defendant has committed the crimes with which he is charged. The decision on whether to proceed to trial then rests with the judge presiding over the hearing. If the prosecutor fails to establish probable cause, the judge dismisses the charges, and the defendant is released. But if probable cause is established, then the defendant is held for trial.

Researchers have discovered wide variation in how jurisdictions conduct their preliminary hearings.[32] In some jurisdictions—for example, in Los Angeles—preliminary hearings resemble miniature trials, with both prosecutor and defense attorney calling and cross-examining witnesses. But in most jurisdictions, preliminary hearings are perfunctory proceedings lasting only a few minutes, with the main evidence presented by a police officer testifying from a police report. In a few jurisdictions also—Chicago is one—the preliminary hearing is used to screen cases, with judges either dismissing cases or reducing charges in a large proportion of the cases brought before them. More typical, however, is David Neubauer's finding that less than two percent of defendants had their cases terminated at preliminary hearings.[33] In jurisdictions in which judges routinely find that probable cause exists, defendants may waive their right to a preliminary hearing.

PLEA BARGAINING

As we have seen, the American system of criminal justice is designed to screen out weak cases early in the process. Thus, those cases which are not screened out are those in which the prosecutor believes that there is strong evidence of guilt. Not surprisingly, therefore, the overwhelming majority of cases that are prosecuted result in convictions. Over two-thirds of defendants who go to trial are found guilty.[34] However, most criminal cases are resolved through a defendant's admission of guilt prior to trial (see Box 6-3). In many instances defendants plead guilty in the expectation that they will receive some consideration in exchange for their plea, such as a reduction in the number or severity of the

---

BOX 6-3 PLEA BARGAINING IN COMPARATIVE PERSPECTIVE*

Other countries share with the United States the need to process large numbers of relatively routine criminal cases. However, they have developed their own mechanisms for doing so. In some countries one finds plea negotiations similar to those found in American criminal courts. In Great Britain, for example, plea bargaining flourishes despite official policies and appellate rulings discouraging the practice. One study found that roughly 85 percent of defendants pled guilty, often changing their plea from "not guilty" shortly before their trial was scheduled to begin. In most cases, defendants were induced to plead guilty by concessions on the sentence they would receive—and by pressure from the judge, who promised defendants a more severe sentence if they went to trial.

However, in Germany—and also, apparently, in other civil law countries—plea bargaining is unknown. Still, most routine cases involving less serious crimes are resolved without trial. The mechanism developed in Germany for disposing of these cases is called the penal order. This order, prepared by the prosecutor and signed by the judge, describes the wrongdoing of the defendant, the evidence gathered by the state, and the penalty to be imposed on the defendant. (The penalty cannot involve imprisonment; the most common penalties are fines or the loss of one's driver's license.) If the defendant accepts the penal order—and about 75 percent of defendants do—then the order becomes effective and has the same effect as a conviction after trial. If the defendant objects, the order is nullified, and the case is scheduled for trial. About 90 percent of those who reject penal orders are found guilty at trial.

The German use of penal orders differs from plea bargaining in several respects. First, the defendant need never appear in court. If in misdemeanor cases the process is the punishment, as Malcolm Feeley has argued,

continued on p. 201

continued from p. 200
that punishment is eliminated by the use of the penal order. The closest analogy to the penal order in American law is the traffic ticket, which allows defendants to mail in the fine or go to court and contest their innocence. Second, the penal order involves no negotiations, no offer and counter-offer. If the accused rejects the penal order, the prosecutor cannot make a second offer; the matter must go to trial. However, the accused's rejection of the penal order is not final; the defendant can accept the penal order (and the punishment it specifies) during the course of the trial or anytime up to the court's announcement of its decision. Finally, the defendant does not risk a harsher punishment by going to trial. The defendant can accept the penal order after the trial has commenced, so the penalty it specifies is not an inducement to forego trial. In addition, studies have shown that German judges do not impose a more severe punishment on those who reject penal orders and demand a trial. Put differently, defendants in Germany are not penalized for asserting their rights.

SOURCE: This analysis is based on John Baldwin and Michael McConville, "Plea Bargaining and Plea Negotiation in England," *Law & Society Review* 13 (Winter 1979): 287-307; William L. F. Felstiner, "Plea Contracts in West Germany," *Law & Society Review* 13 (Winter 1979): 309-325; and Malcolm M. Feeley, *The Process Is the Punishment; Handling Cases in a Lower Criminal Court* (New York: Russell Sage Foundation, 1979).

charges against them and/or a more lenient sentence. Often this expectation is based on a specific agreement negotiated between the prosecutor and the defense attorney and ratified by the judge. The process by which such agreements are negotiated is known as plea bargaining.

The Process of Plea Bargaining

Although "there probably is no such thing as a typical criminal court," certain aspects of plea bargaining are relatively uniform from court to court.[35] Plea negotiations are generally initiated by the defense attorney, whether public defender or private counsel, rather than by the prosecutor. When a defense attorney believes that her client is likely to be convicted at trial, she may approach the prosecutor offering a plea of guilty. In exchange she seeks concessions relating to either the charges against the defendant or the sentence to be imposed.

The fact that defense attorneys typically initiate plea negotiations suggests that most defendants whose cases progress to this stage are in fact guilty of criminal violations or at least that they could not prove their innocence at trial. This is hardly surprising, given the screening of cases that occurs early in the criminal justice process. Experienced defense attorneys readily admit that most of their clients are guilty; as one put it:

> [w]e make an initial determination whether we've got a defense, and many times we don't. When somebody's apprehended in the midst of a break, caught in a store or a house, you have to go some to explain what you're doing there at two or three o'clock in the morning. We get a fair number of these. If you are apprehended fleeing the scene of a crime, you are going to be hard pressed to explain why he's running away from the scene.[36]

Yet the virtual certainty of conviction at trial does not prevent plea bargaining. Prosecutors are willing to offer concessions even in so-called "dead bang" cases, in which the evidence of guilt is conclusive. Thus at times defense attorneys best represent their clients' interests by encouraging them to plead guilty rather than by taking their cases to trial.

Plea bargaining may make sense for the defendant because the prosecutor can offer important concessions in exchange for a guilty plea. A defendant may face multiple charges arising from a series of crimes or even from a single incident. For example, a person who gets drunk and takes a car for a joyride might be charged with grand larceny, possession of a stolen automobile, use of an automobile without authorization from the owner, drunk driving, and reckless driving.[37] The prosecutor may then offer to drop some charges or reduce others—for instance, from grand larceny to petit larceny—in exchange for a guilty plea. In so doing, of course, she also reduces the sentence that a defendant might possibly receive upon conviction. If the"discount" is substantial, the defendant may have a strong incentive to plead guilty. In addition, the prosecutor may agree to recommend a relatively lenient sentence or to refrain from demanding a harsh one in exchange for a guilty plea. Faced with the choice between an assured sentence and the possibility of a more severe one if convicted at trial, the defendant may avoid the risk by pleading guilty.

Plea negotiations characteristically reflect established patterns of interaction between prosecutors and defense attorneys.[38] In many jurisdictions a single prosecutor handles all cases arising in a particular judge's courtroom. Public defenders' offices, which represent the majority of defendants, often operate on the same basis, assigning their defenders to specific courtrooms. Even when defendants can afford private counsel, they typically select someone from the local criminal bar, who has represented numerous defendants in that court. As a result, when a prosecutor and defense attorney (and possibly the judge in the case) enter into plea negotiations, they usually have dealt with each other regularly in the past, including in cases quite similar to the one under discussion.

This personal and professional familiarity facilitates plea negotiations by promoting easy interaction between the attorneys. Even more important, the outcomes of negotiations in previous cases furnishes a basis for resolving the prime issue in any plea bargain, namely, what is an appropriate punishment for the defendant. If the defense attorney is attempting to convince the prosecutor that his client should be given probation, he may bring up previous instances in which the prosecutor had agreed to probation for defendants charged with similar offenses. If previous defendants had received jail time for that offense, he may emphasize factors which distinguish his client from them (such as a stable family life or no prior criminal record) in order to justify a more favorable outcome. The prosecutor, on the other hand, independently considers how this case resembles past cases and whether any factors aggravate the situation and warrant unusual severity. But once the prosecutor and defense attorney have resolved the factual aspects of the case, that is, the nature of the crime and the character of the defendant, their settlement of similar cases in the past guides them in determining what the case "is worth." In other words, because both prosecutor and defense attorney share the assumption that like cases should be treated alike, plea bargains reflect a rough system of precedent in which the outcomes of past negotiations provide standards that govern the resolution of current ones.

If the defendant accepts the settlement they have negotiated, the attorneys then recommend that the judge resolve the case in line with their agreement. Some judges are actively involved in plea negotiations from the very outset, in part to expedite the flow of cases and in part to influence sentencing, which they consider a judicial prerogative. Because they participated in the negotiations, they will of course ratify the plea agreement. However, for judges who do not participate in plea negotiations (and they are probably a majority), their first involvement with a case occurs when they decide whether or not to accept the proposed plea bargain.

Although in theory judges can reject the agreements negotiated by the attorneys, they usually are reluctant to do so. Because both the prosecutor and defense attorney agreed to the plea bargain, the judge may well conclude that their agreement adequately protects the interests of both the community and the defendant. In addition, the prosecutor and defense attorney can supply the judge with information supporting their recommendation, and she usually has little basis for a contrary assessment of the case. Furthermore, if the judge rejects a plea bargain, the defendant may elect to go to trial, something the judge is usually interested in avoiding. Finally, the judge's desire to maintain a harmonious working relationship with attorneys who regularly practice before her promotes an inclination to accept their recommendations. As James Eisenstein and Herbert Jacob have put it, "The higher the proportion of dispositions accounted for by the same set of participants, the more interdependent they become."[39]

Nevertheless, the interdependence of judge, prosecutor, and defense attorney enhances the judge's indirect influence over plea bargains. The prosecutor and defense attorney, mindful that the judge can reject their recommendations, must factor the judge's views into their discussions. This necessity of anticipating and taking account of the judge's perspective means that all participants influence the outcomes of plea negotiations.

Why Plea Bargaining Occurs

The most common view, often endorsed by judges and practicing attorneys, is that plea bargaining is a response to the case pressures that afflict all those involved in the criminal courts.[40] According to this view, escalating crime rates have increased the number of cases coming to the courts, often without any corresponding increase in the resources available for dealing with them. Courts have therefore turned to plea bargaining as a way of resolving cases more expeditiously and reducing delay. Underlying this view are several key assumptions: that plea bargaining, like the burgeoning caseloads that have caused it, is a relatively recent phenomenon; that plea bargaining is a necessary evil rather than a conscious policy choice, a second-best means of dealing with defendants; and that with sufficient resources courts would decide criminal cases through trials rather than by plea bargaining.

Recent research, however, does not support this account of plea bargaining. Although American courts actively discouraged guilty pleas during the early nineteenth century, by the early 1900s plea bargaining had become the primary means of processing cases in many criminal courts.[41] This can be seen not only in the frequency of guilty pleas—in 1926 over ninety percent of all felony convictions in Manhattan and Brooklyn resulted from such pleas—but also in prosecutors' willingness to reduce charges against defendants. In New York in 1926, for instance, 85 percent of all guilty pleas in felony cases were to offenses less serious than the original charges, and in Chicago the figure was 78 percent.[42] Because these figures suggest that plea bargaining was as frequent in the 1920s as it is today, it follows that recent increases in crime cannot explain the prevalence of plea bargaining. Furthermore, if plea bargaining occurs because of a need to deal with heavy caseloads, then those courts with particularly heavy caseloads should rely on plea bargaining more than should courts with lighter caseloads. But this is not the case. Some low-volume courts rely heavily on plea bargaining, while some high-volume courts do not.[43] Indeed, some high-volume courts—for example, those in Baltimore and Los Angeles—

conduct large numbers of trials.[44] Thus caseload pressures alone do not account for plea bargaining.

Another widely held view is that prosecutors plea bargain when they lack sufficient evidence to obtain a conviction at trial.[45] According to this view, a prosecutor's willingness to plea bargain is a sign of weakness, an indication that she must sacrifice her aim of securing the full punishment the law allows in order to ensure that the accused receives some punishment. Although the strength of the evidence affects plea bargaining in some instances, the very frequency of plea negotiations underscores the inadequacy of this explanation. If the evidence were weak in the vast majority of cases, defense attorneys would plea bargain less and take more cases to trial. And if the evidence was strong in most cases, as might be expected after weak cases were screened out, then prosecutors would plea bargain less frequently. This explanation cannot account for the behavior of either defense attorneys or prosecutors because it assumes, quite inaccurately, that prosecutors seek the harshest possible punishment for defendants.

But if neither caseload pressures nor evidentiary problems account for plea bargaining, what does? One view is that attorneys and judges engage in plea bargaining in order to enhance their discretion, so that they can seek *what they perceive* as substantive justice in each case.[46] According to this view, the participants in plea bargaining all concur in the view that strict application of the criminal law does not produce justice. Because the law necessarily defines offenses in general terms (e.g., robbery, assault) and prescribes penalties (or a limited range of penalties) for them, it cannot take into account distinctive elements of the individual case. Therefore an insistence on strict application of the law actually means treating dissimilar cases as similar. Furthermore, when legislators enact criminal laws, the penalties they prescribe may reflect their strong disapproval of the actions they are outlawing rather than a thoughtful consideration of what punishment is appropriate. Thus plea bargaining, according to this view, permits those actually involved in the administration of justice to escape the rigidity and excessive harshness of the criminal law and to focus on the character of the defendant and the actual nature of his offense in determining punishment.

This does not mean, of course, that eavesdroppers on plea negotiations are treated to extended discussions about the nature of justice. Rather, because the participants in plea bargaining have dealt with each other on numerous other occasions, previous understandings usually permit a quick determination of the "worth" of a case and the punishment which is appropriate. According to this explanation, then, plea bargaining is not a sort of assembly-line justice necessitated by heavy caseloads. Rather, it is an attempt to individualize criminal justice.

Other studies have attributed the prevalence of plea bargaining less to a shared concern for substantive justice than to the shared interest of attorneys and judges in processing cases expeditiously.[47] This interest in the speedy disposition of cases does not depend on caseload pressures, for it exists in both low-volume and high-volume courts. For private attorneys, the concern for speedy disposition derives largely from monetary considerations: few defendants can afford the costs associated with an extended trial, such as investigative work, trial preparation, and court time, so private attorneys usually lose money when cases go to trial. But plea bargaining enables them both to benefit their clients (with reduced sentences) and to take on more cases, thereby increasing their income. For judges and for attorneys (prosecutors and public defenders) employed by the state, compensation does not depend on the number of cases processed. However, other incentives promote a common concern for expeditious case processing. Chief among these is the natural desire to reduce one's workload. As Peter Nardulli has observed:

> When the cases on their respective calls are completed in a given day, normally the formal work requirements of the judge, public defender, and prosecutor are fulfilled. Thus, it is in their mutual self-interest to process expeditiously the cases on the call for a given day, regardless of how many cases are scheduled.[48]

Plea bargaining not only allows cases to be disposed of more quickly but also lightens the workloads of judges and attorneys, who can dispense with time-consuming preparation for trial. Moreover, participants in plea bargaining can justify the practice by insisting that trial is rarely warranted because weak cases (those in which there is a serious doubt about guilt) are screened out early in the process. Thus the only question in the remaining cases is the appropriate punishment for the defendant. Furthermore, each participant in plea bargaining recognizes that expeditious case processing requires a willingness to cooperate, that the refusal to do so imposes burdens on other participants and thus may reduce their willingness to cooperate on future cases. In sum, the mutual interdependence of judge, prosecutor, and defense attorney, the prospect of continuing interaction among them, and the common goal of expeditious case processing all serve to dilute adversariness and to promote the cooperative resolution of cases through plea bargaining.

Attacks on Plea Bargaining

Despite the prevalence of plea bargaining, or perhaps because of it, many critics have argued that plea bargaining is an inappropriate and undesirable method of establishing sentencing policy.[49]   According to these critics, plea bargaining diminishes the role of the judge by investing prosecutors with excessive control over sentencing decisions.   In addition, the discretion in sentencing that plea bargaining affords serves to undermine the decisions on punishment established by the state legislature, in effect transferring power from a popularly elected and accountable body to officials whose actions are not subject to public scrutiny.

Critics have also attacked the sentencing policies that plea bargaining promotes.   Some charge that plea bargaining coerces defendants into waiving their constitutional right to assert their innocence by penalizing them for going to trial.[50]   For if pleading guilty guarantees defendants more lenient sentences, the pressure on defendants to plea bargain may be considerable, especially for those who cannot raise bail and must remain in jail until trial.   Other critics complain that plea bargaining results in excessively lenient sentences because prosecutors must offer substantial concessions in order to obtain guilty pleas.[51]   As a result, dangerous offenders escape the harsh punishment they deserve and soon threaten the community once again.   This undermines both respect for the law and its ability to deter crime.   Still other critics, noting the interdependence that develops among the participants in plea bargaining, worry that defense attorneys end up sacrificing their clients' interests in order to maintain good relations with prosecutors.[52]   Finally, some critics insist that because plea bargaining permits the exercise of broad discretion free from regulation and publicity, it fosters favoritism, corruption, and discrimination.[53]   At the very least, it aggravates the problem of securing equal treatment for offenders, because similar offenses may be dealt with differently in various parts of the state or even from courtroom to courtroom in the same community.

Responding to these criticisms, several jurisdictions during the 1970s and 1980s undertook to restrict or abolish plea bargaining.   The most successful effort took place in Alaska.   In 1975 the state's Attorney General, Avrum Gross, prohibited prosecutors from offering concessions as a means of obtaining guilty pleas in felony and misdemeanor cases.   Gross's ban, which effectively abolished plea bargaining in the state, produced some striking and rather surprising results:

contrary to expectations, guilty pleas in criminal cases declined only marginally (from 94 percent to 92 percent of all cases), so the number of trials increased very little;

when trials were held, prosecutorial success increased, so there was no decline in the percentage of defendants convicted;

because the number of trials did not increase substantially after the ban on plea bargaining, the courts did not experience case backlogs; in fact, the time required to process a case actually decreased;

the conviction rates and sentences for persons charged with serious crimes of violence did not change as a result of the ban on plea bargaining, thus suggesting that serious offenders were not escaping punishment as a result of plea bargaining;

persons charged with less serious property offenses—such as burglary, receiving stolen property, and malicious destruction of property—tended to receive more severe sentences than previously, and this was particularly true for first offenders.[54]

Evaluating Plea Bargaining

What conclusions can be drawn from our description of plea bargaining, our survey of the criticisms directed at it, and our review of efforts to abolish it? First of all, as critics claim, plea bargaining does transfer control over sentencing from state legislatures and from judges operating within statutory guidelines to judges, prosecutors, and defense attorneys collectively exercising broad discretion. Yet the critics' charge that this insulates sentencing from popular control is only partially valid. For one thing, as the successful abolition of plea bargaining in Alaska and elsewhere shows, popular efforts to reassert control can succeed. More importantly, studies of criminal courts in various communities confirm that public opinion, as embodied in the broader political and legal culture of the community, does constrain participants in plea bargaining.[55] Of course, the fact that public opinion affects plea bargaining does not by itself legitimate the practice. The fundamental question is whether plea bargaining promotes justice in sentencing.

Some other criticisms of plea bargaining seem on inspection to be complaints about the American criminal justice system in general rather than about plea bargaining. Take, for example, the charge that plea bargaining creates opportunities for favoritism, discrimination, and corruption. Clearly it does, and presumably one could find instances of such abuses.[56] However, the real question is not the potential for abuse but rather the frequency of abuse. Even more, it is whether such abuses are more prevalent in cases that are plea bargained than in cases which go to trial. There simply is no evidence that plea bargaining is more infected by corruption and discrimination than are other modes of disposing of cases.

The charge that plea bargaining promotes excessive leniency in sentencing, endangering the populace by putting violent criminals back on the street, likewise might be better addressed to the American criminal justice system as a whole. For although sentencing in American courts may be too lenient, there is little evidence that plea bargaining by itself promotes lenient sentences.

Contrary to the views of many attorneys and judges, the most sophisticated studies of the issue have discovered no evidence that defendants receive more lenient sentences by plea bargaining.[57] Moreover, the more serious the crime, the less likely plea bargaining is to occur. For one thing, defendants charged with serious offenses, who face the prospect of serving time in prison, are more likely to take their chances at trial and less likely to plea bargain. And prosecutors, mindful of community sentiment, are less willing to cut "sweet" deals with such offenders. When plea bargaining does occur in serious cases, offenders still receive lengthy sentences. The studies of sentencing in Alaska confirm the point: the sentences serious offenders received when plea bargaining was legal were just as severe as those they received after it was abolished.

More troubling is the charge that in plea bargaining defendants are coerced into pleading guilty and waiving their constitutional right to trial. Advocates of plea bargaining observe that most defendants are eager to plead guilty. They even plead guilty when, as in Alaska after the abolition of plea bargaining, they can expect no concessions for their admission of guilt. However, critics insist that defendants' willingness to plead guilty and plea bargain often depends upon their perception that they will be penalized if they go to trial. This fear may be groundless. Judges have insisted that they penalize defendants who demand a trial only when their demand is "frivolous", that is, when they have no basis for contesting the charges against them.[58] And as we have seen, the best empirical evidence suggests that defendants who go to trial do not automatically receive harsher sentences. Yet ultimately this evidence is not decisive. Many judges and attorneys who participate in plea bargaining believe that defendants who go to trial receive harsher sentences.[59] Insofar as defendants take their cues from what their attorneys say, they are likely to share the belief that conviction at trial will lead to a harsher sentence. Whether this perception deters defendants from contesting their innocence remains an open question.

Also troubling is the charge that the established working relationships among participants in plea bargaining deter defense attorneys from vigorously pursuing their clients' interests. Advocates of plea bargaining deny that the strong pressures toward cooperation undermine the vigorous representation of defendants. Prosecutors, they insist, expect defense counsel to pursue legitimate avenues for acquittal and do not penalize such efforts by refusing to plea bargain.[60] Somewhat inconsistently, they also contend that a less adversarial stance usually works to the benefit of defendants, who are usually guilty of the offenses with which they are charged and eager to negotiate a plea. Still, many defense attorneys are ambivalent about their close relationship with prosecutors, concerned that the need to maintain harmonious relations leads them to become "part of the system."[61] Whether plea bargaining is a legitimate and desirable element of American criminal justice thus remains a perplexing and hotly contested issue.

POLICY ISSUES IN CRIMINAL JUSTICE

Over the past three decades, as crime rates in the United States have soared, conservative critics have blamed the courts for much of the rise in crime.[62] By freeing criminals on "legal technicalities" and giving lenient sentences to those who are convicted, these critics contend, the courts have allowed dangerous criminals to return to the streets and have undermined the deterrent effect of the criminal law. To redress the situation, they have proposed several policy changes that would affect the operation of the courts. Among these are the reform or elimination of the exclusionary rule, which prevents the use of illegally obtained evidence to secure convictions; the reform or elimination of the insanity defense in criminal trials; and the establishment of minimum sentences for offenders.

Liberal critics have also challenged the sentencing practices of the courts but from a quite different perspective.[63] They contend that those guilty of the same crime often receive quite different sentences, with particularly harsh sentences meted out to the poor and to members of racial minorities. Reforms must be instituted, they argue, to ensure more equitable sentencing.

Yet not everyone endorses these criticisms. Proponents of the exclusionary rule believe that it deters police from violating constitutional rights and maintains the integrity of the judicial process.[64] Supporters of the insanity defense contend that it reaffirms the moral underpinnings of criminal justice by distinguishing between those who are and those who are not responsible for their actions.[65] And some researchers have challenged claims that courts are unduly lenient or that they discriminate in sentencing offenders.[66]

In this section we examine the policy debates over the exclusionary rule, the insanity defense, and the sentencing of criminals. We analyze both the justifications offered for current policies and practices and the objections to them. We also consider the empirical evidence bearing on the competing claims and assess the likely consequences of the reforms that have been proposed.

The Exclusionary Rule

The exclusionary rule forbids the use in a criminal prosecution of any evidence that is illegally obtained by law enforcement officials. This evidence is usually either physical evidence, such as drugs or weapons, uncovered through illegal searches in violation of the Fourth Amendment, or confessions extracted from defendants in violation of their rights under the Fifth or Sixth Amendments. When a trial judge rules that a police officer violated the defendant's rights in securing some evidence, the prosecution cannot use that evidence to obtain a conviction. Nor can it use any additional evidence the police obtained by following leads generated by the initial illegality—what courts have referred to as "the fruit of the poisonous tree".[67]   Even prior to trial, the exclusionary rule may have an effect. If the only evidence of guilt is inadmissible, the prosecutor has no case and thus is unlikely to charge a suspect.

Yet the exclusionary rule does not immunize lawbreakers from prosecution. Prosecutors can still pursue convictions with any evidence that the police have obtained legally. Put differently, the exclusionary rule merely places the government in the same position it would been in had the illegal search or interrogation not taken place. Moreover, if a conviction is overturned on appeal because illegally obtained evidence was used to secure it, the defendant can be retried with that evidence excluded from consideration.

The Development of the Exclusionary Rule

The United States is unique in its reliance on the exclusionary rule as a means of dealing with police misconduct. Great Britain, Canada, and other common-law countries admit all reliable evidence at trial but permit suits for damages against police officers alleged to have committed illegal acts. No civil-law country disciplines its police by excluding illegally seized evidence. Indeed, for most of the nation's history, American courts too followed the common law rule and permitted the introduction of all probative evidence at trial.

The adoption of the exclusionary rule began early in the twentieth century, when a few states banned the admission of illegally seized evidence as a matter of state law.[68] In *Weeks* v. *United States* (1914), the United States Supreme Court adopted the exclusionary rule for federal prosecutions, maintaining that the exclusion of illegally seized evidence was necessary to protect defendants' Fourth Amendment rights.[69] But *Weeks* had no direct effect on the states, which conduct over 99 percent of criminal prosecutions. Even after the Court applied the Fourth Amendment's search-and-seizure requirements to the states in *Wolf* v. *Colorado* (1949), most states did not adopt the exclusionary rule—as late as 1960, only half the states required the suppression of illegally seized evidence.[70] This changed dramatically after the Court's decision in *Mapp* v. *Ohio* (1961).[71] In *Mapp* the Supreme Court extended the exclusionary rule to the states, inaugurating (in the view of its critics) a constitutional revolution. Although in recent years the Court has limited somewhat the reach of the exclusionary rule, it continues to affect the sorts of evidence admissible at trial.[72]

Underlying the Supreme Court's decisions establishing the exclusionary rule are three complementary arguments. One is that the exclusionary rule is necessary to vindicate the protections of the Fourth and Fifth Amendments. Indeed, advocates of the exclusionary rule have turned the critics' rhetoric back on them. If *Mapp* truly inaugurated a constitutional revolution, the obvious question is why—after all, the ruling did not institute any new requirements regarding searches and seizures. The answer, according to proponents of the exclusionary rule, is that prior to *Mapp* the Fourth Amendment's requirements were routinely ignored. Yet if that is true, it demonstrates that other remedies did not adequately safeguard Fourth Amendment rights.

Advocates argue that the exclusionary rule can safeguard those rights because it deters police misconduct. By preventing convictions on the basis of illegally seized evidence, the exclusionary rule removes the incentive for police to gather evidence illegally. As a result, far fewer unconstitutional searches or interrogations will occur. Thus the exclusionary rule not only vindicates the rights of a defendant subjected to an illegal search or interrogation but also deters future police misconduct, thereby protecting all citizens.

In addition, proponents maintain that the exclusionary rule protects the integrity of the judicial process by preventing the government from benefiting from the misconduct of its agents. To permit the use of illegally obtained evidence in court would signal an implicit approval of the officers' methods in obtaining the evidence. This would convey the message that it is okay to violate constitutional rights for a good cause. But the exclusion of such evidence sends a quite different message: the government must respect rights even as it pursues its legitimate ends.

The Case Against the Exclusionary Rule

Not surprisingly, critics of the exclusionary rule dispute these arguments. They charge, first of all, that the exclusionary rule requires the release of dangerous criminals. For under the exclusionary rule the reliability of the evidence which has been illegally obtained has no effect on its admissibility. If a suspect under extreme duress confesses to a crime, there may be reason to doubt the veracity of his statements. However, if a police officer discovers a stolen wallet during an illegal search of a suspect, the wallet provides clear evidence of guilt. Yet in neither case is the evidence admissible. This holds true no matter how serious the charges against a defendant. Even if the illegally seized evidence conclusively proves that the defendant is guilty of murder, it cannot be used to convict him, and if there is no other evidence adequate to obtain a conviction, the defendant is released. To opponents of the exclusionary rule, this is too high a cost to pay. They insist that all pertinent and reliable evidence should be admitted at trial, so that guilty persons receive their just punishment.

Critics also charge that the exclusionary rule is too inflexible. In determining the admissibility of evidence, the exclusionary rule does not consider how seriously the defendant's rights were infringed in obtaining that evidence. The same penalty of exclusion operates whether the police officer's invasion of the defendant's rights was slight and inadvertent or blatant and intentional. This may mean, in the words of Justice Benjamin Cardozo, that "the criminal is to go free because the constable blundered."[73]   Some critics of the exclusionary rule have therefore proposed a "good faith" exception to the rule, permitting the introduction of evidence resulting from illegal searches or interrogations that officers believed were lawful. This would preserve the rule only for intentional, and therefore serious, invasions of constitutional rights.

Critics contend that the exclusionary rule is ineffective in protecting rights. It can deter police misconduct only if police engage in illegal searches in order to develop evidence for trial. But it has no effect on illegal searches undertaken for other reasons—to harass individuals or to confiscate contraband, for example. Even when police search in order to gather evidence, the exclusionary rule can deter police misconduct only if the offending officer realizes that he is violating Fourth Amendment rights. The officer who mistakenly believes a search is permissible under the Fourth Amendment will not be deterred by the exclusionary rule.

Finally, critics claim that the exclusionary rule protects only criminals, not law-abiding citizens. If police officers illegally ransack a person's house and find evidence of criminality, that evidence is excluded at trial. However, if they discover no evidence of crime, there is no evidence to exclude and no trial at which to exclude it, so the exclusionary rule affords no relief to the victim of the illegal search. Thus opponents propose replacing the exclusionary rule with other mechanisms, such as civil suits against the police by victims of illegal searches or interrogations.

The Evidence on the Exclusionary Rule

The debate over the exclusionary rule largely revolves around competing claims about the rule's effect on criminal justice. Numerous studies have been conducted to assess those claims, and in this section we consider their findings.

Does the Exclusionary Rule Deter Police Misconduct?

If the exclusionary rule has a deterrent effect, one would expect that illegal police searches would decline after *Mapp*. In a few jurisdictions researchers did find a decline in the number of defense motions to suppress evidence as illegally seized, which might signal a decrease in illegal searches.[74]   However, in several jurisdictions there was an increase after *Mapp* in the number of motions to suppress evidence as illegally obtained.[75]   One might attribute this increase to the failure of the exclusionary rule to deter police misconduct.   Alternatively, however, the increase might indicate a greater willingness on the part of defense attorneys to challenge police searches because illegally seized evidence would be excluded at trial. Thus the available evidence does not conclusively resolve the deterrence issue.

What Effect Does the Exclusionary Rule Have on Convictions?

Critics contend that large numbers of guilty persons go free because of the exclusionary rule. However, empirical studies of the effects of the exclusionary rule do not bear out this claim. A study of prosecutions in California, conducted by the National Institute of Justice, found that prosecutors decided not to press charges because of illegal-search problems in 2.4 percent of drug cases and in less than 1 percent of their cases overall.[76] A nine-county study of criminal courts found that defense attorneys filed motions to suppress evidence in over 7 percent of all cases but that only 5 percent of those motions succeeded (with a slightly higher success rate in drugs and weapons cases).[77] The study also found that the defendants were convicted in one-third of those cases in which evidence was suppressed.[78] Thus very few defendants escape conviction because of the exclusionary rule.

Does the Exclusionary Rule Let Dangerous Criminals Go Free?

Even if few defendants avoid conviction as a result of the exclusionary rule, those defendants who do may pose a serious threat to public safety. In general, however, studies of the exclusionary rule do not support that notion. For example, the nine-county study found that most cases "lost" as a result of the exclusionary rule involved so-called victimless crimes (drug possession or possession of a weapon), while fewer than 20 percent involved serious offenses, such as armed robbery, burglary, and arson. Moreover, if the defendants in the "lost" cases had been convicted and received sentences comparable to those given to defendants convicted of the same offenses, almost two-thirds would have received jail sentences of less than six months.[79] These findings suggest that the number of truly dangerous criminals freed by the exclusionary rule is very small—but of course they do not determine whether the release of even a few dangerous criminals is too heavy a price to pay for the exclusionary rule.

Alternatives to the Exclusionary Rule?

Critics concede that if the exclusionary rule is to be eliminated because it is ineffective or results in too many "lost convictions," then some other means must be devised to vindicate constitutional rights and prevent police misconduct.

The two most frequently proposed alternatives are the "good faith" exception to the exclusionary rule and a reliance on civil suits against those who violate constitutional rights.

The idea of a "good faith" exception has received considerable support—it was recommended by the Attorney General's Task Force on Violent Crime in 1981 and has been endorsed in part in recent Supreme Court decisions.[80] Under this proposal, illegally obtained evidence can be used at trial only if the officers who obtained the evidence acted in good faith, that is, with a reasonable belief that they were complying with constitutional requirements. Proponents note that the "good faith" exception retains the exclusionary rule when it might serve a deterrent function. But barring evidence obtained in good faith cannot deter police misconduct because the problem is a lack of knowledge about constitutional requirements, not an unwillingness to observe them. Unfortunately, there are no data establishing how frequently constitutional violations by the police result from good faith mistakes rather than intentional disregard of constitutional mandates.

Many critics who favor abolishing the exclusionary rule have proposed that the United States emulate Great Britain in permitting civil suits against police officers by those whose constitutional rights have been violated.[81] This would not only ensure the availability of all reliable evidence in criminal cases but also offer recourse for innocent victims of illegal searches. Yet proponents of the exclusionary rule caution that juries would sympathize with police officers and be reluctant to decide in favor of "disreputable" plaintiffs, especially those who had committed criminal offenses. The lack of success of citizen suits against police officers offers at least partial support for this contention.[82] It does not appear that the exclusionary rule will soon be eliminated.

The Insanity Defense

In 1981 John W. Hinckley, Jr. fired six shots at President Ronald Reagan. One hit the president in the chest, two wounded members of the president's security detail, and a fourth penetrated to the brain of Press Secretary James Brady, permanently disabling him. Yet a year later, a jury found Hinckley not guilty by reason of insanity, concluding that the government had failed to prove beyond a reasonable doubt that Hinckley was sane at the time of the shooting. Not surprisingly, public opinion was outraged. Some people, thinking that Hinckley had hoodwinked the jury, proposed tightening the legal definition of insanity, while others—including Attorney General William French Smith—demanded the abolition of the insanity defense.

The outrage that greeted the Hinckley verdict recalled earlier controversy over the insanity defense. Queen Victoria herself criticized the acquittal by reason of insanity of Daniel M'Naghten, who in 1843—under the delusion that he was being persecuted by the Pope, the Jesuits, and Prime Minister Robert Peel—mistakenly shot Peel's secretary. (As a verse of the period criticizing the verdict put it, "Ye people of England exult and be glad/For you're now at the will of the merciless mad."[83]) Yet the importance of the M'Naghten case derived less from the unpopularity of its verdict than from the standard it established, the so-called M'Naghten test, for determining whether defendants were responsible for their criminal actions.

Tests of Insanity

The criminal law justifies holding individuals responsible for their conduct on the assumption that they have the ability to choose between acceptable and unacceptable behavior. This assumption also supplies the rationale for the insanity defense: the criminal law should not punish those who are unable to choose between acceptable and unacceptable behavior. But how does one define that inability to choose which exempts a person from the operation of the criminal law? Under the M'Naghten test, a defendant is responsible for criminal actions unless

> the party accused was labouring under such a defect of reason, from disease of the mind, as not to know the nature and quality of the act he was doing; or, if he did know it, he did not know he was doing what was wrong.[84]

Under this test, as under other insanity standards, the incapacity must come from mental disease—an incapacity as a result of drunkenness or drug addiction does not excuse criminal conduct. What is distinctive about the M'Naghten test is its emphasis on the cognitive capacity of defendants, that is, their ability to distinguish right from wrong. Lack of understanding, not an inability to control one's behavior, is decisive.

For most of the twentieth century, efforts to reform the insanity defense have focused on introducing a volitional element into the legal definition of insanity (see Table 6-1). Put simply, defendants would be judged insane not only if they lacked the ability to distinguish right from wrong but also if mental illness prevented them from choosing socially acceptable behavior. This is reflected in the "irresistible impulse" test, which was adopted in some states as a supplement to the M'Naghten test, permitting the acquittal of defendants who could not control their conduct, even though they knew it was wrong. It is also reflected in the American Law Institute's Model Penal Code, which has provided the basis for reform in several states. According to the ALI Code:

TABLE 6-1 INSANITY DEFENSE STANDARDS					
American Law Institute	M'Naghten Rule	M'Naghten Rule and Irresistible Impulse	Guilty But Mentally Ill*	Insanity Test Abolished	No Specific Test
Alabama	Arizona	Colorado	Alaska	Idaho	New Hampshire
Alaska	Delaware	Florida[a]	Delaware	Montana	
Arkansas	Iowa	New Mexico	Georgia	Utah	
California	Kansas	New York[a]			
Georgia	Louisiana	Virginia			
Hawaii	Mississippi	Illinois			
Illinois	*Nebraska	Indiana			
Indiana	Nevada	Kentucky			
Kentucky	New Jersey	Michigan			
Maine	North Carolina	New Mexico			
Maryland	North Dakota[a]	Pennsylvania			
Massachusetts	Oklahoma	South Dakota			
Michigan	Pennsylvania	Utah			
Missouri	South Carolina				
Ohio[a]	South Dakota[a]				
Oregon	Washington				
Rhode Island[a]					
Tennessee					
Texas[a]					
Vermont					
West Virginia					
Wisconsin					

* - States that have instituted the "guilty but mentally ill" verdict appear in other columns listing insanity standards because they employ those standards in determining whether a defendant is mentally ill. Utah has abolished the insanity defense but, somewhat inconsistently, retained the verdict of guilty but mentally ill.

SOURCE: Rita J. Simon and David E. Aaronson, *The Insanity Defense; A Critical Assessment of Law and Policy in the Post-Hinckley Era* (New York: Praeger, 1988), Appendix, pp. 251-263.

KEY: a = With some modification.

A person is not responsible for criminal conduct if at the time of such conduct as a result of mental disease or defect he lacks substantial capacity either to appreciate the criminality of his conduct or to conform his conduct to the requirements of the law.[85]

Although the ALI standard resembles the M'Naghten test, it includes both cognitive and volitional elements and seems, in the use of "appreciate" rather than "know," to permit consideration of whether the defendant was emotionally as well as intellectually aware of the significance of his conduct.[86]

Following the jury's verdict in the Hinckley case, however, reform efforts took a decidedly different direction, as the federal government and over thirty states reconsidered the insanity defense. In the Comprehensive Crime Control Act of 1984, the federal government shifted the burden of proof on the issue of insanity—the defense would have to prove that the accused was insane at the time of the crime, rather than the government having to prove he was not. It also narrowed somewhat the legal definition of insanity by in effect resurrecting the M'Naghten standard for federal prosecutions. Several states also tightened their requirements for insanity acquittals and for the release of offenders acquitted by reason of insanity. Finally, eleven states followed the example of Michigan, which in 1975 had attempted to reduce the use of the insanity defense by establishing the verdict of "guilty but mentally ill."[87]

The Effects of the Insanity Defense

Although no nationwide data exist, various studies indicate that few defendants plead not guilty by reason of insanity (NGRI) and even fewer defendants are acquitted on that basis. According to one study, successful NGRI pleas amounted to only 1/20 of 1 percent of all cases handled by the Office of the Public Defender in New Jersey.[88] However, researchers did find that the test for determining insanity affects both the frequency of insanity pleas and their success—apparently, jurors do attempt to apply the standard outlined by judges in their instructions to the jury.[89] Perhaps surprisingly, the establishment of the "guilty but mentally ill" verdict has not decreased NGRI pleas or acquittals. Instead, it appears that those defendants in Michigan who pled guilty but mentally ill would have simply pled guilty in the absence of that additional verdict.[90]

Just who are the defendants pleading NGRI, and with what crimes are they charged? Highly publicized cases, like that of John Hinckley, suggest that defendants plead insanity only when they face severe punishment for violent crimes. But research on this point is inconclusive. A study of insanity acquittees in Hawaii found that only 22 percent were charged with murder, and that although slightly over half the acquittals were in cases involving crimes against persons (e.g., homicide, rape, assault), a sizable number involved crimes against property (e.g., burglary) or crimes against public order (e.g., indecent exposure).[91] A New York study found that as many as 70 percent of NGRI acquittals involved violent crimes, but research on NGRI acquittees in Colorado found only 19 percent were charged with murder.[92]

Finally, many states commit all defendants found not guilty by reason of insanity for a fifty-day observation period before determining whether they are fit to be released. However, few are released at the conclusion of that observation period. Indeed, several studies have found that in comparison with those convicted and sentenced, insanity acquittees tend to spend an equivalent time in confinement for violent crimes such as murder or attempted murder and more time in confinement for less serious crimes.[93] In sum, recent research suggests that defendants do not "beat the rap" if they successfully plead not guilty by reason of insanity.

Sentencing

From the late 1940s to the early 1970s, the idea of rehabilitation dominated the sentencing of criminals in the United States. It was assumed that the aim of imprisonment was to change the characters, attitudes, and behavior of offenders, both to benefit them and to make them less a threat to the society.[94] Punishment was thus to be tailored to the offender, with the length of confinement depending less upon the character of the offense and more upon how long it took to rehabilitate the offender. To fit the punishment to the offender, sentencing policy emphasized broad discretion for judges in sentencing and the use of indeterminate sentences: prisoners were sentenced for a range of years, and the prison parole board released offenders when they demonstrated sufficient signs of rehabilitation.

In the early 1970s, this understanding of punishment came under attack from a variety of directions. Conservatives charged that the emphasis on rehabilitation promoted excessive leniency in sentencing and argued that punishment should serve the purposes of retribution and incapacitation. Liberals attacked the potential for unfairness and discrimination in a system under which offenders committing the same offense could serve widely disparate sentences, especially when those deciding on sentences (judges and parole boards) did not need to explain or justify their choices. Social science research too undermined the case for rehabilitation, demonstrating that imprisonment rarely promoted rehabilitation and that, even when it did, officials could not reliably determine which offenders had been rehabilitated.[95]

Reforming Sentencing

These criticisms led to reforms designed to curb excessive leniency in sentencing and to eliminate disparities in sentences for the same offense. One such reform was the establishment of "mandatory minimum" sentences for particular offenses. Massachusetts, for example, established a one-year minimum sentence for anyone convicted of carrying a firearm in violation of the state's firearm laws. Michigan prescribed a two-year prison sentence, in addition to the primary sentence, for possession of a firearm during the commission of a felony—as publicized on billboards, "One with a Gun Gets You Two." Virtually all states have enacted mandatory sentencing laws for for drug offenses, firearms crimes, or other felonies.[96]

A second reform has been to limit judicial discretion by establishing guidelines for judges to use in sentencing offenders. Some states—for example, Florida and Maryland—have adopted guidelines that judges might voluntarily adhere to in sentencing. Others, such as California, have enacted specific sentences for various offenses, allowing judges to increase or reduce the prescribed sentence only slightly based on mitigating or aggravating factors. Congress in the Sentencing Reform Act of 1984 adopted a third approach, delegating to a commission the responsibility for devising detailed sentencing criteria. The federal sentencing commission prepared a chart based on the seriousness of the offense and various characteristics of the offender, such as age, mental condition, and prior record, leading to a "score." For each combination of offense and offender scores, a presumptive sentence was established. Federal judges are obliged to justify any sentences outside the guidelines, and both the defendant and the prosecutor can appeal the sufficiency of the justification offered by the judge. (See Box 6-4)

The Effects of Sentencing Reforms

Studies of the Massachusetts and Michigan gun laws suggest that the establishment of mandatory sentences does not guarantee greater severity for offenders or eliminate disparities in sentencing.[97] Prosecutors have circumvented the laws when they believed them unduly harsh, often with the approval of judges and police, either by refusing to charge arrestees with offenses that carry a mandatory sentence or by dismissing cases prior to trial. In addition, defendants charged with crimes carrying a mandatory sentence have more frequently gone to trial, thereby slowing the processing of cases. Those convicted under mandatory-sentence statutes have received more severe sentences. However, mandatory sentence laws have actually increased sentencing disparities among offenders committing the same crime. This is true because for such offenders, the sentence one receives depends on the discretionary decision of the prosecutor as to whether or not to charge them with violating the mandatory-sentence law.

Mandatory sentencing guidelines seem a more promising approach to sentencing reform. Such guidelines have the potential to prevent unjust (e.g., racially discriminatory) disparities in sentencing by eliminating the unchecked discretion of judges or parole boards in determining length of imprisonment. Yet guidelines may not altogether eliminate racial disparities in sentences,

BOX 6-4   THE FEDERAL SENTENCING GUIDELINES: HOW THEY WORK

We begin with a section of the Guidelines:

3. ROBBERY, EXTORTION, AND BLACKMAIL

   Sec. 2B3.1 Robbery

   (a) Base Offense Level: 18

   (b) Specific Offense Characteristics

   (1) If the value of the property taken or destroyed exceeded $2,500, increase the offense level as follows:

Loss	Increase in Level
(A) $2,500 or less	no increase
(B) $2,501 - $10,000	add 1
(C) $10,001 - $50,000	add 2
(D) $50,001 - $250,000	add 3
(E) $250,001 - $1,000,000	add 4
(F) $1,000,001 - $5,000,000	add 5
(G) more than $5,000,000	add 6

Treat the loss for a financial institution or post office as at least $5,000.

   (2) (A) If a firearm was discharged increase by 5 levels; (B) if a firearm or a dangerous weapon was otherwise used, increase by 4 levels; (C) if a firearm or other dangerous weapon was brandished, displayed or possessed, increase by 3 levels.

   (3) If any victim sustained bodily injury, increase the offense level according to the seriousness of the injury:

Degree of Bodily Injury	Increase in Level
(A) Bodily Injury	add 2
(B) Serious Bodily Injury	add 4
(C) Permanent or Life-Threatening Bodily Injury	add 6

Provided, however, that the cumulative adjustments from (2) and (3) shall not exceed 9 levels.

   (4) (A) If any person was abducted to facilitate commission of the offense or to facilitate escape, increase by 4 levels; or (B) if any

continued on p. 222

continued from p. 221

person was physically restrained to facilitate commission of the offense or to facilitate escape, increase by 2 levels.

(5) If obtaining a firearm, destructive device, or controlled substance was the object of the offense, increase by 1 level.

How do the Guidelines operate in practice? Imagine a bank robber, with one prior serious conviction, who robs a bank of $40,000 by pointing a gun at the teller. Then, according to Guideline Sec.2B3.1, the offender would receive an offense score of 23 (18 for the offense, plus 2 for the amount of the robbery and 3 for brandishing the gun), with an additional 3 points for the prior conviction. Looking up the Guideline sentence for such a score, one would find a sentencing range of from 51 to 63 months in prison. If the judge sentences the defendant to a sentence outside the range indicated by the Guidelines, he or she must give reasons for departing from the Guidelines, and an appeals court may then review the reasonableness of the departure.

SOURCE: Stephen Breyer, "The Federal Sentencing Guidelines and the Key Compromises Upon Which They Rest," *Hofstra Law Review* 17 (Fall 1988): 1-50.

either because those determining sentences may still discriminate or because the factors used in determining sentences (such as the existence of prior convictions) may correlate with race.[98] Studies of sentencing guidelines in the states—the federal guidelines are too recent to evaluate—suggest that they have indeed changed sentencing patterns and reduced disparities in sentences for those convicted of the same charges.[99] Still, some evidence exists that prosecutors have sought to limit the guidelines' effects by changing how they charge suspects, and it remains to be seen whether discretion can be eliminated at one stage of the criminal justice process without its reintroduction at another stage.

CONCLUSIONS

While the federal Bill of Rights imposes some basic requirements, the primary responsibility for the administration of justice in the United States rests with state and local governments. As we have seen, this decentralization of authority has encouraged the development of a rich diversity of institutions, laws, and practices for dealing with criminal justice issues. This diversity is reflected in the legal standards defining criminal justice policy—from the rules regulating pretrial release, to the tests for determining responsibility for one's criminal acts, to the laws governing the sentencing of criminals. It is, if anything, even greater in the discretionary practices—such as prosecutorial dismissal of charges and plea bargaining—that have developed in the absence of legal standards, or at times in opposition to them. This diversity suggests that it is probably inaccurate to speak of *the* American system of criminal justice. There are almost as many "systems" as there are states and localities.

Yet states and localities develop their distinctive approaches in the course of confronting a set of common policy problems. For example, both Supreme Court rulings and notions of fundamental fairness demand that indigent defendants be represented by counsel. The policy question is whether to opt for a public defender program, an assigned counsel system, or some other alternative. Similarly, some mechanism must be devised for distinguishing between cases that merit prosecution and cases which do not. The question is whether this judgment should be in the hands of the prosecutor, the judge at the preliminary hearing, or some other official.

Although some issues in the administration of criminal justice do not excite great controversy, others—including some involving the courts—generate intense conflict. Often these conflicts pit defenders of court practices against political conservatives, who charge that American courts have undermined public safety by showing an excessive concern for the rights of criminals and by treating them too leniently. Since the 1970s these conservatives have achieved a number of victories in their campaign to reduce the discretion of judges and mandate harsher treatment for offenders. For example, in some jurisdictions defendants may now be held in "preventive detention" pending trial, may have illegally seized evidence used against them if it was seized in good faith, may find it more difficult to mount an insanity defense, and may face a mandatory or determinate sentence upon conviction.

From another angle, the conflict can be seen as a dispute not only about the substance of policy but about who will set it. Legislators have enacted statutes on a variety of matters—from pretrial release to sentencing—in an effort to seize control of criminal justice policy. On occasion, executive officials too have sought to set basic policy—the ban on plea bargaining by Alaska's attorney general is an obvious example. Yet judges and prosecutors have often opposed these efforts, viewing them as infringements on their prerogatives or as upsetting established modes of operation. At times the opposition has been direct, as when prosecutors and judges in Michigan effectively gutted the state's mandatory sentencing law. More frequently, judges and prosecutors have sought opportunities to exercise discretion despite the new requirements in order to achieve what they view as desirable outcomes.

Whether justice is better promoted by the faithful application of legal standards established by the legislature or by negotiated settlements is, of course, a hotly disputed question. Moreover, it is a question that arises not merely in the criminal justice context but also in the civil justice realm, to which we now turn.

NOTES

1. James Eisenstein and Herbert Jacob, *Felony Justice; An Organizational Analysis of Criminal Courts* (Boston: Little, Brown, 1977), p. 131.

2. Barbara Boland, Catherine H. Conly, Lynn Warner, Ronald Sones, and William Martin, *The Prosecution of Felony Arrests, 1986* (Washington, D.C.: U.S. Department of Justice, Bureau of Justice Statistics, 1989), p. 102.

3. Eisenstein and Jacob, *Felony Justice*, p. 47.

4. *Gideon* v . *Wainwright*, 372 U.S. 335 (1963).

5. *Argersinger* v. *Hamlin*, 407 U.S. 25 (1972).

6. *Report to the Nation on Crime and Justice*, 2nd ed. (Washington, D.C.: U.S. Department of Justice, Bureau of Justice Statistics, 1988), pp. 74-75.

7. Quoted in Jonathan Casper, *American Criminal Justice: The Defendant's Perspective* (Englewood Cliffs, N.J: Prentice-Hall, 1972), p. 101.

8. David W. Neubauer, *Judicial Process; Law, Courts, & Politics in the United States* (Pacific Grove, Calif.: Brooks/Cole Publishing Co., 1991), p. 127.

9. Malcolm M. Feeley, *The Process Is the Punishment; Handling Cases in a Lower Criminal Court* (New York: Russell Sage Foundation, 1979), pp. 30-31. Cf. Eisenstein and Jacob, *Felony Justice*, p. 285.

10. *Report to the Nation on Crime and Justice*, pp. 11-12, 34-35.

11. Ibid., p. 68; cf. Hans Zeisel, *The Limits of Law Enforcement* (Chicago: University of Chicago Press, 1982), p. 98, Figure 23.

12. Vera Institute of Justice, *Felony Arrests*, rev. ed. (New York: Longman, 1981), p. 5, Figure 2; and Zeisel, *Limits of Law Enforcement*, p. 97.

13. *Report to the Nation on Crime and Justice*, p. 69; and Vera Institute, *Felony Arrests*, pp. 4-5.

14. Zeisel, *Limits of Law Enforcement*, p. 32, Figure 9.

15. James Q. Wilson, *Thinking About Crime* (New York: Basic Books, 1975), p. xii.

16. Brian Forst, Judith Lucianovic, and Sarah J. Cox, *What Happens After Arrest?* (Washington, D.C.: National Institute of Law Enforcement and Criminal Justice, 1977), pp. 62-68; and Vera Institute, *Felony Arrests*, pp. 6-22 and *passim*.

17. Zeisel, *Limits of Law Enforcement*, p. 114, and—more generally—pp. 111-112, Table 2.

18. Wayne H. Thomas, Jr., *Bail Reform in America* (Berkeley: University of California Press, 1976), pp. 40-41.

19. On the bail reform movement, see ibid., and Roy B. Flemming, *Punishment Before Trial; An Organizational Perspective of Felony Bail Processes* (New York: Longman, 1982). On the effects of pretrial confinement on case outcomes, see John Goldkamp, "The Effects of Detention on Judicial Decisions: A Closer Look," *Justice System Journal* 5 (Spring 1980): 234-257, and Eisenstein and Jacob *Felony Justice*, pp. 284-285.

20. *Report to the Nation on Crime and Justice*, pp. 76-77.

21. Thomas, *Bail Reform in America*, and Mary A. Torborg, *Pretrial Release: A National Evaluation of Practices and Outcomes* (Washington, D.C.: National Institute of Justice, 1981).

22. Donald E. Pryor and Walter F. Smith, "Significant Research Findings Concerning Pretrial Release," *Pretrial Issues* 4 (Washington, D.C.: Pretrial Services Resource Center, February 1982).

23. Ibid., and Torborg, *Pretrial Release.*

24. Elizabeth Gaynes, *Typology of State Laws Which Permit the Consideration of Danger in the Pretrial Release Decision* (Washington, D.C.: Pretrial Services Resource Center, May 1982), and Barbara Gottlieb, *Public Danger as a Factor in Pretrial Release: A Comparative Analysis of State Laws* (Washington, D.C.: National Institute of Justice, 1985).

25. John Goldkamp, "Questioning the Practice of Pretrial Detention: Some Empirical Evidence from Philadelphia," *Journal of Criminal Law and Criminology* 74 (1983): 1556-1588.

26. *Report to the Nation on Crime and Justice*, p. 77.

27. Deborah Day Emerson, *Grand Jury Reform: A Review of Key Issues* (Washington, D.C.: National Institute of Justice, U.S. Department of Justice, 1983), as reported in *Report to the Nation on Crime and Justice*, p. 72.

28. This discussion of the grand jury is based on Leroy D. Clark, *The Grand Jury* (New York: Quadrangle Books, 1975), and Neubauer, *Judicial Process*, pp. 203-205.

29. *Wood* v. *Georgia*, 370 U.S. 375, 390 (1962).

30. Neubauer, *Judicial Process*, p. 205.

31. Quoted in Lawrence Baum, *American Courts: Process & Policy*, 2nd ed. (Boston: Houghton Mifflin, 1990), p. 176.

32. This research is summarized in Neubauer, *Judicial Process*, pp. 201-203.

33. David Neubauer, *Criminal Justice in Middle America* (Morristown, N.J.: General Learning Press, 1974).

34. *Report to the Nation on Crime and Justice*, p. 84.

35. Martin A. Levin, *Urban Politics and the Criminal Courts* (Chicago: University of Chicago Press, 1977), p. 2.

36. Quoted in Milton Heumann, *Plea Bargaining* (Chicago: University of Chicago Press, 1977), p. 60.

37. Zeisel, *Limits of Law Enforcement*, p. 176.

38. See Eisenstein and Jacob, *Felony Justice*, Chapter 2; Arthur I. Rosett and Donald R. Cressy, *Justice by Consent: Plea Bargaining in the American Courthouse* (Philadelphia: J. B. Lippincott, 1976), Chapters 2 and 5; and Susan R. Thomas Buckle and Leonard G. Buckle, *Bargaining for Justice: Case Disposition and Reform in the Criminal Courts* (New York: Praeger, 1977).

39. Eisenstein and Jacob, *Felony Justice*, p. 248.

40. The caseload-pressure hypothesis is put forth by Abraham Blumberg, *Criminal Justice* (Chicago: Quadrangle Books, 1967). For critical discussions of this hypothesis, see Feeley, *The Process Is the Punishment*, Chapter 8, and Heumann, *Plea Bargaining*, Chapter 3. This latter source also presents statements by judges and criminal lawyers endorsing the caseload-pressure hypothesis.

41. Albert W. Alschuler, "Plea Bargaining and Its History," and Lawrence M. Friedman, "Plea Bargaining in Historical Perspective," *Law and Society Review* 13 (Winter 1979): 211-260.

42. These figures, drawn from Raymond Moley, *Politics and Criminal Prosecution* (New York: Minton, Balch, 1929), and from Illinois Association for Criminal Justice, *The Illinois Crime Survey* (Chicago: Illinois Association for Criminal Justice, 1929), are reported in Alschuler, "Plea Bargaining and Its History," pp. 223 and 231.

43. Heumann, *Plea Bargaining*, Chapter 3, presents data for Connecticut courts.

44. On criminal prosecutions in Los Angeles, see Lynn M. Mather, *Plea Bargaining or Trial?* (Lexington, Mass.: Lexington Books, 1979); and on prosecutions in Baltimore, see Eisenstein and Jacob, *Felony Justice*, Chapter 4.

45. Albert W. Alschuler, "The Prosecutor's Role in Plea Bargaining," *University of Chicago Law Review* 36 (Fall 1968): 50-112.

46. See Feeley, *The Process Is the Punishment*, and Heumann, *Plea Bargaining*. Of course, their perception of what justice requires may be mistaken, either because their understanding of justice is flawed or because they lack sufficient information in order to make an informed judgment.

47. Among the volumes that emphasize this "organizational approach" are Eisenstein and Jacob, *Felony Justice*, and Peter F. Nardulli, *The Courtroom Elite: An Organizational Perspective on Criminal Justice* (Cambridge: Ballinger, 1978).

48. Nardulli, *The Courtroom Elite*, p. 68.

49. Major works critical of plea bargaining include: Blumberg, *Criminal Justice*; Jonathan D. Casper, *American Criminal Justice: The Defendant's Perspective* (Englewood Cliffs, N.J.: Prentice-Hall, 1972); and Kenneth Kipnis, "Criminal Justice and the Negotiated Plea," *Ethics* 86 (1976): 93-106.

50. Kipnis, "Criminal Justice and the Negotiated Plea," and Alschuler, "Prosecutor's Role in Plea Bargaining."

51. See, for example, Ernest van den Haag, *Punishing Criminals* (New York: Basic Books, 1975).

52. Blumberg, *Criminal Justice*.

53. Ibid.

54. For accounts of Alaska's ban on plea bargaining and its effects, see Michael L. Rubinstein and Teresa J. White, "Alaska's Ban on Plea Bargaining," *Law and Society Review* 13 (Winter 1979): 367-383; William F. McDonald and James A. Cramer, *Plea Bargaining* (Lexington, Mass.: Lexington Books, 1980); and Michael L. Rubinstein, Stevens H. Clarke, and Teresa J. White, *Alaska Bans Plea Bargaining* (Washington, D.C.: National Institute of Justice, U.S. Department of Justice, 1980).

55. Levin, *Urban Politics and Criminal Courts*; and Eisenstein and Jacob, *Felony Justice*.

56. See Casper, *American Criminal Justice*, for illustrative material.

57. Major attempts to determine the effect of mode of disposition on sentencing include Eisenstein and Jacob, *Felony Justice*, Chapter 10, and Feeley, *The Process Is the Punishment*, Chapter 5.

58. Heumann, *Plea Bargaining*, p. 142.

59. For the views of attorneys and judges, see ibid., pp. 67, 101, 125, 141.

60. Ibid., pp. 124-126.

61. Ibid., pp. 84-89.

62. See, for example, van den Haag, *Punishing Criminals*.

63. See, for example, George Woodworth, and Charles A. Pulaski, "Comparative Review of Death Sentences: An Empirical Review of Death Sentences," *Journal of Criminal Law and Criminology* 74 (1983): 661-753.

64. Yale Kamisar, "The Exclusionary Rule in Historical Perspective: The Struggle to Make the Fourth Amendment 'More than an Empty Blessing,'" *Judicature* 62 (February 1979): 337-350.

65. See, for example, Abraham Goldstein, *The Insanity Defense* (New Haven: Yale University Press, 1967), and Helen Silving, *Essays on Mental Incapacity and Criminal Conduct* (Springfield, Ill.: Charles C. Thomas, 1967).

66. For a critique of claims that sentencing is "lenient," see Stuart A. Scheingold, *The Politics of Law and Order* (New York: Longman, 1984), pp. 151-153. For a critique of claims that sentencing is discriminatory, see James Eisenstein and Herbert Jacob, *Felony Justice: An Organizational Analysis of the Criminal Courts* (Boston: Little, Brown, 1977), p. 284; John Hagan, "Extra-Legal Attributes and Criminal Sentencing: An Assessment of the Sociological Viewpoint," *Law & Society Review* 8 (Spring 1984), pp. 357-383; and, more generally, William Wilbanks, *The Myth of a Racist Criminal Justice System* (Monterey, Calif.: Brooks/Cole Publishing, 1987).

67. *Silverthorne Lumber Co.* v. *United States*, 251 U.S. 385 (1920).

68. See, for example, *State* v. *Sheridan*, 96 N.W. 730 (Iowa, 1903).

69. *Weeks* v. *United States*, 232 U.S. 383 (1914).

70. *Wolf* v. *Colorado*, 388 U.S. 25 (1949).

71. *Mapp* v. *Ohio*, 367 U.S. 643 (1961).

72. See, for example, *United States* v. *Leon*, 468 U.S. 897 (1984), and *Massachusetts* v. *Sheppard*, 468 U.S. 981 (1984).

73. *People* v. *Defore*, 150 N.E. 585 (1926).

74. Bradley C. Canon, "Is the Exclusionary Rule in Failing Health? Some New Data and a Plea Against a Precipitous Conclusion," *Kentucky Law Journal* 62 (1983-84): 681-730.

75. E. Dallin Oaks, "Studying the Exclusionary Rule in Search and Seizure," *University of Chicago Law Review* 37 (1970): 665-757; and James E. Spiotto, "Search and Seizure: An Empirical Study of the Exclusionary Rule and Its Alternatives," *Journal of Legal Studies* 2 (1973): 243-278.

76. National Institute of Justice, *Criminal Justice Research Report—The Effects of the Exclusionary Rule: A Study in California* (Washington, D.C.: Department of Justice, National Institute of Justice, 1982). For a thought-provoking examination of these and other studies of the effects of the exclusionary rule, see Thomas Y. Davies, "A Hard Look at What We Know (and Still Need to Learn) About the 'Costs' of the Exclusionary Rule: The NIJ Study and Other Studies of 'Lost' Arrests," *American Bar Foundation Research Journal* 1983 (Summer): 611-689.

77. Peter F. Nardulli, "The Societal Cost of the Exclusionary Rule: An Empirical Assessment," *American Bar Foundation Research Journal* 1983 (Summer), p. 595, Table 2, and p. 597, Table 7.

78. Ibid., p. 601, Table 12.

79. Ibid., p. 603, Table 13.

80. The Attorney General's Task Force on Violent Crime: *Final Report* (Washington, D.C.: Department of Justice, 1981), Recommendations, 40, 55-56. For Supreme Court rulings recognizing a "good faith" exception, see note 72 above.

81. Schlesinger, *Exclusionary Injustice*, pp. 77-84.

82. Jonathan D. Casper, Kennette Benedict, and Jo L. Perry, "The Tort Remedy in Search and Seizure Cases: A Case Study in Juror Decision Making," *American Bar Foundation Research Journal* 13 (Spring 1988): 279-303.

83. Quoted in Lincoln Caplan, *The Insanity Defense and the Trial of John W. Hinckley, Jr.* (Boston: David R. Godine, 1984), p. 19. Our account of the Hinckley case relies on this volume.

84. *M'Naghten's Case*, 10 Clark & Fin. 200, 8 Eng. Rep. 718, 722 (1843).

85. American Law Institute, *Modern Penal Code*, sec. 4.01 (1962).

86. Goldstein, *The Insanity Defense*, p. 87.

87. For general surveys of developments in the aftermath of the Hinckley acquittal, see Ingo Keilitz, "Researching and Reforming the Insanity Defense," *Rutgers Law Review* 39 (Winter/Spring 1987): 283-322, and Rita J. Simon and David E. Aaronson, *The Insanity Defense; A Critical Assessment of Law and Policy in the Post-Hinckley Era* (New York: Praeger, 1988).

88. Rodriguez, LeWinn, and Perlin, "The Insanity Defense Under Siege: State Legislative Assaults and Legal Rejoinders," *Rutgers Law Journal* 14 (Winter 1983): 397-430, and—more generally—Richard A. Pasewark and McGinley, "Insanity Plea: National Survey of Frequency and Success," *Journal of Psychiatry and Law* 13 (Spring/Summer 1985): 101-108.

89. Keilitz, "Researching and Reforming the Insanity Defense,"

90. Gare A. Smith and James A. Hall, "Evaluating Michigan's Guilty But Mentally Ill Verdicts: An Empirical Study," *Journal of Law Reform* 16 (1982): 77-114.

91. Robert P. Bogenberger, Richard A. Pasewark, Howard Gudeman, and Stephen L. Beiber, "Follow-up of Insanity Acquittees in Hawaii," *International Journal of Law and Psychiatry* 10 (1987): 283-295.

92. Cornelia Stockman, "The Insanity Defense Reform Act in New York State, 1980-1983," *International Journal of Law and Psychiatry* 7 (1984): 367-384, and Jeffrey L. Rogers, Richard A. Pasewark, and Stephen L. Bieber, "Insanity Plea: Predicting Not Guilty By Reason of Insanity Adjudications," *Bulletin of the American Academy of Psychiatry and Law* 16 (1988): 35-52.

93. Grant T. Harris, Marnie E. Rice, and Catherine A. Cormier, "Length of Detention in Matched Groups of Insanity Acquittees and Convicted Offenders," *International Journal of Law and Psychiatry* 14 (1991): 223-236; Mark Pogrebin, Robert Regoli, and Ken Perry, "Not Guilty By Reason of Insanity: A Research Note," *International Journal of Law and Psychiatry* 8 (1986): 237-241, and Rodriguez, LeWinn, and Perlin, "The Insanity Defense Under Siege."

94. On the centrality of rehabilitation in penological policy, see Francis A. Allen, *The Decline of the Rehabilitative Ideal* (New Haven: Yale University Press, 1981).

95. On the problems of rehabilitation as a penological approach, see Stuart A. Scheingold, *The Politics of Law and Order* (New York: Longman, 1984), pp. 183-185, and Douglas Lipton, Robert Martinson, and Judith Wilks, *The Effectiveness of Correctional Treatment: A Survey of Treatment Evaluation Studies* (New York: Praeger, 1975).

96. A useful overview on mandatory sentencing, and on sentencing reform more generally, is Sandra Shane-DuBow, Alice P. Brown, and Erik Olsen, *Sentencing Reform in the United States: History, Content, and Effect* (Washington, D.C.: Government Printing Office, 1985).

97. On the effects of mandatory sentencing, see Milton Heumann and Colin Loftin, "Mandatory Sentencing and the Abolition of Plea Bargaining: The Michigan Felony Firearm Statute," *Law & Society Review* 13 (Winter, 1979): 393-430; James A. Beha, II, "'And Nobody Can Get You Out:' The Impact of a Mandatory Prison Sentence for the Illegal Carrying of a Firearm on the Use of Firearms and on the Administration of Criminal Justice in Boston," *Boston University Law Review*

57 (1977): 96-146 (Part I), 289-333 (Part II); and more generally, *Sentencing Reform Impacts* (Washington, D.C.: U.S. Department of Justice, National Institute of Justice, 1987), Chapter 3.

98. On the possibilities of racial discrimination even with guidelines designed to reduce discretion, see David C. Baldus, George Woodworth, and Charles A. Pulaski, "Monitoring and Evaluating Contemporary Death Sentencing Systems: Lessons from Georgia," *University of California Davis Law Review* 18 (Summer, 1985): 1375-1467. By a 5-4 vote, the United States Supreme Court rejected such evidence as proof of systematic discrimination in sentencing in capital cases in *McClesky* v. *Kemp*, 481 U.S. 279 (1987). On possible correlations between guideline criteria and race, see Joan Petersilia and Susan Turner, *Guideline-Based Justice: The Implications for Racial Minorities* (Santa Monica, Calif.: Rand Corporation, 1985).

99. On the effect of mandatory sentencing guidelines, see John H. Kramer and Robin L. Lubitz, "Pennsylvania's Sentencing Reform: The Impact of Commission-Established Guidelines," *Crime & Delinquency* 31 (1985): 481-500; and more generally, *Sentencing Reform Impacts*, Chapters 5 and 6.

7 CIVIL JUSTICE AND THE COURTS

"What happened to Kerry was not an act of God; it was an act of Dow."[1] That at least was Michael Ryan's explanation of why, four years after he had returned from military service in Vietnam, his daughter was born with multiple birth defects. Like many other soldiers, Ryan had in Vietnam been exposed to Agent Orange, a chemical defoliant sprayed by American troops on fields and forests to destroy enemy crops and cover. And like them, he was convinced that Agent Orange caused death or debilitating illness in those exposed to the chemical and led to birth defects among their offspring. Ryan, together with other Vietnam veterans, blamed their problems on the chemical companies (such as Dow Chemical) that had produced Agent Orange and demanded justice.

Yet having a sense of injury and injustice is not the same as proving liability in a court of law. Monsanto, Dow, and other producers of Agent Orange consistently denied that it had any toxic effects. Because the cancers suffered by veterans and the birth defects among their children were not distinctive, it would be difficult to prove that they were linked to Agent Orange rather than to other causes. The legal effort to establish such a link would ultimately involve almost 1500 law firms, representing over 2.4 million Vietnam veterans and their families. Against them would be arrayed seven corporate defendants, which together spent roughly $100 million in preparation for the Agent Orange trial.

The litigation began in 1978 when Paul Reutershan, a Vietnam veteran dying of cancer, filed suit against Dow and two other chemical manufacturers. Although Reutershan died before the year ended, other Agent Orange suits followed in several jurisdictions. Early in 1979, Victor Yannacone, an attorney, filed an amended version of the Reutershan complaint as a class action suit. His suit sought damages "in the range of $4 billion to $40 billion" as a trust fund for "all those so unfortunate as to have been and now to be situated at risk, not only during this generation but during generations to come."[2] A panel of federal judges authorized the formation of a class, which would include those allegedly at risk because of Agent Orange. It then consolidated several cases as *In re Agent Orange Product Liability Litigation* for hearing by a federal district court in New York.

Before trial could commence, however, several crucial preliminary legal issues had to be addressed. Were the defendants immune from suit, as they claimed, because they had produced Agent Orange at the request of the government? Should the judge apply state or federal law in deciding the case? In addition to developing legal arguments on these and other questions, the plaintiffs' lawyers had to establish a causal connection between Agent Orange and the disabilities suffered by veterans and their offspring. This was particularly difficult because, as one of their lawyers put it:

> Our clients could not help us prove our case. After all, they had not been hit by a truck, victimized by a doctor, or injured by a drug or other consumer product. They didn't know what had happened to them or when. They only knew that something had gone wrong[3]

Thus, in order to prove their case, the plaintiffs were forced to rely on laboratory studies, epidemiological evidence, and information culled from the files of the defendant companies.

Aggravating these difficulties was the disparity in resources between the parties in the litigation. As Judge George Pratt observed early in the case, the plaintiffs "have limited resources with which to press their claims and [their] plight becomes more desperate and depressing as time goes on," whereas the defendants "have ample resources for counsel and expert witnesses to defend them and . . . probably gain significantly . . . from every delay that they can produce."[4] These problems led to the formation of a huge consortium of interested lawyers to bear the expenses of preparing the case. Even then, the plaintiffs' lawyers often found themselves overmatched.

After five years with little progress, the litigation shifted into high gear with the assignment in October, 1983, of Judge Jack Weinstein to succeed Judge Pratt, who had been elevated to the court of appeals. Determined to move the case to resolution, Judge Weinstein established a trial date of May 7, 1984. His action spurred feverish—but largely unsuccessful—efforts by the plaintiffs' attorneys to develop evidence clearly linking Agent Orange to their clients' afflictions. The prospect of a trial also moved the two sides toward settlement because of uncertainty about its outcome and the calamitous consequences of losing for either side.

On Saturday, May 5, two days before the trial was to begin, Judge Weinstein convened all the attorneys to discuss a settlement, instructing them to "bring their toothbrushes" and to be prepared to stay all night Saturday and Sunday if necessary. His intervention succeeded. At 3:00 A.M. on May 7, just hours before jury selection was to begin, the weary negotiators reached a compromise settlement, under which the chemical companies refused to admit responsibility but agreed to pay the veterans $180 million. The largest class action suit in American history was over.

The Agent Orange litigation highlights several key aspects of civil justice in the United States:

Resolution by negotiation: Despite the intense preparations for trial, the Agent Orange case was eventually resolved through negotiations between counsel for the plaintiffs and counsel for the defendants. It thus fits the pattern for the vast majority of civil cases, which are settled rather than adjudicated. Indeed, although not all judges are as active as Judge Weinstein in promoting settlement, most courts have adopted procedures that promote fact-finding prior to trial in order to encourage the settlement of cases. The negotiations in civil cases occur "in the shadow of the law," that is, with the understanding that either party can demand a trial if a satisfactory agreement cannot be reached.[5] Thus in important respects—the encouragement of negotiated settlements, the prospect of trial should negotiations fail, and the resolution of most cases without trial—the process of civil justice parallels the process of criminal justice in the United States.

Access to justice and the "litigation explosion": The Agent Orange case also highlights an important dispute about the American system of civil justice. One view is that the basic problem in civil justice is ensuring access to the courts for ordinary citizens. From that perspective, one might view the Agent Orange litigation as something of a triumph. For the most part, the plaintiffs were persons of moderate means who had suffered health problems that they attributed to the negligence of large corporations. Yet these plaintiffs were able to secure legal counsel, to gain a hearing for their claims in the courts, and to obtain at least some redress for their suffering—in short, to gain access and secure some measure of justice.[6]

Other commentators, however, insist that the main problem confronting the American system of civil justice is excessive litigation.[7] From their perspective, the American propensity to litigate has in recent years produced a "litigation explosion," overburdening the courts and weakening the American economy.

The Agent Orange case by itself did not cause this problem, though it placed heavy demands on the courts during its six-year duration. But it exemplifies a type of case—mass toxic torts—that have significantly increased the civil case-loads of federal and state courts. Of course, proponents of this view acknowl-edge, those who cause injuries should be called to account. But they contend that mechanisms outside the courts should be devised for dealing with problems such as mass exposure to serious health risks.

The diversity of civil litigation: No single case or set of cases can mirror the diversity of civil litigation in the United States. The Agent Orange case belongs to the category of tort law, that is, cases involving civil wrongs or injuries for which damages are sought. Tort cases may entail, as in the Agent Orange liti-gation, multiple claims by workers or consumers against the actions or products of a limited number of corporations. More often, however, they involve rela-tively simple suits for damages by one individual against another—for example, as compensation for damages or injuries suffered in an automobile accident. (We shall discuss tort litigation in greater detail in Chapter 11.)

Although tort litigation constitutes a highly publicized and growing compo-nent of civil caseloads, American courts also address numerous other sorts of civil cases. Some civil cases involve contractual disputes, either between busi-nesses or—more frequently—between a business, usually attempting to collect a debt, and a consumer. Other civil cases arise out of domestic relationships, involving such matters as divorce, child support, and adoption. Still others involve the legal transfer of property from one party to another, as occurs through the administration of a will or the handling of the estate of someone who died intestate (without a will). Finally, an important category of civil cases involves the legal relationship between governments and citizens. These cases may range from constitutional challenges to governmental actions, such as mandatory drug testing programs, to governmental suits to compel compliance with environmental regulations, antitrust laws, or other statutes.

This description of the types of civil cases, however, raises questions. Why do some conflicts get transformed into legal disputes and taken to court, while oth-ers do not? How do courts deal with civil cases brought before them? And how well is the American system of civil justice operating? Are there ways to make it work better? This chapter seeks to answer those questions.

HOW CASES ARISE

In America's adversarial system of justice, there cannot be a case without a dis-pute. However, not every dispute, even if it has a legal dimension, is brought to court for resolution. Figure 7-1 outlines the process by which disputes arise and the various means available for dealing with disputes. Let us examine the pertinent aspects of this figure.

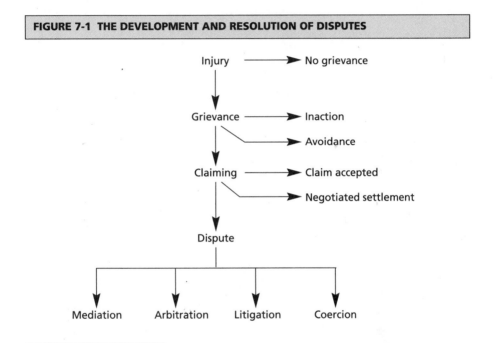

FIGURE 7-1 THE DEVELOPMENT AND RESOLUTION OF DISPUTES

SOURCE: Richard E. Miller and Austin Sarat, "Grievances, Claims and Disputes: Assessing the Adversary Culture," *Law & Society Review* 15 (1980-81): 524-565. Reprinted by permission of the Law and Society Association.

Injuries and Grievances

If cases arise out of disputes, disputes arise out of grievances, and grievances out of injuries. People suffer injuries—physical, economic, psychic—every day. These injuries do not become grievances, however, unless the injured party believes that she is unjustly deprived by another party of something to which she is entitled. Injuries do not become litigable grievances, that is, grievances one could take to court, unless one is deprived of something to which one is legally entitled. A few examples may help clarify this. You have no "grievance" against the government, for example, if it imprisons you for committing a crime, because your loss of liberty is deserved. Or suppose your house is destroyed by a torna-do. In such a case, you suffered an injury that was undeserved, but you have no "grievance" because no one is responsible for the damage. Finally, suppose you operate a pizzeria, and a competitor cuts into your sales. You certainly have suffered a harm and know who caused it, but there is no litigable "grievance" because you had no legal right to a fixed level of sales or profits.

As these examples suggest, by establishing entitlements and imposing obligations, law defines what constitutes a litigable grievance. This definition may vary from one society to another and may change over time within a society, as the law responds to shifts in public opinion. Some scholars attribute part of the increase in litigation in the United States and elsewhere to legal changes brought about by just such a shift in public opinion.[8] They contend that as advances in science and technology have made it possible to control situations of peril or need, the public has begun to claim a right to be free from unnecessary risk. The law, reflecting this claim, has imposed obligations on government and private parties to deliver goods and services that meet achievable standards of safety and usefulness. It has also made it easy to sue when these obligations are not met, and as a result, civil suits have increased.

Responses

Suppose you buy a car that fails to perform up to expectations. You might respond to this problem in various ways.[9] You might do nothing, perhaps justifying your *inaction* by arguing that everyone gets stuck once in a while ("lumping it"). You might also resolve never to purchase another car from that dealer or that manufacturer—social scientists call such a change in behavior, designed to reduce or eliminate contact with a disputant, *avoidance*.[10] Alternatively, you might go to the dealership and *claim* that the car should be repaired or that you should be reimbursed for your inconvenience. The dealer might accept your claim, thereby resolving the matter. Or the dealer might make a counter-offer, perhaps to replace defective parts if you pay the labor costs, and a negotiated settlement might be reached. Finally, the dealer may reject your claim, in which case a dispute exists.

What are your options in such circumstances? One possibility is coercion, the threat or use of force to get what you claim is rightfully yours. Revolutions and fights exemplify the use of coercion to resolve disputes. In our example, however, other forms of dispute resolution are more likely. You might seek the intervention of a third party, such as the Better Business Bureau, to help resolve the dispute through *mediation*. Or you might seek a binding resolution of your dispute outside the courts through *arbitration*. (We shall discuss those modes of dispute resolution later in the chapter.) Finally, you might take your grievance to court (*litigation*).

How do most people deal with their grievances? To some extent it depends upon the grievance. People who believe that they have suffered discrimination are unlikely to take action, whereas people who have suffered physical injuries or damage to their property are more likely to press claims.[11] Overall, however, according to a recent survey of 1,000 randomly selected households nationwide, most resolve their grievances outside the legal system (see Figure 7-2). Several factors explain why people do not usually take their disputes to court:

Adverse consequences of filing suit: Many disputants are reluctant to go to court because they fear that escalating the conflict will produce a backlash. This is particularly true when the disputants have ongoing relationships that might be jeopardized by a suit. Thus family members may prefer to settle their dis-

---

FIGURE 7-2 THE DISPUTING PYRAMID

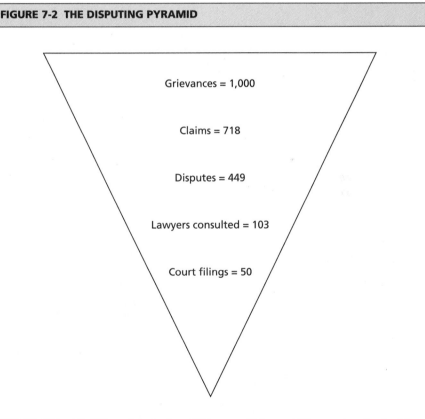

Grievances = 1,000

Claims = 718

Disputes = 449

Lawyers consulted = 103

Court filings = 50

SOURCE: Richard E. Miller and Austin Sarat, "Grievances, Claims, and Disputes: Assessing the Adversary Culture," *Law & Society Review* 15 (1980-81), p. 544, Figure 1-A. Reprinted by permission of the Law and Society Association. Figures indicate the general level of disputing per 1,000 grievances.

putes out of court; so too may neighbors, business partners, and employees involved in disputes on the job. As one victim of sex discrimination explained her refusal to sue: "a lot of people might go against me.... I wouldn't want to ruin the relationships I do have there."[12]

Costs of litigation: Disputants also recognize that litigation, with its attorney fees and court costs, is expensive. A trial also may require plaintiffs to miss work, costing them income or even putting their jobs in jeopardy. Added to these monetary costs may be psychic costs. Disputants may be uncomfortable consulting a lawyer or anxious about appearing in court. Thus, even if they have a legitimate grievance, disputants may conclude that the costs of going to trial outweigh the expected payoff from a successful suit.

Uncertainty: Because they do not know the applicable law, potential litigants may be uncertain about their chances of success. They also may be skeptical about whether a single individual can prevail against a company or against the government. This uncertainty may deter them from filing suit. As one victim of wage discrimination put it, it would be "me against a large corporation" and thus my "word against a [more powerful] someone else's."[13]

Nevertheless, some disputants are willing to consult lawyers and file suit. When they do, their cases proceed through certain legally established steps from initiation to resolution. It is to these steps, and to the law governing them, that we now turn.

RULES AND PROCESSES

Rules

Civil litigation is governed by three sets of rules. One set of rules establishes the substantive legal standards that judges apply in deciding cases. For example, a statute might define and outlaw racial discrimination, an administrative regulation might set water-quality standards, or the common law might determine when one can collect damages for injuries one has suffered. We shall examine these standards in Chapters 9-12.

A second set of rules governs the jurisdiction of courts and thus guides lawyers as to the proper court in which to file a case. We addressed those standards in Chapter 2.

Finally, a third set of rules determines the procedures that lawyers must follow in framing and presenting a case from its inception to the exhaustion of all appeals. For most of American history, these procedural rules were established within each state by state statutes and by rulings announced by state courts. Instead of developing their own procedural rules, each federal court followed the procedures of the state in which it heard cases. Many lawyers complained, however, that this lack of procedural uniformity was confusing, and the American Bar Association campaigned for a standard set of procedural rules for federal litigation. In 1938, in response to these efforts, the Federal Rules of Civil Procedure were adopted. These new rules established a uniform procedure for federal courts that its supporters hailed as "flexible, simple, clear, and efficient."[14] Over half the states have agreed with this assessment, conforming their procedural requirements to the Federal Rules of Civil Procedure.

The Process of Civil Litigation

Because most civil cases are resolved prior to trial, what occurs during the pretrial phase of litigation is vitally important. The pretrial phase serves to identify the law applicable-cable to the case, define the legal issues in the case, and promote the discovery of factual information pertinent to its resolution. The four major steps during the pretrial phase are: (1) pleadings, (2) discovery, (3) motions, and (4) pretrial conference.[15]

Pleadings

A case begins when the plaintiff—or, more likely, the plaintiff's attorney—files a written complaint with the trial court. Under the Federal Rules of Civil Procedure, which greatly simplified pleadings, a complaint must merely (1) describe the factual basis for the plaintiff's suit, (2) explain why the court has jurisdiction over the case, (3) outline the legal theory on which the complaint relies, and (4) indicate the damages or other relief that the plaintiff seeks. The requirements of the Federal Rules of Civil Procedure are met if the complaint reveals enough information so that the defendant can understand the basis for the suit and respond to the complaint.

Once the plaintiff has filed a complaint, the defendant in the case must be "served" with the complaint, that is, formally notified of the complaint and summoned to appear in court at a particular date and time. Should the defendant fail to appear at the appointed time, the judge may rule in favor of the plaintiff without hearing evidence. This is called a default judgment.

Usually, however, defendants file an answer to the plaintiff's complaint. They may deny some or all of the allegations in the complaint. In the Agent Orange case, for example, the chemical companies denied that their product had caused the health problems suffered by the veterans and their children. Those matters on which the plaintiff and defendant differ then become the basis for the dispute. Alternatively, defendants may admit the truth of the plaintiff's allegation but offer an affirmative defense, that is, introduce new facts designed to produce a decision for them. A sky-diving instructor, for instance, may admit that a student died during a jump but reveal that the student signed a form acknowledging the dangers of sky-diving and pledging not to hold the school or instructors responsible for any mishaps. Finally, defendants may respond with a counterclaim, the equivalent of a complaint against the plaintiff. Thus a driver, sued for damages arising out of a traffic accident, might file a counterclaim for the damages to her car.

Even if a plaintiff has no intention of taking a dispute to trial, she may have tactical reasons for filing a complaint. She might file a complaint in order to "engage the authority of the legal system" on her behalf, thereby strengthening her position in the informal resolution of the dispute.[16] Filing a complaint may also signal how seriously the plaintiff views the matter under dispute, thereby inviting the defendant to enter into negotiations to deal with the situation.

Discovery

Discovery involves the pretrial exchange of information between the parties in a lawsuit. Under the Federal Rules of Civil Procedure, every party to a civil action is entitled to the disclosure of all relevant information in the possession of any person.[17] Thus a plaintiff may demand from a defendant (or a defendant from a plaintiff) all information that he possesses relevant to the subject-matter of the case. She may also during discovery question witnesses and others who possess pertinent information. The sole exception to this requirement of full disclosure is for privileged information, such as communications between an attorney and client or between a doctor and patient.

The Federal Rules of Civil Procedure permit such broad scope for discovery in order to prevent a party from hiding damaging evidence or an attorney from springing a surprise on an unwary opponent at trial. In so doing, the Rules promote verdicts at trial based on the weight of the evidence rather than on courtroom tactics.

Full disclosure of facts prior to trial may also encourage litigants to settle cases. Parties sometimes fail to settle cases because they overestimate the strength of their own position or underestimate that of their opponents. Discovery, however, allows an informed assessment of the strengths and weaknesses of the opposing positions and of the likely outcome of a trial.[18]

Lawyers employ three tools during discovery—depositions, interrogatories, and the production of documents and other physical evidence. A deposition involves oral questioning of a witness under trial-like conditions. Attorneys for both sides question and cross-examine witnesses, and their answers are recorded. This testimony may later be introduced at trial—an alert attorney will pounce on any discrepancies between what a witness says at trial and what he said when he was deposed. An interrogatory consists of a set of written questions directed to a party in a case, to which written answers are prepared and signed under oath. A party to a case may also be required during discovery to produce documents or objects for the other party to inspect, photograph, or copy and to permit access to its premises and its files for these purposes. In addition, the plaintiff in a personal injury case may be required to undergo a physical examination by a physician chosen by the defendant or by the court to substantiate an injury claim. Should a party object to questions or to other requests for information or materials, a judge determines whether the requests are legitimate.

In most cases the requests for information or materials during discovery are quite limited. However, discovery in complex cases can be time-consuming and expensive. In the first five years of the IBM antitrust case, for example, 64 million pages of records and documents were obtained through discovery.[19] In some instances, also, "overdiscovery" has led to abuses. As one judge put it:

> For many lawyers, discovery is a Pavlovian reaction. When the lawsuit is filed . . . the word processor begins to grind out interrogatories and requests for production. Deposition notices drop like autumn leaves.[20]

Plaintiffs may file suit with little basis for their claims, hoping that a "fishing expedition" in the defendant's files during discovery might provide them with the evidence they lack. Attorneys may also multiply requests for information during discovery to convince the opposing party it will be less expensive and burdensome to settle the case than to comply with the requests.[21] The Federal Rules of Civil Procedure permit judges to issue protective orders to prevent harassment and to impose sanctions, including the withholding of attorneys' fees, on those who engage in abuses. However, critics contend that these remedies have not curbed abuses of discovery.[22]

Motions

At each stage during the pretrial phase of a case, attorneys for either party can file motions, that is, requests that the judge either issue a legal ruling or take some other action.[23] The Federal Rules of Civil Procedure require that these motions be submitted in writing, specifying the legal basis for the motion and the relief or order sought.

Some motions concern procedural matters relating to the conduct of the case. For example, a defendant may file a motion requesting that the plaintiff be required to amend his complaint to clarify the basis for the suit. Or either party may request that the judge determine whether certain information is subject to discovery. With other motions a party may seek a resolution of the case in its favor prior to trial. In the Agent Orange Case, for example, the defendant corporations sought dismissal of the complaint, claiming that they were immune from suit because they were fulfilling a request from the government. Similarly, if the defendant fails to respond to a complaint, the plaintiff may move for a default judgment. Finally, either the plaintiff or the defendant may move for a summary judgment—a binding determination of the case without a trial. However, a judge can grant a motion for summary judgment only if the law is clear and if there is no dispute between the parties about the facts of the case (and thus no issue to submit to a jury).

How often are cases resolved on the basis of motions, rather than through settlement or through adjudication of the dispute? Our best estimate comes from Herbert Kritzer's intensive study of a sample of over 1600 cases in state and federal courts.[24] Kritzer found that twelve percent of the cases were dismissed for technical reasons or dismissed for cause (such as a failure to state a claim). In another fifteen percent the judge issued a summary judgment, entered a default judgment for the plaintiff, or otherwise decided the case. Thus, although only seven percent of the sample went to trial, judges contributed to the resolution of an additional twenty-seven percent of civil cases.[25]

Pretrial Conference

The Federal Rules of Civil Procedure authorize (but do not mandate) a conference between the judge and attorneys before a case goes to trial. Most states have followed the federal lead in providing for pretrial conferences. At these conferences, which are usually held after discovery is completed, the judge and the attorneys identify the points of agreement and the issues still in dispute. The attorneys also reveal what witnesses they will call and what evidence they will introduce, thereby facilitating the planning of the trial. In complicated cases a judge may schedule earlier conferences with the attorneys as well in order to expedite the process of discovery.[26]

Pretrial conferences not only improve the conduct of trials but can also promote the settlement of cases. As the Agent Orange litigation showed, many judges actively encourage settlement during pretrial conferences. Some initiate discussion of settlement when lawyers are reluctant to do so out of fear that the suggestion might be interpreted as a sign of weakness. Some judges also offer attorneys their own assessment of the strengths and weaknesses of the opposing positions and their views on whether settlement offers are reasonable. Lawyers generally applaud aggressive judicial participation in the settlement process. They are more likely to view a settlement as fair if it has received a judicial endorsement, and such an endorsement may help them persuade a recalcitrant client to accept a reasonable settlement offer.[27]

CIVIL CASES AND THEIR OUTCOMES

The Universe of Cases

Federal district courts decide about 250,000 civil cases each year, and the trial courts of populous states, such as Florida, decide over half a million.[28] It is hard to overestimate the diversity of these courts' civil caseloads. Some cases—like the Agent Orange suit and the IBM antitrust case—involve hundreds of millions of dollars. Others, such as litigation to collect debts, may involve a few hundred dollars at most. Some cases—again, the Agent Orange and IBM cases are prime examples—drag on for years, while others are quickly settled. Still others—for example, uncontested divorces and adoptions—involve no real dispute but merely require judicial ratification of a settlement worked out between the parties.

Types of Civil Cases

One way of capturing the diversity of civil cases is by looking at the types of cases that trial courts hear (see Figure 7-3 and Table 7-1). Taken together, the table and figure reveal that federal and state trial courts each handle a wide range of civil cases and that the mix of civil cases differs considerably from federal to state courts. This is hardly surprising: federal law and state law generally regulate different activities. For example, there is no federal divorce law and no state immigration law. Table 7-2 reveals that the Federal Government is involved, as either plaintiff or respondent, in much of the civil litigation in federal courts. Governmental actions and litigation priorities influence the character and extent of that litigation. Take, for example, Recovery and Enforcement Cases (Table 7-1), which involve the United States as plaintiff seeking to recover overpayments of veterans' benefits and defaulted student loans. In 1980 these cases comprised less than 10 percent of case filings in federal district courts. During the early 1980s, however, the Reagan administration made recovery of money owed to the Federal Government a priority. As a result, the number of these suits increased dramatically, and by 1985 they comprised almost one quarter of all federal civil cases. In the late 1980s, as this campaign

FIGURE 7-3 TYPES OF CASES IN STATE TRIAL COURTS OF GENERAL JURISDICTION, 1990

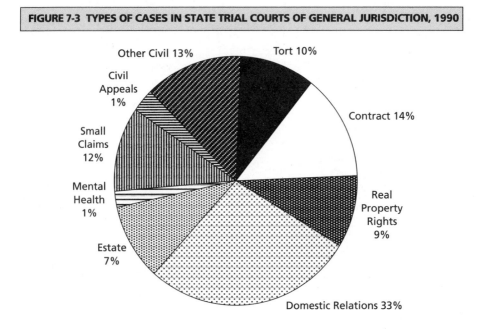

The chart includes data from 24 states.

SOURCE: *State Court Caseload Statistics:Annual Report 1990* (Williamsburg, Va.: National Center for State Courts, 1992), p. 18, Chart I.7.

wound down, the number of recovery and enforcement cases declined precipitously—over 33 percent, for example, from 1989 to 1990.[29]

Federal legislation also affects the types of private cases commenced in federal district courts. A good example is diversity of citizenship cases, which involve suits between citizens of different states. In 1989 Congress raised the amount that must be at stake for diversity cases to be tried in federal court from $10,000 to $50,000. As a result, from 1989-1990 diversity cases dropped 15 percent.[30]

Types of Parties

One may also look at civil cases in terms of the parties involved in the cases. One legal scholar, Marc Galanter, has suggested dividing the parties in civil cases into one-shotters (OS) and repeat players (RP).[31] One-shotters are liti-

TABLE 7-1 TYPES OF CASES IN FEDERAL DISTRICT COURTS, 1990		
Contract actions		46,039
-insurance	6,884	
-marine	3,313	
-negotiable instruments	2,997	
-recovery of overpayments/		
enforcement of judgments	10,328	
-other	21,967	
Real property actions		9,505
-foreclosures	7,196	
-other	2,309	
Tort actions		43,759
-product liability	18,679	
-other personal injury	21,914	
-federal property damage	3,166	
Actions under statutes		118,465
-antitrust	472	
-bankruptcy	5,056	
-civil rights	18,793	
-copyright/patent/trademark	5,700	
-forfeiture and penalty	6,193	
-labor laws	13,841	
-prisoner petitions	42,630	
-securities/commodities/exchanges	2,629	
-social security laws	7,439	
-tax suits	2,604	
-other	13,108	
Other		111
TOTAL CIVIL CASES		217,879

SOURCE: *Annual Report of the Administrative Office of the United States Courts 1990* (Washington, D.C.: Administrative Office of the Courts, 1990), pp. 139-140, Table C-2A.

gants who have only occasional recourse to the courts—for example, spouses in divorce actions and taxpayers in tax cases. In contrast, repeat players are engaged in many similar litigations over time—for example, collection agencies in debt cases and the Internal Revenue Service in tax cases. One-shotters may be either plaintiffs or defendants, as may repeat-players. Table 7-3 categorizes various types of litigation on the basis of the parties in the case. Let us look at each of those categories:[32]

TABLE 7-2 PARTIES IN CIVIL CASES IN FEDERAL DISTRICT COURTS, 1990		
Cases Involving the United States Government:		56,300 (25.8%)
As plaintiff:	31,763	
As defendant:	24,537	
Cases Involving Private Parties Only:		161,579 (74.2%)
Questions of federal law:	103,938	
Diversity of citizenship:	57,183	
Other	458	

SOURCE: *Annual Report of the Director of the Administrative Office of the United States Courts* (Washington, D.C.: Administrative Office of the Courts, 1990), p. 8, Table 6.

OS vs. OS

Much of this litigation merely involves judicial ratification of settlements previously agreed to by the parties. For example, over 90 percent of divorces—by far the most numerous of these cases—are uncontested. However, when the cases involve real disputes, conflict can be intense because the parties often have close personal ties, and spite, resentment, or revenge may fuel the disputes.

RP vs. OS

Many repeat players have legal relationships with large numbers of one-shotters. Owners of apartment complexes, for example, enter into contracts with large numbers of tenants, and finance companies attempt to collect debts from many consumers. These repeat players file suits as part of their normal course of business, using the law to enforce contractual obligations. These case make up a large part of civil litigation, though many cases are settled prior to trial.

OS vs. RP

It is relatively rare for a one-shotter to sue a repeat player. The various factors discussed earlier—the adverse personal consequences of suing, the costs of litigation, and uncertainty about its outcome—deter most one-shotters from filing suit. The sole exception in this category is personal injury cases. Because attorneys take such cases on a contingent basis, that is, their fee is a percentage of the plaintiff's award, one-shotters need not bear the financial costs of litigation. They are therefore more likely to sue.

TABLE 7-3 COMBINATIONS OF PARTIES AND LITIGATION

Initiator, Claimant

	One–Shotter	**Repeat Player**
One-Shotter	Parent v. Parent (Custody) Spouse v. Spouse (Divorce) Family v. Family Member (Insanity Commitment) Family v. Family (Inheritance) Neighbor v. Neighbor Partner v. Partner OS vs OS I	Prosecutor v. Accused Finance Co. v. Debtor Landlord v. Tenant I.R.S. v. Taxpayer Condemnor v. Property Owner RP vs OS II
Repeat Player	Welfare Client v. Agency Auto Dealer v. Manufacturer Injury Victim v. Insurance Company Tenant v. Landlord Bankrupt Consumer v. Creditors Defamed v. Publisher OS vs RP III	Union v. Company Movie Distributor v. Censorship Board Developer v. Suburban Municipality Purchaser v. Supplier Regulatory Agency v. Firms of Regulated Industry RP vs RP IV

Defendant

SOURCE: Marc Galanter, "Why the 'Haves' Come Out Ahead: Speculations on the Limits of Legal Change," *Law & Society Review* 9 (Fall 1974), p. 107, Figure 1. Reprinted by permission of the Law and Society Association.

RP vs. RP

Many repeat players interact frequently with other repeat players. Examples include unions and companies, regulators and regulated firms, and builders and suburbs. In order that litigation not jeopardize these ongoing, mutually beneficial relationships, these repeat players tend to develop mechanisms outside the courts to resolve their disputes.

There are, however, two exceptions to this pattern of low litigation rates. First, some repeat players—for example, the American Civil Liberties Union and the Sierra Club—are committed to furthering particular ends and may be quite willing to reject compromise solutions and take disputes to court. Second, government also tends to be quite heavily involved in litigation with other repeat players, both as plaintiff and as defendant.

Outcomes of Civil Cases

The outcome of a civil case depends largely on the facts of the case, the applicable law, and the presentation of the case by the attorneys—or by the parties in the case, if they are not represented by counsel. While the facts differ from case to case, some generalizations can be made about the latter two factors. Once again, Galanter's distinction between one-shotters and repeat players is useful.[33]

OS vs. OS

In terms of legal representation, one-shotters typically find themselves rather evenly matched. Generally, either both parties have retained counsel or neither has, and neither party is like to hire an attorney from the elite ranks of the legal profession. Because disparities in the quality of counsel are unlikely to determine the outcome of disputes between one-shotters, the substance of the law may have a decisive effect on the outcome of the case.

The effect of the law—and of changes in the law—on case outcomes can be seen if one looks at the most frequent cases pitting one-shotters against one-shotters, namely, divorce cases.[34] Prior to 1970, every state required fault-based grounds for divorce, such as adultery or mental cruelty, with the conduct of the parties during the marriage the key determinant of their financial rights and obligations after divorce. Under this law women fared relatively well in the distribution of marital property and the provision of financial support. In 1970, however, California instituted a system of no-fault divorce, under which marriages could be dissolved on the basis of "irreconcilable differences." The California reform, which was soon adopted by other states as well, also established gender-neutral rules that removed many of the legal and financial protections that the law had provided. Thus the consequence of instituting no-fault divorce, unanticipated and unintended by reformers, was that "women, and the minor children in their households, typically experience[d] a sharp decline in their standard of living after divorce."[35]

RP vs. RP

Because litigation is a normal part of their doing business, repeat players typically retain experienced, specialized counsel. Thus, as in cases involving one-shotters, disputes between repeat players usually involve a rough parity in legal representation. However, because repeat players expect to litigate, they—unlike one-shotters—tend to take steps to ensure that the applicable law is favorable to their interests. They may seek to influence the law that government creates—both business and labor, for example, lobby hard on legislation affecting labor relations. If the applicable law arises out of private agreements, repeat players employ their legal expertise and negotiating skills to fashion favorable contracts. They also attempt to promote a body of judicial precedent favorable to their interests. Thus, in litigation repeat players are concerned not merely with the outcome of individual cases but also with their long-term legal advantage. Repeat players that succeed in securing favorable legislation, contracts, and judicial interpretations can expect to advance their interests through litigation.

RP vs. OS; OS vs. RP

Repeat players enjoy significant advantages in their disputes with one-shotters. Expecting some conflicts in their transactions with one-shotters, repeat players can structure the law at the outset to place themselves at an advantage. As Galanter observes, "it is the RP who writes the form contract, requires the security deposit, and the like," and one-shotters seldom seek to renegotiate the requirements.[36] Moreover, repeat players do not share the one-shotters' concerns about litigating: they understand the process and have sufficient experience to calculate their chances of success. Unlike one-shotters, repeat players usually have hired or retained lawyers, and so their start-up costs for litigating are minimal. Because of this ongoing relationship, the repeat players' lawyers tend to be specialists in the field, whereas those chosen by one-shotters often are not.

The different objectives pursued by one-shotters and repeat players may also work to the repeat players' advantage. As plaintiffs, one-shotters are concerned with having their claims vindicated, and as defendants, with avoiding or minimizing liability. Repeat players, in contrast, are concerned not only with the present case but also with promoting a favorable outcome in future cases. They therefore will be inclined to settle cases that might establish unfavorable precedents and to adjudicate those that will yield favorable ones. As a result, over time repeat players can create a body of law that serves their interests.

Are things really as dismal for one-shotters as Galanter's analysis suggests? The answer is both yes and no. Suits by repeat players against one-shotters comprise the most numerous category of litigation, and several studies suggest that repeat players generally prevail, often by default judgments.[37] (Of course, in many of these cases—for example, creditor-debtor cases—they prevail because one-shotters have failed to meet their clear legal obligations.) On the other hand, one-shotters have enjoyed considerable success as plaintiffs in products liability cases, in which they are suing manufacturers for injuries suffered as a result of alleged product defects.[38] These cases, however, diverge in important respects from other disputes between one-shotters and repeat players. Expert legal representation for one-shotters tends to be readily available—plaintiffs' lawyers in products liability cases are legal specialists, who take cases on a contingent-fee basis. For another, this segment of the bar shares the repeat players' interest in the long-term development of products liability law and acts to secure a body of law favorable to their clients'—and their own—interests. In sum, aggressive attorneys representing one-shotters and their interests may help to equalize the prospects of repeat players and one-shotters involved in a dispute.

A LITIGATION CRISIS?

The Indictment

In recent years, the civil justice system of the United States has come under sustained attack. Consider the indictment: Americans have developed "a mad romance . . . with the civil litigation process."[39] However outrageous the claim, there is a litigant willing to press it and a court to hear it (see Box 7-1). And encouraging this propensity to litigate differences and file frivolous suits is the world's largest legal profession. Not surprisingly, then, "[o]ur society has become the most litigious society in the world. No other nation is even close."[40] "This massive, mushrooming litigation has caused horrendous ruptures and dislocations at a flabbergasting cost to the nation."[41] Litigants themselves bear some of the costs: with overloaded courts, justice is slower and more expensive than ever. The nation's economy also suffers: "Like a plague of locusts, U.S. lawyers with their clients have descended upon America and are suing the country out of business."[42] Only the nation's economic competitors benefit as energies and resources are diverted from "research and development" to "document production and depositions."[43] Fundamental reform of the the civil justice system is essential.

If this harsh assessment is accurate, one could hardly oppose the call for reform. But is it accurate? Let us first consider the basic premise of the indictment, namely, that the United States is today an excessively litigious society.

Is the United States a Litigious Society?

One way to answer that question is to compare litigation rates in the United States with those in other nations. Contrary to the claims of alarmists, such a

---

BOX 7-1 OUTRAGEOUS SUITS?

A man sues a former girl-friend, trying to force her to pay for his time and expenses on a date she did not keep.

A class action suit is filed against General Motors on behalf of "all persons everywhere now alive and all future unborn generations," seeking $6 trillion in damages for pollution.

A high-school student sues her gym teacher and the city after breaking her finger in a school softball game. She alleges that the teacher not only failed to instruct her how to catch a ball but also failed to warn her of the dangers of the sport.

A group of Washington Redskins fans sue to have a court overturn a controversial referee's call that cost the Redskins a win in a football game.

The Italian Historical Society of America sues the Post Office, asking a federal court to bar the issuing of a stamp celebrating Alexander Graham Bell on the grounds that the telephone had actually been invented by Antonio Meucci.

A woman sues the state of California after being told that she did not win the state lottery, because her ball popped out of the winning slot after momentarily entering it.

Of course, filing a suit and collecting damages are two different things. Courts refused to rule for the plaintiffs in all but the last case. However, a jury in that case awarded the disappointed lottery player the $3 million jackpot, plus $400,000 for her emotional trauma.

SOURCES: The first case is described in Lawrence Friedman, *The Republic of Choice; Law, Authority, and Culture* (Cambridge: Harvard University Press, 1990), p. 16; the next four, in Jethro K. Lieberman, *The Litigious Society* (New York: Basic Books, 1981), pp. 4-5; and the final case in Walter K. Olson, *The Litigation Explosion; What Happened When America Unleashed the Lawsuit* (New York: Truman Talley Books, 1991), p. 170.

comparison suggests that the United States is not exceptional. Some countries—most notably, Japan—have litigation rates far lower than those in the United States (see Box 7-2). But several others—among them, Australia, Denmark, England, and Israel—have roughly comparable litigation rates, and still others, such as Yugoslavia, reported substantially higher rates.[44]

One might also consider whether Americans are particularly prone to resolving their disputes by taking them to court. The surveys of potential legal prob-

BOX 7-2 WHY DON'T THE JAPANESE SUE?

If the United States is seen as a litigious society, Japan has just the opposite reputation. In 1986, for example, Japan's per capita litigation rate was only one tenth that of California. This disparity is particularly striking because Japan shares with the United States many characteristics that presumably promote litigation, such as an advanced economy and an urbanized population. Why don't the Japanese sue?

One explanation for the disparity is cultural differences. Traditional Japanese values, it is argued, are oriented toward consensus, toward avoiding conflict and subsuming personal concerns in the interest of the group. Yet if the reluctance to litigate derived from traditional Confucian beliefs, one would expect litigation rates to rise as the modernization of Japanese society undermined those beliefs. In fact, however, litigation rates in Japan today are lower than in the past. More than cultural factors must be involved.

What also keeps litigation rates low, even as Japanese society changes, are governmental policies designed to discourage litigation. The Japanese government has restricted the size of the legal profession, thereby reducing access to legal services. The total number of practicing lawyers in Japan is lower than the number of graduates each year from American law schools, and in Japan only 500 new lawyers annually are permitted to pass the bar exam. In addition, the government has limited the size and effectiveness of the judiciary, so that litigants cannot expect a speedy vindication of their claims. The rules of Japanese courts, such as the ban on class action suits, also discourage individuals from pursuing claims. Finally, when disputes do arise, the Japanese government has developed alternative forums to handle them, such as its system of court-annexed mediation and the Traffic Accident Dispute Resolution Center.

The Japanese experience reveals that when disputes arise, the values and expectations of the society can encourage or discourage litigation. But so too can governmental policies designed to reduce access, increase delay, and deny relief or, alternatively, to facilitate legal redress of grievances. Far from being the inevitable product of societal development, litigation reflects the values and institutions of the society.

SOURCES: Takao Tanase, "The Management of Disputes: Automobile Accident Compensation in Japan," *Law & Society Review* 24 (1990): 651-689; Robert L. Kidder and John A. Hostetler, "Managing Ideologies: Harmony as Ideology in Amish and Japanese Societies," *Law & Society Review* 24 (1990): 895-922, and Lawrence M. Friedman, *Total Justice* (New York: Russell Sage Foundation, 1985).

lems noted previously suggest that Americans are reluctant to litigate and generally do not transform their disputes into litigation. However, their willingness to litigate varies from issue to issue. The only comparative study of the propensity to sue concludes that Americans tend to sue in cases of personal injury somewhat more often than do Britons or Canadians (but not more often than Australians do).[45] This evidence hardly supports the notion of a populace involved in "a mad romance with the civil litigation process."

Finally, one might consider whether Americans are more litigious now than in the past. Certainly, the level of litigation in the United States has risen over time (see Table 7-4). Yet this does not necessarily mean that Americans have become more litigious, because the nation's population has also increased, so there are more Americans to file suits. Indeed, from 1900 to 1960, per capita litigation in the United States remained relatively stable.[46] Since that time, however, the increases in litigation have outstripped population growth.

TABLE 7-4   CIVIL FILINGS IN STATE TRIAL COURTS OF GENERAL JURISDICTION, 1984-1990 (SELECTED STATES)

State	Total Civil Index 1984	Total Civil Index 1990	Total Population Growth 1984-1990
Alaska	100	83	110
California	100	129	120
Florida	100	145	118
Illinois	100	105	99
Kansas	100	136	102
Maine	100	102	106
Missouri	100	124	102
New Jersey	100	149	103
New York	100	173	101
Oklahoma	100	96	95
South Carolina	100	104	99
Texas	100	103	106
Virginia	100	138	110
Wisconsin	100	109	103

SOURCE: Adapted from *State Court Caseload Statistics: Annual Report 1990* (Williamsburg, Va.: National Center for State Courts), p. 18, Text Table I.7.

NOTE: For purposes of comparison, caseload and population levels in each state in 1984 have been set to equal 100. Levels for 1990 therefore represent percentage change for each.

Although this seems to support the notion that Americans have become more litigious, in the sense of eager to sue, one should be cautious in drawing that conclusion.

For one thing, although filings have risen, they have not increased uniformly in all regions of the country and in all areas of the law, as might be expected if Americans had grown more litigious. The greatest single source of the increase in filings is an increase in divorce (and post-divorce) proceedings. As one author wryly noted: "Few of us, I suspect, know many people who filed for divorce because they were enamored of litigation or beguiled by lawyers."[47] In addition, historical studies reveal that although litigation has increased in the United States throughout the twentieth century, its growth has been episodic and uneven.[48] The current "litigation explosion" may thus be merely a short-term phenomenon. Historical studies also show that current levels of per capita litigation in the United States are hardly unprecedented. Higher per capita rates existed in colonial times and during part of the nineteenth century.[49]

In sum, despite widely publicized claims to the contrary, the evidence suggests that the United States is not an unusually litigious society. Nonetheless, litigation in the United States may still adversely affect the legal system and the economy, as critics have charged. We shall analyze the economic effects of litigation in Chapter 11, when we examine tort law and products-liability claims. Let us look here, however, at current efforts to respond to litigation levels and improve the system of civil justice.

IS THERE A BETTER WAY?

Despite their differences, critics of the "litigation explosion" and advocates of greater access to the courts agree on one thing: the American system of civil justice must be improved. The general public seems to share their dissatisfaction, viewing litigation as unduly slow, complex, and costly.[50] Other critics of American civil justice complain that formal legal processes hamper courts in addressing the problems underlying disputes and in fashioning lasting consensual solutions to those problems.[51]

During the 1970s, legal reformers began to propose that less formal forums be created outside the courts to help solve these problems of heavy caseloads, costly justice, and ineffectiveness in settling disputes. Over the last decade, this movement for "alternative dispute resolution"—or ADR, as it is usually called —has enjoyed considerable success. In 1989 alone, state legislatures enacted

more than thirty ADR statutes.[52] A year earlier, Congress had passed the Court
Reform and Access to Justice Act, which authorized pilot ADR programs
attached to federal district courts.[53] Corporations and other private institutions
have also pioneered their own mechanisms for resolving disputes without
recourse to the courts.

Alternatives in Dispute Resolution

Alternative dispute resolution (ADR) encompasses a wide range of forums and
processes. Although considerable differences exist among operating ADR programs, most involve either arbitration or mediation.

Arbitration

Voluntary arbitration

After a period in the major leagues, a baseball player who cannot agree on a
salary with his team is eligible to take the dispute to arbitration. The player
proposes a salary that he believes fair and offers arguments and evidence for his
position. The team submits a different figure and supports its position. The
arbitrator then chooses between the two figures, and both parties are bound by
that decision.

Baseball's system of salary arbitration reveals the basic features of arbitration:
a dispute is submitted to a neutral third party, who hears arguments, reviews
evidence, and renders a decision. As our example suggests, most often voluntary
arbitration is used to resolve labor disputes. In recent years, however, it has also
been employed to settle commercial disputes in various industries, including
construction and insurance.[54]

Although the arbitrator plays a quasi-judicial role, voluntary arbitration differs from litigation in crucial respects. First, voluntary arbitration can occur
only if both parties have consented, usually by contract, to submit their disputes
to arbitration. Baseball's system of salary arbitration, for example, resulted from
a collective bargaining agreement between the players' union and the team
owners. Second, the arbitrators in voluntary arbitration are selected and paid by
the parties. Agreement between the parties determines whether there shall be a
single arbitrator or a panel of arbitrators, the scope of their authority, and how
they shall be selected. Third, voluntary arbitration proceeds according to
ground rules negotiated by the parties. Usually, formal rules of evidence and
procedure are dispensed with in arbitration. This procedural informality simpli-
fies and speeds the process of decision. Fourth, voluntary arbitration promotes

timely decisionmaking. In simple cases the arbitrator may render an immediate decision. Even in complex cases, because they are not obliged to write opinions, arbitrators announce their decisions quickly, usually within thirty days of the conclusion of the arbitration hearing.

Court-annexed arbitration

Court-annexed arbitration might also be called compulsory arbitration.[55] The court assigns selected civil cases, usually those involving relatively small sums of money, to arbitration as a precondition to or as a substitute for trial. Nevada, for example, requires that all civil actions arising out of automobile accidents and involving less than $15,000 be submitted to arbitration.[56] The arbitrator, usually designated by the state, hears arguments and evidence and renders a decision, applying the same legal standards that a judge would apply. If the parties accept the arbitrator's ruling, it is formalized as the court's judgment in the case. If either party objects to the ruling, it can demand a trial of the case; thus the arbitrator's decision is not binding. In most jurisdictions, however, financial penalties discourage frivolous appeals of arbitrators' rulings. In Colorado, for example, unless the party demanding trial improves its position by more than ten percent, it must pay all the costs of the arbitration proceeding, up to $1000.[57]

Since 1952, when the first program was introduced in Pennsylvania, eighteen states and most federal district courts have instituted court-annexed arbitration programs.

Mediation

Mediation attempts to resolve disputes by "assist[ing] the disputants to reach a voluntary settlement of their differences through an agreement that defines their future behavior."[58] In divorce mediation, for example, the agreement may resolve such contentious matters as the division of marital property, child support payments, and visitation rights. In neighborhood disputes, the agreement may specify the actions that each disputant will take or avoid in the future.

Mediators do not render authoritative decisions, like arbitrators or judges at trial, but merely facilitate settlements between the disputants. The success of their efforts thus depends on their interpersonal skills and on their ability to win the trust and cooperation of the disputants. Advocates of mediation view this lack of coercion as an advantage. Requiring that disputants become actively involved in resolving the dispute ensures that the outcome will be one acceptable to both parties.

Mediators promote settlement largely by fostering a productive negotiating climate, in which issues are addressed in an orderly fashion, hostility is controlled, and the need for compromise is recognized. They also may play a more active part in the negotiations, obliging the disputants to clarify their objectives, offering suggestions for settlement, and translating the agreements reached into a written document.[59]

In recent years government programs have promoted the use of mediation to resolve disputes between divorcing couples and within neighborhoods. Many states now offer divorce mediation to promote settlements regarding the division of property, child custody, and visitation rights. California has mandated mediation in all such instances.[60] Although exact figures are unavailable, experts estimated that there were 28,000 divorce mediations in 1980 and over 34,000 a year later—a rise of almost 25 percent.[61] A similar growth has occurred in the use of mediation to deal with neighborhood disputes. In 1975, there were only 11 "neighborhood justice centers" nationwide; a decade later, there were 182.[62] Most of these centers employ mediators to resolve disputes brought by neighborhood residents or referred to them by the courts.

Does ADR Work?

Legal reformers insist that ADR provides fast and inexpensive justice, and the rapid expansion of ADR over the last fifteen years suggests that their arguments have been persuasive. However, ADR has its critics as well.[63] These critics observe that some of the claims for ADR seem contradictory—can it really promote greater access to justice, while at the same time reducing the demands on the courts? Beyond that, they claim that ADR is a class-based reform that shunts the disputes of the average citizen to lesser tribunals while reserving the courts for the concerns and disputes of the elite.[64] Furthermore, they argue that ADR disarms victims of injustice, since their insistence on the full vindication of their rights runs counter to ADR's emphasis on compromise and accommodation.[65]

These are serious charges. Let us look at the actual effects of ADR, focusing on its consequences for access to justice, the caseloads of the courts, the costs of securing justice, and the quality of justice obtained by those whose disputes are addressed through ADR.

Access to Justice

Many ADR programs have been designed to increase the accessibility of justice, especially for those involved in "minor" disputes. These programs do not charge for services nor require lawyers. They may hold hearings at times convenient to all disputants, such as evenings or weekends, and provide multilingual staffs to serve non-English speaking disputants.[66] These features, however, have not attracted large numbers of disputants who were unwilling to bring their disputes to court. The vast majority of cases come to ADR programs on referral from courts or other institutions, rather than from disputants directly seeking their services.[67] Thus ADR programs have not substantially increased access to justice. Whether this will change as ADR programs become institutionalized and well-publicized remains to be seen.

Effects on Court Caseloads

The fact that most disputes come to ADR programs on referral suggests that these programs relieve caseload pressures on the courts. Many proponents of ADR see this as its prime advantage.[68] Although ADR programs have reduced court caseloads somewhat, thus far their impact has been quite limited. In part, this reflects the small size of most ADR programs—an American Bar Association survey found that 60 percent of ADR programs received less than 500 referrals per year and only 4 percent more than 5,000.[69] Of course, as ADR programs increase in number and size, so will their impact on caseloads.

Yet an increase in the disputes handled by ADR programs does not produce a corresponding decrease in court caseloads. Some disputes referred to ADR might have been unsuitable for judicial resolution—a study of five mediation centers found that 22 percent of the cases they handled fit that category.[70] In addition, the parties might have settled their dispute before trial if it had not been referred to an ADR program. Finally, ADR programs may not conclusively resolve the cases referred to them. When the disputants cannot reach an agreement in mediation, they may take their dispute to court. When an arbitrator renders a decision in court-annexed arbitration, the losing party has the option of taking the case to court (although relatively few elect to do so).[71] In sum, ADR programs have the potential to reduce court caseloads but have so far had only a limited impact.

The Costs of Justice

Perhaps the clearest advantage of ADR is that it reduces the costs to government of dispensing justice and to disputants of obtaining it. Nor is this surprising: ADR eliminates judges and juries, streamlines procedures, and disposes of disputes more quickly than courts can. Thus one study found that it cost about $76 to process a case through arbitration and $175 to hear a case.[72] Disputants benefit not only from the greater efficiency of ADR proceedings but also, in most instances, from the opportunity to pursue their claims without incurring the cost of a lawyer.

The Quality of Justice

The absence of judges, lawyers, and jurors, however, raises a serious question: are disputants under ADR receiving "second-class justice"? Critics contend that government uses ADR to get rid of working-class citizens and their disputes, rather than giving them the serious consideration they deserve. Studies of mediation programs that deal with neighborhood problems offer some support for this contention: complainants disproportionately came from the lower-middle class.[73] However, not all ADR programs share this class character. Divorce mediation programs draw disputants from all social classes, as do court-annexed arbitration programs.[74]

Critics also contend that government gives first-class treatment to business cases, while palming off interpersonal disputes to ADR. Undoubtedly, courts are eager to avoid involvement in interpersonal disputes—court personnel often refer to them as "junk cases" and complain that they "don't belong here."[75] Yet their reluctance to deal with interpersonal disputes derives, at least in part, from the recognition that courts are ill-equipped to resolve such disputes. The real question is whether mediation and arbitration do a better job.

Legal scholars have attempted to answer this question by surveying disputants' views about the fairness of the process and outcomes under ADR.[76] Their surveys reveal widespread satisfaction with how disputes were handled and resolved. These responses are particularly striking when compared with litigants' evaluations of court processes. In divorce mediation, for example, where participants were involved both with courts and with mediation, 98 percent of those who had success in mediation expressed satisfaction with the process, as did 57 percent of those who had no success, but only 36 percent were satisfied with the court processes.[77]

Similar results were obtained when disputants were questioned about how effective judicial rulings and mediation agreements were in promoting long-term solutions to their disputes. Surveys reveal that mediation promotes greater understanding, reduced anger, and improved relationships.

While these findings suggest the superiority of mediation and arbitration to adjudication, at least for certain types of cases, they do not necessarily demonstrate that cases should be resolved by ADR programs rather than by courts. Most cases that come to the courts are in fact settled rather than adjudicated. Judges too engage in mediation to settle cases, as our discussion of the Agent Orange case showed. Marc Galanter has referred to the process by which civil cases are resolved as "litigation," emphasizing the blurring of boundaries between litigation and other forms of dispute resolution.[78] This seems an accurate characterization of the current approach for dealing with civil cases in the United States.

CONCLUSIONS

"As a litigant," a learned judge once wrote, "I should dread a lawsuit beyond almost anything else short of sickness and death."[79] Nevertheless, Americans file millions of lawsuits each year. This is not because Americans are unusually litigious—the evidence suggests that the United States is not an overly litigious society. But in a complex, populous society like the United States, disputes are bound to arise. Moreover, advances in technology have transformed expectations of justice, making people less willing to accept injuries as fated or as "nobody's fault." Courts afford one mechanism for resolving those disputes and redressing those injuries.

Litigation, however, is only one among a number of options for dealing with grievances. As we have seen, most grievances do not become disputes, and most disputes do not become court cases. Psychic costs, financial costs, and uncertainty all discourage potential litigants from filing suit. Yet these costs do not fall evenly on all segments of the population. They weigh more heavily on one-shotters than on repeat-players, and this is reflected in the sorts of civil cases brought to the courts for resolution.

Even when litigants do file civil suits, their cases are far more likely to be settled than adjudicated. Indeed, what unites the various reforms of the civil justice system—liberalized rules for discovery, pretrial conferences, and the alternative dispute resolution movement, for example—is the emphasis on promoting settlement and discouraging trials. Indeed, trials seem an anomaly, occurring only when the various mechanisms designed to produce a consensual solution have failed. In this respect the system of civil justice in the United States closely resembles the system of criminal justice, with its emphasis on plea bargaining rather than trial. The question remains whether these systems serve the interests of justice.

NOTES

1. Quoted in Peter H. Schuck, *Agent Orange on Trial: Mass Toxic Disasters in the Courts* (Cambridge: Belknap Press, 1986), p. 256. Our description of the Agent Orange litigation relies on Schuck's account.

2. Quoted in ibid., p. 45.

3. Quoted in ibid., p. 85.

4. Quoted in ibid., p. 68.

5. Robert Mnookin and Lewis Kornhauser, "Bargaining in the Shadow of the Law: The Case of Divorce," *Yale Law Journal* 88 (1979): 950-977.

6. The argument that it is necessary to increase access to justice is presented in Laura Nader, ed., *No Access to Law: Alternatives to the American Judicial System* (New York: Academic Press, 1980); Mauro Capelletti and D. Garth, "Access to Justice: The Newest Wave in the Worldwide Movement to Make Rights Effective," *Buffalo Law Review* 27 (Spring 1978): 181-292; and Daniel McGillis, *Community Dispute Resolution Programs and Public Policy* (Washington, D.C.: U.S. Department of Justice, National Institute of Justice, 1986), Chapter 2.

7. The argument that the United States suffers from too much litigation is presented in Walter K. Olson, *The Litigation Explosion; What Happened When America Unleashed the Lawsuit* (New York: Truman Talley Books, 1991).

8. See Lawrence M. Friedman, *Total Justice* (New York: Russell Sage Foundation, 1985), Part I, and Jethro K. Lieberman, *The Litigious Society* (New York: Basic Books, 1981), Chapter 1.

9. This discussion uses a framework developed by William L. F. Felstiner, "Influences of Social Organization on Dispute Processing," *Law & Society Review* 9 (Fall 1974): 63-94.

10. William L. F. Felstiner, "Avoidance as Dispute Processing: An Elaboration," *Law and Society Review* 9 (Summer 1975), p. 695.

11. Barbara A. Curran, *The Legal Needs of the Public* (Chicago: American Bar Foundation, 1977), pp. 141-142.

12. Quoted in Kristin Bumiller, *The Civil Rights Society; The Social Construction of Victims* (Baltimore: Johns Hopkins University Press, 1988), p. 90.

13. Quoted in ibid., p. 52.

14. Charles Alan Wright, *Law of Federal Courts*, 3rd ed. (St. Paul: West Publishing Co., 1976), p. 293.

15. The discussion of the stages in the process of civil litigation draws on Wright, *Law of Federal Courts*, Chapter 10; Mary Kay Kane, *Civil Procedure in a Nutshell*, 2nd ed. (St. Paul: West Publishing Co., 1985), Chapter 3; William P. McLauchlan, *American Legal Processes* (New York: John Wiley & Sons, 1977), Chapter 3; and David W. Neubauer, *Judicial Process; Law, Courts, and Politics in the United States* (Pacific Grove, Calif.: Brooks/Cole Publishing Co., 1991), Chapter 11.

16. Sally Engle Merry, *Getting Justice and Getting Even; Legal Consciousness Among Working-Class Americans* (Chicago: University of Chicago Press, 1990), p. 87.

17. Wright, *Law of Federal Courts*, p. 398.

18. Richard Posner, "An Economic Approach to Legal Procedure and Judicial Administration," *Journal of Legal Studies* 2 (June 1973): 399-458.

19. Olson, *The Litigation Explosion*, p. 119.

20. Judge William Schwarzer, quoted in Robert E. Litan, "Speeding Up Civil Justice," *Judicature* 73 (October-November 1989), p. 162.

21. Kane, *Civil Procedure in a Nutshell*, pp. 141-143.

22. Olson, *The Litigation Explosion*, Chapter 6, and Litan, "Speeding Up Civil Justice." See also recommendations 4-6 of the President's Council on Competitiveness, discussed in Deborah R. Hensler, "Taking Aim at the American Legal System: The Council on Competitiveness's Agenda for Legal Reform," *Judicature* 75 (1992), pp. 246-247.

23. David W. Neubauer, *Judicial Process: Law, Courts, and Politics in the United States* (Pacific Grove, Calif.: Brooks/Cole Publishing Co., 1991), pp. 285-287.

24. Herbert M. Kritzer, "Adjudication to Settlement: Shading in the Gray," *Judicature* 70 (October-November 1986): 161-165.

25. Kritzer, "Adjudication to Settlement," p. 164, Table 3.

26. This discussion of pretrial conferences draws on Wright, *Law of Federal Courts*, pp. 444-447, and Kane, *Civil Procedure in a Nutshell*, pp. 149-154.

27. Wayne D. Brazil, *Settling Civil Suits; Litigators' Views About Appropriate Roles and Effective Techniques for Federal Judges* (Chicago: American Bar Association Press, 1985), pp. 45-46 and *passim*.

28. For data on civil cases in federal district courts, see *Annual Report of the Director of the Administrative Office of the United States Courts 1990* (Washington, D.C.: Administrative Office of the Courts, 1990), p. 7, Table 5. For data on civil cases in state trial courts, see *State Court Caseload Statistics: Annual Report 1990* (Williamsburg, Va.: National Center for State Courts, 1992), p. 14, Chart I.6.

29. *Annual Report of the Director of the Administrative Office of the United States Courts 1990*, pp. 6-7.

30. Ibid., p. 8.

31. Marc Galanter, "Why the 'Haves' Come Out Ahead: Speculations on the Limits of Legal Change," *Law & Society Review* 9 (Fall 1974): 97-107 and *passim*.

32. Ibid.

33. Ibid.

34. This analysis follows that of Lenore J. Weitzman, *The Divorce Revolution* (New York: Free Press, 1985). Subsequent studies have tempered Weitzman's conclusions. See, for example, Herbert Jacob, *Silent Revolution; The Transformation of Divorce Law in the United States* (Chicago:

University of Chicago Press, 1988), and Stephen D. Sugarman and Herma Hill Kay, eds., *Divorce Reform at the Crossroads* (New Haven: Yale University Press, 1990).

35. Weitzman, *The Divorce Revolution*, p. x.

36. Galanter, "Why the 'Haves' Come Out Ahead," p. 98.

37. See generally Craig McEwen and Richard Maiman, "Small Claims Mediation in Maine: An Empirical Assessment," *Maine Law Review* 33 (1981): 237-268; Austin Sarat, "Alternatives in Dispute Processing: Litigation in a Small Claims Court," *Law & Society Review* 10 (Spring 1976): 339-376; and Barbara Yngvesson and Patricia Hennessey, "Small Claims, Complex Disputes: A Review of the Small Claims Literature," *Law & Society Review* 9 (Winter 1975): 219-274. For a cautionary perspective on those findings, see Neil Vidmar, "The Small Claims Court: A Reconceptualization of Disputes and an Empirical Investigation," *Law & Society Review* 18 (1984): 515-550.

38. Robert Roper and Joanne Martin, "Jury Verdicts and the 'Crisis' in Civil Justice: Some Findings from an Empirical Study," *Justice System Journal* 11 (Winter 1986): 321-348.

39. Quoted in Marc Galanter, "The Day After the Litigation Explosion," *Maryland Law Review* 46 (1986), p. 3.

40. Quoted in Richard D. Catenacci, "Hyperlexis or Hyperbole: Subdividing the Landscape of Disputes and Defusing the Litigation Explosion," *Review of Litigation* 8 (Fall 1989), p. 320.

41. Quoted in Galanter, "Day After the Litigation Explosion," p. 3.

42. Quoted in ibid., p. 4.

43. Quoted in Gregory Brian Butler and Brian David Miller, "Fiddling While Rome Burns: A Response to Dr. Hensler," *Judicature* 75 (February-March 1992), p. 251.

44. Marc Galanter, "Reading the Landscape of Disputes: What We Know and Don't Know (And Think We Know) About Our Allegedly Contentious and Litigious Society," *U.C.L.A. Law Review* 31 (1983), pp. 54-59.

45. Herbert M. Kritzer, "Propensity to Sue in England and the United States: Blaming and Claiming in Tort Suits," *Journal of Law and Society* 18 (Winter 1991): 400-427.

46. David W. Neubauer, "Are We Approaching Judicial Gridlock? A Critical Review of the Literature," *Justice System Journal* 11 (Winter 1986), p. 365.

47. Galanter, "Day After the Litigation Explosion," p. 10.

48. Stephen Daniels, "Ladders and Bushes: The Problem of Caseloads and Studying Court Activities Over Time," *American Bar Foundation Research Journal* (1984): 751-796; and Wayne V. McIntosh, *The Appeal of Civil Law; A Political-Economic Analysis of Litigation* (Urbana: University of Illinois Press, 1990), Chapter 7.

49. Galanter, "Day After the Litigation Explosion," p. 5; and McIntosh, *Appeal of Civil Law*, esp. p. 166, Table 7.4.

50. For public opinion data on courts and their operations, see Yankelovich, Skelly and White, Inc., *The Public Image of Courts: Highlights of a National Survey of the General Public, Judges, Lawyers and Community Leaders* (Williamsburg, Va.: National Center for State Courts, 1978).

51. A representative exposition of this viewpoint is Stephen B. Goldberg, Eric D. Green, and Frank E. A. Sander, *Dispute Resolution* (Boston: Little Brown & Co., 1985). Not all commentators share this assessment; see, for example, Christine B. Harrington, *Shadow Justice; The Ideology and Institutionalization of Alternatives to Court* (Westport, Conn.: Greenwood Press, 1985), Chapter 3.

52. Standing Committee on Dispute Resolution, American Bar Association, *Legislation on Dispute Resolution* (Washington, D.C.: American Bar Association, 1990), p. 63.

53. 28 U.S.C. 651 (1988).

54. This discussion of arbitration draws upon John W. Cooley, "Arbitration vs. Mediation— Explaining the Differences," *Judicature* 69 (February-March, 1986): 263-269, and Susan M. Leeson and Bryan M. Johnston, *Ending It* (Cincinnati: Anderson Publishing Co., 1988), Chapter 3.

55. This analysis draws upon the treatment of court-annexed arbitration in Leeson and Johnston, *Ending It*, Chapter 4; Deborah Hensler, "What We Know and Don't Know About Court Administered Arbitration," *Judicature* 69 (February-March, 1986): 270-278; and Note, "Court-Annexed Arbitration: The Verdict Is Still Out," *Review of Litigation* 8 (Fall 1989): 327-346.

56. Standing Committee on Dispute Resolution, *Legislation on Dispute Resolution*, p. 75.

57. Colorado Mandatory Arbitration Act, reprinted in *Legislation on Dispute Resolution*, p. 80.

58. Cooley, "Arbitration vs. Mediation—Explaining the Differences," p. 266, and Leeson and Johnston, *Ending It*, Chapter 6.

59. Kenneth Kressel, *The Process of Divorce; How Professionals and Couples Negotiate Settlements* (New York: Basic Books, 1985), pp. 179-180.

60. Ibid., p. 182.

61. Ibid.

62. McGillis, *Community Dispute Resolution Programs and Public Policy*, p. 7.

63. Major works critical of alternative dispute resolution include: Richard Abel, *The Politics of Informal Justice* (Orlando, Fla.: Academic Press, 1982); Jerold Auerbach, *Justice Without Law* (New York: Oxford University Press, 1984); Harrington, *Shadow Justice*; and Lisa Lerman, "Mediation of Wife Abuse Cases: The Adverse Impact on Women," *Harvard Women's Law Journal* 7 (1984): 57-113.

64. Abel, *Politics of Informal Justice*.

65. Owen M. Fiss, "Against Settlement," *Yale Law Journal* 93 (1984): 1073-1090.

66. McGillis, *Community Dispute Resolution Programs and Public Policy*, p.87.

67. Merry, *Getting Justice and Getting Even*, pp. 182-188.

68. Harrington, *Shadow Justice*, Chapter 1.

69. McGillis, *Community Dispute Resolution Programs and Public Policy*, p. 77.

70. Ibid., p. 76.

71. Hensler, "What We Know and Don't Know About Court Administered Arbitration," p. 275.

72. Ibid., p. 274.

73. See the excellent summary of these studies in Merry, *Getting Justice and Getting Even*, pp. 182-188.

74. See Kressel, *The Process of Divorce*, and Hensler, "What We Know and Don't Know About Court Administered Arbitration," p. 275.

75. Merry, *Getting Justice and Getting Even*, p. 14.

76. These paragraphs rely on the summary of survey data in McGillis, *Community Dispute Resolution Programs and Public Policy*, pp. 61-67. For a dissenting interpretation, see Harrington, *Shadow Justice*, Chapter 5.

77. McGillis, *Community Dispute Resolution Programs and Public Policy*, p. 63.

78. Marc Galanter, "'. . . A Settlement Judge, Not a Trial Judge': Judicial Mediation in the United States," *Journal of Law and Society* 12 (Spring 1985): 1.

79. Learned Hand, "The Deficiencies of Trials to Reach the Heart of the Matter," in Association of the Bar of the City of New York, *Lectures on Legal Topics* (New York: Macmillan, 1926), p. 105.

CHAPTER

8 JUDICIAL DECISIONMAKING

Consider the following two accounts of a recent decision of the United States Supreme Court:

In *Stanford* v. *Kentucky* (1989), the Supreme Court upheld the death sentences imposed on two murderers, who had committed their crimes before reaching their eighteenth birthday.[1] Speaking for a five-member Court majority, Justice Antonin Scalia argued that the Eighth Amendment's ban on cruel and unusual punishments did not preclude imposition of the death penalty on those who were juveniles at the time they committed their offenses. Scalia asserted that the understanding of cruel and unusual punishments at the time the Bill of Rights was ratified offered no support for the appellants' claim. Rather, under the common law at the time of the Founding, one could be tried as an adult when one was fourteen years old. Thus, those who adopted the Bill of Rights did not view it as cruel or unusual to treat teenagers as adults in the criminal-justice process.

Nor did the Supreme Court's prior rulings require invalidation of the offenders' death sentences. While these precedents had established that the Eighth Amendment was to be interpreted in light of the "evolving standards of decency that mark the progress of a maturing society," they also recognized that the statutes enacted by the people's representatives provided the most important evidence of the society's standards of decency.[2] Surveying those statutes, Scalia found that most states permitted capital punishment for sixteen or seventeen-year-old offenders. He therefore concluded that there was neither a historical nor a modern consensus rejecting capital punishment for juveniles who murder. Consequently, speaking for the Court majority, he upheld the death sentences.

* * * *

In *Stanford* v. *Kentucky* (1989), the Supreme Court's five-member conservative majority upheld the imposition of death sentences on two murderers, who had committed their crimes while still juveniles. The Court's ruling marked yet another defeat for those mounting constitutional challenges to capital punishment in the states. It also continued the tough-minded approach to the rights of defendants that has characterized the Court since the elevation of William Rehnquist to Chief Justice.

President Ronald Reagan deserves much of the credit—or blame—for the Court's increasingly conservative stance in criminal-justice cases. Reagan had vowed to appoint conservatives to the Court, and he apparently succeeded. As in many previous cases, all four of Reagan's appointees (all of whom were Republicans) voted together against the defendants' claims. Joining the four to establish the majority was Justice Byron White, who has often provided the crucial fifth vote on criminal-justice issues. The decision in *Stanford,* together with other recent conservative rulings, suggest that President Reagan has indeed reversed the orientation of the Supreme Court.

*   *   *

These two accounts present strikingly different explanations of why the justices rejected the constitutional challenge to the death sentences in *Stanford* v. *Kentucky.* The first account analyzes the legal reasoning offered by the Supreme Court in support of its decision. Thus, it explains the Court's ruling in terms of the original understanding of the Eighth Amendment, the Court's precedents, and the approach traditionally employed by the Court in determining the "standards of decency" prevailing in the society. The second account, in contrast, altogether ignores those legal factors. Instead, it explains the ruling in terms of the political orientation of the justices, the political agenda of the president who appointed them, and interpersonal dynamics on the Supreme Court.

These accounts illustrate two distinct approaches to understanding judicial decisionmaking. The first approach, which we shall call the *legal perspective,* distinguishes judicial decisionmaking from the decisionmaking of other political actors, such as legislators and executives. What is distinctive about judicial decisionmaking, according to this perspective, is that judges are expected to decide cases according to law, rather than on the basis of personal predilection or public opinion, and must justify their rulings through a process of legal reasoning.

The second approach, which might be called the *political perspective,* insists that judicial decisionmaking closely resembles decisionmaking by other political actors. What is decisive in judicial decisionmaking, according to this perspective, are extralegal factors, such as the attitudes of the judges, their conceptions of how they should behave, and the institutional context in which they operate. Although judges must justify their rulings on the basis of law, law merely provides the rationale for judicial decisions; it does not constrain judicial choice.

This chapter describes and compares these two perspectives on judicial decisionmaking. In doing so, it focuses primarily on decisionmaking on appellate courts because those courts—in contrast with trial courts—are primarily concerned with the analysis of legal questions and usually present their analyses in written opinions.

THE LEGAL PERSPECTIVE

The Phases of Judicial Decisionmaking

According to the legal perspective, judicial decisionmaking involves two phases—discovery and justification. "Discovery" involves the judge's initial determination of how a case should be resolved, and "justification" involves the elaboration of the legal bases for the decision in a written opinion.[3] These two phases are interrelated. In the discovery phase, the judge may be said to "intuit" the proper resolution of the case, that is, to arrive at the resolution without proceeding through a step-by-step reasoning process. However, this judicial intuition differs from the intuitive judgment of the average citizen, because the judge's intuition is a professional judgment. More specifically, a judge's intuition is informed by her legal training and her experience on the bench. Thus, one may say that the legal bases for resolving the case play a role in the discovery phase as well as in the justification phase of judicial decisionmaking.[4]

In the justification phase, the judge presents the bases for her decision in a written opinion. Because judges do not reach their decisions by a process of formal reasoning, the opinions that judges write do not describe the psychological processes by which they arrived at their decisions. Nevertheless, the requirement that judges publicly justify their rulings is crucial to judicial decisionmaking. This requirement forces the judge to examine whether there are persuasive legal bases supporting the decision she intuited. If there are, she explains those bases in her opinion. If there are not, she must modify her initial position to bring it in line with the weight of legal authority.

The Tools of Judicial Decisionmaking

To decide cases, judges must determine what law is applicable, determine its meaning, and apply the law to the facts of the case. This inquiry may lead them to consult a variety of legal or extralegal materials. Three of these are of particular importance.

The Legal Text

Judicial decisionmaking begins with the text of the applicable constitution, statute, or administrative regulation. (In cases involving the common law, of course, there is no text because there is no legal enactment to interpret.) The text is basic because it is authoritative—the function of the judge is to give effect to the law enacted by the constitution-maker or lawmaker. In addition, the words used in an enactment constitute the best guide to its meaning. It is with this in mind that Justice Felix Frankfurter offered his famous three-step guide to statutory interpretation: (1) Read the statute; (2) read the statute; (3) read the statute![5]

If the meaning of an enactment is clear on its face, then judges need search no further but may merely apply it in the case before them. Legal commentators refer to this as the "plain meaning rule."[6] Often, however, the meaning of an enactment is not immediately obvious; indeed, litigation arises precisely because it is possible to disagree about the meaning of the law. Judges must then analyze the language of the enactment more closely. Consider, for example, the Mann Act—also known as the White Slave Traffic Act—enacted by Congress in 1910. This law made it a felony to "transport or cause to be transported . . . in interstate commerce . . . any woman or girl for the purpose of prostitution or debauchery, or for any other immoral purpose." While the meaning of "prostitution" is plain, the same cannot be said for the other terms of the act, "debauchery" and "any other immoral purpose." Suppose a robber paid for a woman's airline ticket so that she could join him in robbing a bank. Assuming bank robbery is immoral, has he violated the Mann Act?

Looking merely at the text of the Mann Act, a judge would answer that the robber had not violated the law. To understand why, one must look at how judges interpret legal texts. They begin with the presumption that the enactment is a coherent effort to accomplish some purpose.[7] Thus, determining the general purpose of a statute or other enactment is crucial to clarifying the meaning of its various parts. In our hypothetical case, for example, the language of the Mann Act ("prostitution" and "debauchery") suggest that it was designed to prevent the transportation of women for the purpose of sexual misconduct. Therefore the law did not forbid the transportation of women for bank robbery. Judges also read the words in a legal enactment in context rather than merely giving them their dictionary meaning. Justice Oliver Wendell Holmes explained why context is so crucial to interpretation: "A word is not a crystal, transparent and unchanged, it is the skin of a living thought and may vary greatly in color and content, according to the circumstances and the time in which it is used."[8] This context may serve to give specificity to the general language in an enactment. Thus, in the context of the Mann Act, the meaning of "any immoral purpose" is clarified by its appearance in juxtaposition to other language ("prostitution" and "debauchery") dealing with sexual immorality.

As our example illustrates, recurrence to the legal text means more than simply reading the words. The judge examines the text as an integrated whole, determining the purpose of the enactment (which may not be immediately apparent), comparing and reconciling its various provisions, and clarifying its general language through analysis of the context in which the phrases appear. If this analysis does not suffice to answer the legal questions confronting the judge, she may turn to other legal materials.

Legislative History

In their interpretive quest, judges may also consult the "legislative history" of the enactment, that is, materials generated in the course of adopting a statute or constitutional provision.[9] To determine the meaning of a statute, a judge may trace its evolution through the records of committee hearings, through committee reports summarizing the legislation and its purposes, and through the statements of legislators during floor debates. In interpreting provisions of the United States Constitution, for example, a judge may consult James Madison's Notes of the debates at the Constitutional Convention, the debates in the conventions called to ratify the proposed constitution, and the *Federalist Papers* and other commentary contemporaneous with the ratification process.[10] By mining the legislative history of an enactment, a judge may better determine the purposes of the enactment and how its authors believed it should be interpreted.

Legal scholars have long debated the desirability of relying on legislative history. Courts in Great Britain have steadfastly refused to consider legislative materials to determine the intention of Parliament in passing a statute.[11] At least in recent years, however, courts in the United States have been quite willing to look to legislative history, particularly in interpreting statutes.[12] Proponents believe that legislative history helps judges to resolve ambiguities and interpret enactments in line with the intentions of those who adopted them. For example, a judge interpreting the Mann Act could consult the congressional debates surrounding its adoption to determine how its sponsors understood the terms "debauchery" and "other immoral purposes." Even more important, by consulting legislative history, a judge could ensure that her interpretation of the law's purposes coincided with the intentions of the legislators. This is crucial because the legislature's power to enact law necessarily entails the power to prescribe the authoritative meaning of the law that it enacts.[13]

Those who oppose the use of legislative history deny that one can ascribe an intention to a group, such as a legislative body or constitutional convention.[14] They note that statutes and constitutional provisions are the product of group deliberations. Many of those who vote for a measure never state their view of what it means or how it should be interpreted. Those who do speak may do so primarily to influence the judicial interpretation of the provision.[15]   However, there is no reason to assume that the views of those who speak during legislative debates are representative—legislators may have quite different understandings of the enactments they adopt.[16]   Given the unreliability of legislative history, opponents argue that judges should ignore it in favor of analysis of the enactment and of judicial rulings interpreting it.

Precedent

A precedent is a prior judicial decision that might be used as a basis for deciding a current case. In a hierarchical legal system, lower-court judges are obliged to decide cases in line with the precedents established by higher courts. For example, a ruling by the Minnesota Supreme Court on a matter of Minnesota state law is authoritative and binding on judges in the state's trial courts. A ruling by a court of similar rank, however, does not constitute authoritative precedent, in the sense that it need not be followed. For example, a federal court of appeals may interpret a federal law in a particular way, but another federal court of appeals is not obliged to accept the first court's interpretation of the law. Nor is a court legally obliged to adhere to its own prior decisions, at least in the United States. The Supreme Court, for example, may overrule its earlier decisions interpreting the Constitution or federal statutes.

Of course, even when precedents are not authoritative, they may still be persuasive. Thus, a federal court of appeals may, after learning how another appeals court interpreted a federal law, decide that that interpretation was correct and adopt it. Or the Supreme Court may conclude that its earlier rulings interpreting, say, the Eighth Amendment's ban on cruel and unusual punishment were correct and use them to justify its ruling in a current case. Similarly, judges in Alabama or Oregon may seek guidance in the rulings of judges from other states in interpreting the common law.

The system of case law in the United States and Great Britain relies heavily on the doctrine of precedent (or *stare decisis*). Basically, this doctrine states that cases should be decided today as they were decided in the past. Indeed, from

1898-1966 the House of Lords, which serves as the highest court in Great Britain, subscribed to a strict doctrine of precedent, holding itself absolutely bound by its earlier decisions.[17] While courts in the United States have never embraced this extreme position, they too have recognized that strong arguments support judicial adherence to precedent and that departures from precedent therefore require justification.

The doctrine of precedent is particularly important in the resolution of cases at common law, because there is no legal text or legislative history on which to base decisions. However, *stare decisis* also operates in statutory interpretation and, to a lesser extent, in constitutional adjudication. Box 8-1, which surveys the range of opinion on the use of precedent in judicial decisionmaking, reveals the four reasons that are usually offered for adherence to precedent.[18]

Predictability: Adherence to precedent assures a certainty of result which would otherwise be difficult to obtain. This certainty enables people to predict the legal consequences of their actions and to act accordingly. For example, I am more willing to enter into a contract if I can be sure that the law will support me if the other party violates the contract. And I can have that assurance if the law currently upholds contractual obligations and judges adhere to precedent in contract law.

Reliance: Just as people rely on promises in ordering their affairs, so also do they rely on judicial decisions authoritatively establishing the meaning of the law and gauge their behavior accordingly. A departure from precedent, then, is analogous to the breaking of a promise. "Having induced people to act in a certain manner, the legal system could only be blameworthy if it subsequently sought to punish or in any other way thwart the previously announced consequences of action."[19] Simply put, the legal system should give effect to the expectations that it has itself engendered.

Equality: Equality before the law (uniformity of treatment) is an essential element in a just legal system.[20] The doctrine of precedent obliges judges to decide similar cases in the same way. By doing so, it reduces the discretion of judges, thereby ensuring that extraneous factors (such as the race, religion, gender, or social status of the parties) do not infect the process of decision.

Efficiency: The doctrine of *stare decisis* provides judges with a quick and easy basis for justifying their rulings and thus relieves them of the burden of returning to first principles in each case. Instead of having to "reinvent the wheel" in each case, judges can turn to the experience and wisdom of earlier judges in resolving cases. This in turn promotes the timely disposition of cases.

BOX 8-1   PERSPECTIVES ON PRECEDENTS

"Precedents only prove what was done, but not what was well done." (Thomas Hobbes, English philosopher)

"It is better that the law should be certain than that every judge should speculate upon improvements in it." (Lord Eldon, English jurist)

"The question whether the doctrine of stare decisis should be adhered to . . . is always a choice between relative evils. When it appears that the evil resulting from a continuation of the accepted rule must be productive of greater mischief to the community than can possibly ensue from disregarding the previous adjudications on the subject, courts have frequently and wisely departed from precedent." (Chief Justice Arthur Vanderbilt, New Jersey Supreme Court)

"The force of precedent in the law is heightened by an additional factor: that curious, almost universal sense of justice which urges that all men are properly to be treated alike in like circumstances." (Karl Llewellyn, law professor)

"This search for a static security—in the law or elsewhere is misguided. The fact is that security can only be achieved through constant change, through the wise discarding of old ideas that have outlived their usefulness, and through the adapting of others to current facts." (Justice William O. Douglas, U.S. Supreme Court)

"The labors of judges would be increased almost to the breaking point if every past decision could be reopened in every case, and one could not lay one's own course of bricks on the secure foundation of the courses laid by others who had gone before him." (Chief Justice Benjamin Cardozo, New York Court of Appeals)

"It is revolting to have no better reason for a rule of law than that so it was laid down in the time of Henry IV. It is still more revolting if the grounds upon which it was laid down have vanished long since, and the rule simply persist from blind imitation of the past." (Justice Oliver Wendell Holmes, then on the Massachusetts Supreme Judicial Court and later on the U.S. Supreme Court)

SOURCES: Thomas Hobbes, *A Dialogue Between a Philosopher and a Student of the Common Laws of England*, ed. Joseph Cropsey (Chicago: University of Chicago Press, 1971), p. 129; Lord Eldon: *Sheddon* v. *Goodrich*, 8 Ves. 497; Arthur Vanderbilt: *Fox* v. *Snow*, 76 A.2d 877 (1950); Karl Llewellyn, "Case Law," *Encyclopedia of the Social Sciences*, vol. 3 (New York: Macmillan, 1930), p. 249; William O. Douglas, "Stare Decisis," *Columbia Law Review* 49 (1949), p. 735; Benjamin Cardozo, *The Nature of the Judicial Process* (New Haven: Yale University Press, 1921), pp. 149-150; Oliver Wendell Holmes, "The Path of the Law," *Harvard Law Review* 10 (1897), p. 439.

As Box 8-1 indicates, these arguments for *stare decisis* can be countered by arguments against strict adherence to precedent. Moreover, adherence to precedent is not as easy as it may initially appear. To understand why, we must examine the process of judicial reasoning.

Legal Reasoning as Deductive Reasoning

In 1984 Gregory Johnson was convicted of violating a Texas law prohibiting flag desecration after he burned an American flag as part of a political protest. He appealed his conviction to the United States Supreme Court, contending that the Texas statute impinged on his First Amendment right of freedom of speech.[21] Assume that you are a Supreme Court justice confronted with this claim. How do you go about deciding whether Johnson's conviction should be upheld or whether the Texas law should be struck down as unconstitutional?

One possible approach is deductive reasoning. According to the deductive model of judicial reasoning, depicted in Figure 8-1, you as a justice would first

FIGURE 8-1 THE DEDUCTIVE MODEL OF JUDICIAL DECISIONMAKING

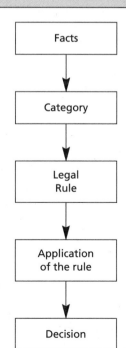

analyze the facts of the case to determine the legal category into which the case fit. In *Texas* v. *Johnson*, for example, the category would be First Amendment cases and, more particularly, cases involving "symbolic speech" (expressive conduct). Next, you would identify the legal rule or standard that governed that category of cases. In constitutional cases, such as our example, you might find that legal rule in the Constitution itself or more likely in earlier rulings interpreting the applicable provision. By applying the rule to the facts of the case, you would then determine whether, according to the rule, the Texas law was constitutional or whether Johnson's expressive conduct was protected by the Constitution. Finally, on the basis of this analysis, you would arrive at your decision.

Is the deductive model an accurate depiction of how judges decide cases? The answer is both yes and no. The more settled the legal rule, the more likely judicial decisionmaking is to resemble the deductive model. In many cases judges can straightforwardly resolve the dispute on the basis of settled law. Indeed, one thoughtful commentator on the judicial process, Justice Benjamin Cardozo, estimated that roughly ninety percent of the cases that come before courts are "predestined," in that they could only be decided in one way.[22]

Yet if judicial decisionmaking were always so simple, then a computer with all the pertinent legal rules stored in its memory could fill the position of a judge. More to the point, judges who knew the law would always agree as to how cases should be decided. In fact, of course, courts often do not display such unanimity. The justices of the United States Supreme Court, for example, decide less than one-third of their cases unanimously.

Why is the deductive model not a fully adequate description of judicial decisionmaking? For one thing, for legal reasoning to follow the deductive model, there must be a single legal rule for the judge to apply in deciding the case. But for some cases there is no controlling precedent or established legal rule. This may occur when a judge interprets a recently enacted statute, or addresses a novel constitutional claim, or confronts an unprecedented situation at common law. For other cases there may be more than one category or rule that seems applicable. In fact, the issue in dispute may be which rule should be applied. Thus, the deductive model of judicial decisionmaking cannot explain how judges deal with novel issues or choose between competing rules. Finally, the deductive model portrays the law as static, with judges consistently applying existing legal standards. In actuality, however, judicial decisions may change the law by overruling precedents or by announcing new legal standards. The deductive model may explain legal stability, but it cannot account for legal change. It cannot explain why judges depart from precedent nor when they should do so.

Legal Reasoning as Reasoning by Example

The deficiencies of the deductive model led a group of legal scholars, known as the Legal Realists, to propose alternative explanations of judicial decisionmaking.[23] One influential Legal Realist, Edward Levi, has suggested that legal reasoning is best understood as reasoning by example and analogy rather than as deductive reasoning.[24] Figure 8-2 offers a schematic representation of Levi's theory.

Levi's Theory

To explain Levi's theory, let us return to our example of *Texas* v. *Johnson*, the flag-burning case.[25] According to Levi, a justice deciding that case would examine how the Supreme Court had previously dealt with expressive conduct that violated state or federal statutes. Presumably, she would discover that in some instances the Court had ruled that the First Amendment protected the expressive conduct and in other instances that it did not.[26] The judge would

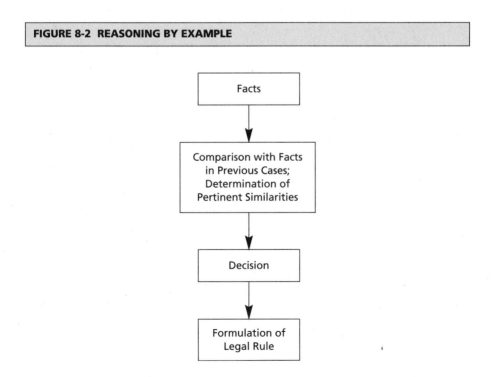

FIGURE 8-2 REASONING BY EXAMPLE

SOURCE: Based on Edward H. Levi, *An Introduction to Legal Reasoning* (Chicago: University of Chicago Press, 1949).

then consider whether the facts in the flag-burning case more closely resembled those in the cases in which the Court had vindicated the expressive conduct or in which it had refused to do so. Presumably, if the *Johnson* case more closely resembled those instances in which the Court had ruled that the expressive conduct was constitutionally protected and struck down the statutes regulating it, the judge would rule in favor of Johnson. If it more closely resembled those instances in which the Court had denied constitutional protection to the expressive conduct and upheld the laws regulating it, the judge would rule in favor of Texas.

As Levi recognized, however, the issue is not that simple. Both sets of prior cases—those upholding and those striking down laws regulating expressive conduct—presumably resemble the flag-burning case in some respects and differ from it in others. A judge must therefore determine which similarities and which differences are decisive. According to Levi, this judicial determination of similarity and difference is the key step in the legal process.

In making this determination, the judge not only decides the case but also devises the legal rule by which the decision is justified. Assuming that she ruled in favor of the flag-burner, her opinion would announce a legal rule that reconciled her ruling with previous decisions protecting expressive conduct. It would also explain why the present case differed from those in which the Court had ruled against First Amendment claims. Put differently, whereas the deductive model suggests that judges decide by applying known rules to diverse facts, Levi insists that "the rules arise out of *a process which, while comparing fact situations, creates the rules and then applies them.*"[27]

Applying Levi's Theory: The Right to Privacy

Levi's theory offers a much more dynamic model of the process of judicial decisionmaking. The Supreme Court's rulings on the right to privacy can serve to illustrate this. The Court first recognized a constitutional right to privacy in *Griswold* v. *Connecticut* (1964).[28] At issue in *Griswold* was a Connecticut law that forbade the use of contraceptives and made it a criminal offense for anyone to give birth-control information. Although the Constitution does not expressly deal with contraception, William O. Douglas, speaking for the Court, ruled that the Connecticut law violated the constitutional right to privacy, which he found implicit in various other guarantees of the Bill of Rights. The statute, Douglas emphasized, invaded the "intimate relation of husband and wife," and its enforcement would require police to search the bedrooms of married couples for evidence of contraceptive use.[29] Thus, in recognizing the constitutional right to privacy, Douglas portrayed it as inhering in a particular relationship (marriage).

Seven years later, in *Eisenstadt* v. *Baird* (1972), the contraception issue again came before the Court.[30] Ex-priest William Baird claimed that a Massachusetts law, which forbade the distribution of contraceptives to unmarried people, violated the constitutional right to privacy recognized in *Griswold*. Clearly, there were similarities between the two cases. Both involved laws that forbade the distribution and use of contraceptives to prevent procreation. Yet there were also differences. The Massachusetts law did not interfere with marital relations, since it only restricted distribution to unmarried people, and its enforcement did not require police to invade the bedroom. The justices thus had to decide whether the situations in the two cases were fundamentally similar, in which case they would invalidate the Massachusetts law on the basis of their precedent in *Griswold*, or different, in which case they could uphold it.

The Supreme Court in *Eisenstadt* struck down the Massachusetts law as a violation of the constitutional right to privacy. Speaking for the Court, Justice William Brennan noted:

> If the right to privacy means anything, it is the right of the individual, married or single, to be free from unwarranted governmental intrusion into matters so fundamentally affecting a person as the decision whether to bear or beget a child.[31]

Although the Court in *Eisenstadt* based its decision on the right to privacy, the quotation indicates that the Court's definition of the right—what Levi refers to as the rule or legal standard—had changed. No longer did the Court view the right to privacy as rooted in certain legally sanctioned relationships, such as marriage (the position it had taken in *Griswold*). Instead, it argued that the right to privacy belonged to the individual. In addition, the Court expanded the right from a safeguard against unreasonable invasions of the bedroom into a right to choose whether or not to procreate.

One year later, the Supreme Court in *Roe* v. *Wade* confronted a constitutional challenge to state laws restricting abortion.[32] Those attacking the laws argued that the restrictions on abortion resembled the restrictions on contraception invalidated in *Griswold* and *Eisenstadt*, in that they intruded on a woman's decision whether or not to bear a child and therefore violated her constitutional right to privacy. Those defending the laws insisted that even if the right to privacy includes the choice whether or not to procreate, that choice had been made when the woman became pregnant. They further argued that the state's valid interest in the life of the fetus and in the safety of medical procedures for abortion distinguished this situation from those on which the Court had already ruled. They thus concluded that the Court's rulings in *Griswold* and *Eisenstadt* did not require invalidation of the Texas law.

The Supreme Court in *Roe*, however, disagreed. The right to privacy, it held, extended to "activities relating to marriage, procreation, contraception, family relationships, and child rearing and education."[33] This represented an elaboration—or extension—of the Court's position in *Eisenstadt*. Having established a realm of freedom from unwarranted governmental regulation, the Court held that "a woman's decision whether or not to terminate her pregnancy" fit within this realm and therefore was protected by the right to privacy.[34]

Thirteen years later, the Supreme Court in *Bowers* v. *Hardwick* (1986) addressed the question of whether the right to privacy extended to consensual homosexual activity.[35] In challenging a Georgia statute prohibiting sodomy, Michael Hardwick noted that the Court's previous privacy rulings—*Griswold*, *Eisenstadt*, and *Roe*—had all struck down governmental regulations affecting sexual relations. He argued that the Georgia statute resembled the laws struck down in earlier cases, in that it likewise regulated choices associated with the realm of sexual intimacy. Therefore, it too represented an unconstitutional invasion of the right to privacy.

A five-member majority on the Court, however, rejected Hardwick's portrayal of the Court's earlier cases. Those cases, Justice Byron White argued for the Court, all involved a connection to "family, marriage, or procreation," a connection absent in the present case.[36] Because the situation in *Bowers* differed in this crucial respect from those in earlier cases, the Court concluded that those cases did not require the extension of the right to privacy to protect homosexual activity. It therefore held that Georgia's sodomy statute was constitutional.

Implications

Our survey of the Supreme Court's privacy rulings illustrates one way that legal change occurs in a system of precedent. Judges may not apply precedent in the mechanical fashion suggested by the deductive model. Rather, they may reason by example, and in doing so they may expand or narrow the reach of earlier decisions. In *Eisenstadt* and *Roe*, for example, the Court discovered similarities to *Griswold* that led it to extend the right to privacy to new situations. In contrast, the Court found that the situation in *Bowers* was fundamentally different from that in previous cases and concluded that the right to privacy did not prevent legal regulation of homosexual activity.

Yet if judicial decisionmaking does not proceed by deductive reasoning, can't judges manipulate precedents and other legal materials in order to decide cases on the basis of their personal values? Unfortunately, there is no simple answer to that question. One check on judges is that they must explain and justify their rulings in written opinions. The fact that these opinions are subject to public scrutiny and criticism imposes some limitation on judges. In addition, judges operate within constraints imposed by the craft of judging and the traditions of the law. Among these constraints is the notion that the judge should decide according to law, even though it may conflict with her personal views. Box 8-2 suggests that judges take this responsibility seriously. However, it also suggests that how judges interpret the law may be affected by their backgrounds, their experience, and their personal values. It is this recognition that leads us to the political perspective on judicial decisionmaking.

THE POLITICAL PERSPECTIVE

The political perspective on judicial decisionmaking begins with the phenomenon of dissenting opinions on multi-member courts. In over two-thirds of the cases decided by the United States Supreme Court in recent years, one or more justices dissented.[37] Although dissent rates are lower on federal courts of appeals and state appellate courts, the judges on those courts also disagree on how a sizable proportion of their cases should be resolved.[38] According to the political perspective, these disagreements cannot be attributed to legal factors. When a multi-member court decides a case, all the judges are construing the same enactments, interpreting the same precedents, and applying the same law to the same set of facts. Thus, difference in the law or in the facts cannot explain differences in judgment.

These differences in judgment occur, according to the political perspective, because the law does not really determine the outcome of most cases. Rarely is the law so clear and definite that only a single position is legally defensible. Rather, in most cases the plaintiff and the defendant can each make a substantial legal argument for ruling in their favor. In such circumstances judges must choose among possible outcomes, and those choices reflect the judges' personal political views. It is those views, then, and not the law, that ultimately determine how cases are resolved.

As Figure 8-3 indicates, however, judicial decisionmaking involves more than judges reading their policy preferences into the law. As James Gibson has observed, "[j]udges' decisions are a function of what they prefer to do, tempered by what they think they ought to do, but constrained by what they perceive is feasible to do."[39] The attitudes of judges determine what they want to do, their role conceptions—their conceptions of proper judicial behavior—affect what the judges believe they ought to do, and public opinion and the institu-

BOX 8-2 JUDICIAL PERSPECTIVES ON PERSONAL VALUES AND DECISIONMAKING

"One who belongs to the most vilified and persecuted minority in history is not likely to be insensitive to the freedoms guaranteed by our Constitution. Were my purely personal attitude relevant, I should whole-heartedly associate myself with the general libertarian views in the Court's opinion, representing as they do the thought and action of a lifetime. But as judges we are neither Jew nor Gentile, neither Catholic nor agnostic.... As a member of this Court, I am not justified in writing my private notions of policy into the Constitution, no matter how deeply I may cherish them or how mischievous I may deem their disregard." (Justice Felix Frankfurter, dissenting in *West Virginia Board of Education* v. *Barnette* [1943])

"The language of the judicial decision is mainly the language of logic... Behind the logical form lies a judgment as to the relative worth and impor-tance of competing legislative grounds, often an inarticulate and uncon-scious judgment, it is true, and yet the very root and nerve of the whole proceeding." (Justice Oliver Wendell Holmes, at that time a member of the Massachusetts Supreme Judicial Court [1897])

"Since 1879 Connecticut has had on its books a law which forbids the use of contraceptives by anyone. I think this is an uncommonly silly law ... But we are not asked in this case to say whether we think the law is unwise, or even asinine. We are asked to hold that it violates the United States Constitution. And this I cannot do." (Justice Potter Stewart, dissenting in Griswold v. Connecticut [1965])

"Here, indeed, is the point of contact between the legislator's work and [the judge's]. The choice of methods, the appraisement of values, must in the end be guided by like considerations for the one as for the other... [Y]et the judge, even when he is free, is still not wholly free.... He is to exercise a discretion informed by tradition, methodized by analogy, disci-plined by system, and subordinated to 'the primordial necessity of order in social life.'" (Justice Benjamin Cardozo, then of the New York Court of Appeals [1921])

"Cases such as these provide for me an excruciating agony of the spirit. I yield to no one in the depth of my distaste, antipathy, and, indeed, abhor-rence, for the death penalty.... Were I a legislator, I would vote against the death penalty ... I do not sit on these cases, however, as a legislator.... Although personally I may rejoice at the Court's result, I find it difficult to accept or justify as a matter of history, of law, or of constitutional pronounce-ment." (Justice Harry Blackmun, dissenting in Furman v. Georgia [1972])

SOURCES: The quotations from extra-judicial writings are from Oliver Wendell Holmes, "The Path of the Law," *Harvard Law Review* 10 (1897), p. 444; and from Benjamin A. Cardozo, *The Nature of the Judicial Process* (New Haven: Yale University Press, 1921), p. 141.

FIGURE 8-3 THE POLITICAL PERSPECTIVE ON JUDICIAL DECISIONMAKING

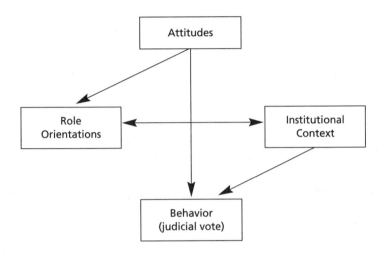

SOURCE: Based on the analysis in James L. Gibson, "From Simplicity to Complexity: The Development of Theory in the Study of Judicial Behavior," *Political Behavior* 5 (1983): 7-49.

tional context in which they operate circumscribe what judges find it feasible to do.[40] Figure 8-3, which summarizes the political perspective on judicial decisionmaking, provides the basis for our analysis. Moreover, as Figure 8-3 suggests, these factors are often interrelated.

Attitudes

As we saw in Chapter 3, judicial selection is a political process. Presidents typically nominate active members of their political party for federal judgeships and inquire into potential nominees' legal and political views, especially before filling vacancies on the Supreme Court. Politics also affects judicial selection in the states. Partisan election systems, of course, reward loyal and active party members. Political considerations also affect gubernatorial appointments, even when governors are choosing judges under the process of "merit selection." Not surprisingly, given the extensive political backgrounds of those who become judges, they tend to bring to the bench consistent and long-established political views.

The Development of Attitudes

What factors shape the attitudes, the values and beliefs, of judges? Assuming, as the political perspective does, that judicial decisionmaking closely resembles all other political decisionmaking, it follows that the same factors that influence political behavior generally should also influence, either directly or indirectly, how judges decide cases. The formation of politically relevant attitudes begins in early childhood.[41] Numerous studies have demonstrated the influence of various background factors, such as family background, religion, and socioeconomic status, on the development of individuals' political beliefs and behavior.[42]

Judges' values and beliefs, like those of other citizens, may also be influenced by significant political events and by nationwide changes in the pattern of opinion. For one generation, the crucial event was the Great Depression; for another, the Vietnam War; for a third, the rise of conservatism during the Reagan era. As Justice Benjamin Cardozo has put it, "The great tides and currents which engulf the rest of men do not turn aside in their course and pass the judges by."[43]

The established social practices and patterns of opinion within a particular region may likewise influence judicial attitudes. The values and beliefs of those growing up in the South prior to the Civil War, for example, were inevitably affected by the institution of slavery, although reactions to that system varied among individuals. More recently, scholars have documented differences in political culture among the various states, differences in patterns of thought and behavior that presumably affect all within those states.[44] Given the political character of judicial selection, one would expect only those who supported the reigning values in the state to attain positions as judges.

According to "Mr. Dooley," a political commentator of the early twentieth century, "the judges follow the election returns."[45] Although Dooley's remark probably exaggerates the influence of immediate political factors on judicial decisions, it points to an important truth. The legal safeguards of judicial independence do not altogether shield judges from the political environment. They, like everyone else, follow the news and are aware of societal developments and of trends in public opinion, including reactions to their decisions. While one would not expect judges to tailor their rulings to conform to public opinion, the political environment may nonetheless influence judicial decisionmaking.

The Effects of Attitudes on Decisions

Do judges' personal attitudes influence the outcome of cases? Despite judges' efforts to banish personal views from their decisions (see Box 8-2), many studies indicate that judges' attitudes do affect their votes. What is particularly significant is that the judges' votes often follow clear patterns, dividing along what might be considered liberal and conservative lines. The United States Supreme Court furnishes a prime example.

As Table 8-1 shows, when Supreme Court justices disagreed in civil liberties cases, some justices (such as William Brennan and Thurgood Marshall) consistently took the liberal position, voting in favor of those who claimed that their rights had been violated. Other justices (Antonin Scalia and William Rehnquist, for instance) have regularly adopted the conservative position, voting to uphold challenged laws or governmental actions. In cases involving economic issues, a similar division has occurred. Liberal justices have tended to favor economic "underdogs," such as labor unions and small businesses, while conservative justices have more frequently ruled in favor of economic "upperdogs."[46] Justices who voted along liberal lines in civil liberties cases also tended to do so in economic cases, and justices who were conservative on civil liberties issues tended to be conservative on economic issues as well.

These findings might seem to suggest that the law is nothing but an elaborate charade, designed to fool a credulous public, while freeing judges to pur-

TABLE 8-1 THE VOTING BEHAVIOR OF SUPREME COURT JUSTICES, 1969-1986

| | Percentage liberal in nonunanimous cases | | | |
Justice	Civil liberties	N	Economics	N
Rehnquist	5.6	959	22.8	285
Burger	17.6	1,099	25.0	328
O'Connor	24.5	318	31.0	87
Harlan	27.6	105	29.6	27
Powell	31.2	940	29.7	256
White	33.7	1,103	50.6	328
Blackmun	39.5	1,056	46.5	310
Stewart	43.6	782	32.1	234
Black	43.9	107	65.4	26
Stevens	61.4	676	52.6	211
Brennan	85.5	1,086	74.2	329
Marshall	88.5	1,078	68.2	321
Douglas	94.1	374	78.4	111

SOURCE: Jeffrey A. Segal and Harold J. Spaeth, "Decisional Trends on the Warren and Burger Courts: Results from the Supreme Court Data Base Project," *Judicature* 73 (1989): 103-107.

sue their own policy goals. In fact, however, the connection between judges' attitudes and their votes is more subtle. When the appropriate legal outcome in a case is clear, decisions are unanimous, regardless of the judges' attitudes. But when the appropriate legal outcome is not immediately clear, when appellate judges are confronted with persuasive legal arguments on both sides of an issue, they must determine which arguments are stronger. According to the political perspective, the judges' attitudes inevitably affect this determination. They do so by influencing the judges' perception of the issues in the case and their judgment about the strength of the competing legal arguments. The judges are not engaged in duplicity; they simply cannot altogether escape who they are.

If political attitudes affect the votes of judges on the United States Supreme Court, presumably they should on other courts as well. This is difficult to confirm directly, however, because state and federal judges do not readily grant interviews to discuss their political views. Researchers have therefore approached the issue indirectly by looking for connections between judges' party affiliations and their voting behavior. This research assumes that because Republicans and Democrats have different political perspectives, party membership will be a good indicator of judges' attitudes. Therefore, if judges' attitudes decisively influence their votes, one should be able to predict the overall pattern of a judge's votes by knowing her party affiliation. Table 8-2 summarizes the results of studies that have examined the link between judges' partisan affiliations and their decisions.

As this table reveals, the researchers' findings are mixed. Several studies—for example, those of Schubert, Goldman, and Tate—found connections between the party affiliations of judges and their voting behavior.[47] However, the divisions on some courts, as the studies by Walker and Dolbeare revealed, bore no relation to the judges' partisan affiliations.[48] Moreover, as Goldman's initial study revealed, partisan divisions may be found on some issues and not on others.[49] In addition, as Carp and Rowland's study of voting behavior on federal district courts demonstrated, partisan divisions may operate during some periods but not during others.[50]

Other studies have examined connections between judges' social backgrounds or other attributes (such as their state of birth, their gender, and their race) and their voting behavior on the bench. Underlying these studies is the assumption that the judges' backgrounds and attributes shape their attitudes, which in turn affect their decisions.[51] For example, some studies have found that judges who had prior experience as prosecutors are likely to be judicial conservatives.[52]

TABLE 8-2 PARTISAN AFFILIATION AND JUDICIAL VOTING BEHAVIOR

Court	Study	Cases	Findings
U.S. Supreme Court	Tate	Civil liberties and economics decisions (1946-1978)	Democrats more liberal than Republicans on both sets of issues
U.S. Courts of Appeals	Goldman	Sample of all cases (1961-1964)	Democrats more liberal on economic issues; no difference in civil liberties cases
	Goldman	Sample of all cases (1965-1971)	Democrats more liberal generally, especially outside the South
	Songer	Sample of all cases (1935-1939 and 1965-1971)	Panels with Democratic majorities considerably more liberal than those with Republican majorities
U.S. District Courts	Richardson/ Vines	Civil liberties and labor cases (1956-1961)	Democrats marginally more sympathetic to workers; Republicans somewhat more favorable to civil liberties
	Walker	Civil liberties cases (1963-1968)-	No relationship between party and vote
	Carp/ Rowland	All cases (1956-1977)-	Pre-1969: little relationship; post-1969: Democrats considerably more liberal, particularly in civil liberties and criminal justice cases
Michigan Supreme Court	Schubert	Worker compensation cases (1954-1957)	Democrats more liberal than Republicans
	Ulmer	Personal injury and unemployment cases (1958-1960)	Democrats more favorable to injured and to the unemployed
Wisconsin Supreme Court	Adamany	Worker and unemployment compensation cases	Party identification did not explain votes
New York Court of Appeals	Beiser/ Silberman	Worker compensation cases	Party identification did not explain votes

SOURCES: C. Neal Tate, "Personal Attribute Models of the Voting Behavior of U.S. Supreme Court Justices' Liberalism in Civil Liberties and Economics Decisions, 1946-1978," *American Political Science Review* 75 (June 1981): 355-367; Sheldon Goldman, "Voting Behavior on the United States Courts of Appeals, 1961-64," *American Political Science Review* 60 (1966): 370-385; Sheldon Goldman, "Voting Behavior on the United States Courts of Appeals Revisited," *American Political Science Review* 69 (1975): 491-506; Donald Songer, "Consensual and Nonconsensual Decisions in Unanimous Opinions of the United States Courts of Appeals," *American Journal of Political Science* 26 (1982): 225-239.   Richard J. Richardson and Kenneth N. Vines, *The Politics of Federal Courts: Lower Courts in the United States* (Boston: Little, Brown, 1970); Thomas G. Walker, "A Note Concerning Partisan Influences on Trial-Judge Decision Making," *Law and Society Review* 6 (1972): 645-649; Robert A. Carp and C. K. Rowland, *Policymaking and Politics in the Federal District Courts* (Knoxville: University of Tennessee Press, 1983); Glendon Schubert, *Quantitative Analysis of Judicial Behavior* (New York: Free Press, 1959); S. Sidney Ulmer, "The Political Party Variable in the Michigan Supreme Court," *Journal of Politics* 11 (1962): 352-362; David W. Adamany, "The Political Party Variable in Judges' Voting: Conceptual Notes and a Case Study," *American Political Science Review* 63 (March 1969): 57-74; Edward N. Beiser and Jonathan J. Silberman, "The Political Party Variable: Workmen's Compensation Cases in the New York Court of Appeals," *Polity* 3 (1971): 521-531.

The impact of judges' background characteristics on their decisions, however, also tends to vary from study to study.[53]   Often it is difficult to disentangle causal connections—for example, are judges conservative because of their experience as prosecutors, or are lawyers likely to seek a position as prosecutor because they are conservative? In addition, some attributes that one might expect to be important, such as the race or gender of judges, have surprisingly little documented effect on their behavior on the bench.[54]

If one cannot consistently predict judges' voting behavior from their social backgrounds, the reason may lie in the influence of other factors on judicial decisionmaking. Among the most important of these are judicial role orientations.

Judicial Role Orientations

As the quotations in Box 8-2 show, judges generally believe that they should submerge their personal beliefs, however deeply felt, and decide cases in accordance with the law. They also hold numerous other beliefs about what is appropriate and inappropriate judicial behavior. To some extent, the judge's beliefs mirror societal views about the responsibilities of a judge. But the judge's views are elaborated and refined during the professional socialization of law school, through work as a practicing attorney, and through involvement with other members of the legal profession. Once on the bench, a judge's beliefs are further influenced by her experience as a judge and by the expectations of those with whom she interacts, especially her fellow judges.[55]

This process of socialization to the norms of a profession is, of course, not unique to judges. Teachers, doctors, insurance agents, and others—all undergo a similar process of learning the norms of conduct for their professions. These beliefs about the sorts of behavior appropriate for judges are referred to as judicial role orientations.[56]

Judicial role orientations operate as self-imposed obligations, restricting the actions that a judge will undertake. They are important because they can affect judicial decisions. For example, role orientations may prevent judges from voting in line with their personal beliefs. As Box 8-2 shows, in *Furman* v. *Georgia* Justice Harry Blackmun voted to uphold the constitutionality of the death penalty, despite his abhorrence of capital punishment on moral grounds. Similarly, Felix Frankfurter voted to sustain state laws requiring students to salute the American flag, despite his opposition to such laws. In both instance, the justices voted as they did because of their conceptions of proper judicial behavior, in particular, their belief that a judge's personal convictions should not affect his vote.

As these examples illustrate, judicial role orientations usually do not require that a judge vote for a particular outcome. Rather, they affect how judges go about making their decisions. More specifically, role orientations indicate the sorts of factors that judges can legitimately consider in making their decisions and the weight to be assigned to those factors.[57]

The influence of judicial role orientation can be seen in the way that judges treat precedent. If judicial attitudes alone determined judicial decisions, then judges would uphold precedents that supported outcomes they favored and overrule those precedents that produced disagreeable results. In actuality, however, some judges believe that they should adhere to the court's prior rulings, even if they might decide the case differently in the absence of precedent. Thus, when Sandra Day O'Connor was appointed to the Supreme Court by President Ronald Reagan, it was assumed that she shared the president's conservative philosophy and would vote accordingly. Yet when the justices had the opportunity to overrule *Roe* v. *Wade*, the Court's controversial abortion decision, in *Planned Parenthood of Southeastern Pennsylvania* v. *Casey* (1992), O'Connor refused to do so, citing the necessity to respect precedent.[58] Similarly, despite the Bush administration's urgings in an amicus curiae brief, Justice David Souter disappointed the president who appointed him by voting to strike down religious invocations at graduation ceremonies as a violation of the Establishment Clause.[59] He too justified his position as compelled by long-established Court precedents.

Although role orientations affect judicial decisions, their exact impact is difficult to determine. For one thing, there is no consensus about what constitutes proper judicial behavior. Rather, the norms of appropriate conduct vary somewhat from court to court and within courts over time. The practice of filing dissenting opinions is a good example. The norms of judicial behavior on some courts discourage public expressions of dissent, whereas on other courts judges are free to dissent whenever they disagree with the court majority.[60] And whereas dissent was once frowned upon on the United States Supreme Court, today dissenting opinions are filed in most cases.[61]

In addition, despite broad areas of agreement—for instance, judges should not engage in partisan politics while on the bench—sitting judges may have quite different conceptions of the judicial role.[62] Some judges subscribe to a philosophy of judicial restraint, which limits the factors that they can validly consider in reaching a decision and the circumstances in which they can legitimately overrule a precedent or strike down a legislative enactment. Others judges embrace the philosophy of judicial activism, which places less emphasis on the doctrine of stare decisis and on deference to legislative judgment. Appropriate judicial behavior, then, depends on the judge's choice of a particular role orientation. Conceivably, a judge's choice among possible role orientations may be influenced by the judge's attitudes and political values. Thus, during the 1960s and 1970s, liberal judges also tended to be activists.[63] Since the mid-1980s, however, judicial conservatives have been interested in reversing many of the rulings of their liberal predecessors, and thus one finds conservative judges, such as Justices Anthony Kennedy and Antonin Scalia, exhibiting an activist role orientation.[64]

Institutional Factors

The decisions of appellate courts are group decisions. By itself, the vote of a single judge cannot determine the outcome of a case. Thus, if a judge wishes to ensure that a case is decided in line with her views, she must convince other judges to endorse her position.[65] Similarly, other judges may seek to persuade her to their position. These interactions among judges also influence judicial decisionmaking.

As noted in Chapter 7, the norms of appropriate judicial behavior limit the means that a judge may use to gain acceptance of her position. Whatever their efficacy in international conflicts, force or intimidation cannot be used by a judge to achieve her goals. She cannot, like a legislator, trade her vote in one case to gain votes for her position in another.[66] Nor can she promise political support for those who vote with her or threaten political ruin for those who oppose her.

Perhaps the most potent weapon available to a judge is legal expertise, together with the ability to bring that expertise to bear in a well-crafted judicial opinion.[67] As one judge on a federal court of appeals put it, "Some judges are simply better than others. Some know more, think better. It would be strange if among nine men all had the same ability. Some simply have more respect than others."[68] The importance of legal expertise is hardly surprising. Committed to deciding cases in accordance with the law, judges are receptive to legal arguments from their colleagues, and if those arguments are compelling, they can be persuaded to switch their votes. As Justice Robert Jackson put it: "I myself have changed my opinion after reading the opinions of the other members of this Court. And I am as stubborn as most."[69] Of course, the arguments that judges find compelling may to some extent depend upon their attitudes and their role conceptions. Thus, judges are more likely to be persuaded by colleagues who generally share their perspective on legal issues. Still, in the absence of compelling legal arguments, judges do not change their votes.

If judges may persuade their colleagues to vote with them by the strength of their arguments, they may also threaten to write an opinion attacking the position taken by those who reject their arguments. The effectiveness of this threat generally depends on the ability of the judge to present a persuasive legal argument. As Box 8-3 shows, judges do not shrink from stinging attacks on the reasoning ability of their colleagues and the coherence of their views. Perhaps surprisingly, these attacks usually do not interfere with the day-to-day working relationships within a court.

An appellate court is in reality a small group working together over a prolonged period. It is not surprising, then, that personal relations with fellow judges also play a role in judicial decisionmaking. Judges, like other human beings, are more receptive to arguments from colleagues who treat them with respect and consideration than from those who are disagreeable.[70] Although warm personal relationships develop more often among those who share common legal views, they can flourish even among judges who frequently disagree. For example, when William Rehnquist was appointed to the Supreme Court, he was its most conservative member. But that did not prevent him from quickly becoming a close friend of William O. Douglas, the most liberal justice on the Court.[71]

Ultimately, though, judges usually come to the bench with firmly established views, and their fellow judges have few weapons beyond legal argument to induce them to change their minds. Group interaction therefore has only a limited effect on how judges vote.

ANALYZING THE TWO PERSPECTIVES

This chapter has described two perspectives on judicial decisionmaking. The legal perspective on judicial decisionmaking views it as a process of reasoning

BOX 8-3 JUDICIAL ATTACKS

Because appellate courts are small groups in which judges must work together over a long period, one might expect that judges would refrain from harshly criticizing the rulings and opinions of their colleagues. As these excerpts from the opinions of Supreme Court justices reveal, however, judges are quite willing to attack the views of colleagues who disagree with them in a case:

"Nothing in the letter or the spirit of the Constitution or in the precedents squares with the heavy-handed and one-sided action that is so precipitously taken by the court in the name of fulfilling its constitutional responsibilities." (Justice John Marshall Harlan, dissenting in *Miranda* v. *Arizona*)

"Not in my memory has a plurality gone about its business in such a deceptive fashion. At every level of its review, from its effort to read the real meaning out of the Missouri statute, to its intended evisceration of precedents and its deafening silence about the constitutional protection it would jettison, the plurality obscures the portent of its analysis." (Justice Harry Blackmun, dissenting in *Webster* v. *Reproductive Health Services*)

"Once we depart from the text of the Constitution, just where . . . do we stop? The most amazing feature of the Court's opinion is that it does not even purport to give an answer. . . . Evidently, the governing standard is to be what might be called the unfettered wisdom of a majority of this Court, revealed to an obedient people on a case-by-case basis." (Justice Antonin Scalia, dissenting in *Morrison* v. *Olson*)

"A number of Justices just short of a majority of the majority that promulgates today's passionate dialectics joined in answering them in [a decision just four years prior]. The distinction attempted between that case and this is trivial, almost to the point of cynicism . . . . Today's judgment will be more interesting to students of psychology and of the judicial processes than to students of constitutional law." (Justice Robert Jackson, dissenting in *Zorach* v. *Clauson*)

"A few citations to 'research in psychology' that have no particular bearing upon the precise issue here cannot disguise the fact that the Court has gone beyond the realm where judges know what they are doing. The Court's argument . . . is, not to put too fine a point on it, incoherent." (Justice Antonin Scalia, dissenting in *Lee* v. *Weisman*)

"One wonders whether the majority still believes that race discrimination—or, more accurately, race discrimination against nonwhites—is a problem in our society, or even remembers that it ever was." (Justice Harry Blackmun, dissenting in *Wards Cove Packing Co.* v. *Atonio*) based on legal principles and judicial precedents. These principles and precedents prescribe a particular outcome in many cases. Even where there is a realm of choice for the judge, law circumscribes the range of choice and guides its exercise. Thus the law is the most important determinant of judicial decisions.

The political perspective on judicial decisionmaking views it as a process in which extralegal factors, such as the judges' attitudes and role orientations, are the primary influences on judicial decisions. According to this view, judges' attitudes and orientations color how they view the law and the facts in a case and thereby determine the decisions they reach.

Which of these accounts of judicial decisionmaking is more accurate? Unfortunately, there is no clear-cut answer to that question. As we have noted, numerous studies have documented the relationship between judges' political beliefs and their rulings. Judges insist, however, that their rulings reflect the law rather than their personal views, and some recent studies back them up. Jeffrey Segal, for example, has shown that legal considerations (the pattern of facts in the case and the Court's legal doctrine) are better predictors of the Supreme Court's search-and-seizure rulings than are the attitudes of the justices. Other studies have systematically demonstrated the importance of legal factors in the Court's rulings on obscenity, church and state, and women's rights.[72] When scholars have attempted to assess the adequacy of the two perspectives, their findings have offered support for both perspectives on judicial decisionmaking, although somewhat stronger support for the political perspective.[73]

These varying findings suggest that an adequate account of judicial decisionmaking must acknowledge the importance of both legal and extralegal factors. Judges take an oath to dispense equal justice under law, and it seems reasonable to assume that most judges take that obligation seriously. Thus, when the law is clear, judges can be expected to follow it. As the Legal Realists have shown, however, often the law is not clear, and the judge must choose between two plausible legal arguments. Though they recognize that they must choose the stronger legal argument, the judges' perceptions of the facts of the case and the strength of the competing arguments is to some extent influenced by their experience and beliefs. Their choices, then, cannot be divorced from their backgrounds and beliefs.

Nevertheless, judges are members of the legal profession, and their beliefs have been formed by their legal training. They therefore recognize an obligation not to read their own beliefs into the law. Indeed, their understanding of their responsibilities as judges—their role orientations—encourages them to guard against it. Even though judges' efforts to banish personal views from their decisions are unlikely to be fully effective, they do have some effect. Thus, in the words of Justice Felix Frankfurter:

> The judicial process demands that a judge move within the framework of relevant legal rules and the covenanted modes of thought for ascertaining them. He must think dispassionately and submerge personal feeling on every aspect of a case. There is a good deal of shallow talk that the judicial robe does not change the man within it. It does. The fact is that *on the whole* judges do lay aside private views in discharging their judicial functions. This is achieved through training, professional habits, self-discipline, and that fortunate alchemy by which men are loyal to the obligations with which they are entrusted.[74]

NOTES

1. *Stanford* v. *Kentucky*, 492 U.S. 361 (1989).

2. The Supreme Court's recognition of "evolving standards of human decency" as the basis for interpreting the Eighth Amendment stems from *Trop* v. *Dulles*, 356 U.S. 86 (1958).

3. This distinction is drawn from Richard A. Wasserstrom, *The Judicial Decision: Toward a Theory of Legal Justification* (Stanford, Calif.: Stanford University Press, 1961), pp. 26-27.

4. Joseph C. Hutcheson, Jr., "The Judgment Intuitive: The Function of the 'Hunch' in Judicial Decision," *Cornell Law Quarterly* 14 (1929), p. 274.

5. Felix Frankfurter, "Some Reflections on the Reading of Statutes," *Columbia Law Review* 47 (1947), p. 527.

6. As the United States Supreme Court put it in *Lake County* v. *Rollins*, 130 U.S. 662, 670 (1889): "If the words convey a definite meaning, which involves no absurdity, nor any contradiction of other parts of the instrument, then that meaning apparent on the face of the instrument, must be accepted."

7. See Reed Dickerson, *The Interpretation and Application of Statutes* (Boston: Little, Brown, 1975), Chapter 8.

8. *Towne* v. *Eisner*, 245 U.S. 418, 425 (1925).

9. For a discussion of the uses and abuses of legislative history, see Dickerson, *The Interpretation and Application of Statutes*, Chapter 10.

10. The usefulness and limitations of these materials are surveyed in James H. Hutson, "The Creation of the Constitution: The Integrity of the Documentary Record," *Texas Law Review* 65 (November 1986): 1-40.

11. Dickerson, *The Interpretation and Application of Statutes*, pp. 161-162.

12. Ibid., Chapter 10.

13. This argument has also been used to justify interpretation of the United States Constitution in line with the intentions of the Founders. See Edwin Meese, "Toward a Jurisprudence of Original Intention," *Benchmark* 2 (1986): 1-10.

14. See, for example, Paul Brest, "The Misconceived Quest for the Original Understanding," *Boston University Law Review* 60 (March 1980): 204-238.

15. As Justice Robert Jackson put it in *Schwegmann Bros. v. Calvert Distillers Corp.*, 341 U.S. 385, 395 (1951): "[T]o select casual statements from floor debates, not always distinguished for candor or accuracy, as a basis for making up our minds what law Congress intended to enact is to substitute ourselves for the Congress in one of its important functions." More generally, see Dickerson, *The Interpretation and Application of Statutes*, pp. 156-157.

16. See Lief H. Carter, *Reason in Law* (Boston: Little, Brown, 1979), pp. 71-72, and Brest, "The Misconceived Quest for the Original Understanding."

17. William L. Reynolds, *Judicial Process in a Nutshell* (St. Paul: West, 1980), p. 168.

18. These arguments are summarized and critiqued in Wasserstrom, *The Judicial Decision*, Chapter 4.

19. Ibid., p. 68.

20. As Karl Llewellyn put it: "The force of precedent in law is heightened by an additional factor: that curious, almost universal sense of justice which urges that all men are properly to be treated alike in like circumstances." ("Case Law," *Encyclopedia of the Social Sciences* 3 [New York: Macmillan, 1930], p. 249.)

21. *Texas v. Johnson*, 491 U.S. 397 (1989).

22. Benjamin Cardozo, *The Nature of the Judicial Process* (New Haven: Yale University Press, 1921), p. 149.

23. For an excellent overview of Legal Realist thought, see Wilfrid E. Rumble, Jr., *American Legal Realism: Skepticism, Reform, and the Judicial Process* (Ithaca, N.Y.: Cornell University Press, 1968).

24. Edward H. Levi, *An Introduction to Legal Reasoning* (Chicago: University of Chicago Press, 1949).

25. 491 U.S. 397 (1989). Levi does not discuss this recent case in his volume.

26. Compare, for example, *Cohen v. California*, 403 U.S. 15 (1971), with *United States v. O'Brien*, 391 U.S. 367 (1968).

27. Levi, *An Introduction to Legal Reasoning*, p. 4.

28. *Griswold v. Connecticut*, 381 U.S. 479 (1965).

29. 381 U.S. 479, 486.

30. *Eisenstadt v. Baird*, 405 U.S. 438 (1972).

31. 405 U.S. 438, 453.

32. *Roe* v. *Wade*, 410 U.S. 113 (1973).

33. 410 U.S. 113, 153.

34. Ibid.

35. *Bowers* v. *Hardwick*, 478 U.S. 186 (1986).

36. 478 U.S. 186, 191.

37. Thomas G. Walker, Lee Epstein, and William J. Dixon, "On the Mysterious Demise of Consensual Norms in the United States Supreme Court," *Journal of Politics* 50 (May 1988): 361-389.

38. For federal courts of appeals, see Donald R. Songer, "The Circuit Courts of Appeals," in John B. Gates and Charles A. Johnson, eds., *The American Courts: A Critical Assessment* (Washington, D.C.: CQ Press, 1991), and J. Woodford Howard, *Courts of Appeals in the Federal Judicial System: A Study of the Second, Fifth, and District of Columbia Circuits* (Princeton, N.J.: Princeton University Press, 1981). For state supreme courts, see Henry Glick and George Pruet, Jr., "Dissent in State Supreme Courts: Patterns and Correlates of Conflict," in Sheldon Goldman and Charles M. Lamb, eds., *Judicial Conflict and Consensus: Behavioral Studies of American Appellate Courts* (Lexington, Ky.: University of Kentucky Press, 1986).

39. James L. Gibson, "From Simplicity to Complexity: The Development of Theory in the Study of Judicial Behavior," *Political Behavior* 5 (1983): 9.

40. Ibid. We employ a modified version of Gibson's framework for analysis in this chapter.

41. See Robert D. Hess and Judith V. Torney, *The Development of Political Attitudes in Children* (Chicago: Aldine, 1967), and David Easton and Jack Dennis, *Children in the Political System: Origins of Political Legitimacy* (Chicago: University of Chicago Press, 1980).

42. See Allan M. Winkler, "Public Opinion," in Jack Greene, ed., *The Encyclopedia of American Political History* (New York: Charles Scribner's Sons, 1988), and Lloyd Free and Hadley Cantril, *The Political Beliefs of Americans* (New York: Simon & Schuster, 1968).

43. Cardozo, *The Nature of the Judicial Process*, p. 168.

44. Daniel J. Elazar, *American Federalism: A View from the States*, 3rd ed. (New York: Harper & Row, 1984).

45. Finley Peter Dunne, *The World of Mr. Dooley*, ed. by Louis Filler (New York: Collier Books, 1962), p. 89.

46. For a discussion of how to distinguish economic "underdogs" from economic "upperdogs", see Jeffrey A. Segal and Harold J. Spaeth, "Decisional Trends on the Warren and Burger Courts: Results from the Supreme Court Data Base Project," *Judicature* 73 (August-September 1989): 103-107.

47. Glendon Schubert, *Quantitative Analysis of Judicial Behavior* (New York: Free Press, 1959); Sheldon Goldman, "Voting Behavior on the United States Courts of Appeals Revisited," *American Political Science Review* 69 (June 1975): 491-506; and C. Neal Tate, "Personal Attribute

Models of the Voting Behavior of U.S. Supreme Court Justices: Liberalism in Civil Liberties and Economic Decisions, 1946-1978," *American Political Science Review* 75 (June 1981): 355-367.

48. Thomas G. Walker, "A Note Concerning Partisan Influence on Trial-Judge Decision Making," *Law & Society Review* 6 (May 1972): 645-659; and David W. Adamany, "The Political Party Variable in Judges' Voting: Conceptual Notes and a Case Study," *American Political Science Review* 63 (March 1969): 57-74.

49. Sheldon Goldman, "Voting Behavior on the United States Courts of Appeals, 1961-64," *American Political Science Review* 60 (June 1966): 370-385.

50. Robert A. Carp and C. K. Rowland, *Policymaking and Politics in the Federal District Courts* (Knoxville: University of Tennessee Press, 1983).

51. Gibson, "From Simplicity to Complexity," pp. 23-26.

52. See, for example, Tate, "Personal Attribute Models of the Voting Behavior of U.S. Supreme Court Justices."

53. See the discussions in Joel B. Grossman, "Social Backgrounds and Judicial Decision-Making: Notes for a Theory," *Journal of Politics* 29 (May 1967): 334-351, and Walter Murphy and Joseph Tanenhaus, *The Study of Public Law* (New York: Random House, 1972), pp. 107-109.

54. Gibson, "From Simplicity to Complexity," pp. 21-22.

55. James L. Gibson, "Judges' Role Orientations, Attitudes, and Decisions: An Interactive Model," *American Political Science Review* 73 (September 1978): 918.

56. Ibid.

57. See, for example, Henry A. Glick, *Supreme Courts in State Politics* (New York: Basic Books, 1971), Chapter 2.

58. *Planned Parenthood of Southeastern Pennsylvania* v. *Casey*, 60 LW 4795 (1992).

59. *Lee* v. *Weisman*, 60 LW 4723 (1992).

60. See the sources cited in notes 37 and 38 above.

61. See Walker, Epstein, and Dixon, "On the Mysterious Demise of Consensual Norms."

62. See Glick, *Supreme Courts in State Politics*, Chapter 2; John T. Wold, "Political Orientations, Social Backgrounds, and the Role Perceptions of State Supreme Court Judges," *Western Political Quarterly* 27 (1974): 239-248; and Gibson, "Judges' Role Orientations, Attitudes, and Decisions."

63. See James L. Gibson, "Decision Making in Appellate Courts," in Gates and Johnson, *American Courts: A Critical Assessment*, p. 264, Table 10-2.

64. Ibid. See also Justice Scalia's subsequent opinions ignoring *stare decisis* and urging new directions for the Court in *Webster* v. *Reproductive Health Services*, 109 S.Ct. 3040 (1989); *R.A.V.* v. *City of St. Paul*, 60 LW 4667 (1992); and *Planned Parenthood of Southeastern Pennsylvania* v. *Casey*, 60 LW 4795 (1992).

65. Of course, other judges may independently come to the same conclusion.

66. For the highly controversial suggestion that justices have on occasion done so, see Robert Woodward and Scott Armstrong, *The Brethren; Inside the Supreme Court* (New York: Simon & Schuster, 1979).

67. This analysis follows that of Walter F. Murphy, *Elements of Judicial Strategy* (Chicago: University of Chicago Press, 1964), Chapter 3.

68. Howard, *Courts of Appeal in the Federal Judicial System*, p. 230.

69. Quoted in Alan Westin, *The Anatomy of a Constitutional Law Case* (New York: Macmillan, 1958), pp. 123-124.

70. See Murphy, *Elements of Judicial Strategy*, pp. 98-104.

71. Lawrence Baum, *The Supreme Court* (3rd ed; Washington, D.C.: Congressional Quarterly Press, 1989), p. 156.

72. Jeffrey A. Segal, "Predicting Supreme Court Cases Probabilistically: The Search and Seizure Cases, 1962-1984," *American Political Science Review* 78 (December 1984): 891-900; Jeffrey A. Segal, "Supreme Court Justices as Human Decision Makers: An Individual-Level Analysis of the Search and Seizure Cases," *Journal of Politics* 48 (November 1986): 938-955; Timothy M. Hagle, "Constitutional Decision Making: The Obscenity Decisions of the Warren, Burger, and Rehnquist Courts," paper presented at the 1989 meeting of the American Political Science Association; Joseph A. Ignagni, "Explaining and Predicting Supreme Court Decision Making: The Establishment Clause Cases, 1970-1986," paper presented at the 1990 meeting of the Midwest Political Science Association; and Robin M. Wolpert, "Explaining and Predicting Supreme Court Decision-Making: The Gender Discrimination Cases, 1971-1987," paper presented at the 1991 meeting of the Midwest Political Science Association.

73. Tracey E. George and Lee Epstein, "On the Nature of Supreme Court Decision Making," *American Political Science Review* 86 (June 1992): 323-337.

74. *Public Utilities Commission* v. *Pollack*, 343 U.S. 451, 466 (1959). (Italics added).

3

STRUCTURES AND PARTICIPANTS IN THE JUDICIAL PROCESS

9 JUDICIAL POLICYMAKING: AN INTRODUCTION

Throughout American history, judges have been accused of deciding cases based on their own policy preferences rather than in accordance with the law. During the first third of the twentieth century, it was political liberals who levelled the charge of judicial usurpation. The justices of the United States Supreme Court, they claimed, based their rulings on a particular economic theory (laissez-faire capitalism) rather than on the Constitution. From the 1950s through the 1970s, it was conservatives' turn to express outrage. They denounced the Supreme Court's rulings on pornography, abortion, school prayer, and the rights of defendants as elements of a liberal social agenda with little or no constitutional basis. Over the past decade or so, it has again been liberals who have attacked the Supreme Court, charging that its decisions reflect nothing more than the justices' political conservatism.[1]

One need not accept all these charges as accurate. Critics often see a dereliction of judicial duty in every decision with which they disagree. Nevertheless, these criticisms of the Supreme Court's rulings sound a common theme: the task of the judge is to "say what the law is," not to make law.[2] Policymaking is the responsibility of the other branches of government, and judges who engage in policymaking are usurping power and behaving improperly.

Viewed from another perspective, however, judicial policymaking is neither exceptional nor suspect. Courts "say what the law is" in the course of deciding cases, and this inevitably enmeshes them in public policy. Their rulings may announce authoritative legal standards that define public policy within the jurisdiction they serve. In some cases, too, their rulings may influence political action and stimulate or retard societal change. This holds true regardless of whether judges decide the cases properly or not and regardless of whether their rulings uphold or strike down governmental actions. A recent Supreme Court ruling, *Edwards* v. *Aguillard* (1987), illustrates the point.[3]

In *Edwards* the Court struck down a Louisiana law that required teachers to devote as much time to "creation science" as to evolution in teaching about human origins. In doing so, the Court established educational policy by defining, in part, what might be taught in public schools. In addition, the Court's ruling presumably discouraged other efforts to infuse religious doctrines into public education. However, had the Court upheld the Louisiana statute, that ruling likewise would have had policy consequences. Validation of the Louisiana statute would have established creation science as a legitimate part of a public-school curriculum. It might also have encouraged the enactment of "equal time" statutes in other states and promoted other measures designed to forge a closer connection between religion and public education.

Although the *Edwards* example reveals that judges cannot altogether avoid policymaking, it does not prove that critics of judicial policymaking are mistaken. Rather, the two perspectives on judicial policymaking can be viewed as complementary. Whereas one view emphasizes that judicial rulings inevitably have policy consequences, the other view cautions that judicial rulings rooted solely in the policy views of the judges are inappropriate. Before examining how one might distinguish appropriate from inappropriate judicial policymaking, however, let us look more closely at the character and types of judicial policymaking, which are summarized in Table 9-1.

THE OCCASIONS OF JUDICIAL POLICYMAKING

Judicial Review and Constitutional Policymaking

Constitutions specify the scope of governmental powers, divide those powers among the various branches of government, and confer rights that government cannot violate. When the government exceeds the powers granted to it, when a branch of government exercises powers conferred on another branch, or when government infringes on constitutionally protected rights, its actions are unconstitutional. Those who are injured by the government's unconstitutional actions may challenge them in the courts and call upon judges to invalidate those actions. The power of the courts to determine whether the government's actions are consistent with the Constitution and to invalidate those which are not, is known as judicial review.

TABLE 9-1 TYPES OF JUDICIAL POLICYMAKING

Type of Policymaking	Definition	Major Policymakers	Legal Basis	Eras of Greatest Policymaking
Constitutional	Judicial review of governmental action to determine its consistency with constitutional requirements	United States Supreme Court; state supreme courts	Federal Constitution, state constitution	For Federal courts, since the late nineteenth century; for state courts, 1900-1930s and 1970s to the present
Remedial	Establishment and implementation of requirements to eliminate constitutional violations or meet constitutional requirements	Federal district courts	Use of equity power to achieve constitutionally mandated situation	Since the late 1950s (*Brown v. Board of Education*)
Statutory interpretation	Interpretation and application of legislative enactments	Federal courts of appeals; state appellate courts	Federal legislation, state legislation	Since the increase in legislation in the late nineteenth and early twentieth centuries
Oversight of administrative activity	Review of administrative activity to ensure that it is consistent with constitutional, statutory, and/or agency requirements	Federal courts of appeals; state appellate courts	Federal or state constitution; federal or state legislation; agency rules or other requirements	Since the growth of regulatory agencies, beginning in the early twentieth century, with major increases during the New Deal (1930s) and Great Society (1960s)
Common-law	Judicial enunciation and application of legal standards in the absence of legislation or administrative action	State appellate courts	Judicial precedents, societal standards	During the first half of the nineteenth century and in tort law since World War II
Cumulative	Judicial development of policy through the exercise of discretion in resolving a large number of similar cases	State trial courts	Established practices within the court or jurisdiction	No particular period

Since the United States Supreme Court first used the power of judicial review to strike down congressional legislation in *Marbury* v. *Madison* (1803), judicial review has furnished a prime basis for judicial involvement in policymaking.[4] Often courts exercise this power of judicial review in ruling on the constitutionality of federal or state legislation. Since *Marbury*, the U.S. Supreme Court has struck down as unconstitutional about 125 Federal statutes and over 1000 state laws.[5] However, other governmental actions are likewise subject to constitutional scrutiny. In the celebrated case of *United States* v. *Nixon* (1973), for example, the Supreme Court ruled that President Richard Nixon did not have the power to withhold tapes of White House conversations from a federal district court seeking them for use in a criminal prosecution.[6] More frequently, however, it is lower level officials, such as police officers, whose actions are subject to constitutional scrutiny. From 1980-1990, for example, the Supreme Court decided on average over twenty cases per year involving the rights of suspects in criminal cases.[7]

The U.S. Supreme Court's constitutional rulings establish binding precedent for all courts in the United States, and their effects are felt nationwide. However, all federal and state courts can consider whether governmental actions coincide with federal constitutional requirements. The rulings of these courts, although they affect only a limited geographic area, may also involve important policy matters. In *James* v. *Wallace* (1974), for example, a federal district court ruled that confinement in certain Alabama prisons, which were plagued by overcrowding, violence, and grossly inadequate health care, violated the constitutional ban on cruel and unusual punishments.[8] To remedy the constitutional violation, Judge Frank Johnson ordered extensive reforms in the prison, requiring substantially increased state expenditures, and established his own guidelines for prison operations.[9] State courts' authority to consider constitutional violations under their state constitutions, as well as under the Federal Constitution, may furnish an additional basis for judicial intervention. In 1990, for example, the Ohio Supreme Court recognized that the state's constitution guarantees an absolute right to non-excessive bail in non-capital cases, and the Montana Supreme Court ruled that the Montana Constitution prohibits purposefully setting bail at a level beyond the means of indigent defendants.[10]

In ruling on constitutional questions, courts operate within clear constraints. Because the power of judicial review is the power to enforce constitutional norms, the Federal Constitution or its state counterpart must furnish the basis for judicial decisions.[11] Judges are expected not to substitute their own personal policy views for those of other governmental bodies (though they are sometimes accused of doing so). Nor are they free to validate governmental actions that violate the constitutional norms. Moreover, in reaching their decisions judges do not act in a vacuum. Only rarely do they consider a constitutional provision without seeking guidance from previous judicial decisions (precedents) interpreting the same provision. Both the force of precedent and the need to justify decisions as constitutionally based serve to guide and confine judges in their exercise of judicial review.

Yet as Chapter 8 made clear, this does not mean that constitutional interpretation is a merely mechanical process. Judges do not—and could not—merely "lay the article of the Constitution which is involved beside the statute which is challenged and decide whether the latter squares with the former."[12] Most of the federal constitutional provisions that have generated extensive litigation are phrased in general terms. Examples include the Fourth Amendment's ban on "unreasonable searches and seizures," the Fifth and Fourteenth Amendments' requirement of "due process of law," and the Fourteenth Amendment's guarantee of "the equal protection of the laws." The generality of these phrases requires judges to look beyond the text of the Constitution in determining their meaning.

One source which judges may look to is judicial precedents. Although judges can rely on these earlier decisions interpreting a constitutional provision, these decisions do not altogether resolve the problem. In some instances, the validity of the court's earlier rulings may be precisely what is at issue. A case in point is the famous case of *Brown* v. *Board of Education* (1954), challenging the constitutionality of legally mandated, racial segregation in public schools.[13] If the Supreme Court had decided on the basis of precedent, it would have upheld the practice of racial segregation, based on its earlier decision in *Plessy* v. *Ferguson* (1896), which permitted states to maintain "separate but equal" facilities.[14] However, the ultimate touchstone of constitutionality is the Constitution itself, not the precedents of the Supreme Court. Thus judges may, as they did in *Brown*, depart from precedent when they conclude that previous cases were wrongly decided.

Finally, even when the meaning of a constitutional provision is clear, its application in the specific case may be problematic. In *Chaplin & Drysdale, Chartered* v. *United States* (1989), for instance, all nine Supreme Court justices recognized that the Sixth Amendment guarantees criminal defendants a right to be represented by counsel at trial.[15] However, the justices disagreed sharply about whether the federal government could confiscate assets acquired through drug trafficking, when the defendant planned to use them to pay his legal fees. As these examples show, constitutional interpretation involves the exercise of judgment, and reasonable judges, equally devoted to the Constitution, often arrive at quite different understandings of the document.

Remedial Policymaking

As our earlier reference to *James* v. *Wallace* suggested, judicial involvement in constitutional cases may extend beyond determining whether the constitution has been violated. Once a constitutional violation is discovered, it must be remedied. *Remedial policymaking* refers to judicial imposition of requirements on officials in order to eliminate unconstitutional conditions or practices.

In most cases, all that is required is for judges to order officials to stop their unconstitutional conduct and to refrain from it in the future. Thus in *Reed* v. *Reed* (1971), its first major ruling on gender discrimination, the Supreme Court ruled that Idaho (and other states) could no longer give an automatic preference to men over women as administrators of estates, and this sufficed to dispose of the problem.[16] However, when the constitutional violation entails a failure by government to meet its constitutional obligations, judges may direct that specific remedial actions be undertaken to correct unconstitutional situations. Abraham Chayes has described what is distinctive about such judicial involvement:

> [The judge's decree] seeks to adjust future behavior, not to compensate for past wrong. It is deliberately fashioned rather than logically deduced from the nature of the legal harm suffered. It provides for a complex, on-going regime of performance rather than a simple, one-shot, one-way transfer. . . . [I]t prolongs and deepens, rather than terminates, the court's involvement with the dispute.[17]

As Chayes suggests, such remedial policymaking can involve judges in prolonged and detailed supervision of public facilities. Judge Johnson's ruling in *Jones* v. *Wallace*, for example, required that the prison hire a nutrition consultant and even prescribed the maximum number of inmates per toilet.[18] Such judicial intervention can occur even if courts do not assume immediate policymaking responsibility. In *Brown* v. *Board of Education* II (1955), the Supreme Court required that school districts take affirmative steps to eliminate racial segregation in their public school systems.[19] However, the Court left it up to the various school districts to determine how best to implement this requirement. Federal district court judges could intervene only if districts failed to meet their constitutional responsibility to desegregate their schools. Nevertheless, the refusal of many states and communities to comply with *Brown* compelled federal judges to devise and impose their own school desegregation plans.[20] (We shall consider this judicial involvement in detail in Chapter 10.)

Sometimes courts rule that an unconstitutional situation exists but refrain from announcing a remedy. For example, in *Robinson* v. *Cahill* (1972), the New Jersey Supreme Court ruled that the state's system of school finance violated the New Jersey Constitution but left it to the governor and legislature to devise a replacement.[21] While this approach puts an issue on the political agenda and gives the other branches of government an opportunity to act, it succeeds only if the political authorities are willing to meet their constitutional responsibilities.

Although the federal or state constitution might provide the basis for invalidating government actions, it offers little guidance as to how to remedy unconstitutional practices or their effects. Consequently, as Chayes noted, in seeking to remedy constitutional violations, judges necessarily exercise considerable discretion. In determining whether a judge has acted appropriately, one must consider the effectiveness of the judge's approach and whether it intrudes excessively on the powers of other branches of government.[22]

Statutory Interpretation and Judicial Policymaking

Although constitutional cases receive the most attention, they comprise a miniscule portion of court caseloads. Typically, judges are involved in enforcing legislative mandates rather than in invalidating them. The judge deciding a criminal case must determine what the defendant has done and whether those actions violate the criminal law. Judges in civil cases often must apply statutes in reaching their decisions. Thus, the responsibility to "say what the law is" frequently requires the judge to determine the meaning of legislative enactments and how they apply in specific cases.

This responsibility appears to provide little occasion for judicial policymaking. Most disputes are of interest only to the litigants themselves. Even when a dispute has broader significance, the legislature has supplied the standard for resolving it by enacting the statute. Moreover, because statutes are designed to serve particular purposes, they can—at least in theory—state precisely the aims to be achieved and the means for their achievement. Thus, the courts' function in cases involving statutory interpretation appears distinctly subsidiary: to determine what the law means and to decide cases in line with that meaning.

Yet as Chapter 8 has suggested, this picture, although not altogether inaccurate, is misleading.[23] In civil cases in particular, the fact that judges interpret statutes in the course of deciding cases usually means that the litigants differ about the statute's meaning or application. In resolving these differences, judges must choose between the competing interpretations of the law proposed by the parties to the case. Frequently, this choice, which is necessary to resolve the specific dispute, can have much wider effects. Indeed, one critic of judicial policymaking has charged that judges have all too often "embark[ed] on ambitious ventures of judicial reform in the name of statutory construction."[24] To understand how the judicial responsibility to interpret the law enmeshes judges in policymaking, one must look more closely at the factors that produce the need for statutory interpretation.

First, disputes about the meaning of a statute may arise if its provisions are unclear or appear to conflict with one another. On occasion, this lack of clarity may be inadvertent, the result of poor draftsmanship or inconsistent amendments added during legislative consideration of the measure. At other times, however, statutory ambiguity may reflect the technical complexity of the subject matter or what Justice Felix Frankfurter once referred to as "the intrinsic difficulties of the language."[25] Finally, unclear statutes may result from legislative efforts to avoid controversial policy choices through broad and general language. For example, Title VII of the Civil Rights Act of 1964 outlaws discrimination in employment on the basis of race, color, religion, sex, or national origin but fails to define what constitutes discrimination. This enabled its supporters to avoid divisive issues, such as whether discrimination must be intentional and whether affirmative action is permissible under the statute.[26] Some observers have contended that this "intentional" ambiguity is particularly prevalent in recent statutes.[27] But whatever the validity of this assertion, it is clear that judges frequently confront ambiguous statutory language. In such circumstances, their responsibility to resolve legal disputes obliges them to give meaning to unclear statutory provisions.

Second, disputes may arise over whether a law applies to a situation which was not contemplated by those who enacted the legislation. *Mortenson* v. *United States* provides a classic example.[28] Mr. and Mrs. Mortenson operated a (legal) house of prostitution in Grand Island, Nebraska. When they travelled to Salt Lake City to visit Mrs. Mortenson's parents, they took two of their employees along for the trip. After the vacation, they drove back to Nebraska, where their employees resumed their work. The Mortensons were subsequently prosecuted under the Mann Act, a federal statute that (as Chapter 8 indicated) forbade transporting women across state lines "for the purpose of prostitution or debauchery, or for any other immoral purpose."[29] Clearly the authors of the act never imagined the Mortensons' situation; they were primarily concerned with preventing coercion of young women into prostitution. Nevertheless, the government argued that when the Mortensons brought their employees back to work, they were in fact transporting them across state lines for the purpose of prostitution. Eventually, the United States Supreme Court by a 5-4 vote overturned the Mortensons' conviction.

Social and technological changes may also produce situations that not even the most farsighted legislator could have anticipated. *Diamond* v. *Chakrabarty* (1980) illustrates how such changes may provide occasions for judicial policymaking.[30]   Chakrabarty had created a living micro-organism under laboratory conditions and applied for a patent for his invention. Not surprisingly, in enacting the current federal patent law in 1952, Congress had not considered whether living organisms could be patented, and nothing in the law directly permitted or forbade the patenting of living organisms. The United States Supreme Court was therefore called upon to determine whether the broad language of the patent law, indicating an intention to reward ingenuity and invention, extended to the creation of such organisms. As the Court recognized, its decision could significantly influence whether genetic research was "accelerated by the hope of reward or slowed by the want of incentive."[31]   In ruling in favor of Chakrabarty and permitting the patenting of micro-organisms, the Court made important policy, but it did so in the course of fulfilling its responsibility to interpret and apply the law.

Third, disputes may also arise about how a statute affects prior legislation. Although the legal principles governing such situations are clear, their application can produce disputes that require judicial intervention. One principle is that if a new congressional or state statute is inconsistent with an existing one, the more recent enactment supersedes the earlier one. However, unless the legislature clearly indicates its intention to supersede an earlier enactment or unless two laws directly conflict, courts may be asked to determine if they are in fact inconsistent.

Another principle is that congressional legislation "preempts" (supersedes) inconsistent state legislation. But Congress rarely indicates how its enactments relate to existing state legislation. Thus when Congress enters a field that had previously been dominated by state legislation, courts often must determine whether the state law has been preempted. Similarly, when states legislate in an area in which congressional legislation exists, litigation often results. For example, when California enacted a statute outlawing "record piracy" (unauthorized duplication of recordings), several persons challenged their convictions under the act by claiming that it was preempted by the federal copyright law.[32]   They lost.

Oversight of Administrative Activity and Judicial Policymaking

Over the past sixty years, both the size of the federal and state governments and the scope of their activities have increased dramatically. Accompanying this unprecedented growth in government has been a major expansion in administrative policymaking. Through their power to issue regulations that further define legislative mandates and have the force of law, administrative agencies "legislate." Through their power to determine whether persons or organizations have violated law or regulations, agencies "adjudicate." Through their power to award or withhold authorizations and licenses and to establish and enforce eligibility requirements for government benefit programs, agencies control the distribution of important economic goods. This expansion in administrative policymaking has created new opportunities for judicial policymaking, as those injured by administrative actions challenge those actions in court.

Just as litigants may challenge the constitutionality of legislative enactments, so also may they challenge the constitutionality of administrative actions. More frequently, however, when litigants claim that an agency has exceeded its legal authority, the basis for the claim is statutory rather than constitutional. Because an agency can make policy only in pursuance of its statutory mandate, litigants may claim that an agency's action is inconsistent with its mandate. In such circumstances, the courts must determine whether the agency has exceeded its authority or has adopted policies inconsistent with its authorizing legislation. In doing so, the courts encounter the same difficulties of interpretation that they confront in statutory interpretation.

In other instances the challenge may be to administrative inaction rather than to administrative action. If a law imposes responsibilities on an agency, a litigant may charge that the agency has failed to carry out its responsibilities. This may involve total inaction by the agency. More frequently, however, the issue involves the adequacy of the agency's response to the legislative mandate. In *Allen* v. *Wright,* for example, a group of parents sued the Internal Revenue Service, alleging that it had not adopted sufficient standards and procedures to fulfill its obligation to deny tax-exempt status to racially discriminatory private schools.[33] In such cases also, judges must analyze the statutory requirements imposed on governmental agencies.

Even if an agency has statutory authorization for its actions, litigants may challenge the processes by which the agency arrived at its policy. This is a particularly fertile basis for litigation. The Administrative Procedure Act, enacted by Congress in 1946, specifies the basic procedures that federal agencies must follow in their rulemaking. Subsequent statutes have multiplied procedural requirements, and many agencies have supplemented these statutory requirements with their own rules of procedure. Although judges have sometimes been reluctant to challenge agencies' policy determinations, recognizing that they lack the technical expertise to evaluate agency assessments, they have been much more willing to intervene to ensure procedural regularity.[34] Yet judicial rulings on procedural issues can often have important policy consequences by requiring agencies to delay or reconsider their actions. Take, for example, the requirement under the National Environmental Protection Act that all agencies prepare an environmental impact statement for any proposal for legislation or "major federal action."[35]   Environmental groups have used this requirement as a weapon to delay or seek modifications in projects they opposed by filing suits challenging the failure to file the statements or the adequacy of those which were filed.[36]

In sum, as administrative policymaking has expanded, so has judicial intervention designed to ensure that agencies observe the substantive and procedural requirements imposed upon them. Yet this intervention has inevitably enmeshed courts in policy disputes and led them to issue rulings that have had a major impact on public policy.

The Common Law and Judicial Policymaking

As we have seen, constitutions, statutes, and administrative regulations can furnish legal standards for judges to apply in deciding cases. Yet in the United States, the scope of these types of law, although vast, is hardly comprehensive. Thus, when a dispute arises regarding, say, whether A is liable for injuries that B has suffered, a judge cannot look to the other branches of government for applicable legal standards. Instead, the judge must, in the course of resolving the dispute, establish the law that will govern it. As we have noted, this body of judge-made law, developed to resolve legal conflicts in the absence of legislative or executive enactments, is termed the common law.

Through their decisions enunciating the common law, the courts clearly make policy. Nevertheless, several factors serve to channel and control this policymaking. First, judges have only limited discretion in devising common-law legal policy. They are not free merely to incorporate their own policy preferences into law. Rather, as the term itself implies, the common law is to reflect the values and practices of the community. As noted in Chapter 1, during the thirteenth and fourteenth centuries, when the common law originated in England, judges drew their standards directly from the common practices of the society. Over time, as the body of judicial decisions elaborating these societal standards grew, recourse to legal precedent gradually replaced the direct invocation of community standards. Today, courts generally rely on precedent in deciding cases at common law. This reliance on precedent, fortified by the doctrine of *stare decisis*, ensures continuity in the law and effectively limits the range of judicial discretion in deciding cases.

Second, the common-law principles that a court announces have only a limited authority. When a state supreme court announces a principle of common law, it does so in the course of deciding a particular case. When subsequent cases arise that appear similar to the initial case, the court must decide whether to extend, modify, or abandon the principle it initially announced. Thus, the common law is established not so much by an individual decision as by an accumulation of decisions dealing with a particular area of the law. Moreover, although a state court's decision may constitute authoritative precedent within the state, its acceptance beyond the state's borders depends not upon the authority of the court but upon the persuasiveness of the arguments supporting the decision. This is particularly true when a court departs from established principles of the common law and charts a new direction.

Finally, although the common law is dynamic rather than static, decisive breaks with past decisions are rare. Change in the common law tends to be incremental, a gradual case-by-case modification of legal standards in response to shifts in the character and values of the society. At each step of the process, the movement can be halted or reversed if it appears to be heading in the wrong direction.

Yet ultimately these constraints channel, rather than prevent, judicial policymaking: courts inevitably make policy in their interpretation and development of the common law. Nor is this necessarily undesirable. The legal principles that were appropriate for the largely agrarian America of the eighteenth century could hardly serve the legal needs of the late twentieth century. Social and technological changes have created new problems that require the courts to extend or modify common-law principles. New relationships have developed in the society that must be taken into account in applying common-law principles. New aspirations have emerged, and the law must be sufficiently flexible to permit their fulfillment.

In sum, the courts' responsibility to resolve disputes in the absence of legal enactments obliges them to make law. Although no single court or decision establishes policy, legal standards emerge from the multiplicity of common-law rulings that judges are called upon to make. Although change is typically gradual and may in some instances only be discernible in retrospect, the common law must be dynamic to serve the needs of a changing society. These changes in the common law generally grow out of changes in the broader society. At the same time, the courts' decisions can also encourage or retard societal trends. Common-law policymaking thus both reflects and affects American society.

Cumulative Policymaking

Although some cases clearly raise important policy issues, most court cases involve more mundane disputes that are of concern only to the disputants. No new legal principles emerge from these cases, and the societal impact of individual judicial decisions is minimal. However, one should not distinguish too sharply between the few decisions that announce new policy and those decisions that comprise the bulk of court business. For although those latter cases, taken individually, may be relatively insignificant, they may in the aggregate embody important policy choices.

Moreover, judges often exercise considerable discretion in resolving these more mundane disputes. Ordinarily, judges decide cases by applying the law. However, at times the society's sense of justice cannot readily be reduced to precise legal standards. In such circumstances the legislature may merely announce a general standard and rely on judges to use their discretion to do justice on a case-by-case basis. When this occurs, the state's policy, instead of being defined by legislative mandate, actually emerges from the totality of judicial decisions.

Sentencing in criminal cases illustrates this sort of cumulative policymaking. Until recent reforms (see Chapter 6), the criminal law in the United States tended to define the minimum and maximum penalties for various offenses—for example, five to ten years for armed robbery—but allow the judge considerable discretion in sentencing within those guidelines. (If anything, plea bargaining has increased the range of discretion available in sentencing.) Although the sentence meted out to an individual offender does not establish policy, the overall pattern of sentencing in criminal cases does constitute important policymaking. This is not merely because of the large number of offenders who are sentenced. Rather, the pattern of sentencing may reveal how the society regards various crimes. The lower sentences for possession of marijuana during the late 1960s, for example, indicated a change in societal standards even before state legislatures acted to reduce penalties. In addition, a comparison of the sentences meted out to members of various racial and economic groups provides one indication of the society's commitment to equal justice. Charges of racial bias in sentencing and complaints about judges who are "soft on crime," whether justified or not, indicate that cumulative policymaking can be highly controversial.

A second example of cumulative policymaking is child custody awards in contested divorce cases.[37] When parents cannot agree on a custody arrangement, trial-court judges determine which parent shall retain custody or whether joint custody shall be awarded. Although the judge's award is to serve the "best interests of the child," this vague standard affords considerable leeway for the exercise of judicial discretion.[38] Once again, the decision in individual cases may be of concern chiefly to the contending parties. However, the cumulative effect of those decisions is to define how the society weighs the various factors that might be considered in determining the child's "best interest." During the early twentieth century, for example, judges—rhapsodizing that "there is but a twilight zone between a mother's love and an atmosphere of heaven"—consistently supported maternal claims for custody.[39]   Over the past three decades, however, fathers have become more willing to seek custody and more successful in obtaining it.   As this change suggests, cumulative policymaking can both respond to and influence developments occurring in the broader society.

In sum, then, cumulative policymaking occurs when the courts, by deciding a series of essentially similar cases, in effect define policy in a given area. Although legislation or rulings by appellate courts may circumscribe the range of judicial choice, trial judges often retain considerable leeway in deciding individual cases.   In exercising this discretion, judges rarely announce broad policy standards.   Indeed, they may give little consideration to the broader policy that their decisions are creating.   Nonetheless, the results of their decisions constitute the state's policy.

THE INCIDENCE OF JUDICIAL POLICYMAKING

The Level of Judicial Policymaking

Although judicial policymaking is not a recent phenomenon, judges are more involved in policymaking today than in the past.   What accounts for this increased judicial policymaking?   It may be that today's judges are more willing, even eager, to take an active role in policymaking than were judges in earlier eras.[40] Recognizing this, groups may also be more willing to use the courts to advance their policy objectives.[41]   Perhaps the primary reason for increased judicial policymaking, however, is simply that there is now more law and more litigation.

At one time, many state constitutions mandated that the state legislature meet every other year for a limited period. Today, most state legislatures meet annually, and longer, and enact more laws.[42]   Except when its members are campaigning for reelection, Congress is almost continually in session.[43] Perhaps the biggest change, however, involves administrative lawmaking. The creation of regulatory agencies during the twentieth century has produced an explosion of federal rules and regulations.[44]   In 1936, for example, the Code of Federal Regulations, which includes all regulations issued by federal agencies, numbered 2,619 pages.   Today, these regulations stretch over more than 67,000 pages.[45]   This increase in law creates new rights and responsibilities and, in so doing, stimulates litigation. Many of these cases do not involve judicial policymaking: judges merely enforce preexisting legal standards, and the outcomes of the cases are of consequence only to the litigants. However, many others create new opportunities for—and indeed, may oblige judges to engage in—judicial policymaking.

Historical Shifts in Judicial Policymaking

Changes have occurred over time not only in the amount but also in the character of judicial policymaking (see Table 9-1):

Constitutional policymaking: The twentieth century has been the main era for constitutional policymaking in the United States. The United States Supreme Court invalidated only two Federal statutes and 34 state statutes before 1860.[46] (However, some rulings upholding Federal laws against state challenge also had important policy consequences.[47]) State supreme courts during the nation's first century were more involved in constitutional policymaking: the Virginia Supreme Court, for example, considered constitutional challenges to 35 state laws before 1860.[48] However, since 1970 the Supreme Court has struck down 26 Federal statutes, more than 20 percent of all it has invalidated (see Figure 9-1).[49] Over the past two decades, state courts also have shown renewed willingness to strike down statutes violating state declarations of rights, a phenomenon we shall analyze in Chapter 11.

**FIGURE 9-1 CONGRESSIONAL STATUTES RULED UNCONSTITUTIONAL BY THE
UNITED STATES SUPREME COURT**

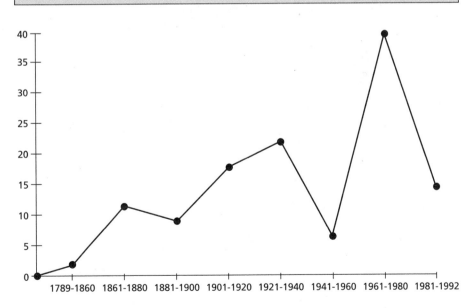

SOURCE: Compiled from Library of Congress, *The Constitution of the United States; Analysis and Interpretation,* S. Doc., 99-16, 99th Congress, 1st session, 1987. Updated to 1992.

Remedial policymaking: The imposition of detailed plans of action to remedy constitutional violations began in the 1950s with the the effort to implement *Brown* v. *Board of Education*, the Supreme Court's school desegregation decision.[50]

Statutory policymaking: As we noted previously, federal and state legislation has increased during the twentieth century. As the amount of legislation has increased, so has the volume of litigation over its interpretation and the level of statutory policymaking by judges. Equally important has been a change in the character of legislation. During the nineteenth century, federal statutes primarily involved the distribution of benefits to citizens—the Homestead Act, which made public lands available to settlers, is a prime example—and such legislation rarely provoked disputes. During the twentieth century, however, the expansion of federal and state regulation of private conduct has prompted challenges by those affected by the statutes. Often these disputes about the interpretation and application of regulatory statutes have wound up in the courts.[51]

Oversight of administrative agencies: Although some state regulatory agencies were created during the nineteenth century, most federal administrative agencies were established in bursts of creative energy during the Progressive Era (roughly 1900-1920), the New Deal (1932-1940), and the Great Society period (roughly 1963-1970).[52] The establishment of new agencies prompted increased administrative activity and expanded judicial involvement in the oversight of that activity.

Common-law policymaking: As we have noted, during the nation's first century, most American law was enunciated by courts rather than enacted by legislatures. Common-law policymaking represented the most important judicial policymaking of that era.[53] From 1800-1870, American courts introduced important innovations in the common law. Judges adapted English common-law doctrines to the more democratic and egalitarian society found in the United States. They also eased and encouraged the transition from an agrarian society to a more industrialized one.[54]

During the twentieth century, the scope of the common law has contracted, as statutes and administrative regulations have replaced the common law in fields such as employer-employee relations. However, since World War II, state appellate courts have introduced revolutionary changes in the tort law, that is, the law governing liability for injuries that one has caused. We shall discuss some of these changes in Chapter 11.

Cumulative policymaking: Cumulative policymaking has occurred throughout the nation's history.

The Agenda of Judicial Policymaking

As American society changes, so too do the sorts of issues coming before the courts. This in turn affects the focus of judicial policymaking. The changing agenda of the United States Supreme Court illustrates the point. During the nineteenth century, the vast majority of cases coming before the Court did not involve constitutional issues; today, they do.[55] Even more important are the changes in the sorts of constitutional issues the Court addresses. Prior to the Civil War, the Court's cases usually involved disputes about the respective spheres of the national and state governments. After the Civil War, industrialization and the growth of large corporations prompted governmental efforts to deal with those developments, and the Court's constitutional agenda focused on the scope of federal and state power to regulate economic enterprises. Since the late 1930s, when the Court recognized broad federal and state authority to regulate economic matters, it has been most involved in delineating the scope of constitutional rights.[56]

The policymaking agendas of other courts likewise reflect societal changes. For example, a study of the dockets of state supreme courts over a one-hundred year period documented a shift from commercial to noncommercial cases and concluded that the courts "seem to be less concerned with the stabilization and protection of property rights, more concerned with the individual and the downtrodden, and more willing to consider rulings that promote social change."[57] A similar study of federal courts of appeals concluded that criminal cases and cases involving the federal government had risen dramatically, confirming the importance of legislation in stimulating litigation. Whereas private economic disputes had dominated the dockets of courts of appeals early in the twentieth century, they constituted a much smaller proportion of their caseload by the late twentieth century.[58]

ASSESSING JUDICIAL POLICYMAKING

Criteria for Evaluation

Most people evaluate judicial policymaking on the basis of results. They praise judicial policies which they favor and condemn those they dislike. In doing so, they treat courts as indistinguishable from other political institutions: what matters is the substance of the policy, not its legal basis. Thus if they are pro-life, they applaud Supreme Court rulings that restrict abortion. If they are politically conservative, they deplore lenient sentences for offenders.

This section, however, focuses on two other criteria for evaluating judicial policymaking, namely, *legitimacy* and capacity or *policy effectiveness*. To determine whether a judicial decision enunciating policy is legitimate, one must ask: is the issue one which judges may properly address, and is there an adequate legal basis for the court's position? Note that one's answer to those questions might not coincide with one's policy views. We might condemn as illegitimate a judicial ruling that advances a policy we favor; alternatively, we may acknowledge another judicial ruling as legitimate, even while deploring the specific policy announced by the court.

To assess judicial policymaking in terms of judicial capacity or policy effectiveness, one asks a different question: has the policy announced by the court succeeded in achieving its goals? Applying this criterion, one would evaluate court-ordered busing by examining whether it in fact promotes racial integration in schools (see Chapter 10). Or one would evaluate the exclusionary rule by analyzing whether it in fact deters police misconduct (see Chapter 6). It is to the issue of judicial policymaking capacity that we turn first.

Judicial Capacity and Policy Effectiveness[59]

Every governmental institution has its own characteristic approach to defining and dealing with policy issues. This approach reflects the particular background and expertise of the policymakers, the way they make their policy decisions, and the resources they command to ensure that their policies are carried out. Comparing courts with other governmental bodies on these bases, some commentators have concluded that courts are ill-equipped to devise and implement policy. Donald Horowitz, the most well-known of these critics, identifies several problems with judicial policymaking.[60]

Timeliness of Addressing Problems

Timing is important in successful policymaking. If a problem is addressed too early, without adequate understanding of its dimensions or of the range of possible solutions, remedial efforts are unlikely to succeed and may merely produce other problems. Conversely, if a problem is addressed too late, it may be more difficult to solve.

Courts do not control when they will confront policy issues because they do not control their own agendas. Rather, they must passively await the decision of litigants to bring policy issues before them for resolution. With the exception of the United States Supreme Court (and to a lesser extent, some state high courts), they cannot decline to hear properly brought cases, even if the cases raise policy issues that are not ripe for resolution. In sum, although timing may be essential to effective policymaking, it is largely a matter of chance whether courts will address problems at the time most conducive to their successful resolution.

Adequacy of Information

The wisdom of policy choices often depends upon the quality of the information policymakers receive and the uses to which they put it. Yet according to Horowitz, courts are less likely than other institutions to obtain relevant information and use it effectively.

First of all, courts announce broad policy—for example, the inadmissibility of illegally seized evidence—in the course of deciding specific cases. This poses no difficulty if the case the court decides is representative of all possible situations that the court's ruling will affect. But, according to Horowitz, this is rarely the case. Rather, courts make policy without information about many situations that their policy will affect, and the result of such ill-informed policymaking is likely to be bad policy.

In addition, because courts must decide issues on the basis of law, the information they receive in legal briefs and in oral argument tends to focus on legal considerations rather than on the desirability of a policy or the likely consequences of alternative approaches to a problem. Moreover, even if such information were conveyed, judges could hardly refuse to recognize a constitutional or legal right because of doubts about its desirability. Whereas other policymakers tend to view policy issues in terms of ranges of alternatives and costs and benefits, courts necessarily view them in terms of legal rights and legal duties.

Furthermore, courts confront policy issues only in adversarial proceedings, with the issues framed as disputes between two specific parties. Although other groups and interests may be affected by the court's decision, they have no legal standing to present their views and concerns and may not even know about the litigation. Even if the parties do not monopolize the transmission of information, the input the court receives is typically less rich and complete than that available to a legislature or administrative agency considering a policy issue. For example, rules of evidence may keep relevant information from the court. And whereas other governmental bodies can seek out additional information on their own, as in legislative hearings, or commission studies of a problem, courts must rely on the information they receive through legal briefs and oral argument.

Even if that information is inadequate, courts cannot decline to decide or post-pone their decision.

Finally, judges in general jurisdiction courts decide cases in a variety of fields. They thus approach cases that involve issues of public policy as generalists rather than as experts. In theory, this allows them to bring a fresh perspective to prob-lems. However, it also means that they lack the background that specialization in a particular field brings. Because of this, judges typically lack the ability to understand and make use of sophisticated policy-relevant information even when it is made available to them. Confronted with expert testimony, they lack the skills necessary to evaluate the experts' claims or, if the experts disagree, to choose among conflicting views. Whether the issue be the carcinogenic effects of Agent Orange, the environmental consequences of opening public lands to private development, or the deterrent effects of capital punishment, judges con-front technical problems as amateurs.

Flexibility of Response

The more flexibility policymakers have in devising solutions to problems, the more likely they are to deal with them successfully. According to Horowitz, however, courts have far fewer options than do other policymakers. Because courts must decide cases on the basis of law, they cannot impose a compromise solution on disputants, no matter how desirable. Moreover, if persons possess a right, they possess it regardless of cost, and thus cost-benefit analysis, the prime approach to contemporary policymaking, plays little role in judicial policymak-ing. Finally, courts have fewer means of remedying illegal situations than do other governmental institutions. They can forbid, permit, or require actions, but they can neither tax nor spend (although their orders may require expendi-tures by other branches). They can neither create new agencies to administer their directives nor appoint officials to oversee their implementation.

Monitoring the Effects of Decisions

Once a policy is established, policymakers must monitor its implementation to ensure that the policy is carried out (compliance) and that it has its desired effects. This policy review also allows policymakers to modify their policies when earlier approaches have proven ineffective in achieving the desired results.

According to Horowitz, courts cannot effectively monitor the effects of their decisions, nor can they respond to those effects as easily as can other policymak-ers. Instead of overseeing the consequences of their decisions, judges typically turn to other cases, once they have announced a decision. When the target population for a decision is large—for example, police officers who interrogate suspects—judges have no way to monitor compliance with their ruling. Even when the target population is relatively small, courts often do not know whether their decisions are being carried out unless affected groups sue, bringing instances of non-compliance to the attention of the courts

A further problem plagues judicial efforts to ensure that their policies have their desired effects. Because the American legal system emphasizes adherence to precedent, courts are generally reluctant to overrule earlier decisions, particularly recent ones. Yet this means that courts cannot readily change course when confronted with evidence that their policy directives have failed to achieve their desired results. Thus, even when they can determine the consequences of their decisions, respect for precedent renders judges less able than other policymakers to benefit from that information.

Evaluating Horowitz's Critique

Not all observers agree with Horowitz that courts are particularly ill-equipped to devise policy.[61] The recent proliferation of remedial policymaking, they claim, shows that Horowitz underestimates courts' ability to devise new approaches to deal with unfamiliar problems. Beyond that, courts fare badly in Horowitz's analysis because he unfairly compares the actual operation of courts to an idealized picture of legislatures and administrative agencies. Legislators—just like judges—are generalists, confronting a wide array of issues on the basis of incomplete information. Like judges also, they do not control their own agendas, but instead must address those issues on which the public demands action. Frequently, these legislative issues arise—just like judicial issues—because of a single occurrence. For example, the riots in Los Angeles after the acquittal of the police officers charged with beating Rodney King prompted Congress to enact an urban aid program. In addition, legislators and administrators, just like judges, have difficulty supervising the operation of their policies—the Savings and Loan debacle is a prime example. Finally, as *Brown* v. *Board of Education* and the Alabama prison litigation demonstrated, the choice is often not between the courts or some other institution addressing a problem but between judicial intervention and governmental inaction.

Some commentators also insist that insofar as judges do have a distinctive approach to policymaking, this may prove an advantage rather than a disadvantage. The emphasis on reasoned justification in judicial decisionmaking, for example, may promote more thoughtful policy pronouncements. Furthermore, judges—especially federal judges—enjoy an independence from partisan pressures and the importunings of special interests. Their relative insulation may enable them to pursue policies that serve the public interest rather than short-term political advantage.[62]

Finally, insofar as Horowitz's critique is accurate, it applies primarily to situations in which a judge announces broad policy in a single case. As we have seen, not all judicial policymaking fits that pattern. Common-law policymaking and cumulative policymaking generally involve an incremental, case-by-case approach. Judges usually do not announce broad policy in the course of statutory policymaking or judicial oversight of administrative activity. Horowitz's critique therefore seems particularly applicable to constitutional policymaking and remedial policymaking.

Legitimacy

Even if judges cannot altogether avoid policymaking, this does not mean that all judicial policymaking is legitimate. Judges may announce decisions that have no basis in law but merely reflect their personal policy views. Or their rulings may clearly invade the powers and prerogatives of the other branches of government. In such circumstances, few people would deny that the rulings were illegitimate. However, people may well disagree about what constitutes an adequate legal basis for a decision or about the judiciary's proper role in governing in a democratic society. Indeed, almost from the establishment of the Constitution, the scope of judicial authority has prompted fierce debate.

In recent years this debate has been framed in terms of "judicial activism" versus "judicial restraint." Unfortunately, these terms obscure as much as they clarify. The term "judicial activism" has frequently been used to criticize judicial rulings. However, some scholars and judges have applauded such activism, particularly when it resulted in a broad definition of individual rights.[63] Thus, characterizing a decision as activist or restrained does not necessarily resolve whether it is legitimate or not.

In addition, the meaning of the terms themselves is far from clear. In an effort to replace polemics with precision, political scientist Bradley Canon identified several dimensions for characterizing decisions as activist or restrained (see Box 9-1).[64]

Useful though Canon's list is in clarifying the various understandings of activism and restraint, it also underscores the limitations and confusions in the contemporary debate over judicial activism and restraint. Most obviously, as Canon himself acknowledges, the criteria for activism and restraint apply best to

---

BOX 9-1 DIMENSIONS OF JUDICIAL ACTIVISM AND RESTRAINT

1. *Majoritarianism:* Activist decisions negate policies adopted through democratic processes; restraintist decisions uphold them.

2. *Interpretive Stability:* Activist decisions modify or overrule earlier court decisions, doctrines, or interpretations; restraintist decisions leave them intact.

3. *Interpretive Fidelity:* Activist decisions interpret constitutional provisions in a manner that diverges from the clear intentions of their drafters or the clear implications of the language used; restraintist decisions adhere to the text and the original understanding of provisions.

4. *Substance-Democratic Process Distinction:* Activist decisions make substantive policy; restraintist decisions merely preserve the democratic process.

5. *Specificity of Policy:* Activist decisions announce detailed policy directives; restraintist policy leave discretion to other agencies or individuals.

6. *Availability of an Alternative Policymaker:* Activist decisions supersede serious consideration of the same problem by other governmental agencies; restraintist decisions promote it.

SOURCE: Adapted from Bradley C. Canon, "A Framework for the Analysis of Judicial Activism," in Stephen C. Halpern and Charles M. Lamb, *Supreme Court Activism and Restraint* (Lexington, Mass.: Lexington Books, 1982), pp. 386-387.

constitutional policymaking. Statutory policymaking and cumulative policymaking by definition do not overturn legislation. Common-law policymaking does not preclude policymaking by other branches of government.

Even if one limits one's attention to constitutional policymaking, the distinction between activism and restraint is not altogether satisfactory. Whereas some judicial decisions might be characterized as clearly activist and others as clearly restraintist, many decisions may be activist on some dimensions and restrained on others. When the United States Supreme Court reversed course in 1937 and began to uphold New Deal legislation, its rulings were activist, in that they overruled precedent, but restrained in that they upheld congressional legislation.[65] Similarly, the Court in *Brown* v. *Board of Education* rejected the prevailing standard of "separate but equal" and overturned laws in several states but arguably did so in order to bring the interpretation of the Equal Protection

Clause in line with the clear implications of its language.[66] Thus, depending on the criteria one employed, one could characterize those rulings as either activist or restrained.

The main problem with discussions of judicial activism and restraint, however, is that they distract attention from what should be the primary concern in assessing the legitimacy of judicial policymaking, namely, whether the court's rulings are legally defensible. Put differently, the most important criterion for judging the legitimacy of judicial decisions and judicial policymaking is what Canon has termed "Interpretive Fidelity." Judicial policymaking is legitimate, whether or not it overturns congressional statutes and judicial precedents, if the court's ruling is consistent with the text and intention of the provision being interpreted. Conversely, a judicial decision is illegitimate if it follows precedent or upholds legislation when fidelity to the Constitution demands their invalidation. Of course, acceptance of interpretive fidelity as the primary criterion does not eliminate disputes. Judges disagree, often vehemently, about how to interpret constitutional provisions and other legal texts. Commentators constantly debate whether courts have adequately justified their rulings. Chapter 8 has suggested why such disagreements may occur, even among those committed to the disinterested interpretation of the law.

CONCLUSIONS

This chapter has served to dispel several myths about judicial policymaking. One myth is that judicial policymaking necessarily involves a judicial usurpation of power. At times this may be the case. But generally, judicial policymaking is the unavoidable result of judges' fulfilling their responsibility to decide cases in accordance with the law. In the course of doing so, they interpret constitutions and statutes, oversee the actions of administrative agencies, and elaborate the common law. The decisions they render have policy consequences, often regardless of how they rule, and μthus judges are unavoidably involved in the development of public policy.

A second myth is that the growth of judicial policymaking reflects an effort by activist judges to exercise power. Although there may be individual judges who abuse their positions, more seems involved than the character of the judges. After all, over a decade of judicial appointments by Presidents Reagan and Bush, both of whom expressed fervent opposition to judicial activism, have not eliminated judicial policymaking. Rather, it is the expansion of government and increases in law, rather than the composition of the judiciary, that is primarily responsible for judicial policymaking.

A third myth is that judicial policymaking is necessarily undemocratic, in that the will of the judge is prevailing over the will of the populace. In actuality, much judicial policymaking does not place courts at odds with the popular will. In statutory policymaking and in judicial oversight of administrative agencies, judges are presumably giving effect to, rather than overriding, the will of the legislature. In common-law policymaking they are acting in the absence of legislation, and in cumulative policymaking they are exercising discretion within bounds set by the legislature.   Constitutional policymaking sometimes places judges at odds with legislatures, but often the judges are invalidating actions of officials—for example, police officers—who are themselves not directly accountable to the public. Finally, in remedial policymaking judges sometimes displace other policymakers but typically do so only when those policymakers have failed to act to meet constitutional requirements.

Of course, this does not mean that judicial policymaking is beyond criticism. Judges at times exceed their legitimate powers, render unwise decisions, or announce policies that fail to achieve their objectives. However, it does mean that to understand and assess judicial policymaking, one must look closely at how judges reach their decisions and at the effects their decisions actually have. Thus, in Chapter 10 we examine in detail federal court policymaking on two important issues, school desegregation and abortion, and in Chapter 11 we look at state court policymaking involving school finance and products liability.

NOTES

1. See generally David M. O'Brien, *Storm Center; The Supreme Court in American Politics* (2nd ed.; New York: Norton, 1990); Alpheus Mason, *The Supreme Court from Taft to Burger* (3rd ed.; Baton Rouge: Louisiana State University Press, 1979); Lawrence Tribe, *God Save This Honorable Court* (New York: Random House, 1985); and Christopher Wolfe, *The Rise of Modern Judicial Review* (New York: Basic Books, 1986).

2. The quotation is from Chief Justice John Marshall's opinion for the Court in *Marbury* v. *Madison*, 1 Cranch (5 U.S.) 137, 173 (1803), the first case in which the United States Supreme Court struck down a congressional statute as unconstitutional.

3. *Edwards* v. *Aguillard*, 482 U.S. 578 (1987).

4. *Marbury* v. *Madison*, 1 Cranch (5 U.S.) 137 (1803). There are a few instances of state exercise of judicial review prior to 1800. For a discussion of these cases and of the roots of judicial review, see Sylvia Snowiss, *Judicial Review and the Law of the Constitution* (New Haven: Yale University Press, 1990).

5. These data are drawn from Library of Congress, *The Constitution of the United States: Analysis and Interpretation*, S. Doc. 99-16, 99th Congress, 1st Session, 1987.

6. *United States* v. *Nixon*, 418 U.S. 683 (1974).

7. These data are computed from the yearly statistics on the work of the Supreme Court, published in the *Harvard Law Review*, volumes 94-104, 1980-1990.

8. *James* v. *Wallace*, 382 F.Supp. 1177 (M.D. Ala. 1974); *James* v. *Wallace*, 406 F.Supp. 318 (M.D. Ala. 1976).

9. For an account of Judge Frank Johnson's involvement, see Tinsley E. Yarbrough, *Judge Frank Johnson and Human Rights in Alabama* (University, Ala.: University of Alabama Press, 1981); and Jethro K. Lieberman, *The Litigious Society* (New York: Basic Books, 1981), Chapter 5.

10. *State ex rel. Baker* v. *Troutman*, 553 N.E.2d 1053 (Ohio 1990), and *City of Billings* v. *Layzell*, 789 P.2d 221 (Mont. 1990).

11. This is more complicated than it sounds. For representative efforts by constitutional theorists to address this issue, see Sotirios Barber, *On What the Constitution Means* (Baltimore: Johns Hopkins University Press, 1984); Robert Bork, *The Tempting of America; The Political Seduction of the Law* (New York: Free Press, 1990); John Hart Ely, *Democracy and Distrust; A Theory of Judicial Review* (Cambridge: Harvard University Press, 1980); and Gary L. Jacobsohn, *The Supreme Court and the Decline of Constitutional Aspiration* (Totowa, N.J.: Rowman & Littlefield, 1986).

12. The quotation is from Justice Owen Roberts's opinion for the Court in *United States* v. *Butler*, 297 U.S. 1 (1936).

13. *Brown* v. *Board of Education*, 347 U.S. 483 (1954).

14. *Plessy* v. *Ferguson*, 163 U.S. 537 (1896).

15. *Caplin & Drysdale, Chartered* v. *United States*, 109 S.Ct. 2646 (1989).

16. *Reed* v. *Reed*, 404 U.S. 71 (1971).

17. Abram Chayes, "The Role of the Judge in Public Law Litigation," *Harvard Law Review* 89 (1976), p. 1298.

18. *James* v. *Wallace*, 406 F.Supp. 318 (M.D. Ala. 1976).

19. *Brown* v. *Board of Education* [*Brown* II], 349 U.S. 294 (1955).

20. The role of Federal judges in desegregation efforts is discussed in Chapter 10.

21. *Robinson* v. *Cahill* [*Robinson* I], 303 A.2d 273 (N.J. 1973), and *Robinson* v. *Cahill* [*Robinson* II]. 339 A.2d 193 (N.J. 1975). See the discussion of school finance in Chapter 11.

22. For discussion of these limits, see Gary L. McDowell, *Equity and the Constitution; The Supreme Court, Equitable Relief, and Public Policy* (Chicago: University of Chicago Press, 1982).

23. A useful summary of the problems involved in statutory interpretation is found in Cass Sunstein, *After the Rights Revolution* (Cambridge: Harvard University Press, 1990), Chapter 4.

24. Donald L. Horowitz, *The Courts and Social Policy* (Washington, D.C.: Brookings, 1977), p. 13.

25. Felix Frankfurter, "Some Reflections on the Reading of Statutes," *Record of the Association of the Bar of the City of New York* 2 (1947), reprinted in Walter F. Murphy and C. Herman Pritchett, *Courts, Judges, and Politics,* 2nd ed. (New York: Random House, 1974), p. 414.

26. Important cases spawned by this failure to define discrimination include: *Griggs* v. *Duke Power Co.,* 401 U.S. 424 (1970); *United Steelworkers of America* v. *Weber,* 443 U.S. 193 (1979); and *Wards Cove Packing Co.* v. *Atonio,* 109 S.Ct. 2115 (1989).

27. Theodore J. Lowi, *The End of Liberalism,* 2nd ed. (New York: W.W. Norton, 1979), especially Chapter 5.

28. 322 U.S. 369 (1944).

29. 18 U.S.C.A. sec. 398.

30. *Diamond* v. *Chakrabarty,* 447 U.S. 303 (1980).

31. Ibid., at 317.

32. *Goldstein* v. *California,* 412 U.S. 546 (1973).

33. *Allen* v. *Wright,* 468 U.S. 737 (1984).

34. Martin Shapiro, *Who Guards the Guardians? Judicial Control of Administration* (Athens, Ga.: University of Georgia Press, 1988), especially Chapter 3.

35. According to section 102 (2)(C) of the Act, the environmental impact statement must address (1) the environmental impact of the act; (2) any adverse environmental effects which cannot be avoided should the proposal be implemented; (3) alternatives to the proposed action; (4) the relation between local short-term uses of man's environment and the maintenance of long-term productivity; and (5) any irreversible and irretrievable commitments of resources which would be involved in the proposed action should it be implemented.

36. See, for example, *Environmental Defense Fund, Inc.* v. *Corps of Engineers,* 470 F.2d 289 (1973).

37. See generally G. Alan Tarr and Mary Cornelia Porter, "Gender Equality and Judicial Federalism: The Role of State Appellate Courts," *Hastings Constitutional Law Quarterly* 9 (Summer 1982), pp. 942-950.

38. Ibid., pp. 963-969, Table E.

39. *Tuter* v. *Tuter,* 120 S.W.2d 203, 205 (Mo. Ct. App. 1938).

40. In part this both reflects and further promotes the support for judicial activism within the academic and legal communities. For a summary of the arguments for judicial activism, see Christopher Wolfe, *Judicial Activism; Bulwark of Freedom or Precarious Security* (Pacific Grove, Calif.: Brooks/ Cole, 1991).

41. See, for example, Karen O'Connor, *Women's Organizations' Use of the Courts* (Lexington, Mass.: Lexington Books, 1980); Stephen L. Wasby, "Civil Rights Litigation by Organizations: Constraints and Choices," *Judicature* 68 (April-May 1985): 337-352, and Clement Vose, *Caucasians Only* (Berkeley: University of California Press, 1959).

42. See Rich Jones, "The State Legislatures," *Book of the States, 1992-93* (Lexington, Ky.: Council of State Governments, 1992), pp. 128-129.

43. The 102nd Congress convened its first session on January 3, 1991, and adjourned on November 27, 1991; it convened its second session on January 3, 1992, and adjourned on October 9, 1992. (*Topical Law Review: Congressional Index* [Chicago: Commerce Clearing House, 1992])

44. For the history of the creation of such agencies, see James Q. Wilson, "The Rise of the Bureaucratic State," *The Public Interest* 41 (Fall 1975): 77-103, and Richard Harris and Sidney Milkis, *The Politics of Regulatory Change; A Tale of Two Agencies* (New York: Oxford University Press, 1989).

45. George C. Greanias and Duane Windsor, "Is Judicial Restraint Possible in an Administrative Society?" *Judicature* 64 (April 1981), p. 402.

46. Library of Congress, *The Constitution of the United States*, pp. 1915-1921.

47. Important rulings upholding congressional power include *McCulloch* v. *Maryland*, 17 Wheat. 316 (1819), and *Gibbons* v. *Ogden*, 19 Wheat. 1 (1824).

48. Margaret V. Nelson, *A Study of Judicial Revision in Virginia, 1789-1928* (New York: Columbia University Press, 1946).

49. Library of Congress, *The Constitution of the United States*, pp. 1909-1912, and *1988 Supplement*, pp. 187-190.

50. *Brown* v. *Board of Education* [*Brown* II], 349 U.S. 294 (1955).

51. On the changing character of Federal legislation, see Theodore J. Lowi and Benjamin Ginsberg, *American Government; Freedom and Power* (New York: W.W. Norton, 1990), p. 70, Table 3.1.

52. Wilson, "The Rise of the Bureaucratic State."

53. William E. Nelson, *Americanization of the Common Law* (Cambridge: Harvard University Press, 1975).

54. Morton J. Horwitz, *The Transformation of American Law, 1780-1860* (Cambridge: Harvard University Press, 1977).

55. For an overview of changes in the Supreme Court's agenda over time, see O'Brien, *Storm Center*, pp. 244-250.

56. This analysis relies on Ralph A. Rossum and G. Alan Tarr, *American Constitutional Law; Cases and Interpretation*, 3rd ed. (New York: St. Martin's Press, 1991), pp. 28-29.

57. Robert A. Kagan, Bliss Cartwright, Lawrence M. Friedman, and Stanton Wheeler, "The Business of State Supreme Courts, 1870-1970," *Stanford Law Review* 30 (November 1977), p. 155.

58. Lawrence Baum, Sheldon Goldman, and Austin Sarat, "The Evolution of Litigation in the Federal Courts of Appeals, 1895-1975," *Law & Society Review* 16 (1981-82): 291-309.

59. This account relies on G. Alan Tarr and Russell S. Harrison, "Legitimacy and Capacity in State Supreme Court Policymaking: The New Jersey Court and Exclusionary Zoning," *Rutgers Law Journal* 15 (Spring 1984), pp. 542-547.

60. Donald L. Horowitz, *The Courts and Social Policy* (Washington, D.C.: Brookings Institution, 1977).

61. See Ralph Cavanagh and Austin Sarat, "Thinking About Courts: Toward and Beyond a Jurisprudence of Judicial Competence," *Law & Society Review* 14 (Winter 1980): 371-420; and Stephen L. Wasby, "Arrogation of Power or Accountability: Judicial Imperialism Revisited," *Judicature* 65 (October 1981): 208-219.

62. See, for example, Michael J. Perry, *The Constitution, the Courts, and Human Rights* (New York: Yale University Press, 1982); and Arthur S. Miller, "In Defense of Judicial Activism," in Stephen C. Halpern and Charles M. Lamb, eds., *Supreme Court Activism and Restraint* (Lexington, Mass.: Lexington Books, 1982).

63. See, for example, Perry, *The Constitution, the Courts, and Human Rights*; Ronald Dworkin, *Taking Rights Seriously* (Cambridge: Harvard University Press, 1977); and John Hart Ely, *Democracy and Distrust; A Theory of Judicial Review* (Cambridge: Harvard University Press, 1980).

64. Bradley C. Canon, "A Framework for the Analysis of Judicial Activism," in Halpern and Lamb, *Supreme Court Activism and Restraint*.

65. *National Labor Relations Board* v. *Jones & Laughlin Steel Corporation*, 301 U.S. 1 (1937), overturning such rulings as *United States* v. *E. C. Knight Company*, 156 U.S. 1 (1895) and *Carter* v. *Carter Coal Company*, 298 U.S. 298 (1936).

66. *Brown* v. *Board of Education*, 347 U.S. 483 (1954), overturning *Plessy* v. *Ferguson*, 163 U.S. 537 (1896).

10 FEDERAL COURT POLICYMAKING

This chapter focuses on two of the most controversial issues that have confronted the federal courts in the last few decades, namely, school desegregation and abortion. Certainly no account of federal court policymaking can pretend to be comprehensive, given the variety of policy issues that these courts address. Nonetheless, the rulings on school desegregation and abortion, as well as the reactions to them, illustrate crucial features of federal court policymaking. Our analysis (1) reveals the process by which these policy issues were transformed into legal disputes and brought before the courts for resolution; (2) shows how federal court policy on these issues has changed over time; (3) describes the interplay between judicial rulings and the political process; and (4) assesses how effective the federal courts have been in achieving their policy objectives.

SCHOOL DESEGREGATION

Brown v. *Board of Education* is one of the most celebrated rulings ever announced by the United States Supreme Court.[1] Prior to *Brown*, the Supreme Court's record on racial injustice was best exemplified by the infamous Dred Scott case and by *Plessy* v. *Ferguson* (1896), in which it upheld racial segregation under the doctrine of "separate but equal."[2] But in *Brown* the Court repudiated its dismal past and enshrined racial equality as a fundamental constitutional principle. Yet proclamation of this principle did not dispel disagreement about its meaning, nor ensure its acceptance. In this section we examine the Supreme Court's constitutional policymaking regarding school desegregation and the remedial policymaking of lower federal courts charged with implementing *Brown*. Table 10-1 provides a chronology of the Supreme Court's most important desegregation rulings.

TABLE 10-1 MAJOR SUPREME COURT RULINGS ON SCHOOL DESEGREGATION

Case	Ruling
Brown v. Board of Education [Brown I] (1954)	Declared that state-mandated racial segregation in public schools violated the Equal Protection Clause.
Brown v. Board of Education [Brown II] (1955)	Required local school districts to dismantle their dual school systems with "all deliberate speed"
Green v. County School Board of New Kent County (1968)	Required local school districts to devise school desegregation plans that would *immediately* promote integration
Swann v. Charlotte-Mecklenburg Board of Education (1970)	Upheld a variety of remedies—including busing, school pairing, and redrawing attendance zones—as means to promote school desegregation
Keyes v. School District No. 1, Denver, Colorado (1973)	Held that the use of racial considerations in drawing attendance boundaries, assigning teachers, and locating new schools violated *Brown* and justified imposition of a desegregation plan
Milliken v. Bradley [Milliken I] (1974)	Ruled that lower courts could not order interdistrict busing without evidence that suburban districts had acted to promote racial segregation in schools
Pasadena City Board of Education v. Spangler (1976)	Ruled that once a district has achieved desegregation, school authorities need not readjust attendance zones annually to keep up with population shifts, even if failure to do so would result in some resegregation
Missouri v. Jenkins (1990)	Upheld in large part judicial imposition of a desegregation plan that required expensive educational innovations and ordered the state to fund them

The Road to Brown

Brown represented the culmination of a litigation campaign designed to overturn the system of racial segregation endorsed in *Plessy* v. *Ferguson*.[3] Spearheading this fight against segregation was the Legal Defense Fund of the National Association for the Advancement of Colored People (NAACP), under the direction of Charles Houston and later of Thurgood Marshall. During the early 1930s, when the NAACP began its campaign, *Plessy* was firmly established, precluding a frontal assault on the "separate but equal" doctrine. But Houston believed that a long-term strategy of undermining segregation could succeed. The Legal Defense Fund began by bringing before the courts particularly egregious denials of equality. It hoped thereby not only to combat particular injustices but also to mobilize support for the NAACP's fight for racial equality and to inform the judiciary about the evils of segregation.

One area of particular concern was public education. The Southern and Border states had eagerly accepted *Plessy*'s invitation to institute racial separation, requiring white and black students to attend separate schools, but had ignored its requirement of equality.[4] Thus, a study in the 1920s reported that Georgia spent eight times as much on white students as it did on African-American students, and Mississippi five times as much.[5] The Legal Defense Fund enjoyed particular success in challenging segregation in graduate and professional schools. For one thing, because fewer students were involved, challenges to segregation at the graduate level aroused less controversy. More importantly, denials of equality at that level were easier to document. Because all states operated elementary and secondary schools for African-Americans, a successful constitutional challenge required a detailed demonstration of inequalities between the white and black schools. In contrast, many states did not offer graduate programs for African-American students, and thus their refusal to admit qualified black applicants to existing programs was an obvious violation of equality. During the two decades prior to *Brown*, the U.S. Supreme Court upheld several of the Legal Defense Fund's challenges to educational inequalities in graduate and professional schools.[6] These victories paved the way for the direct attack on racial segregation in *Brown*.

In retrospect, the series of cases leading to *Brown* resemble a carefully plotted campaign, with central direction of the course and pace of litigation.[7] Indeed, many other groups—for example, women's groups and environmental groups— have looked to these cases for a model of how to pursue policy ends through the courts.[8] In actuality, however, the Legal Defense Fund's campaign was less systematic than it seemed. While the aim of eliminating racial subordination did not change, the Legal Defense Fund litigated cases in a variety of fields. Often it attacked targets of opportunity rather than following a long-term plan. As favorable precedents accumulated in school cases, the Legal Defense Fund did decide to concentrate more attention on school desegregation. But as Mark Tushnet has observed, "If the military metaphor referring to a litigation campaign is helpful, the campaign was conducted on a terrain that repeatedly required changes in maneuvers."[9]

Brown I and Brown II

In 1952 the Supreme Court granted certiorari to consider a direct challenge to racial segregation in the public schools of Topeka, Kansas. Similar cases from Delaware, South Carolina, and Virginia were consolidated with *Brown* on appeal.[10] The Court also heard argument in a fifth case, *Bolling* v. *Sharpe*, dealing with segregation in the public schools in Washington, D.C.[11] The appointment of a new chief justice, the reargument of the cases before the reconstituted Court, and intracourt negotiations to secure unanimity among the justices all delayed a decision in the cases.[12] Finally, on May 17, 1954, the Court announced its rulings. Speaking for the Court, Chief Justice Earl Warren found that African-American children were psychologically injured by being forced to attend separate schools. He therefore concluded that "in the field of education the doctrine of 'separate but equal' has no place."[13]

The Court in *Brown* offered two somewhat incompatible explanations for its claim of psychological harm. On the one hand, it suggested that the harm to African-American students came from *state-enforced* segregation, which communicated a message of black inferiority. From this it would follow that the replacement of racial criteria with color-blind criteria for school attendance would suffice to remedy the injury. On the other hand, the Court also argued that African-American students were injured by lack of contact with their white peers. Insofar as this was the case, elimination of racial criteria was not enough. The remedy required was racial integration of the schools, because only integrated education could be equal education.[14]

The Court did not resolve this ambiguity in *Brown* I, as the decision came to be called, because it postponed consideration of how to implement its ruling until its next term. The justices recognized that, given the "wide applicability" of its ruling and the "great variety of local conditions," implementation would be no easy task. At the time of the ruling, seventeen Southern and Border states, plus the District of Columbia, mandated racial segregation in their elementary and secondary schools. Four other states—Arizona, Kansas, New Mexico, and Wyoming—permitted segregation by local option. Altogether, over seventy percent of African-American children attended schools in those states.[15]

In *Brown* II, the Court conducted over thirteen hours of oral argument, permitting all interested parties to state their views on how to dismantle the system of segregated education. Arguing for the NAACP, Thurgood Marshall pressed for an immediate start to desegregation. In contrast, counsel for the Southern states—seeking "a gradualism with infinity as the deadline"—warned of dire consequences if the Court required immediate desegregation.[16]

On its face, the Court's decree in *Brown* II seemed to side with the NAACP. The justices reaffirmed their commitment to *Brown* I and insisted that "the vitality of these constitutional principles cannot be allowed to yield simply because of disagreement with them."[17] They imposed on local school districts the responsibility for solving problems associated with the implementation of *Brown* and admitting students on a non-discriminatory basis "with all deliberate speed." Finally, they authorized federal district courts to oversee the process of desegregation and to use their equity powers to ensure compliance if local officials deviated from the mandate of *Brown*.

Nevertheless, *Brown* II posed problems. For one thing, the Court failed to clarify whether *Brown* required racial integration of previously segregated schools or merely the assignment of children to schools on a non-racial basis. Equally important, the Court's ruling could be read as permitting, even condoning, delay. By exaggerating the administrative problems that might be encountered in desegregation, *Brown* II seemed to be telling Southern school districts that they could delay desegregation. The absence of deadlines for starting or completing desegregation, as well as the language of "all deliberate speed", conveyed the same message. Indeed, *Brown* II seemed to encourage proponents of segregation to create local problems in order to justify delay. Small wonder, then, that Southern officials were elated. As a Southern attorney explained: "We couldn't ask for anything better than to have our local, native Mississippi district judges consider [the integration problem].... Our local judges know the local situation, and it may be 100 years before it's feasible."[18] NAACP officials, meanwhile, considered *Brown* II "a great mistake."[19]

The Response to Brown, 1954-1964

For the most part, desegregation proceeded without excessive controversy or resistance in the Northern and Border states, as those districts that had maintained dual school systems complied in good faith with *Brown*'s requirements.[20] Topeka, Kansas, for example, the city which produced the *Brown* case, introduced a desegregation plan in 1955, assigning all students to their neighborhood schools.[21] The school board of Washington, D.C., prepared a desegregation plan even before *Bolling* v. *Sharpe* was decided and adopted the plan only eight days after the decision.[22] By 1961, over half of the black students in the

Border States were attending school with whites, and this percentage increased in succeeding years.[23] In sum, *Brown* succeeded in eliminating dual school systems in those Northern and Border states that had required or permitted them.

The South was another story. In some areas efforts to implement *Brown* met with defiance. In Little Rock, Arkansas, Governor Orval Faubus deliberately provoked a violent confrontation over the desegregation of Central High School. Only after President Dwight Eisenhower dispatched federal troops to protect the black students who were to attend Central from hostile mobs, and after the Supreme Court sternly denied the school board's request to postpone desegregation, did a fragile peace return.[24] The Virginia legislature empowered the governor to seize and close any school threatened with racial integration and forbade the use of state funds for any school operating on an integrated basis. In fact, the public schools in Prince Edward County, Virginia, closed for four years, while white students attended "private" schools supported by tuition grants from the state. Eventually, the Supreme Court halted the charade and authorized the district court to reopen the public schools on a desegregated basis and require funding for them.[25] Meanwhile, several Southern States launched campaigns of legal harassment against the NAACP and other civil rights organizations. These efforts, together with the violence and intimidation practiced by the Ku Klux Klan and the White Citizens' Councils, put advocates of desegregation on the defensive. For example, despite the rigid segregation in the state, no desegregation suits were filed in Mississippi until 1961.[26] As Richard Kluger summed it up, an "exorcism is seldom a pretty spectacle."[27]

Not all Southern resistance was overtly illegal. Opponents of *Brown* appealed to public opinion, seeking to inflame hostility toward the Supreme Court and desegregation. The most influential of these appeals was the "Southern Manifesto," which denounced *Brown* as an abuse of judicial authority and pledged to overturn it "by all lawful means." Over one hundred Southern senators and representatives signed the Manifesto. School boards masked their intransigence in inaction, offering ingenious justifications for delay instead of desegregation plans. State legislatures meanwhile enacted myriad laws designed to fortify segregation and discourage desegregation. A Louisiana law, for example, denied promotion or graduation to any student of a desegregated school, and a Georgia law deprived police officers of their retirement and disability benefits if they failed to enforce the state's segregation laws. From 1954-1957 alone, Southern States enacted over 136 new laws and constitutional amendments designed to preserve segregation.[28] As commentators wryly noted, in Southern school desegregation, there was far more deliberation than speed.

Faced with obstructionism by Southern political officials, civil rights groups sought relief from the federal district courts. However, these courts often could not—or did not—help. Some Southern district-court judges, reflecting the political milieu in which they served, sought to contain, rather than enforce, *Brown*. Thus, Judge Davidson, whose rulings in a Dallas desegregation case were reversed six times, lamented that the "white man has a right to maintain his racial integrity, and it can't be done so easily in integrated schools."[29] Even those judges committed to upholding *Brown* found it difficult to know what to do. The Supreme Court's mandate in *Brown* II was ambiguous at best, yet the Court refused to hear cases in which it might clarify its position. In the absence of guidance from the Court, some federal judges used their discretion to narrow the effect of *Brown*, maintaining that it merely required the use of race-neutral criteria for assigning pupils.[30] Thus, school districts met their constitutional obligations even if their schools remained almost completely segregated. Other judges were "content with [desegregation at] the pace of an extraordinarily arthritic snail."[31] Those judges who recognized that *Brown* required real deseg-regation often found themselves stymied by ingenious efforts to preserve racial separation. They would no sooner invalidate one law as inconsistent with *Brown* than the state legislature would pass another. As the Southern saying went, "as long as we can legislate, we can segregate."[32]

Figure 10-1 dramatically illustrates the failure of school desegregation in the South in the decade following *Brown*. As late as 1963, less than one percent of

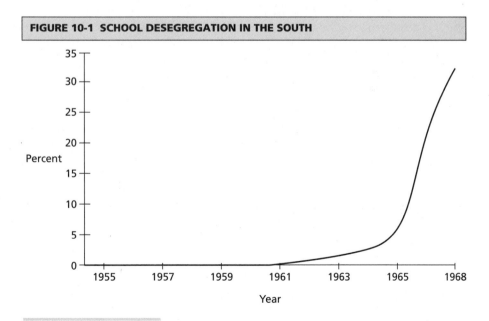

FIGURE 10-1 SCHOOL DESEGREGATION IN THE SOUTH

SOURCE: Gerald Rosenberg, *The Hollow Hope; Can Courts Bring About Social Change?* (Chicago: University of Chicago Press, 1991), p. 50, Table 2.1. This table depicts the percentage of all African-American schoolchildren in the South attending public elementary or secondary school with whites.

black students in the South were attending school with white children. Even in localities where the Supreme Court had intervened directly, the results were discouraging. For example, in 1963, only 69 of the 7,700 students at the supposedly desegregated, "formerly" white, junior and senior high schools in Little Rock were black.[33] In the South, at least, *Brown*'s tenth anniversary offered no cause for celebration.[34]

School Desegregation, 1964-1971

Yet if Figure 10-1 reveals that school segregation continued in the South through 1964, it also documents a dramatic shift in attendance patterns in the second decade after *Brown*. Whereas in 1964 only 1.2 percent of African-American students in the South were attending school with whites, by 1973 91.3 percent were. What accounts for this remarkable shift? First, after 1964 Congress and the federal executive branch joined with the Court in promoting school desegregation. Second, the Supreme Court forcefully intervened, clarifying what constituted a violation of *Brown* and what measures lower courts might impose to remedy violations.

Congress's enactment of the Civil Rights Act of 1964 "represented a gathering and coalescence of the nation will on the whole question of Southern school segregation."[35] Title II of the Act authorized the Department of Justice to sue "for the orderly achievement of desegregation in public education." This relieved the NAACP of much of the burden and expense of litigating desegregation and effectively undercut the Southern strategy of deterring desegregation suits by attacking civil rights organizations. Title VI of the Act prohibited the dispersal of federal funds to units of government, including school districts, that practiced racial discrimination. This provision became important with the passage of Elementary and Secondary Education Act (ESEA) in 1965. ESEA established a program of federal financial aid to school districts, and given the poverty in many Southern States, their districts stood to benefit from the aid program. However, if a school district refused to desegregate, its federal funds could be cut off. Thus, if the Civil Rights Act proffered the stick of federal enforcement, ESEA offered the carrot of federal inducements. By 1969 federal funds made up between 11 and 21 percent of state budgets for public schools in the Southern States.[36] Southern school districts therefore could no longer afford to defy court orders to desegregate, for that might jeopardize the flow of federal dollars, on which they had become dependent. As one expert concluded, "the change [in Southern resistance to desegregation] would have been impossible without the lure of money from the Elementary and Secondary Education Act."[37]

In 1968 the Supreme Court also clarified what compliance with *Brown* entailed. The Court's way was prepared by rulings of the Fifth Circuit Court of Appeals and by guidelines developed by the Department of Health, Education, and Welfare (HEW) to implement the Civil Rights Act of 1964. In a series of cases in the mid-1960s, Judge John Minor Wisdom argued that compliance with *Brown* entailed more than the elimination of racial criteria in assigning students. States had not to only cease segregating but also to start integrating their schools.[38] The HEW guidelines sounded a similar theme, measuring desegregation by the number of blacks and whites in school together. In *Green* v. *County School Board* (1968), the Supreme Court endorsed this understanding of *Brown* in invalidating a "freedom-of-choice" plan under which students could choose which school they would attend.[39] This "freedom" was illusory, the Court held, because pressure might be applied to discourage black students from selecting the white school. More importantly, the Court rejected "freedom-of-choice" because it failed to produce meaningful integration. Implicit in this ruling were two assumptions. First, without state segregation laws, racial integration would have occurred, and second, the responsibility of previously segregated school systems was to achieve the level of integration that would have existed in the absence of segregation. In portraying *Brown* as requiring racial integration, the Court ensured that racial balance would thereafter be a crucial element in its decisions.

The Court's new forcefulness can also be seen in the measures it endorsed for remedying violations of *Brown*. In *Green* the Court bluntly stated that the time for "deliberate speed" had passed, that desegregation must be immediate.[40] In *Swann* v. *Charlotte-Mecklenburg Board of Education* (1971), the Court specifically endorsed a variety of remedial measures that some district court judges had used to promote desegregation.[41] Among these were the alteration of student attendance zones and the busing of students to achieve integration. Although the Court cautioned that busing could not "risk the health of the children or significantly impinge on the educational process," the main effect of *Swann* was to fortify district-court judges in their aggressive efforts "to eliminate from the public schools all vestiges of state-imposed segregation."[42]

The Courts and School Desegregation in the 1970s

The Changing Context of School Desegregation

During the late 1960s and the 1970s, school desegregation litigation entered a new phase. Plaintiffs expanded the scope of desegregation efforts, challenging racial segregation in Northern urban districts as well as in the South. The decision to confront Northern school segregation seemed logical. With the massive emigration of African-Americans from the South in the decades after World War II, a large and increasing percentage of black schoolchildren attended school in Northern urban areas, and many of these children found themselves in single-race schools.

Several factors complicated desegregation litigation in the North. For one thing, whereas Southern school districts had forthrightly maintained segregated systems, most Northern cities never expressly mandated separate schools for blacks and whites. Because *Brown* outlawed only *intentional* school segregation, the mere fact of segregated schools did not violate the Constitution. Proving constitutional violations therefore was more difficult than it had been in Southern school cases. Some Northern districts did pursue blatantly discriminatory policies: in Dayton, Ohio, for example, African-American teachers were forbidden to teach white students.[43] But in most cases Northern school officials had contrived to promote racial segregation through a series of undramatic and—on their face—race-neutral policy choices. In Denver, for example, the school board gerrymandered school-attendance zones to maintain racially homogeneous schools and set up mobile classrooms at black schools rather than transferring the overflow of students to underutilized white schools.[44] In Boston the school board established feeder patterns that ensured that students from white elementary schools attended white middle schools and constructed new schools with sizes and locations designed to maintain racial separation.[45] Plaintiffs in Northern desegregation suits had to prove that such actions, which on their face were racially neutral, were intended to promote segregation, rather than to serve other valid purposes, and therefore violated the mandate of *Brown*.

Even if they did so, plaintiffs—and the courts providing relief—faced a further hurdle. To a considerable extent, patterns of racial segregation in Northern schools mirrored long-standing residential segregation. This complicated efforts to prove that school segregation resulted from official discrimination rather than from private housing choices. Even if official discrimination contributed to school segregation, it was difficult to determine its precise effect. Yet *Brown* only permitted district judges to eliminate the effects of intentional segregation, and therefore the scope of the district court's remedy had to coincide with the scope of the constitutional violation.

Designing an effective remedy for segregation was likewise problematic. Given the degree of residential segregation in Northern cities, judges could not achieve substantial integration merely by assigning students to their neighborhood schools. Even busing students to other schools within a school district might not produce substantial integration. School districts in Northern cities did not encompass the entire metropolitan area. Rather, suburban school districts, whose student population was primarily white, typically ringed urban school districts whose student population was heavily non-white. This posed an obstacle to meaningful integration. It also ensured a ready "escape" for families reluctant to send their children to predominantly non-white schools. If enough families exited the school district, that too could frustrate judicial efforts to achieve desegregation.

Judicial Rulings and Popular Responses

At the outset of the 1970s, the Supreme Court adopted an aggressive approach to school desegregation. In Swann it upheld a federal district court's desegregation plan that ordered busing for over 13,000 students.[46] While denying that the Constitution required "any particular degree of racial balance and mixing," the Court endorsed reliance on the racial composition of the whole school district in determining the scope of constitutional violations.[47] In doing so, it rescued plaintiffs from the task of proving the effect of discriminatory policies. Instead, the Court simply assumed that in the absence of state-imposed segregation, the proportion of black and white students in specific schools would generally coincide with their distribution in the school district as a whole.

In its first Northern desegregation case, *Keyes* v. *School District No. 1, Denver, Colorado* (1973), the Court upheld the federal district court's finding that the school board's various efforts to maintain racially homogeneous schools violated *Brown*.[48] Moreover, it eased the burden of proof on plaintiffs seeking to prove intentional segregation. If they could prove intentional segregation in one part of the school system, the justices held, then the burden of proof shifted to the school board to show that segregation in other parts of the school system did not result from official action. Because proving this was virtually impossible, *Keyes* in effect permitted district-wide desegregation remedies, including busing, based on violations occurring in only one part of the district.

The public response to this sort of aggressive judicial intervention was overwhelmingly negative. Congress cut off federal funds for busing in 1972 and in 1978 forbade the Department of Health, Education, and Welfare to terminate federal funds to school districts when compliance with desegregation would require busing. Over two hundred representatives supported a constitutional amendment to outlaw busing for racial balance.[49] In some Northern communities, the response recalled the violence in Little Rock. In Pontiac, Michigan, arsonists firebombed ten school buses, and after a white student was stabbed at South Boston High, an angry mob trapped 135 black students in the school for four hours, until a police decoy operation extricated them.[50] In many cities, court-ordered busing prompted "white flight" to private schools or to the suburbs. In Memphis, Tennessee, 35 percent of white students left the public school system during the first year of busing, and in New Castle County, Delaware, white enrollments following busing declined 50 percent.[51] Instead of promoting racial integration, busing in these communities accelerated the transition to a virtually all-black school system.

In the face of such widespread opposition, the Supreme Court retreated. In *Milliken* v. *Bradley* [*Milliken* I] (1973), the Court curtailed the power of district-court judges to remedy segregation.[52] The judge in *Milliken* had ordered busing between Detroit and surrounding suburban school districts in order to relieve segregation in the city's schools. By a 5-4 vote, the Court reversed the lower court, holding that since the suburban districts had not participated in the segregation of the Detroit schools, they were not obliged to participate in efforts to desegregate them. By prohibiting interdistrict busing except when suburban districts had connived to segregate inner-city schools, the Court effectively undercut efforts to integrate Northern urban school districts. In the wake of *Milliken* I, some district courts turned from the reassignment of students to the mandating of programs of educational improvements as the remedy for constitutional violations.[53]

Dayton Board of Education v. *Brinkman* [*Dayton* I] (1977) increased plaintiffs' burden of proof in desegregation cases and further curtailed the remedial powers of lower-court judges.[54] No longer, the Court held, would discrimination in one part of a school district create a presumption of system-wide discrimination, as it had in *Keyes*. Instead, the Court held that "isolated" violations did not justify system-wide desegregation plans. The justices cautioned that judicial remedies must not go beyond redressing the "incremental segregative effect" of the district's constitutional violations.[55]

Finally, in *Pasadena Board of Education* v. *Spangler* (1976) the Court suggested that the time for judicial supervision of school desegregation was coming to a close.[56] Once again reversing a district-court judge, the Court held that once a school district had met its duty to desegregate, school authorities did not have to continue to adjust attendance zones to promote integration. Even if shifts in the district's population promoted the resegregation of schools, the mandate of Brown was to eliminate the effects of intentional segregation, not to guarantee integrated schools.

The Legacy of Brown

As we have noted, in 1954 21 states and the District of Columbia, enrolling over 70 percent of African-American students, either required racial segregation in their schools or permitted by local option. *Brown* succeeded in desegregating public schools in Northern and Border States that had maintained dual school systems, but a decade after *Brown*, 99 percent of African-American students in the South attended segregated schools. Congressional intervention encouraged the desegregation of Southern schools in the late 1960s and early 1970s. By 1972, 91 percent of African-American students in the South were attending integrated schools.[57] Yet despite desegregation suits in the North, racial segregation in public education did not decline.[58] Moreover, civil rights advocates no longer viewed integration of the public schools as a high priority.[59] Although one hesitates to call the Court's intervention a failure, *Brown* and succeeding cases did not guarantee racial integration in public education.

ABORTION

More than the normal contingent of reporters was on hand for the final day of the Supreme Court's 1991-1992 term. A large crowd of demonstrators and spectators had also gathered outside the Supreme Court, anticipating—or dreading—the Court's ruling in *Planned Parenthood of Southeastern Pennsylvania* v. *Casey*.[60] At issue in *Casey* was the constitutionality of a Pennsylvania law that restricted the availability of abortion by imposing various requirements on women seeking abortions and on facilities providing them (see Table 10-2). Many Court-watchers believed that those restrictions interfered with the right of women to terminate their pregnancies, a right that the Court had recognized twenty years earlier in *Roe* v. *Wade*.[61] They thus expected that *Casey* would provide the vehicle for the Court to overrule *Roe*.

The Court's decision in *Casey*, however, defied expectations, pleasing neither pro-life nor pro-choice groups. On the one hand, a coalition of five justices upheld all the provisions of the Pennsylvania statute except the requirement that a woman notify her spouse before obtaining an abortion. In doing so, the Court apparently circumscribed the constitutional right announced in *Roe*. On the other hand, a different coalition of five justices expressly reaffirmed *Roe* and the abortion right recognized in that case. What was clear from the five opinions issued by the various justices was that they were bitterly divided on the abortion issue. Four justices—Rehnquist, Scalia, Thomas, and White—insisted that the Pennsylvania statute was constitutional and that *Roe* should be overruled. Two justices—Blackmun and Stevens—maintained that *Roe* should be affirmed and the Pennsylvania law struck down in its entirety. The three remaining justices—O'Connor, Kennedy, and Souter—cast the decisive votes in the case. While upholding most provisions of the Pennsylvania law, they

TABLE 10-2 MAJOR SUPREME COURT RULINGS ON ABORTION

Case	Holding
Roe v. *Wade*; *Doe* v. *Bolton* (1972)	Recognized a woman's constitutional right to terminate her pregnancy, struck down state laws restricting abortion, and established a framework for determining the validity of state regulations of abortion
Planned Parenthood of Central Missouri v. *Danforth* (1976)	Struck down state requirements of spousal and, for minors, parental consent for abortions; invalidated various regulations of medical procedures for abortion
Harris v. *McRae* (1980)	Upheld congressional legislation banning the use of federal Medicaid funds for abortions, unless abortion was necessary to preserve the life of the mother or in cases of rape or incest
Akron v. *Akron Center for Reproductive Health* (1983)	Invalidated a requirement that abortions after the first trimester be performed in a hospital; reaffirmed the Court's ruling in *Roe*
Webster v. *Reproductive Health Services* (1989)	Upheld a prohibition on abortions by state employees or in state facilities, except to save the life of the mother, and a requirement of viability tests for fetuses over 20 weeks old
Planned Parenthood of Southeastern Pennsylvania v. *Casey* (1992)	Reaffirmed the abortion right announced in *Roe*; upheld requirements that certain information be furnished to women 24 hours prior to an abortion, that minors obtain parental consent for an abortion (with the possibility of judicial approval as an alternative), and that medical facilities performing abortion file medical information with the state; invalidated a spousal notification requirement

refused—largely on the basis of *stare decisis*—to repudiate *Roe*. Justice Scalia and Chief Justice Rehnquist attacked the three justices' interpretation of history and *stare decisis* in scathing terms.[62]

Although *Casey* was the most recent confrontation over abortion on the Supreme Court, it was hardly the first. Abortion had stirred controversy ever since it emerged as a legal issue in the 1960s. Let us look more closely at the emergence of abortion as an issue and at judicial decisions dealing with it.

Abortion Becomes a Legal Issue

Like most important policy issues that make their way to the Supreme Court, abortion did not emerge as a constitutional issue by happenstance or through the dogged efforts of a single person. While there was never a fully orchestrated plan to test the constitutionality of restrictions on abortion, a loose network of groups committed to liberalizing state abortion laws had formed in the decade prior to *Roe*. Thus *Roe* v. *Wade*, like *Brown* v. *Board of Education*, is best understood as the culmination of a broader campaign to promote legal reforms.[63]

In the early 1960s, the laws in most states permitted abortion only in very limited circumstances, such as to save the life of the mother. These laws, which dated from the late nineteenth century, effectively restricted legal abortions: only eight thousand were performed nationwide in 1966. However, they did little to deter illegal abortions: roughly a million illegal abortions were performed that same year.64

Beginning in the 1950s, support for the state restrictions on abortion began to erode. Physicians at medical conferences questioned state restrictions on abortion as an infringement on their exercise of medical judgment. Of even greater significance was the publication in 1962 of a model penal law by the American Law Institute (ALI), which permitted abortion when pregnancy was the result of rape or incest, when its continuation threatened the physical or mental health of the mother, or when there was a risk of birth defects. During the early 1960s, reports about the fertility drug Thalidomide and about an outbreak of German measles, both of which caused birth defects, brought the issue of abortion before the general public. When the California State Board of Medical Examiners brought disciplinary charges against two prominent physicians who had performed abortions on women with German measles, the state's medical profession rallied behind the doctors and urged the California legislature to liberalize the state's abortion law.

As abortion became a more salient issue and as opinion on abortion shifted, groups such as the National Association for Repeal of Abortion Laws (NARAL) formed to campaign for more permissive abortion policies. In the seven years prior to *Roe* (1966-1972), these groups enjoyed considerable success. Fourteen states enacted more liberal abortion laws, generally modeled on the ALI guidelines, and four states—Alaska, Hawaii, New York, and Washington—repealed their existing laws, making abortion an unrestricted medical procedure.[65] As Figure 10-2 shows, passage of these laws dramatically increased the number of legal abortions performed in the United States. Nevertheless, because the reform laws still placed restrictions on abortion, large numbers of illegal abortions continued to be performed, even in states that had modified their laws.[66] Abortion reformers concluded that even the ALI-style laws did not ensure adequate access to abortion.

At the same time that they pursued legislative reform, abortion advocates also contemplated taking the issue to the courts—and particularly to the United States Supreme Court. This was not surprising. During the 1960s, under the leadership of Chief Justice Earl Warren, the Supreme Court had established a record of liberal activism and had demonstrated a commitment to the expansion of constitutional rights. Even with the appointment of Chief Justice Warren Burger as Warren's replacement, opponents of abortion expected a sympathetic hearing from the Court.

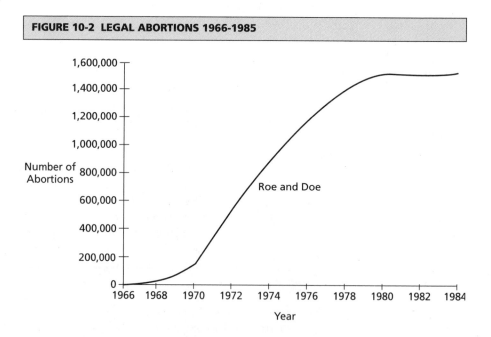

FIGURE 10-2 LEGAL ABORTIONS 1966-1985

SOURCE: Gerald Rosenberg, *The Hollow Hope; Can Courts Bring About Social Change?* (Chicago: University of Chicago Press, 1991), p.179, Figure 6.1.

From the reformers' perspective, judicial resolution of the abortion issue had significant advantages. Whereas legislative reform required a state-by-state effort, a single Supreme Court ruling could establish policy nationwide. Moreover, once the Supreme Court recognized a constitutional right to choose whether to terminate a pregnancy, it would require a constitutional amendment or a shift on the Court to overturn the ruling. In addition, the Court's ruling in *Brown* v. *Board of Education* had convinced liberal reformers that judicial rulings could inaugurate far-reaching social changes.[67] Abortion reform thus seemed an obvious issue to bring to the courts. Finally, a judicial ruling would provide a firmer foundation for legalized abortion, establishing it as a woman's right rather than merely a matter of physicians' interests or health concerns.

Yet if the potential rewards of litigation were great, so too were the risks. If a pregnant woman challenged a state abortion law, she would no longer be pregnant by the time her case reached the Supreme Court. In such circumstances, the Court might avoid the issue on technical grounds, much as it had dismissed an early challenge to Connecticut's ban on the sale and use of contraceptives.[68] Even worse (from the reformers' perspective), the Court might uphold state abortion laws, dealing the reformers a major setback. Advocates of abortion reform, therefore, faced two problems. First, they had to find an appropriate plaintiff to challenge a state abortion law. As Box 10-1 indicates, the discovery of "Jane Roe" occurred largely by chance. Second, they had to develop persuasive arguments for the unconstitutionality of state abortion laws. This task was complicated by the fact that the Constitution does not expressly deal with the right to terminate a pregnancy. Abortion reformers therefore devoted considerable energy to legal research, hoping to influence legal thinking on the abortion issue. The Association for the Study of Abortion, for example, funded the research and writing of an article by law professor Cyril Means on the history of the abortion right. This legal research paid dividends when the Supreme Court cited the article seven times in support of its ruling in *Roe* v. *Wade*.[69] When the Supreme Court agreed to hear constitutional challenges to the abortion laws in Texas and Georgia, groups within the abortion-rights movement worked together to write the legal briefs and prepare the attorneys for oral argument.[70]

Roe v. Wade

In *Roe* v. *Wade* the Supreme Court invalidated Texas's traditional abortion statute, and in the companion case of *Doe* v. *Bolton,* it struck down Georgia's reformed (ALI-style) abortion law.[71] Speaking for a seven-member majority, Justice Harry Blackmun concluded that the right to privacy, initially recognized in *Griswold* v. *Connecticut*[72] eight years earlier, "is broad enough to encompass a woman's decision whether or not to terminate her pregnancy."[73] This right,

BOX 10-1 WHO IS JANE ROE?

Marbury v. *Madison, Brown* v. *Board of Education, Miranda* v. *Arizona*—
the cases are familiar to any student of the Supreme Court. Less familiar
are the persons behind the cases— William Marbury, Louise Brown, and
Ernesto Miranda. If anything, the plaintiff in *Roe* v. *Wade* was even more
obscure; for her attorneys used a pseudonym, "Jane Roe," to protect her
from the social stigma of acknowledging that she was pregnant but
unmarried.

Years after the case, Norma McCorvey disclosed that she was "Jane Roe."
At the time the case was initiated, Norma McCorvey—or "Pixie," as she
was called by her carnival co-workers—was 21. Married at age 16,
divorced, and the mother of a five-year-old daughter, McCorvey felt that
she could not care for another child. She claimed—falsely, she later admitted—that her pregnancy was the result of rape, hoping that this would
enable her to get an abortion. But Texas's law outlawed abortions except
to save the life of the mother, and McCorvey could not find a physician
who would perform an illegal abortion. She resigned herself to having the
baby and giving it up for adoption. When she spoke to a lawyer about
this, he referred her to Linda Coffee and Sarah Weddington, two lawyers
who were eager to challenge the Texas abortion statute. After discussing
the matter with them, McCorvey agreed to serve as plaintiff in the case.

How did *Roe* v. *Wade* affect Norma McCorvey? It did not enable her to get
an abortion. Her child was born and given up for adoption before the
Supreme Court ever heard her case. She was ecstatic about the Court's ruling: "It makes me feel like I'm on top of Mount Everest." Yet she played
little role in the litigation and did not even attend the oral argument
before the Supreme Court. Indeed, when told that her case was being
appealed to the Court, her reaction was: "My God, all those people are so
important. They don't have time to listen to some little old Texas girl who
got in trouble."

In 1980 McCorvey told a reporter that she was "Jane Roe." She became
actively involved in abortion politics in the late 1980s, speaking at pro-
choice rallies. Her notoriety brought her both opportunities and problems.
A television movie was made, depicting her involvement in *Roe* v. *Wade*.
But in 1989, shortly before she was to participate in an abortion-rights
rally, early morning shotgun blasts shattered the windows of her home
and car.

As Norma McCorvey's story illustrates, the people whose cases reach the
Supreme Court may be quite ordinary people. But the litigation is not
ordinary litigation. Except in criminal cases, the litigants have often "disappeared" by the time the Court hears their cases. This is hardly surprising, for the Supreme Court does not review cases to correct injustices to

continued on p. 351

> *continued from p. 350*
> particular individuals but to decide legal issues of national importance. Thus, what is at stake is not so much the fate of the litigants—indeed, in McCorvey's case, the ruling in *Roe* had no direct effect on her situation— but the legal principles that will govern the nation.

SOURCES: McCorvey's quotations and basic information about her background were drawn from Marian Faux, *Roe v. Wade* (New York: Macmillan, 1988), pp. 174, 304, and *passim.* Additional information was drawn from Steven Waldman, "Attacking the Real 'Jane Roe'," *Newsweek,* April 17, 1989, p. 22; and Lisa Belkin, "Woman Behind the Symbols in Abortion Debate," *New York Times,* May 9, 1989, p. A18.

the Court cautioned, was not absolute. During the first trimester (first twelve weeks) of pregnancy, a woman—in conjunction with her physician—could decide whether to terminate her pregnancy without state interference. During the second trimester, states could regulate the abortion procedure, but only in order to safeguard maternal health. During the third trimester, which coincides with the viability of the fetus (that is, its ability to survive outside the womb), states could regulate or even ban abortion, except when it was necessary to preserve the life or health of the mother.

Roe and *Doe* had implications far beyond Texas and Georgia. Thirty-one states had abortion laws like Texas's, thirteen had reformed laws like Georgia's, and three banned all abortions. Presumably, the Court's rulings required those states to abandon their abortion laws. Only the four states that had repealed their abortion laws were unaffected. Moreover, the opinion of the Court also enunciated unusually detailed guidelines governing how states could regulate abortion in the future. The clarity of the Court's guidelines stands in sharp contrast to the vague "all deliberate speed" formula in *Brown* v. *Board of Education.* After *Roe,* states for the most part knew what sorts of regulations of abortion would survive judicial scrutiny. Yet the detail of the guidelines, particularly in the absence of clear support in the text of the Constitution, opened the Court to criticism that it was legislating rather than judging.[74]

The Response to Roe

The general public's immediate response to *Roe* was rather muted; former President Lyndon Johnson died on the day that *Roe* was decided, and his death, not the Court's decision, captured the day's headlines.[75] Those groups most interested in the litigation reacted in predictable fashion. Lawrence Lader, Chairman of the NARAL, hailed the Court's ruling as "a thunderbolt" and "even more conclusive than any of us had dared to hope."[76] Meanwhile, John

Cardinal Krol, president of the National Catholic Conference, charged the Court with opening the door to "the greatest slaughter of innocent life in the history of mankind."[77]

The Pro-Life Offensive

When a supporter went to the pro-choice headquarters in New York after *Roe* was decided, she found it shut tight, with a sign posted that they had won and that everyone had gone home.[78]　In a sense this typified the response of pro-choice groups to *Roe*. They assumed that *Roe* had ended the battle, and they relied upon the courts to repel any efforts to restrict a woman's right to terminate her pregnancy. But for pro-life advocates, the battle had just begun. *Roe* galvanized pro-life forces, creating a grass-roots movement committed to overturning the Court's ruling and opposing the spread of abortion.[79]　The pro-life forces sought to influence public opinion through picketing, demonstrations, and pray-ins, tactics they had learned from the civil rights movement. More radical pro-life groups, such as Operation Rescue, attempted to prevent abortions, descending en masse on abortion clinics and forcibly blocking access to staff and patients. Most importantly, however, pro-life groups put pressure on public officials to oppose and limit abortion. If they had lost in the judicial arena, they sought in other arenas to reverse or limit the Court's ruling.

The most direct way to overturn a Supreme Court ruling is by constitutional amendment; indeed, five amendments have been adopted, in whole or in part, to overturn Supreme Court decisions.[80]　Pro-life forces, however, failed to persuade Congress to support an anti-abortion amendment. Although 275 amendments were proposed in Congress from 1973-1985, only one received committee approval and reached the floor of the House, and it failed to win a simple majority vote.[81]　Senator Jesse Helms of North Carolina introduced a Human Life Bill, which would have defined human life as beginning at conception, but it too found little support. The only success pro-life forces enjoyed in Congress was the passage of the Hyde Amendment, which barred the use of Medicaid funds for abortions except to save the life of the mother. When this legislation was challenged, the Supreme Court backed away from a confrontation with Congress, ruling the Hyde Amendment constitutional by a 5-4 vote.[82]

Pro-life forces fared better with the executive branch during the Reagan and Bush administrations. Presidents Reagan and Bush were both elected with a Republican platform calling for an anti-abortion constitutional amendment. They initiated administrative actions designed to discourage abortion, from banning the use of foreign aid money to support abortions, to prohibiting the use of fetal tissue in medical research, to banning counselling or referring for abortion at federally funded clinics. This last directive—labelled the "gag rule" by critics—was challenged in the courts; but in *Rust* v. *Sullivan* (1991), the Supreme Court sustained the ban.[83] Perhaps most importantly, the Reagan and Bush administrations sought to undermine *Roe* v. *Wade* in the courts by appointing judges opposed to abortion and by filing *amicus curiae* briefs urging the Supreme Court to overrule its decision.

The election of President William Clinton marked a setback for pro-life forces. Clinton campaigned on a pro-choice platform and promised to appoint judges solicitous of privacy rights. Early in his administration, he issued executive orders lifting the "gag rule" at federally funded clinics, removing anti-abortion restrictions on foreign aid, and otherwise reversing pro-life policies of previous administrations. He also announced his support for a "Freedom of Choice Act," which would preclude virtually all state restrictions on abortion.

The reaction of state legislatures to *Roe* varied enormously. While some states sought to bring their laws in line with *Roe*, others attempted to impede access to abortion. Some states blatantly defied the Court's ruling. North Dakota and Rhode Island, for example, enacted laws banning abortion except to save the life of the mother. Other states, while not challenging *Roe* directly, adopted legislation that sought to exploit "loopholes" in the decision. Illustrative of these laws were spousal and parental consent requirements, mandatory waiting periods, hospitalization requirements, and elaborate statistical reporting requirements. These laws served three purposes. First, they discouraged abortions by increasing the expense or difficulty of obtaining an abortion. Second, they drained the time and resources of the pro-choice groups that challenged the laws and of the courts that had to hear those challenges. Third, they provided opportunities for opponents of abortion to urge the Supreme Court to reconsider its ruling in *Roe*.[84]

Abortion Rulings After Roe

In contrast with the field of school desegregation, where the Supreme Court virtually abandoned the field for a decade after announcing its landmark ruling in *Brown*, the Court remained actively involved with abortion policy. In the two decades after *Roe*, the justices ruled on twenty-one abortion cases.[85] From 1973-1986, the Court consistently reaffirmed the basic holding of *Roe* and closely policed state efforts to curtail the right recognized in that case. Thus, it invalidated spousal and parental consent requirements, counselling requirements, hospitalization requirements, and various regulations of abortion procedures.[86] Only governmental refusals to fund abortions and a requirement that parents be notified before a minor received an abortion survived the Court's scrutiny.[87] Since 1986, however, the Court's composition has changed, and so have its rulings (see Table 10-2). From 1986-1992, four members of the *Roe* majority retired, and Presidents Reagan and Bush replaced them with justices much less sympathetic to *Roe*. These changes brought a reversal of roles for pro-life and pro-choice groups. Opponents of abortion, sensing victory, turned their attention to the courts, appealing cases to the newly constituted Court in the hope that the justices would seize the opportunity to reverse *Roe*. Pro-choice groups, meanwhile, turned to the political arena, mobilizing to support pro-choice candidates, and urging Congress to enact legislation safeguarding abortion rights.

In *Webster* v. *Reproductive Health Services* (1989) and in *Planned Parenthood of Southeastern Pennsylvania* v. *Casey* (1992), the justices did discard the trimester framework used by Justice Blackmun in *Roe*. They also upheld a number of state regulations that limited the availability of abortion, including some—e.g., a mandatory waiting period prior to abortions—that they had struck down in earlier cases. However, five votes could not be obtained for overruling *Roe*. In his dissent in *Webster*, Justice Harry Blackmun, who wrote the opinion of the Court in *Roe*, warned that "the signs are evident and very ominous, and a chill wind blows."[88] With the election of President Clinton, who pledged during his campaign to fill vacancies on the Court with judges supportive of abortion rights, and the appointment of Ruth Bader Ginsburg to replace Justice Byron White, it appears that *Roe* has weathered the storm.

The Effects of Roe

Though they agree on little else, both pro-life and pro-choice groups believe that *Roe* v. *Wade* inaugurated an abortion revolution. Certainly, the aim in *Roe* was, according to Justice Blackmun, to secure "the fundamental constitutional right of women to decide whether to terminate a pregnancy."[89] Yet given the criticisms frequently voiced about judicial policymaking capacity, the question arises: did *Roe* in fact ensure that women could secure legal abortions?

Figure 10-2, which depicts the incidence over time of legal abortions in the United States, permits several observations.[90] First, as noted earlier, the trend toward the availability of legal abortions began prior to *Roe*, following the enactment of reform statutes in some states and the repeal of abortion laws in others. Second, although *Roe* did not initiate the trend toward increased access to abortion services, it certainly continued that trend. The rate of increase in legal abortions actually declined slightly after *Roe*. Still, there is no way to know whether legal abortions would have increased as much without the Court's rul-

ing. Third, by 1980 the level of legal abortions in the United States had stabi-
lized, and it remains relatively stable to the present day. This is interesting
because of the efforts of abortion opponents, through the Hyde Amendment
and various state laws, to decrease access to abortion. Whatever their symbolic
value, these measures had little discernible effect on the incidence of abortion.
Indeed, a study of the Center for Disease Control found that approximately 94
percent of women who would have been eligible for Medicaid funding prior to
the Hyde Amendment were able to obtain some kind of funding for their abortions.[91] Similarly, bans on abortions in public hospitals or by public employees
have not decreased abortion levels. Private clinics, responding to market
demand, have filled the gap.[92]

From another angle, however, one might view the Court's aim in *Roe* as settling the issue of abortion. If that was its goal, the Court did not achieve it.
Prior to *Roe*, abortion reform was proceeding in various states with a minimum
of fanfare and with only moderate political conflict. *Roe*, however, changed
that. The decision became a rallying point for pro-choice and pro-life forces
alike. It increased the visibility of abortion, nationalized the issue, and intensi-
fied the conflict over it. One must wonder whether, as in Western Europe,
abortion would have become widely available with less conflict if the Court had
not intervened.[93]

BROWN, ROE, AND BEYOND

The federal courts' policymaking on school desegregation and abortion illustrate how political issues come before the federal courts for resolution, how
judicial policies change over time, how those affected by the judicial policies
may respond to them, and why judicial policies achieve or fail to achieve their
objectives. Let us look at each of these topics.

The Development of Legal Issues

Both *Brown* and *Roe* resulted from campaigns by groups to change public policy through the courts. These campaigns resembled each other in certain
respects. In both the groups sought to dictate the focus and timing of litigation.
Yet in both they had to respond to unexpected opportunities, such as the discovery of a suitable plaintiff in *Roe*, and to fortuitous developments, such as the
accumulation of favorable precedents in the graduate-school cases litigated prior
to *Brown*. The two campaigns, however, also reveal the different uses that
groups seeking legal reforms may make of litigation. Realizing that Southern
school districts would not voluntarily desegregate their schools, the NAACP

relied exclusively on litigation to achieve this goal. In contrast, abortion reformers used litigation not as an alternative to political action but as an additional weapon in their effort to liberalize abortion laws. In fact, abortion reformers enjoyed considerable success in the legislative arena before challenging restrictions on abortion in the courts.

Most constitutional policymaking by the federal courts involves group sponsorship of litigation, as in *Brown* and *Roe*. Groups may also pursue their political or ideological aims in cases involving statutory interpretation or the oversight of administrative activity. In doing so, they may seek to use the courts to build on victories won in the political arena or to reverse the losses they suffered there. The phenomenon of group sponsorship is hardly surprising, given the costs of litigation and the lack of financial incentives for individual plaintiffs. The main exception to group sponsorship involves criminal justice, where defendants who claim that their rights were violated have a strong personal stake in the outcome of the case.

Policy Change

The Supreme Court's rulings on school desegregation and abortion reveal the various ways that judicial policies may change over time. Sometimes the changes are dramatic, occurring through landmark rulings like *Brown* that overrule previous decisions and announce a fundamental shift in direction. More frequently, however, changes in judicial policies are gradual or incremental. A court may explicitly modify its position in the light of changing circumstances, as the Supreme Court did in dispensing with "all deliberate speed" and demanding immediate desegregation in the late 1960s after gaining the support of Congress and the presidency in its desegregation efforts. A court may also expand a legal principle in applying it to a new situation, as the Supreme Court did in *Roe* v. *Wade* in extending the right to privacy to encompass the right to terminate a pregnancy. In addition, a court may signal a change in policy by narrowing a legal principle announced in previous cases or by refusing to apply it to new situations. The Supreme Court's rejection of interdistrict busing in *Milliken* v. *Bradley* is a prime example. Finally, a court may subtly modify policy by undermining precedents even as it claims to be adhering to them. The Supreme Court's refusal to overrule *Roe* v. *Wade*, while upholding regulations inconsistent with it in *Planned Parenthood of Southeastern Pennsylvania* v. *Casey*, is a case in point.

What causes changes in judicial policy? In part, these changes result from changes in judicial personnel. As judges are replaced by others with different legal and political views, one can expect to see those differences reflected in judicial decisions. However, personnel changes on the courts, unlike those in other branches, rarely produce dramatic shifts in policy. For as Chapter 8 indicated, the authority of precedent, judicial role conceptions, and other legal constraints may all limit the speed and scope of policy change. Indicative of this is the Supreme Court's unwillingness to overrule *Roe* v. *Wade* out of respect for *stare decisis.*

Policy changes may also result from judicial dissatisfaction with the results of previous judicial policies. The Supreme Court's ruling in *Green* v. *County School Board of New Kent County* exemplifies this. The Court in *Green* had thirteen years experience with Southern efforts to delay compliance with *Brown* or evade it through programs that produced minimal desegregation. This convinced the justices to set more specific and forceful standards for the implementation of *Brown*'s mandates, requiring immediate elimination of dual school systems and asserting that districts' plans were to be judged by the level of integration they produced.

In formulating new judicial policies, judges may rely on counsel for the contending parties or on *amicus curiae* briefs for guidance. Thus, both Thurgood Marshall for the NAACP and the attorneys for the Southern states influenced the desegregation guidelines established in *Brown* II. Judges may also borrow from the experience of other courts that have addressed similar problems in the past. The Supreme Court drew upon the rulings of appeals courts in clarifying the meaning of desegregation and the experience of district courts in determining the sorts of measures that might be undertaken to implement *Brown*.

Finally, judicial policies may also be shaped to some extent by the political environment in which judges operate. Some commentators have suggested, for example, that the Supreme Court's rulings in *Brown* and *Roe* followed shifts in public opinion rather than leading them.[94] The Supreme Court's willingness to accord the South a period of adjustment through the mechanism of "all deliberate speed" likewise suggests a sensitivity to political environment. So too does the Court's curtailment of aggressive district-court intervention, as in *Milliken* v. *Bradley*, in the face of widespread public opposition.

Legal Obligation

A judicial ruling imposes legal obligations on the parties to the case and on lower-court judges, who must apply the legal principles enunciated by the court in future cases. Judicial rulings also have legal implications for a broader "target population" that is in the same situation as the parties to the case. The size of this target population depends on the breadth of the legal principles a court announces. This in turn depends to a considerable extent on the breadth of the enactment the court is interpreting. Constitutional provisions, for example, tend to be more broadly applicable than statutes or administrative regulations. To some extent, however, courts themselves may determine the legal implications of their rulings by choosing on what legal principles they will base their decisions. For example, prior to *Brown*, the Supreme Court tied its rulings in school cases to the particular facts of the cases, so that they primarily affected the parties in the cases. In *Brown*, however, the Court held that state-mandated segregation in education was unconstitutional, thus expanding the target population to include all states and localities that had established segregated school systems.

What legal obligations are imposed on a target population by a judicial ruling? Unfortunately, there is no consensus. Some legal scholars insist that a judicial ruling announces legal standards which are authoritative throughout the jurisdiction served by the court. Thus, a district court's ruling invalidating a practice requires all those within the district to refrain from the practice, and a Supreme Court ruling has the same effect nationwide.[95] Other legal scholars maintain that what is authoritative is the court's ruling in the case, not the legal principles on which it was based. Thus, one may dispute those legal principles and engage in practices which, if legally challenged, would furnish the court with an opportunity to reconsider the principles it had announced.[96] Still other legal scholars distinguish between settled and unsettled law, arguing that one may engage in actions inconsistent with the legal principles announced in a case only until those principles have become firmly established.[97] Under that standard, any racial discrimination in education would violate a legal principle established in *Brown* and confirmed in succeeding cases.

In most cases those affected by judicial rulings comply with them. Yet as *Brown* and *Roe* reveal, the mere existence of legal obligations does not guarantee compliance.

Communications Problems

Lower-court judges or members of the target population may not comply with judicial mandates if they are unclear about what actions are required. For example, after *Brown* II many district-court judges were unsure about whether school districts had to integrate their schools or merely cease using racial criteria in student assignment. They also were unclear about what sorts of remedial measures they could employ if districts failed to meet their obligations under *Brown*. The Court's lack of clarity in *Brown*, together with its refusal to hear subsequent school cases and resolve ambiguities, increased the discretion of district-court judges and officials involved in school desegregation. Many used the opportunity to confine the effects of *Brown*.

In contrast, clear mandates reduce discretion and encourage actions in line with the Court's aims. The Supreme Court's early abortion rulings exemplify this. The Court in *Roe* v. *Wade* announced detailed legal standards, and over the next decade it further elaborated their implications in reviewing post-*Roe* legislation. So does *Swann* v. *Charlotte-Mecklenburg Board of Education*, in which the Supreme Court clarified what compliance with *Brown* required and specifically endorsed various remedial measures employed by district courts to implement *Brown*. Yet the effects of a clear initial mandate can be undermined by subsequent rulings that are inconsistent with it or that suggest a change in policy direction. The Supreme Court's rulings on abortion since 1987, which have raised questions about the continuing authority of *Roe*, illustrate this phenomenon.

Finally, although it did not affect the response to the Supreme Court's school desegregation or abortion rulings, a target population cannot comply with a ruling unless that ruling is transmitted to it. Beyond officially promulgating their decisions, courts have no control over the transmission of their mandates. Usually this poses no problem: those affected by a judicial ruling are aware of the court's action. But this is not always the case, particularly when the target population is large. For example, when the Supreme Court announces a ruling affecting the power of police officers to conduct searches or interrogations, not all officers may hear of the ruling.[98] Similarly, many taxpayers may be unaware of Tax Court rulings that affect their tax liability.

Even if members of the target population are aware of a judicial ruling, they may misunderstand it. For example, some school officials erroneously interpreted the Supreme Court's invalidation of prayer in the public schools as merely forbidding coercion of students who did not wish to pray.[99] Such misinterpretations may occur because of ambiguities in the judicial ruling. Even if a ruling is clear, it may be simplified or distorted in the course of transmission. Most police officers, for example, get their information about rulings on police practices from non-judicial sources, such as local officials, police training sessions, and the mass media. They can comply with the rulings only if those sources faithfully and accurately convey what the court has said.[100]

Noncompliance

Usually people conform to the legal requirements announced in judicial decisions. Indeed, the effectiveness of the judicial policy prescriptions depends in large measure on voluntary compliance. Yet at times the parties to a case, lower-court judges, and/or members of the target population may refuse to undertake or refrain from actions as required by judicial rulings. Several state legislatures, for example, either ignored *Roe* v. *Wade* or enacted laws clearly inconsistent with its mandates. Most Southern school districts did not desegregate their schools in the decade after *Brown* II, and some district-court judges abetted their noncompliance by refusing to enforce *Brown*. Even those district-court judges who sought to implement *Brown* often found themselves outmaneuvered. Only the intervention of Congress, which enacted the 1964 Civil Rights Act and the Elementary and Secondary Education Act, and of the executive branch, which enforced those laws, produced compliance in the South.

The federal judiciary's difficulties in implementing *Brown* underscore its limited power to compel compliance, particularly when opposition is widespread. As Alexander Hamilton noted in *The Federalist Papers*, the judiciary does not control "either the sword or the purse" and must "ultimately depend upon the aid of the executive arm even for the efficacy of its judgments."[101] When the executive and legislative branches support the federal judiciary, compliance with its mandates is likely. Thus, when the power of the sword and of the purse were brought to bear on Southern school districts after 1964, noncompliance rapidly ended. But when the other branches of the national government maintain neutrality or oppose judicial policies, the ability of the federal courts to ensure compliance declines dramatically.[102]

Policy Effectiveness

A basic question to be asked of any judicial policymaking is whether the court achieved its objective. But answering this question is not always easy. For one thing, it may be difficult to determine what the court's objective was. *Brown* v. *Board of Education* is a case in point. If the aim in *Brown* and succeeding cases was to eliminate official support for racial segregation, then the Court clearly succeeded. Overt discrimination in education has virtually disappeared. If the Court's aim, however, was to ensure that children attended integrated schools, then the Court did not completely succeed. Today, most urban school districts, North and South, are racially homogeneous. In addition, some districts in which racial integration existed have, with population shifts, moved toward resegregation. If the Court's objective in *Brown* was to guarantee a good education to all students without regard to race, then again the Court has had only limited success. Indeed, as Chapter 11 will show, reformers interested in improving education for the disadvantaged have in recent years focused their attention more on school finance than on desegregation.

It may also be difficult to disentangle whether judicial decisions or other factors produced particular effects. Take, for example, the phenomenon of white flight, that is, the movement of white families (and schoolchildren) from urban to suburban school districts. Opponents of court-ordered busing charged that it produced white flight and that judicial policies aimed at promoting integration were counter-productive, leading instead to racial isolation for minority students in urban school districts.[103] Other commentators, however, denied that court-ordered busing precipitated the white exodus from the cities and from urban school districts. That, they maintained was a national phenomenon, not limited to municipalities with court-ordered busing, and busing itself did not accelerate the process.[104]

Similarly, when the goals of judicial policy are achieved, one cannot always assume that judicial decisions produced the effects. The late 1960s, for example, witnessed a rapid and sweeping desegregation of Southern schools, as required by Brown. Yet as we have seen, congressional legislation and executive enforcement had more to do with the change than *Brown* did.

Even when judicial decisions achieve their objectives, other factors—unanticipated by the judges or by those who brought suit—may play a key role. The aftermath of *Roe* v. *Wade* illustrates this. In *Roe* the Supreme Court attempted to make the option of abortion more widely available. Increases in legal abortions after 1973 indicate that the Court succeeded. But this did not occur as abortion reformers—and probably the justices—had expected. The reformers had assumed that hospitals would perform abortions once they were legal. The vast majority of public and private hospitals, however, continued to refuse to perform abortions even after 1973.[105] This created the possibility that the Court would be stymied by the opposition of institutions it had depended upon to implement its policy, just as it had been in *Brown*.

But hospitals, it turned out, were not crucial to the success of *Roe*. When they refused to perform abortions, medical clinics were opened to meet the demand for abortions.[106] These alternative institutions developed, because there was a financial incentive for providing abortions. Ironically, neither abortion reformers nor the justices foresaw how critical clinics would be. Indeed, the issue of where abortions were to be performed was ignored in the briefs submitted by the parties in *Roe* and was addressed only briefly in Justice Blackmun's opinion for the Court. In that sense, the success of *Roe* was as much the result of chance as of planning.[107]

Ultimately, the effectiveness of judicial policies may depend on the adequacy of the judges' understanding of the social processes that they are trying to influence. As we saw in Chapter 9, those who criticize judicial policymaking assert that judges lack the expertise and cannot acquire the knowledge necessary for effective policymaking.[108] While we offer no conclusions about the adequacy of this critique, our survey of federal judicial policymaking on school desegregation and abortion should provide a basis for evaluating that claim.

NOTES

1. *Brown* v. *Board of Education*, 347 U.S. 483 (1954). This case is commonly referred to as *Brown* I.

2. *Scott* v. *Sandford*, 60 U.S. (19 Howard) 393 (1857), and *Plessy* v. *Ferguson*, 163 U.S. 537 (1896).

3. Our discussion of the school desegregation litigation prior to *Brown* relies on Daniel M. Berman, *It Is So Ordered: The Supreme Court Rules on School Segregation* (New York: W.W. Norton, 1966); Richard Kluger, *Simple Justice* (New York: Alfred A. Knopf, 1975); Mark V. Tushnet, *The NAACP's Legal Strategy Against Segregated Education, 1925-1950* (Chapel Hill: University of North Carolina Press, 1987); and Stephen Wasby, "Interest Groups in Court: Race Relations Litigation," in Allan Cigler and Burdett Loomis, eds., *Interest Group Politics* (Washington, D.C.: Congressional Quarterly Press, 1983).

4. The classic account of the development of racial segregation is C. Vann Woodward, *The Strange Career of Jim Crow* (New York: Oxford University Press, 1966).

5. Cited in Tushnet, *The NAACP's Legal Strategy Against Segregated Education*, p. 5.

6. Important victories included *Missouri ex rel. Gaines* v. *Canada*, 305 U.S. 337 (1938); *Sweatt* v. *Painter*, 339 U.S. 629 (1950); and *McLaurin* v. *Oklahoma State Regents for Higher Education*, 339 U.S. 637 (1950).

7. Our argument here follows that of Tushnet, *The NAACP's Legal Strategy Against Segregated Education*, Chapter 8.

8. See, for example, Karen O'Connor, *Women's Organizations' Use of the Courts* (Lexington, Mass.: Lexington Books, 1980), and Robert Rabin, "Lawyers for Social Change: Perspectives on Public Interest Law," *Stanford Law Review* 28 (January 1970): 207-261.

9. Tushnet, *The NAACP's Legal Strategy Against Segregated Education*, pp. 145-146.

10. For a discussion of these cases and their aftermath, see Raymond Wolters, *The Burden of Brown; Thirty Years of School Desegregation* (Knoxville: University of Tennessee Press, 1984).

11. *Bolling* v. *Sharpe*, 347 U.S. 497 (1954).

12. On the intracourt politics surrounding *Brown*, see Kluger, *Simple Justice*, Part III; S. Sidney Ulmer, "Earl Warren and the *Brown* Decision," *Journal of Politics* 33 (1971): 689-702; and Mark Tushnet with Katya Lezin, "What Really Happened in *Brown* v. *Board of Education*," *Columbia Law Review* 91 (December 1991): 1867-1930.

13. *Brown* v. *Board of Education*, 347 U.S. 483, 495.

14. Our analysis follows those of Robert L. Carter, "A Reassessment of *Brown* v. *Board*," and of Diane Ravitch, "Desegregation: Varieties of Meanings," both found in Derrick Bell, ed., *Shades of Brown; New Perspectives on School Desegregation* (New York: Teachers College Press, 1980).

15. By Southern states, we mean Alabama, Arkansas, Florida, Georgia, Louisiana, Mississippi, North Carolina, South Carolina, Tennessee, Texas, and Virginia. By Border States, we mean Delaware, Kentucky, Maryland, Missouri, Oklahoma, and West Virginia. The state of the law at the time of *Brown* is drawn from Gerald R. Rosenberg, *The Hollow Hope; Can Courts Bring About Social Change?* (Chicago: University of Chicago Press, 1991), p. 42.

16. J. Harvie Wilkinson, *From Brown to Bakke; The Supreme Court and School Integration, 1954-1968* (New York: Oxford University Press, 1979), pp. 64-77. Our account of the aftermath of *Brown* relies on, in addition to Wilkinson's volume, Rosenberg, *The Hollow Hope*, Chapters 2-5; Stephen L. Wasby, Anthony A. D'Amato, and Rosemary Metrailer, *Desegregation from Brown to Alexander* (Carbondale, Ill.: Southern Illinois University Press, 1977); and Raymond Wolters, *The Burden of Brown*.

17. *Brown* v. *Board of Education* [*Brown* II], 349 U.S. 294, 300 (1955).

18. Quoted in Wilkinson, *From Brown to Bakke*, p. 65.

19. Quoted in ibid., p. 66.

20. Ibid., pp. 69-70.

21. Wolters, *The Burden of Brown*, p. 256. Racial segregation was not the only form that racial discrimination took in Topeka's schools; see Wolters, pp. 254-55, and Kluger, *Simple Justice*, pp. 381-382.

22. Wolters, *The Burden of Brown*, p. 12.

23. Rosenberg, *The Hollow Hope*, p. 50, Table 2-1.

24. The Supreme Court's ruling was *Cooper* v. *Aaron*, 358 U.S. 1 (1958). Background on the Little Rock debacle is found in Wilkinson, *From Brown to Bakke*, pp. 88-95.

25. The Supreme Court's ruling was *Griffin* v. *County School Board*, 375 U.S. 391 (1964). Background on the closing of schools in Prince Edward County is found in Wilkinson, *From Brown to Bakke*, pp. 95-102, and Wolters, *The Burden of Brown*, pp. 65-128.

26. On the war against the NAACP, see Robert H. Birkby and Walter F. Murphy, "Interest Group Conflict in the Judicial Arena: The First Amendment and Group Access to the Courts," *Texas Law Review* 42 (1964): 1018-1048. Pertinent cases include *NAACP* v. *Alabama*, 357 U.S. 449 (1958), and *Gibson* v. *Florida Legislative Investigating Committee*, 372 U.S. 539 (1963). On the absence of school desegregation suits in Mississippi, see Jack W. Peltason, *Fifty-Eight Lonely Men* (Urbana, Ill.: University of Illinois Press, 1971), p. 99.

27. Kluger, *Simple Justice*, p. 748.

28. Rosenberg, *The Hollow Hope*, p. 79.

29. Quoted in Reed Sarrat, *The Ordeal of Desegregation* (New York: Harper, 1966), p. 201.

30. See, for example, Judge John J. Parker's influential opinion in *Briggs* v. *Elliott*, 132 F.Supp. 776, 777 (E.D.S.C. 1955).

31. Walter Gellhorn, "A Decade of Desegregation—Retrospect and Prospect," *Utah Law Review* 9 (1964), p. 6.

32. Quoted in Harrell R. Rodgers, Jr., and Charles S. Bullock III, *Law and Social Change: Civil Rights Laws and Their Consequences* (New York: McGraw-Hill, 1972), p. 72.

33. Rosenberg, *The Hollow Hope*, p. 84.

34. Wilkinson, *From Brown to Bakke*, p. 102.

35. Ibid., p. 108.

36. These data are drawn from Rosenberg, *The Hollow Hope*, p. 98.

37. Gary Orfield, *The Reconstruction of Southern Education* (New York: Wiley, 1969), p. 228.

38. This analysis follows that of Wilkinson in *From Brown to Bakke*, pp. 108-118. The pertinent Fifth Circuit cases are *Singleton* v. *Jackson Municipal Separate School District I*, 348 F.2d 729 (CA5 1965); *Singleton* v. *Jackson Municipal Separate School District II*, 355 F.2d 865 (CA5 1966); and *United States* v. *Jefferson County Board of Education*, 372 F.2d 836 (CA5 1966).

39. *Green* v. *County School Board*, 391 U.S. 430 (1968).

40. 391 U.S. 430, 439. See also *Alexander* v. *Holmes County Board of Education*, 396 U.S. 19 (1969).

41. *Swann* v. *Charlotte-Mecklenburg Board of Education*, 402 U.S. 1 (1971).

42. 402 U.S. 1, 30-31 and 15.

43. Paul R. Dimond, *Beyond Busing: Inside the Challenge to Urban Segregation* (Ann Arbor, Mich.: University of Michigan Press, 1985), Chapters 1 and 6.

44. Wilkinson, *From Brown to Bakke*, p. 197.

45. Ibid., p. 206.

46. *Swann* v. *Charlotte-Mecklenburg Board of Education*, 402 U.S. 1 (1971).

47. Ibid., at 30-31.

48. *Keyes* v. *School District No. 1, Denver, Colorado*, 413 U.S. 189 (1973).

49. *Statement of the United States Commission on Civil Rights on School Desegregation* (Washington, D.C.: Government Printing Office, 1982); James Bolner and Robert Shanley, *Busing: The Political and Judicial Process* (New York: Praeger, 1974); and Dimond, *Beyond Busing*, pp. 385-386.

50. Wilkinson, *From Brown to Bakke*, pp. 202 and 207.

51. Ibid., p. 180, and Wolters, *The Burden of Brown*, pp. 246-247.

52. *Milliken* v. *Bradley* [*Milliken* I],. 418 U.S. 717 (1974).

53. See, for example, *Milliken* v. *Bradley* [*Milliken* II], 433 U.S. 267 (1977), and *Missouri* v. *Jenkins*, 110 S.Ct. 1651 (1990).

54. *Dayton Board of Education* v. *Brinkman* [*Dayton* II], 433 U.S. 406 (1977). The Dayton litigation is chronicled in Dimond, *Beyond Busing*, Chapters 6-8 and 15-16.

55. See, for example, *Dayton Board of Education* v. *Brinkman* [*Dayton* II], 443 U.S. 526 (1979), and *Columbus Board of Education* v. *Penick*, 443 U.S. 499 (1979).

56. *Pasadena City Board of Education* v. *Spangler*, 427 U.S. 424 (1976); for a more recent ruling likewise curtailing judicial supervision of school districts, see *Freeman* v. *Pitts*, 112 S.Ct. 1430 (1992).

57. See Rosenberg, *The Hollow Hope*, p. 50, Table 2.1.

58. See, for example, Micheal Giles, Douglas Gatlin, and Everett Cataldo, "White Flight and Percent Black: The Tipping Point Reexamined," *Social Science Quarterly* (June 1976): 85-92.

59. See, for example, Robert L. Carter, "A Reassessment of *Brown* v. *Board*," and Ronald R. Edmonds, "Effective Education for Minority Pupils: *Brown* Confounded or Confirmed," in Bell, ed., *Shades of Brown*.

60. *Planned Parenthood of Southeastern Pennsylvania* v. *Casey*, 60 U.S.L.W. 4795 (1992).

61. *Roe* v. *Wade*, 410 U.S. 113 (1972).

62. Such criticism is, of course, not unique to this case. See the discussion in Chapter 8.

63. Our account of the origins of abortion legislation and of the movement to liberalize state abortion laws relies primarily on Marian Faux, *Roe v. Wade* (New York: Macmillan, 1988); Lawrence Lader, *Abortion II: Making the Revolution* (Boston: Beacon Press, 1973); Eva R. Rubin, *Abortion, Politics, and the Courts*, rev. ed. (Westport, Conn.: Greenwood Press, 1987); and Gerald R. Rosenberg, *The Hollow Hope*, Chapters 6-9.

64. Rosenberg, *The Hollow Hope*, p. 180, Table 6.1.

65. Rubin, *Abortion, Politics, and the Courts*, p. 164.

66. Faux, *Roe v. Wade*, p. 117.

67. See, for example, Aryeh Neier, *Only Judgment: The Limits of Litigation in Social Change* (Middletown, Conn.: Wesleyan University Press, 1982); Jennifer L. Hochschild, *The New American Dilemma* (New Haven: Yale University Press, 1984); and Owen Fiss, "The Supreme Court, 1978 Term—Foreword: The Forms of Justice," *Harvard Law Review* 93 (November 1979): 1-58.

68. *Poe* v. *Ullman*, 367 U.S. 497 (1961). For an enlightening discussion of the considerations underlying the Court's initial avoidance of the birth-control case, see Alexander M. Bickel, *The Least Dangerous Branch; The Supreme Court at the Bar of Politics* (Indianapolis: Bobbs-Merrill, 1962), pp. 143-156.

69. The article was Cyril Means, "The Phoenix of Abortional Freedom: Is a Penumbral or Ninth Amendment Right About to Arise from the Nineteenth-Century Legislative Ashes of a Fourteenth-Century Common Law Liberty?" *New York Forum* 17 (Fall 1971): 335-410. The role of abortion reformers in the development of the article is documented in Faux, *Roe v. Wade*, p. 217.

70. See Faux, *Roe v. Wade*, Chapter 13.

71. *Roe* v. *Wade*, 410 U.S. 113 (1973), and *Doe* v. *Bolton*, 410 U.S. 179 (1973).

72. *Griswold* v. *Connecticut*, 381 U.S. 479 (1965).

73. *Roe* v. *Wade*, 410 U.S. 113, 153.

74. Such criticism even came from some scholars who had endorsed previous activist rulings of the Warren Court. See, for example, John Hart Ely, "The Wages of Crying Wolf: A Comment on *Roe* v. *Wade*," *Yale Law Journal* 82 (1973): 920-949

75. Our account of the response to *Roe* draws particularly on Barbara H. Craig and David M. O'Brien, *Abortion and American Politics* (Chatham N.J.: Chatham House, 1993); Rubin, *Abortion, Politics, and the Court*; Rosenberg, *The Hollow Hope*; and Raymond Tatalovich, "Abortion: Prochoice Versus Prolife," in Raymond Tatalovich and Byron W. Dayner, eds., *Social Regulatory Policy; Moral Controversies in American Politics* (Boulder, Colorado: Westview Press, 1988).

76. Lader, *Abortion II*, frontpiece.

77. Quoted in Faux, *Roe v. Wade*, p. 305.

78. Michele McKeegan, *Abortion Politics; Mutiny in the Ranks of the Right* (New York: Free Press, 1992), p. 130.

79. On the pro-life movement and abortion politics, see Raymond Tatalovich and Byron W. Daynes, *The Politics of Abortion: A Study of Community Conflict in Public Policy Making* (New York: Praeger, 1981); Frederick S. Jaffe, Barbara L. Lindheim, and Philip R. Lee, *Abortion Politics: Private Morality and Public Policy* (New York: McGraw-Hill, 1981); and Robert J. Spitzer, *The Right to Life Movement and Third Party Politics* (Westport, Conn.: Greenwood Press, 1987).

80. The Eleventh Amendment overruled *Chisholm* v. *Georgia*, 2 U.S. 419 (1793); the Fourteenth Amendment, *Scott* v. *Sandford*, 60 U.S. 393 (1857); the Sixteenth Amendment, *Pollock* v. *Farmers' Loan & Trust Co.*, 157 U.S. 429 (1895); the Twenty-Fourth Amendment, *Breedlove* v. *Suttles*, 302 U.S. 277 (1937); and the Twenty-Sixth Amendment, *Oregon* v. *Mitchell*, 400 U.S. 112 (1970).

81. Tatalovich, "Abortion: Prochoice Versus Prolife," p. 200.

82. *Harris* v. *McRae*, 448 U.S. 297 (1980). 238 members of Congress submitted an *amicus curiae* brief in the case, urging the Court to uphold the Hyde Amendment.

83. *Rust* v. *Sullivan*, 111 S.Ct. 1759 (1991).   For a discussion of the Reagan and Bush administrations' initiatives, albeit from a critical perspective, see McKeegan, *Abortion Politics*, Chapters 4-8.   President Clinton rescinded the gag rule by executive order during his first month in office.

84. Rosenberg, *The Hollow Hope*, pp. 187-188.

85. Early post-*Roe* cases include: *Bigelow* v. *Virginia*, 421 U.S. 809 (1975); *Connecticut* v. *Mentillo*, 423 U.S. 9 (1975); *Planned Parenthood of Central Missouri* v. *Danforth*, 428 U.S. 52 (1976); *Beal* v. *Doe*, 432 U.S. 438 (1977); *Maher* v. *Roe*, 432 U.S. 464 (1977); *Poelker* v. *Doe*, 432 U.S. 519 (1977); *Colautti* v. *Franklin*, 439 U.S. 379 (1979); *Bellotti* v. *Baird*, 443 U.S. 622 (1979); *Harris* v. *McRae*, 448 U.S. 297 (1980); *Williams* v. *Zbaraz*, 448 U.S. 358 (1980); *H.L.* v. *Matheson*, 450 U.S. 398 (1981); *Akron* v. *Akron Center for Reproductive Health, Inc.*, 462 U.S. 416 (1983); *Simopoulos* v. *Virginia*, 462 U.S. 506 (1983); *Planned Parenthood Associated of Kansas City, Missouri* v. *Ashcroft*, 462 U.S. 476 (1983); and *Thornburgh* v. *American College of Obstetricians and Gynecologists*, 476 U.S. 747 (1976).

86. See *Planned Parenthood of Central Missouri* v. *Danforth* (spousal consent and parental consent); *Akron* v. *Akron Center for Reproductive Health* (counselling and hospitalization requirements); and *Thornburgh* v. *American College of Obstetricians and Gynecologists* (burdensome medical procedures).

87. See *Harris* v. *McRae* (ban on Medicaid funding for abortions), and *H.L.* v. *Matheson* (parental notification requirement).

88. *Webster* v. *Reproductive Health Services*, 109 S.Ct. 3040, 3079 (1989).

89. *Roe* v. *Wade*, 410 U.S. 113, 153.

90. Our analysis in this section follows that of Rosenberg, *The Hollow Hope*, pp. 189-201.

91. Ibid., p. 187.

92. Ibid., p. 190.

93. For an enlightening comparative analysis, see Mary Ann Glendon, *Abortion and Divorce in Western Law* (Cambridge: Harvard University Press, 1987), Chapters 1 and 3.

94. On *Roe*, see ibid., and on *Brown*, see Lewis Steel, "Nine Men in Black Who Think White," *New York Times Magazine*, October 13, 1968. More generally, see, Rosenberg, *The Hollow Hope*, Chapters 5-6.

95. For an analysis of scholarly support for this position, see Gary L. Jacobsohn, *The Supreme Court and the Decline of Constitutional Aspiration* (Totowa, N.J.: Rowman & Littlefield, 1986), Chapter 7.

96. See ibid., and Sanford Levinson, *Constitutional Faith* (Princeton, N.J.: Princeton University Press, 1988).

97. See Jacobsohn, *The Supreme Court and the Decline of Constitutional Aspiration*, Chapters 6-7.

98. See, for example, Neil A. Milner, *The Court and Local Law Enforcement; The Impact of Miranda* (Beverly Hills, Calif.: Sage Publications, 1971).

99. See William K. Muir, Jr., *Prayer in the Public Schools: Law and Attitude Change* (Chicago: University of Chicago Press, 1967), and Richard Johnson, *The Dynamics of Compliance* (Evanston, Ill.: Northwestern University Press, 1967).

100. On communications problems and judicial impact, see Charles A. Johnson and Bradley C. Canon, *Judicial Policies; Implementation and Impact* (Washington, D.C.: Congressional Quarterly Press, 1984), pp. 205-210.

101. Alexander Hamilton, John Jay, and James Madison, *The Federalist Papers*, ed. by Clinton Rossiter (New York: New American Library, 1961), #78, p. 465.

102. See Rosenberg, *The Hollow Hope*, Chapter 1 and *passim*.

103. For an overview of the controversy over busing, see Johnson and Canon, *Judicial Policies*, pp. 131-134. The most influential argument against busing was James S. Coleman, Sara D. Kelly, and John Moore, *Recent Trends in School Desegregation* (Washington, D.C.: Urban Institute, 1975).

104. Thomas Pettigrew and Robert L. Green, "School Desegregation in Large Cities: A Critique of the Coleman 'White Flight' Thesis," *Harvard Educational Review* 46 (February 1976): 1-53; and Christine H. Rossell, "School Desegregation and White Flight," *Political Science Quarterly* 90 (Winter 1975-76): 673-695.

105. See Rosenberg, *The Hollow Hope*, p. 190, Table 6.2. Our analysis in this section follows that of Rosenberg, pp. 189-201.

106. Ibid., p. 197, Tables 6.4 and 6.5.

107. Ibid., pp. 200-201.

108. See Donald L. Horowitz, *The Courts and Social Policy* (Washington, D.C.: Brookings, 1977), and—more generally—the discussion in Chapter 9.

11 STATE COURT POLICYMAKING

While rulings such as *Brown* v. *Board of Education* and *Roe* v. *Wade* attract national attention, less publicized judicial decisions also enunciate important policy. Many of these rulings come from state courts. Indeed, according to Justice William Brennan of the United States Supreme Court, "[t]he composite work of the courts in the fifty states probably has greater significance [than that of the U.S. Supreme Court] in measuring how well America attains the ideal of equal justice for all."[1]

This chapter focuses on state courts' constitutional policymaking dealing with public school finance and on their common-law policymaking on products liability (the legal standards governing suits for damages for injuries caused by defective products). State court policymaking in these fields, in addition to its intrinsic importance, reveals basic features of how state courts participate in governing. In particular, it highlights the influence on state judicial policymaking of state courts' relationships with federal courts, with courts in other states, and with the state legislature and other institutions of state government.

SCHOOL FINANCE

Initially, federal courts—not state courts—were in the forefront of legal efforts to reform state systems for financing public education. In 1971 Demetrio Rodriguez filed a class-action suit in federal district court, arguing that Texas's system of school finance violated the equal protection clause of the United States Constitution. The system that Rodriguez challenged resembled those in most other states. Funding for elementary and secondary schools came primarily from local property taxes.[2] Thus, the level of spending for education varied from school district to school district, depending on the value of taxable property in the district and on the rate at which it was taxed. The inter-district differences in spending per child could be substantial. At the time of Rodriguez's suit, the Edgewood Independent School District in San Antonio annually spent $356 per pupil, while the neighboring Alamo Heights district spent $564.[3]

According to Rodriguez, the disparities in funding among school districts, produced by this heavy reliance on local property taxes, resulted in unequal and inadequate education for students in property-poor districts.[4] More to the point, he asserted that they violated the Federal Constitution. A federal district court agreed and struck down Texas's system of school finance as inconsistent with the equal protection clause of the Fourteenth Amendment. In *San Antonio Independent School District* v. *Rodriguez* (1973), however, the United States Supreme Court by a 5-4 vote reversed the district court's decision.[5] The Court majority maintained that the equal protection clause did not require equal expenditures in school districts, and thus Texas's system of school finance was constitutional.

Although *Rodriguez* precluded further challenges under the Federal Constitution, it did not end school-finance litigation. Over the next two decades, ten state supreme courts struck down their state's system of school finance as unconstitutional.[6] Among these courts was the Texas Supreme Court which, sixteen years after *Rodriguez*, unanimously ruled that the state's system of school finance violated the Texas Constitution.[7] Let us look more closely at the transformation of school-finance litigation and its consequences.

The Development of School–Finance Litigation

Litigating for Change

For courts to rule on the constitutionality of state systems of school finance, there must be litigants willing to raise the issue and a legal basis for their claim. *Brown* v. *Board of Education* was crucial in stimulating school-finance litigation.[8] *Brown* focused attention on the detrimental effects of inequalities in education, prompting social commentators and political activists to consider the impact of other forms of educational inequality.[9] In addition, *Brown*— together with other egalitarian rulings of the Supreme Court—signalled the justices' willingness to use the equal protection clause to combat inequalities.[10] It thus encouraged potential litigants to believe that they would have a forum receptive to their claims. Finally, *Brown* also appeared to show that the Supreme Court could successfully inaugurate major social change. Given the slow pace and uncertain results of state-by-state legislative reform of school finance, this made the judicial path to reform particularly attractive. Not surprisingly, then, school-finance reformers pinned their hopes on the U.S. Supreme Court.

But the reformers had miscalculated badly. By the early 1970s, when *Rodriguez* came to the Supreme Court, the Supreme Court's composition and orientation had changed. Republican President Richard Nixon had appointed four new justices, and these new justices, more committed to judicial restraint than their predecessors, were not interested in egalitarian crusades. In *Rodriguez* the Nixon appointees supplied four of the five votes needed to uphold Texas's system of school finance, ensuring that federal courts would not play a role in school-finance reform.

State Courts and State Law

Thirteen days after the Supreme Court announced its decision in *Rodriguez*, however, the New Jersey Supreme Court in *Robinson* v. *Cahill* unanimously ruled the state's system of school finance unconstitutional.[11] New Jersey's system for financing education closely resembled Texas's, which—according to the U.S. Supreme Court—met federal constitutional requirements. Thus, the New Jersey justices could not base their ruling on the federal equal protection clause. Instead, they held that New Jersey's system of school finance violated the state constitution's requirement that the state provide to all children a "thorough and efficient education."[12]

Robinson transformed and reinvigorated the campaign for school-finance reform through the courts. It reminded potential litigants—and government officials—that state systems of school finance had to satisfy state, as well as federal, constitutional requirements. Moreover, it showed that the applicable state provisions were not identical with those in the Federal Constitution—there was no federal analogue to the "thorough and efficient" clause or to other state constitutional requirements (see Box 11-1). *Robinson* also reminded potential litigants that a favorable ruling on school finance under the state constitution could not be reversed by the U.S. Supreme Court. State supreme courts are the authoritative interpreters of their state constitutions, so state rulings interpreting their provisions are not subject to Supreme Court review. Thus, victories won in state court would not turn into defeats in federal court. Finally, *Robinson* demonstrated that state courts might prove more sympathetic to school-finance challenges than had the federal courts. As a result, *Robinson* encouraged reformers to look to their state constitutions and their state courts

---

BOX 11-1   STATE CONSTITUTIONAL PROVISIONS AND SCHOOL FINANCE

Many states have distinctive constitutional provisions which are relevant to school finance:

Illinois: The Illinois Constitution states that "[a] fundamental goal for the People of the State is the educational development of all persons to the limits of their capacities" and requires the state to "provide for an efficient system of high quality public educational institutions and services." (Art. X, sec. 1)

Montana: The Montana Constitution requires the state to provide "a system of education which will develop the full educational potential of each person. Equality of educational opportunity is guaranteed to each person of the state." (Art. X, sec. 1)

New Jersey: "The Legislature shall provide for the support of a thorough and efficient system of free public schools."(Art. VIII, sec. 14)

New Mexico: "Children of Spanish descent in the state of New Mexico ... shall forever enjoy perfect equality with other children in all public schools." (Art. XII, sec. 10)

Texas: "It shall be the duty of the legislature of the state to establish and make suitable provision for the support and maintenance of an efficient system of public free schools." (Art. VII, sec. 1)

Wyoming: The Wyoming Constitution mandates a "complete and uniform system of public instruction." (Art. 7, sec. 1)

---

in challenging state systems of school finance. As the attorney in Connecticut's school-finance case testified, *Robinson* "fired my imagination."[13]

School-Finance Litigation in State Courts

After Robinson, reformers in several states initiated state constitutional challenges to school-finance systems. They based their claims either on equal protection guarantees in state constitutions or on state education provisions, such as New Jersey's requirement of a "thorough and efficient education." In the seven years after Rodriguez, twelve state supreme courts heard challenges to their states' systems of school finance (see Table 11-1).[14] Reformers enjoyed some success, prevailing in half the cases. After 1980, however, interest in school-finance litigation waned. From 1981-1988, litigants filed only seven suits against school-finance programs, and in all but one of those cases the state supreme court upheld the states' programs.[15] Since 1989, however, reformers have launched a new wave of litigation, challenging school-finance programs in five states.   In four of those cases, state supreme courts have invalidated the challenged programs.[16] One successful suit was in New Jersey, where the state's

TABLE 11-1 SCHOOL-FINANCE LITIGATION IN THE STATES		
	State Law Invalidated	**State Law Upheld**
Period One (1973-1980)	New Jersey (1973) California (1976) Connecticut (1977) Washington (1978) Wyoming (1978) West Virginia (1979)	Arizona (1973) Montana (1974) Idaho (1975) Oregon (1976) Pennsylvania (1978) Ohio (1979)
Period Two (1981-1988)	Arkansas (1983)	Georgia (1981) Colorado (1982) Maryland (1983) New York (1983) Oklahoma (1987) South Carolina (1988)
Period Three (1989-)	Kentucky (1989) Montana (1989) Texas (1989) New Jersey (1990)	Wisconsin (1989)

supreme court ruled that the "reformed" program established after Robinson did not remedy "the constitutional failure of education in poorer urban districts" and mandated greater aid to those districts.[17]

The twenty years of school-finance litigation confirmed that state courts, looking to their state constitutions, could engage in constitutional policymaking independent of the U.S. Supreme Court.   But they also also raised a question. In fourteen states the courts upheld school-finance programs, and in ten they invalidated the programs. Given the similarities among the challenged programs, why did state courts disagree about their constitutionality?

Differences in state law do not seem to account for the courts' disparate rulings. State courts, interpreting virtually identical constitutional provisions, have reached opposite results. The Kentucky, New Jersey, and Washington supreme courts, for example, interpreted the education articles of their state constitutions to require the invalidation of existing school-finance programs. But the Colorado, Missouri, and New York supreme courts upheld comparable school-finance programs in their states on the basis of very similar provisions. The Arkansas and California supreme courts ruled that the systems of school finance in their states violated state constitutional guarantees of equality, but the Michigan, Ohio, and Oregon courts—looking at similar provisions—reached the opposite conclusion.[18]

More helpful in explaining the conflicting interpretations of similar provisions are differences in the judges' role conceptions (discussed in Chapter 9). Some state judges, stressing the importance of judicial restraint, upheld school-finance programs because they believed it proper to defer to the state legislature. Thus, New York's supreme court noted that it was "particularly appropriate for . . . the legislative body (reflective of and responsive as it is to the public will)" to make decisions about the allocation of public funds.[19] Other judges, rejecting judicial activism, expressed the fear that their "unwise and unwarranted entry into the controversial area of public school financing" would transform their court into a "super-legislature," and embroil it "in a turbulent field of social, economic, and political policy."[20]

Even some judges who invalidated state programs of school finance insisted that judicial restraint guided their actions. Their intrusion into a field traditionally reserved to the legislature, they asserted, was compelled by the state's violation of clear constitutional commands.[21] Moreover, troubled by the apparent conflict between fidelity to the state constitution and respect for legislative prerogatives, they attempted to minimize the conflict by leaving the design of remedial measures to the legislature. Nevertheless, some judges who invalidated state programs forthrightly embraced judicial activism. West Virginia's high court, for example, not only struck down the state's system of school finance but designated eight specific areas in which schools would have to help students to develop their capacities.[22] The Kentucky Supreme Court meanwhile established seven output goals that had to be met for children to have a constitutionally adequate education.[23]

One might also expect that the justices' political views would explain, at least in part, the different rulings on such a controversial policy issue. Yet it is difficult to determine how much *direct* influence these views exerted on the judges' decisions. Take, for example, the Texas school-finance case. The opinion of the court was written by Justice Oscar Mauzy, a Democrat who had formerly chaired the state senate's Education Committee.[24] One might easily attribute his vote, requiring the reform of school finance, to his background and political perspective. Yet if political backgrounds and views directly determined votes, one would not expect the eight other members of the Texas Supreme Court—

five Democrats and three Republicans—to have endorsed joined Justice Mauzy's position and joined his opinion. The New Jersey Supreme Court's rulings in *Robinson* v. *Cahill* and in *Abbott* v. *Burke*, its more recent school-finance ruling, also defy explanation in simple political terms. Despite the justices' extensive political experience and their differing partisan affiliations, both decisions were unanimous.[25]

State Courts and State Legislatures

Once a court has detected a constitutional violation, it must act to remedy the violation. In many cases, the action required is straightforward: a court may order officials to cease their unconstitutional conduct, or it may award damages to those whose constitutional rights were violated. In the school-finance cases, however, the remedial task was more complicated. If a court concluded that the existing system of school finance violated the state constitution, it would have to ensure that a constitutionally adequate system replaced it.

But could state supreme courts meet that responsibility? State judges possessed no special expertise in education policy. They could not raise revenues to guarantee adequate funding for poorer districts. They were ill-equipped to supervise the implementation of policy. In short, they exhibited the very limitations that had led some scholars to despair of effective judicial policymaking.[26]

State supreme courts dealt with this problem in a variety of ways. Perhaps the simplest solution was that adopted by the California Supreme Court in *Serrano* v. *Priest* (1976).[27] In *Serrano* the court held that the state violated the equal protection clause of the California Constitution by allowing school expenditures per student to vary from district to district on the basis of property values. Given that definition of the constitutional violation, the court merely required the state to ensure that in the future funding per student not depend on the wealth of the school district. The clarity of the court's standard facilitated compliance by the state legislature. It also produced a reallocation of school funds without involving the court in designing education policy. Indeed, this ruling, together with Proposition 13—a subsequent anti-tax amendment to the California Constitution—produced a virtual equality of expenditures per student across the state.[28] Nevertheless, the California Supreme Court avoided entanglement in the details of education policymaking at some cost. It did so only by treating education policy as rather simple, by assuming that additional funding in poor districts would necessarily improve education.[29]

A more complex situation confronted those courts which invalidated school-finance programs for failure to provide a "thorough and efficient education" or to meet other requirements established by the education articles of their state constitutions. Such provisions imposed on state governments the obligation to provide a quality education for all students and on courts a duty to ensure that the state met that responsibility. But if the other branches of state government failed to meet their responsibility, would the state supreme court have to intervene with its own education plan?

Mindful of their limitations as policymakers, most state supreme courts sought to achieve their educational goals through agenda-setting policymaking.[30] Under agenda-setting policymaking, state supreme courts did not attempt to devise and impose their own policy, a task for which they were ill-suited. Rather, they invalidated existing policy and, with only the broadest of guidelines, left it to the governor and state legislature to come up with a policy that satisfied constitutional requirements. Thus, the courts' agenda-setting policymaking reordered the political priorities of the other branches of state government. Invalidation of existing policy forced governor and legislature to address the issue of school finance. At the same time, it allowed them considerable latitude in devising their own approaches to remedying the constitutional violations identified by the court.[31] Judicial intervention thus did not diminish opportunities for legislative policymaking.

Agenda-setting policymaking was attractive to state courts because it kept them from getting bogged down in the details of education policy. At the same time, however, it involved them in ongoing oversight of legislative efforts to meet constitutional requirements. In New Jersey, for example, the supreme court announced its initial ruling in *Robinson* v. *Cahill* (*Robinson* I) in 1971 but did not issue its final ruling in the case until 1976 (*Robinson* VI).

Agenda-setting policymaking did not always promote prompt and effective reform of public education. One notable success was in Kentucky, where the governor and state legislature cooperated to produce landmark legislation overhauling the state's system of public education and imposing the new taxes necessary to support the changes.[32] In many other states, however, the legislative response was slow and begrudging. In retrospect, this was hardly surprising. The fact that the state legislature had not previously initiated reforms on its own testified to the strong interests attached to the existing system of school finance. Moreover, school-finance reform often became tied up in political maneuvering in the state. In Texas, for example, it took four special legislative sessions and two gubernatorial vetoes before a new school funding plan was enacted.[33] In New Jersey, over a year passed after *Robinson* v. *Cahill* without any legislative action, because the lame-duck governor lacked the political muscle for effective leadership. Indeed, it took five years to get school-finance reforms enacted and implemented.[34]

Even when the legislature did act, that did not always resolve matters. Agenda-setting policymaking gave legislators considerable leeway in determining how to satisfy constitutional requirements. Yet the broader the leeway, the more difficult it was for legislators to determine what the requirements were—what, after all, is "a thorough and efficient education," and how does one determine when it has been achieved?   In addition, legislators were sometimes loath to take responsibility for court-mandated reforms, particularly if they required tax increases or were otherwise unpopular.   Some state legislators thus enacted laws that failed to meet fully the constitutional requirements enunciated by the court or that sought to circumscribe the effects of the court's ruling.   In doing so, they were implicitly negotiating with the state supreme court about the sort of policy that it would accept.

In such circumstances, the state supreme court was faced with two choices. It could invalidate the new law, provoking a confrontation with the legislature. Or it could avoid a confrontation by upholding the new law, even though it did not fully conform to the court's mandates.   In actuality, state supreme courts followed both courses.   Indeed, sometimes a court pursued both courses simultaneously, as the New Jersey Supreme Court's rulings following *Robinson* I illustrate.   Initially, the New Jersey court granted a nine-month extension after its deadline for legislative action ran out, a move interpreted as indicating a wavering judicial commitment to school-finance reform.   Four months later, however, the court reversed course, threatening to redistribute school aid itself if the legislature failed to act. Yet when legislation was enacted which only partially fulfilled the court's mandate, the justices upheld it against constitutional challenges.   Then, when the legislature balked at funding the new law, the court set a deadline after which the state was forbidden to operate the schools under the old school-finance program.   The deadline passed, the state's schools closed, and a week later the New Jersey legislature appropriated funds for the implementation of the new law.[35]

The Broader Context of State Constitutional Policymaking

Our description of school-finance litigation has emphasized how constitutional policymaking involves state supreme courts with other institutions of state government.   State courts' interactions with federal courts and with supreme courts in other states, however, are also crucial to state constitutional policymaking.

Federal Courts and State Court Policymaking

The rulings on school finance reveal how state supreme courts engage in independent constitutional policymaking.   Through the interpretation of their state constitutions, these courts had a major impact on educational policy in their states, and their rulings were not subject to review or reversal by the U.S. Supreme Court. In fact, school finance is only one of several areas in which state courts have relied on state constitutions to protect rights not guaranteed by the Federal Constitution. State bills of rights contain various other guarantees which have no parallel in the federal bill of rights (see Box 11-2). Even rights protected by the Federal Constitution may, as a result of distinctive constitutional language or state constitutional history, have a different scope under state constitutions. For example, whereas inequalities in school funding did not offend the equal protection clause of the Federal Constitution, the California Supreme Court held that they violated the equality requirements of the California Constitution. Since the early 1970s, state courts have increasingly looked to state guarantees to develop a body of state civil-liberties law, a phenomenon known as "the new judicial federalism."[36]

Perhaps because state courts have primary responsibility for the administration of criminal justice, the main focus of the new judicial federalism has been the elaboration of state guarantees of defendants' rights.[37] Some state courts have announced interpretations of state provisions—for example, on search and seizure, double jeopardy, and self-incrimination—that diverge from the U.S. Supreme Court's interpretation of analogous federal guarantees.[38] In other cases, state courts have interpreted state provisions that have no federal analogue, such as Oregon's prohibition on "unnecessary rigor" in punishment.[39]

State courts have also announced pioneering rulings outside the criminal justice area. Particularly noteworthy are state rulings on the right to privacy, gender equality, and the separation of church and state.[40] State judges have even begun to develop their own approaches to areas of law, such as freedom of speech and equal protection, long dominated by the Supreme Court and federal constitutional law.[41]

While the development of the new judicial federalism shows the independent policymaking role played by state courts, it also illustrates the connection between federal court policymaking and state court policymaking. From the 1930s to the 1960s, federal courts took a more expansive view of civil liberties than did state courts. This led litigants seeking to protect or expand rights to file their suits in federal court or to base their claims in state courts on the Federal Constitution. Only when the Supreme Court, as a result of personnel changes, became less receptive to their claims, did civil-liberties advocates turn their attention to state courts and state law. School-finance litigation exemplifies the pattern. Until *Rodriguez* dashed their hopes, reformers expected their victory would come in the U.S. Supreme Court. Only when they failed there did they begin to consider seriously state provisions dealing with education. In sum, the orientation of the U.S. Supreme Court—and litigants' response to that orientation—have a major influence on the opportunities for state constitutional policymaking.[42]

BOX 11-2 DISTINCTIVE STATE CONSTITUTIONAL GUARANTEES

State constitutions protect a number of rights not expressly mentioned in the United States Constitution, as the following provisions illustrate:

Right to privacy: "The right of individual privacy is essential to the well-being of a free society and shall not be infringed without the showing of a compelling state interest." (Mont. Const., Art. II, sec. 10)

Ban on public aid to parochial schools: "No public money or property shall be appropriated for or applied to any religious worship, exercise or instruction, or the support of any religious establishment." (Wash. Const., Art. I, sec. 11) "All schools maintained or supported wholly or in part by the public funds shall be forever free from sectarian control or influence." (Wash. Const., Art. IX, sec. 4)

Right to a legal remedy: "All courts shall be open, and every person, for an injury done to him in his person, property or reputation, shall have remedy by due course of law." (Conn. Const., Art. I, sec. 10)

Gender equality: "Equality of rights under the law shall not be denied or abridged by the State on account of sex." (Hawaii Const., Art. I, sec. 21)

Right to bear arms: "All persons ... have certain inherent and inalienable rights; among these are ... the right to keep and bear arms for security or defense of self, family, home, and others, and for lawful common defense, hunting, recreational use, and all other lawful purposes, and such rights shall not be denied or infringed by the state or any subdivision thereof." (Neb. Const., Art. I, sec. 1)

Right to bail: "All persons shall be bailable by sufficient sureties, except for capital offenses where the proof is evident or the presumption great." (Ohio Const., Art. I, sec. 9)

Freedom from excessive punishments: "Persons arrested or imprisoned shall not be treated with unnecessary rigor." (Utah Const., Art. I, sec. 9)

Right to safe schools: "Such public safety extends to public primary, elementary, junior high, and senior high school campuses, where students and staff have the right to be safe and secure in their persons." (California Const., Art. I, sec. 28)

Interstate Influences

The school-finance cases show that state supreme court rulings can have important effects beyond the borders of the state. The New Jersey Supreme Court's
ruling in *Robinson* v. *Cahill*, for example, stimulated litigation in a number of
states by showing the potential for state constitutional challenges to school-
finance programs. Indeed, the proliferation of groups using litigation to pursue
policy reforms virtually ensures that battles won on one front will be refought
on others.[43] In mounting these challenges, groups often drew upon arguments
made by courts in other states. Thus, after the New Jersey court relied on the
state constitution's "thorough and efficient education" clause to invalidate the
state's system of school finance, reformers in other states with a similar constitutional provision argued that its state supreme court should adopt the New
Jersey court's interpretation. When state supreme courts announced their rulings, their opinions often relied heavily on arguments from school-finance rulings in other states.

These precedents were not controlling: each state supreme court is the
authoritative interpreter of its own state constitution. Nevertheless, the positive
orientation toward precedent in the United States promoted interstate borrow-
ing. This orientation toward precedent created an expectation that judges
would consult and give weight to earlier rulings, even when they were not
strictly controlling. It also encouraged attorneys to rely on out-of-state precedents to bolster their legal arguments. Finally, because state supreme courts
confronted common legal problems, they found it useful to consult how other
states had handled those problems.[44]

THE TORT LAW REVOLUTION AND PRODUCTS–LIABILITY LAW

Tort law deals with civil wrongs (other than breach of contract) that result in
death, personal injury, or property damage, for which a person can sue to recover damages. Thus, tort law cases range from suits in "fender-bender" traffic
accidents, to cases of medical malpractice, to personal-injury cases resulting
from defective or dangerous consumer products. For the most part, state courts
prescribe the rules that govern the resolution of tort-law cases through their
decisions elaborating the common law.

Over the past four decades, these rules have changed dramatically. State
appellate courts have transformed the standards for determining liability, abolished long-standing immunities from suit, and reduced or eliminated many
other barriers to plaintiffs recovering damages for injuries they have suffered.
Particularly controversial have been state courts' innovations relating to prod-

ucts liability, that is, the responsibility of manufacturers or sellers for the injuries suffered by consumers of their products. Some commentators believe that these rulings have enhanced the safety of consumers by raising the costs for businesses of accidents, negligence, and poorly designed products. These higher costs, it is assumed, give businesses an incentive to remove dangerous items from the market and to develop safer products. Other commentators, however, argue that the nation's tort-law system retards innovation and reduces the competitiveness of American firms without enhancing safety.

In this section we examine how state judges have established new policy regarding the obligations of producers to consumers. We document the policy changes that have occurred, consider the factors that have led state courts to inaugurate these changes, review the claims of proponents and opponents about the effects of the tort law revolution, and assess the evidence bearing on those claims. Box 11-3 contains a glossary of terms that may be helpful in understanding the debate over products-liability law.

The Changing Face of Products-Liability Law

The "First Regime" in Products-Liability Law

The "first regime" in tort law (and hence in products-liability law) lasted into the nineteenth century. During this first regime, people were generally held responsible for any harms their actions may have caused. Underlying this standard was the notion that tort law exists primarily to redress injuries. This standard served to retard change in the society. Because a person was responsible for any adverse effects her actions might produce, even inadvertently, the prudent course was to refrain from action, and particularly from risky actions. Put simply, under the first regime one acted at one's own peril.[45]

The "Second Regime" in Products-Liability Law

The "second regime" developed during the nineteenth century, as state courts adapted the common law in response to the shift from an agrarian economy to an industrial one. The key question confronting the courts was how to treat accidental injuries caused by risky, although socially useful, activities.[46] For industrial capitalism to flourish, it was widely assumed, entrepreneurs had to be free to take risks and launch new enterprises without the constraint of legal responsibility for every adverse consequence of their actions. Society would presumably benefit if producers' freedom of action was maximized, even if this

BOX 11-3   A PRODUCTS LIABILITY GLOSSARY

ASSUMPTION OF RISK: The rule that persons accept the risks inherent in situations they willingly enter, like the taking of a dangerous job, and therefore cannot claim damages if they are injured.

COMPARATIVE NEGLIGENCE: The rule that plaintiff's recovery will be reduced in proportion to the degree that his own negligence was responsible for his injury.

CONTRIBUTORY NEGLIGENCE: The rule that plaintiff may not recover damages if he is wholly or partially responsible for his injury.

DESIGN DEFECT: A defect in a product resulting from the fact that, although the product was manufactured as it was designed, the design was not as safe as it should have been.

ENTERPRISE LIABILITY: Under this standard, liability rests upon each member of an industry that produced a product that harmed consumers, with liability usually apportioned according to each member's share of the market for that product.

FAILURE TO WARN: The failure of a defendant in a products liability case to have provided adequate warnings or instructions regarding the use of its product.

FELLOW SERVANT RULE: The rule that employers were not liable for workers' injuries brought about by the negligence of a fellow worker; they were liable only when they were personally at fault.

MANUFACTURING DEFECT: A defect resulting from a product's not having been manufactured as it had been designed.

NEGLIGENCE: Breach of a duty by the defendant to exercise due care.

PRIVITY OF CONTRACT: The contractual relationship between buyer and seller, which provided a basis for liability for defective products. Traditionally, however, consumers under this doctrine could not sue manufacturers for defective goods unless they had bought the goods directly from the manufacturer.

PUNITIVE DAMAGES: In cases in which it is proved that the defendant acted willfully, maliciously, or fraudulently, a plaintiff may be awarded punitive or exemplary damages in addition to compensatory damages to punish the defendant or set an example for similar wrongdoers.

STATE-OF-THE-ART DEFENSE: The defense that permits a defendant to avoid liability in a design defect case if at the time of manufacture there was no safer design available, or in a failure to warn case if at the time of

continued on p. 383

continued from p. 382
manufacture there was no way for the defendant to have known of the danger he failed to warn against.

STRICT LIABILITY: Under this standard, one who sells a product in a defective condition unreasonably dangerous to a consumer is held liable for harm caused by the defect.

TORT: Any civil legal wrong, other than a breach of contract, that results in personal injury, death, or property damage, and for which a person can sue to recover damages.

meant that the "quiet citizen must keep out of the way of the exuberantly active one."[47]

One crucial aspect of the shift from the first regime to the second was a reconceptualization of the aims of tort law. State judges during the nineteenth century began to view tort law as primarily concerned with deterring injurious conduct. This switch in orientation, from redressing injuries to deterring misconduct, had far-reaching consequences. No longer was one responsible for all injuries caused by one's actions. Under the second regime, only if those injuries were foreseeable, and if one failed to exercise due care to avoid them, was one liable. In thus enshrining *negligence* as the standard for determining liability, state courts imparted a moral dimension to tort law; one was liable only when one's actions were blameworthy. But adoption of the negligence standard also made it more difficult for plaintiffs to secure redress for injuries, because they had to prove not only that the defendant's actions injured them but also that the defendant had acted negligently. As Oliver Wendell Holmes summed it up, "the general principle of our law is that loss from accident must lie where it falls, and that principle is not affected by the fact that a human being is the instrument of misfortune."[48]

State courts also limited producers' tort liability by modifying the traditional understanding of to whom obligations were owed. Under the first regime, one's duty of care was universal, extending to all people. Under the second regime, however, contract emerged as the primary basis for establishing obligations. If a producer entered into a contract with a purchaser, then they were in privity of contract, and courts would enforce the obligations established by the contract. But if one did not enter into a contract with another person, then the common law generally assumed that one had no duties toward that person. Moreover, producers could reduce the risk of products–liability suits by disclaiming responsibility in sales contracts for injuries that their products might cause.

Finally, state courts developed various other legal doctrines—the fellow servant rule, assumption of risk, and contributory negligence—that served to immunize producers from liability. Perhaps the most important of these was the contributory negligence doctrine, under which plaintiffs were barred from recovery if their own negligence had contributed, no matter how slightly, to the injury they suffered. Although state courts during the early twentieth century devised various exceptions that eased the burdens on plaintiffs, the general thrust of legal developments during the second regime was to restrict the compensatory function of the law of torts.[49]

Liability Under the Second Regime

To clarify the implications of the policies adopted by state courts under the second regime, consider the following scenarios:[50]

* - Helen Henningsen was injured when the ten-day-old Plymouth she was driving crashed as a result of defects in the vehicle's steering system. She sued both the dealer who sold the car to her husband and the manufacturer, seeking reimbursement for her medical expenses and for the cost of repairs to the car.

* - When David Larsen's Chevrolet Corvair collided head on with another car, the force of the collision thrust the Corvair's steering column into Larsen's head. He sued General Motors, which manufactured the car, claiming that its design was unsafe.

* - In the late 1940s several firms produced and marketed DES, a drug given to pregnant women to prevent miscarriages. In 1971 scientists discovered a link between DES and a form of cancer occurring in the daughters of women who took the drug. Because none of the "DES daughters" could identify which firm manufactured the DES taken by her mother, they sued all the manufacturers of DES.

Under the products-liability law that existed in most states from the mid-nineteenth century through the 1950s, the plaintiffs would likely have lost all three cases. In the first case, Mrs. Henningsen had not purchased the car; her husband had. Because she had not formed a contract with the Plymouth dealer, he had no contractual obligation to her. Moreover, even if her husband had been driving when the accident occurred, he could not have collected damages for medical expenses, because the standard purchase agreement he signed limited the dealer's liability to replacement of defective parts. Nor could the Henningsens have collected from the car's manufacturer, even if the vehicle was defective when it left the assembly line. Neither of the Henningsens had privity of contract with Plymouth, and thus the manufacturer had no legal obligations to them. Finally, they could not collect from the dealer who sold them the car, because the defect did not result from negligence on his part.

In the second scenario, David Larsen, the driver of the Corvair, would also not have collected damages under the second regime. Like the Henningsens, he had no contract with the car's manufacturer, and thus he did not meet the requirement of privity of contract. In addition, the collision which led to his injury did not result from a defect in the manufacture of the car; all Corvairs had the same steering column. Finally, Larsen's injury occurred in part because of driver error, and thus the doctrine of contributory negligence, under which plaintiffs are barred from recovery if their actions also contributed to an injury, immunized General Motors.

In the final scenario, no company that produced DES would be held liable because none could be proven to have produced the DES that injured the "DES daughters." In addition, the plaintiffs would also have to prove that the companies either knew of or should have foreseen the carcinogenic properties of DES. For under a negligence standard, one is liable for injuries one causes only if they are foreseeable and preventable.

The "Third Regime" in Products-Liability Law

Beginning in the late 1950s, a fundamental shift occurred in products-liability law, as legal doctrines were developed that facilitated plaintiffs' efforts to obtain redress for injuries. Indicative of this shift is the fact that, under this third regime (contemporary products-liability law), the plaintiffs in all three scenarios were legally entitled to damages for their injuries.

Privity of Contract and Strict Liability

In the first scenario, Mrs. Henningsen was able to recover damages because of the elimination of the requirement of privity of contract. In *Henningsen* v. *Bloomfield Motors* (1960), the New Jersey Supreme Court ruled that when manufacturers offer a product for purchase, the product is accompanied by an implied warranty that it is reasonably suitable for use.[51] Those who are injured by defective products may sue for damages, even if they have no contractual relations with the manufacturer. The court further held that manufacturers could not use contractual provisions to escape liability for injuries caused by their defective products.

Three years after *Henningsen,* the California Supreme Court went even further, adopting strict liability as the standard in products-liability cases.[52] Under the strict-liability standard, the *Henningsen* court's fiction of an implied warranty was no longer necessary; for the manufacturer of a defective product is responsible for any injuries it causes. Strict liability shifts the focus from the conduct of the producer, which was crucial under the negligence standard, to the product itself. All that the plaintiff must prove is that the product was defective and caused the injury.

Once the New Jersey and California supreme courts pioneered these doctrinal changes, other state appellate courts quickly followed their lead. Within a decade and a half, over two-thirds of the states had embraced strict liability and eliminated the requirement of privity of contract. As Lawrence Baum and Bradley Canon put it, "Never before had such a momentous change in tort law swept the American states so rapidly."[53]

Design Defect and Comparative Negligence

In the second scenario, Larsen's injuries did not result from negligence or errors in the construction of his Corvair; the car was manufactured exactly as it had been designed. Under current products-liability law, however, conformity to design specifications is not decisive. State courts have recognized that a defendant may also be liable if the design of the product that caused an injury is defective, that is, if there was a safer alternative design for the product. In Larsen's case, for example, there were ways to design a steering column so that it would not impale the driver's head or chest in the event of a collision. Chevrolet's failure to do so unreasonably created dangers, and thus, Larsen could sue for damages for injuries suffered because of the design defect.

Under the tort doctrines of the second regime, Larsen's contributory negligence—his partial responsibility for the crash would have barred him from recovering for his injuries. In recent years, however, most states have abandoned the contributory negligence standard and adopted the comparative negligence standard in its place. Under this new standard, a plaintiff's partial responsibility does not preclude recovery for his injuries. Rather, the damages he receives are merely reduced in proportion to the degree that his own negligence was responsible for his injury.

It is hard to overestimate the importance of these changes in expanding plaintiff's opportunities to obtain redress. Adoption of the comparative negligence has eliminated a major barrier to products-liability suits. And as Jethro Lieberman has noted, "Strict liability for design defect has become a dominant part of the law governing products because it seems to be the only standard that can reach a large class of injuries left untouched by the earlier doctrines."[54]

Failure to Warn, Enterprise Liability, and Punitive Damages

The third scenario, the DES case, exhibits three more important innovations in contemporary products-liability law. The drug DES did serve the purpose of preventing miscarriages, and arguably no better alternative design may have been available at the time it was produced. Nonetheless, DES was dangerous if used for other than its intended purpose, and even if used for its intended purpose, it had certain residual hazards. The manufacturers of DES, however, did not warn women of the dangers of the drug. Under modern products-liability law, their failure to warn made them strictly liable for injuries caused by the drug. The only recognized exception to this warning requirement is if, at the time of manufacture, there was no way the defendant knew or could have known of the dangers he failed to warn against (the so-called "state of the art defense"). Some states do not allow even this defense against failure-to-warn claims.[55]

Courts have also permitted recovery even when, as in the DES case, plaintiffs could not identify which company had manufactured the product that harmed them. Rather than deny relief, courts established the doctrine of enterprise liability, under which all manufacturers of a product are required to pay damages for injuries it caused. Thus, in the DES case the court apportioned liability among the companies that had produced the drug on the basis of their market shares. The doctrine of enterprise liability has proved particularly helpful in assessing liability in so-called toxic torts cases, such as those involving exposure to asbestos or Agent Orange, in in which a very large number of plaintiffs have been injured by a generic product.[56]

Finally, when the defendant's conduct was willful, malicious, or fraudulent, courts may award punitive damages as well as compensation for injuries. Punitive damages punish defendants by imposing costs on them greater than the injuries they caused. They also warn other potential wrongdoers of the costs of misconduct and therefore may deter such behavior. Because jury imposition of punitive damages can substantially increase the liability of defendants, they have become very controversial.

Causes of the Revolution in Products-Liability Law

The dramatic transformation of judicial policy from the second to the third regime, like that from the first regime to the second, reflected changes in both social conditions and social philosophy. The industrialization of the American economy in the last half of the nineteenth century led to increased work-related accidents, as workers dealt with more dangerous machinery and materials. Consumers benefited from the wider range of products on the market but often lacked the technical expertise to assess the engineering or safety of modern goods. Moreover, they could not individually bargain with mass producers for guarantees that the goods they bought were safe and durable. Yet when consumers and workers were injured, the system of products-liability law during the second regime made it difficult for them to collect damages.[57]

This policy on products liability meshed with the laissez-faire economic theory and the philosophy of rugged individualism that were dominant in the late nineteenth and early twentieth centuries. But over time, the prevailing social and legal philosophy changed, and as it did, it affected perspectives on the relationship between producers and consumers. Lawrence Friedman has characterized the new perspective as an expectation of "total justice," a notion that one should obtain redress for any harm one suffers.[58] Jethro Lieberman has described the emergence of a "fiduciary ethic," a sense that individuals have a duty to see that their actions do not harm others.[59] If policy on products liability was to reflect these changing societal conditions and views, it would have to do more than mitigate the harshness of privity of contract and other legal doctrines.[60] The new policy would have to take compensating the victims of accidents rather than deterring misconduct as its primary aim.[61]

Although changing conditions and views may have provided the impetus for a shift in policy, the shift could not occur unless state judges were willing to overrule precedents and enunciate new legal standards.[62] Initially, some judges refused to do so, maintaining that the doctrine of *stare decisis* required them to adhere to established legal principles. As one judge put it, "The judicial wastebasket should not be filled with precedents only a few years old."[63] Other judges, likewise insisting on judicial restraint, argued that policymaking was the province of legislatures, not courts. Yet some activist state judges concluded that neither respect for precedent nor judicial role constraints prevented them from reforming products-liability law. Alteration of policies on products liability, they argued, could not be a usurpation of legislative authority, because those policies had been established by judges. Furthermore, courts were responsible for the growth of the common law as well as for maintaining legal stability. Thus, the New Jersey Supreme Court forthrightly declared: "The law should be based on current concepts of what is right and just, and the judiciary should be alert to the never ending need for keeping common law principles abreast of the times."[64]

When activist courts, like the New Jersey and California supreme courts, initiated changes in products-liability law, they dramatically altered the situation.

Legal principles that had previously appeared settled were settled no longer, and indeed the movement appeared to be away from previously established positions. Moreover, the rulings of these activist courts appeared to have vindicated the legitimacy of court-initiated policy changes. Finally, although most state appellate courts were reluctant to take a leadership role, they were equally reluctant to defend legal doctrines that had been repudiated by a majority of their sister courts. In sum, by challenging the established doctrines in products-liability law, the activist courts created a momentum that carried less adventuresome courts along the path of reform.[65]

The Consequences of Policy Change

According to their proponents, the reforms in products-liability policy have ensured safer consumer goods by inducing manufacturers to improve product safety rather than risk costly suits for injuries caused by their products.[66] Although producers would bear the costs of injuries under the new products-liability policy, proponents assumed that this was not a problem, because producers could figure those costs into the prices of the goods they sold and could purchase liability insurance to reduce their risks.[67]

According to critics of the products-liability reforms, however, that is not the way things have worked out. The changes in products-liability law, they claim, have transformed "the doers, the makers, and the providers of this world ... into perpetual prey, pursued and worried at every turn by a hound-like legal profession."[68] Erratic and excessive jury awards have prompted insurance companies to refuse coverage—one company official found the United States "as unpredictable from an underwriter's point of view as a banana republic."[69] And American firms, deterred from innovation by the threat of lawsuits, have found themselves at a competitive disadvantage in the global marketplace. Let us examine these charges.

The Critique of Products-Liability Reforms

Innovation and the Range of Goods

Critics claim that changes in products-liability policy have deterred entrepreneurial innovation, to the detriment of consumers and of the nation's place in the world economy.[70] Under a system of strict liability, jurors focus on the defects in products rather than on the care taken in design and production to reduce risks for consumers. These jurors, critics claim, tend to sympathize with accident victims and are predisposed to assume that the new is more dangerous than the familiar. Therefore, they tend to award damages whenever a plaintiff using a new product is injured, even in the face of strong scientific evidence against the plaintiff's claim.[71] Even when defendants ultimately prevail, the costs of defending liability suits can be ruinous. For example, although manufacturers of light aircraft won more than 80 percent of products-liability cases brought to trial, liability costs added an estimated $70,000 to the price of each light airplane built in 1987.[72]

Faced with the prospect of excessive and at times capricious damage awards, firms may cease production of safe products or withhold new products from the market. A survey of the nation's 500 largest corporations found that 25 percent claimed to have withdrawn products from the market because of liability or liability insurance problems.[73] Firms also may opt out of particularly risky fields. For example, whereas in the early 1970s there were thirteen pharmaceutical companies pursuing research in contraception and fertility, by the late 1980s there was only one.[74] Other firms may decide to stick with products whose risks are known, rather than develop new products, even if they believe the new products safer. Indeed, a firm that develops a safer product opens itself up to suits by plaintiffs who use the advances to argue that there was a design defect in the earlier, less safe version.

As one commentator summed it up, the "risk of lawsuits is so great, and the consequences so potentially disastrous, that the inevitable result is for more caution in product innovation [in the United States] than in other advanced nations."[75] This not only places American firms at a competitive disadvantage with foreign firms but also deprives Americans of new, desirable, and often safer consumer goods.

Unjustifiable Awards and Frivolous Claims

Critics also charge that contemporary products-liability law exacerbates the worst tendencies of civil juries. Jurors lack the expertise to evaluate complex technical information, but under the strict-liability standard, cases often turn on testimony by scientific experts on the causes of injuries or on defects in product design. Not surprisingly, then, jurors' decisions in products–liability cases often are capricious and unpredictable. In addition, critics allege that jurors tend to be sympathetic to accident victims, hostile to corporations, and eager to impose the costs of accidents on "deep pockets" defendants rather than on individuals.[76] Judgments under current products-liability law reflect those biases, with plaintiffs reaping excessive and undeserved damage awards and defendants saddled with punitive damages.[77] No plaintiff was awarded a million dollars until 1964; now million dollar verdicts are routine.[78]

These unjustified verdicts and excessive awards, the critics charge, merely encourage more products-liability litigation, as plaintiffs seek to cash in and attorneys to earn large contingent fees at the expense of producers.[79] The pro-plaintiff bias of civil juries, as well as the capriciousness of their verdicts, also affects the settlement of products-liability cases. Fearful of an excessive award if they take a case to trial, defendants may settle cases, even when the claims against them lack merit.[80] Yet this too promotes more products-liability suits.

Costs and Benefits

What are the costs of this system of products liability? According to the Institute on Civil Justice, the United States spent between $29 billion and $36 billion on tort litigation in 1985.[81] (Products-liability cases are only a part, though an important part, of overall tort litigation.) Accident victims receive only about half of this sum, with the remainder going to attorneys and insurers for administering the claims settlement process.[82] Despite these enormous expenditures, critics charge, Americans are not significantly safer than they were under the second regime.[83] In sum, the policy adopted by state courts has proven to be an extremely costly but ineffective means of promoting consumer safety.

Evaluating the Evidence

Researchers have only recently begun to systematically gather evidence about these claims. The rather fragmentary research that is available does not fully support either the proponents or the critics of the products-liability policy developed by the courts.

A products-liability litigation explosion?

Critics have charged that the changes in products-liability policy have led to an explosion in litigation against producers. The strongest evidence supporting this claim is the astronomical increase in products-liability suits in federal courts: in 1974, there were less than 2000, but by 1986, there were over 13,000.[84]

Unfortunately, the available data on the caseloads of state courts, which hear the vast majority of products-liability cases, report all tort filings, not merely products-liability cases.[85] Nevertheless, these data do not show an explosion in products-liability filings. During the 1980s, overall tort filings in state courts rose on average roughly three percent annually.[86] Even if products-liability cases increased somewhat faster than tort cases did generally, the change is still modest. Moreover, in many states these increases in tort filings were outstripped by increases in contract and property-rights cases.[87] Instead of an explosion of tort cases, these data suggest that in several states tort cases formed a smaller part of judicial caseloads during the 1980s.

A boon for plaintiffs?

Critics have also charged that the products-liability revolution, combined with jury sympathies for plaintiffs and biases against businesses, has resulted in unwarranted victories for plaintiffs and overgenerous awards when they do prevail. But the reports of outrageous rulings typically used to support these contentions are unconvincing. For one thing, many of these "horror stories" are inaccurate. Critics, for example, often cite a California case in which the company which designed a phone booth was allegedly held liable when a drunk driver crashed into it, injuring a man in the booth. In fact, however, the driver was not drunk, the plaintiff had time to get out of the booth but the door jammed, and the court merely said that the issues raised were appropriate for a jury to consider.[88] Even when case reports are accurate, one cannot generalize on the basis of isolated and unrepresentative cases.

Systematic data on outcomes in products-liability cases are available for only two counties, San Francisco County and Cook County (Chicago). These data reveal that the success rate for plaintiffs in products liability cases has risen—in the 1960s, plaintiffs in Cook County won only one quarter of products-liability cases, but by the 1980s they won roughly one half. The data also show that median jury awards have risen dramatically.[89] Moreover, juries in these jurisdictions award more money when plaintiffs are severely injured and defendants are "deep pockets" organizations, such as businesses.[90]

Although these data seem to support the critics' claims, they should be interpreted cautiously. For one thing, Cook County and San Francisco may be unrepresentative, and plaintiffs may not have fared as well in other jurisdictions. Moreover, the rise of damage awards need not reflect pro-plaintiff or anti-business biases. Part of the rise in damage awards can be attributed to cases involving more serious injuries and larger medical expenses than cases tried at the start of the period.[91] Furthermore, figures on jury awards may be inflated because trial judges or appellate courts may subsequently reduce them. In Cook County and San Francisco, for example, the percentage reduction for jury awards of over $1 million was close to 40 percent.[92] Finally, contrary to critics' claims, interviews with jurors reveal not a bias against business but rather a suspicion of plaintiffs' motives and actions.[93]

What effects on safety and on innovation?

Proponents and critics of the products-liability reforms disagree sharply about how they have affected product safety. Proponents believe that changes in products-liability law and in levels of litigation would prompt producers to devote greater attention to product safety, thereby leading to fewer accidents. The very limited research which is available, however, has found no relationship between these legal changes and accident rates.[94]   Even acknowledging that factors such as technological change and consumer demands may also affect accident rates, there is no concrete evidence vindicating the hopes of products-liability reformers.

Aside from these data, the only other evidence is expert opinion.   One group of economists surveyed product safety in various industries and economic sectors.   They concluded that, except in the chemical industry, changes in products liability law had done little to improve product safety.[95]   When safety improvements did occur, they resulted primarily from adverse publicity generated by litigation about a product's safety and the manufacturer's reputation, which reduced consumer demand.[96]   The economists also concluded that, again with the exception of the chemical industry, changes in products-liability law tended to retard the development and marketing of new products.[97]

Responses to the Products-Liability "Crisis"

Concerns about a crisis in products liability, whether justified or not, have prompted changes in products-liability policy aimed at relieving the burdens on defendants. State legislatures, which have the power to overturn common-law doctrines by statute, have initiated some of the changes.   For example, in 1984 the New Jersey Supreme Court held social hosts responsible for their guests' automobile accidents, when the hosts served them liquor knowing that they were intoxicated and would be driving.[98]   But when three other state courts followed New Jersey's lead in extending liability, they were promptly overruled by statute.[99]   Indeed, from 1985-1988 forty-eight state legislatures enacted reforms affecting products liability.[100]   Some established caps on damages, particularly for non-economic injuries, such as pain and suffering.[101]   Others sought to discourage litigation by placing limits on attorneys' contingent fees or by imposing sanctions on attorneys who file frivolous suits.[102]

Several state supreme courts also modified their policies on products liability during the 1980s.[103]   Some declined to extend doctrines that benefit plaintiffs to new situations.   Thus, they refused to impose strict liability on producers of dangerous but "defectless" products, such as handguns, alcohol, and swimming pools, or on producers who failed to warn victims of scientifically unknown risks.[104]   Other state courts retreated from pro-plaintiff positions.   The New Jersey Supreme Court, for example, limited the imposition of enterprise liability solely to asbestos cases.[105]   Similarly, the California Supreme Court refused to extend liability to a drug company based, among other things, on the effect that would have on drug research and the development of new drugs.[106]

Researchers have also reported changes in the outcomes of products-liability cases.   One study found that plaintiffs prevailed in 40 percent of products-liability cases in federal district courts in 1983 but in only 32 percent three years later.[107] At this point, it is difficult to tell whether this decline in plaintiffs' success rate was due to legal changes or other factors and whether it carried over into state courts as well.

CONCLUSIONS

As the school-finance cases revealed, constitutional policy-making in state courts is influenced by those courts' relations with federal courts, with the supreme courts of other states, and with the other institutions of state government. The development of products-liability law suggests that federal courts have considerably less influence on common-law policymaking. On occasion, it is true, federal rulings may guide state legal developments—for example, charitable institutions were immune from tort suits in most states until a ruling in a federal court of appeals led states to reconsider and eliminate the immunity.[108] But overall, federal courts decide such a miniscule proportion of common-law cases that their opportunities for influence are quite limited. In addition, state courts have traditionally assumed responsibility for the development of the common law and thus have no reason to look to the federal courts for direction.

Considerably more important is the influence of state courts in other states. In dealing with the common law, there is no legal text—no statute, constitutional provision, or administrative regulation—to interpret. Consequently precedent, including the rulings of courts in sister states, becomes more important in guiding judicial decisions. Reliance on precedent contributes to stability in the law when the rulings in various states coincide. But when they diverge, state courts' reliance on precedent can, paradoxically, be a force for legal change. Success by a litigant in one state can encourage litigants in other states to raise the same legal issue. When they do so, they can point to favorable precedents in other states in arguing for legal change. If a state court only consults its own prior cases, respect for precedent, *stare decisis*, would promote legal continuity. But if a court considers precedents from beyond the state's borders, then it may well find conflicting interpretations of the common law. When it does, this conflict diminishes the authority of the court's prior rulings, because those precedents then represent only one possible interpretation of the common law. Or, from a different perspective, the availability of precedents to support both sides in a case gives judges the opportunity to choose which precedent they will follow. Thus, once some states had adopted the strict liability standard, judges in other states could decide whether to follow their own precedents or to join the movement to strict liability.

The development of products-liability law during the third regime also reveals that common-law policymaking takes place within the context of state politics. State legislators can by statute overturn legal principles enunciated by judges and redirect the course of the common law. For example, during the 1980s, when the products-liability rulings of state judges were viewed as tilting the balance too much in favor of plaintiffs, several state legislatures acted to redress the balance. Moreover, state legislatures may affect the course of the common law even without legislating. After all, the potential for legislative intervention may itself act as a constraint on judicial decisions. Still, it would be a mistake to view the relation between state courts and legislators as simply conflictual. Most judicial decisions interpreting the common law provoke no response from legislators. In fact, judicial decisions and legislative responses (or non-responses) can be viewed as a form of implicit negotiation, through which judges and legislators each seek to leave their mark on the common law.

NOTES

1. William J. Brennan, Jr., "State Supreme Court Judge Versus United States Supreme Court Justice: A Change in Function and Perspective," *University of Florida Law Review* 19 (1966), p. 236.

2. See William E. Thro, "To Render Them Safe: The Analysis of State Constitutional Provisions in Public School Finance Reform Litigation," *Virginia Law Review* 75 (1989), p. 1647. For data on the contributions of federal, state, and local sources to school budgets, see *Digest of Educational Statistics 1992* (Washington, D.C.: Department of Education, 1992), p. 152, Table 150.

3. *San Antonio Independent School District* v. *Rodriguez*, 411 U.S. 1, 11-13 (1973).

4. See the discussion of this contention in K. Forbis Jordan and Kern Alexander, "Constitutional Methods of Financing Public Schools," in Kern Alexander and K. Forbis Jordan, eds., *Constitutional Reform of School Finance* (Lexington, Mass.: Lexington Books, 1973).

5. *San Antonio Independent School District* v. *Rodriguez*, 411 U.S. 1 (1973).

6. These cases include: *DuPree* v. *Alma School District No. 30*, 651 S.W.2d 90 (Ark. 1983); *Serrano* v. *Priest* [*Serrano* II], 557 P.2d 929 (Cal. 1976); *Horton* v. *Meskill*, 376 A.2d 359 (Conn. 1977); *Rose* v. *Council for Better Education*, 790 S.W.2d 186 (Ky. 1989); *Helena Elementary School District No. 1* v. *State*, 769 P.2d 684 (Mont. 1989); *Robinson* v. *Cahill*, 303 A.2d 273 (N.J. 1973); *Seattle School District No. 1* v. *State*, 585 P.2d 71 (Wash. 1978); *Pauley* v. *Kelly*, 255 S.E.2d 859 (W.Va. 1979); and *Washakie County School District No. 1* v. *Herschler*, 606 P.2d 310 (Wyo. 1980).

7. *Edgewood Independent School District* v. *Kirby* [*Edgewood* I], 777 S.W.2d 391 (Tex. 1989).

8. *Brown* v. *Board of Education*, 347 U.S. 483 (1954).

9. See, for example, John E. Coons, William H. Clune III, and Stephen D. Sugarman, *Private Wealth and Public Education* (Cambridge: Belknap Press, 1970); and Kern Alexander and K. Forbis Jordan, eds., *Constitutional Reform of School Finance.*

10. See, for example, *Griffin* v. *Illinois*, 351 U.S. 12 (1958); *Douglas* v. *California*, 372 U.S. 353 (1963); and *Harper* v. *Virginia State Board of Elections*, 383 U.S. 663 (1966).

11. *Robinson* v. *Cahill*, 303 A.2d 273 (N.J. 1973).

12. New Jersey Constitution, Article VIII, sec. 14, para. 1.

13. Wesley W. Horton, "Memoirs of a Connecticut School Finance Lawyer," *Connecticut Law Review* 24 (Spring 1992), p. 706.

14. The cases during this period in which plaintiffs' challenges succeeded are listed in note 6 above. Unsuccessful challenges included: *Thompson* v. *Engleking*, 537 P.2d 635 (Ida. 1975); *Milliken* v. *Green*, 203 N.W.2d 457 (Mich. 1972); *Woodahl* v. *Straub*, 520 P.2d 776 (Mont. 1974); *Board of Education* v. *Walter*, 390 N.E.2d 813 (Ohio 1979); *Olsen* v. *Oregon*, 554 P.2d 139 (Ore. 1976); and *Danson* v. *Casey*, 399 A.2d 476 (Pa. 1978).

15. School-finance reformers enjoyed their only success during this period in *Dupree* v. *Alma School District No. 30*, 651 S.W.2d 90 (Ark. 1983). Unsuccessful challenges included: *Lujan* v. *State Board of Education*, 649 P.2d 1005 (Col. 1982); *Thompson* v. *McDaniels*, 285 S.E.2d 156 (Ga. 1981); *Hornbeck* v. *Somerset County Board of Education*, 458 A.2d 758 (Md. 1983); *Board of Education* v. *Nyquist*, 439 N.E.2d 359 (N.Y. 1982); *Fair School Finance Council of Oklahoma, Inc.* v. *State*, 746 P.2d 1135 (Okla. 1987); and *Richland County* v. *Campbell*, 364 S.E.2d 470 (S.C. 1988).

16. The cases during this period in which plaintiffs' challenges succeeded are listed in note 7 above. The only unsuccessful challenge was *Kukor* v. *Grover*, 436 N.W.2d 568 (Wisc. 1989).

17. *Abbott* v. *Burke*, 575 A.2d 359, 394 (N.J. 1990).

18. As William E. Thro has observed, "Regardless of when the case was brought, the state constitutional provision ruled upon, or the wording of the state constitutional provision, the outcomes were totally unpredictable." See his "The Third Wave: The Impact of the Montana, Kentucky, and Texas Decisions on the Future of Public School Finance Reform," *Journal of Law and Education* 19 (Spring 1990), pp. 231-232.

19. *Board of Education* v. *Nyquist*, 439 N.E.2d 359, 369 (1982). Our analysis in this paragraph is similar to that in *State Constitutions in the Federal System; Selected Issues and Opportunities for State Initiatives* (Washington, D.C.: Advisory Commission on Intergovernmental Relations, 1989), p. 112.

20. *Thompson* v. *Engleking*, 537 P.2d 635, 640-41 (Id. 1975).

21. See, for example, *Helena Elementary School District No. 1* v. *State*, 769 P.2d 684, 689-90 (Mont. 1989).

22. *Pauley* v. *Kelly*, 255 S.E.2d 859, 877 (W. Va. 1979).

23. *Rose* v. *Council for Better Education*, 790 S.W.2d 186, 212 (Ky. 1989).

24. Janice C. May, "Financing Public Schools in Texas: A Protracted Imbroglio," *State Constitutional Commentaries and Notes* 2 (Fall 1990), p. 9.

25. The New Jersey Supreme Court has a tradition of unanimity in major cases. See G. Alan Tarr and Mary Cornelia Aldis Porter, *State Supreme Courts in State and Nation* (New Haven: Yale University Press, 1988), Chapter 5.

26. Donald L. Horowitz, *The Courts and Social Policy* (Washington, D.C.: Brookings, 1977). For a detailed discussion of Horowitz's critique of judicial policymaking capacity, see Chapter 9.

27. *Serrano* v. *Priest*, 557 P.2d 929 (Cal. 1977). For a comparison of the *Serrano* approach with that in later cases, see Charles S. Benson, "Definitions of Equity in School Finance in Texas, New Jersey, and Kentucky," *Harvard Journal on Legislation* 28 (Summer 1991): 401-421.

28. Ibid., p. 405, n. 20.

29. Debate on the relation between levels of funding and quality of education has been a constant aspect of finance-reform efforts. Recent contributions to this literature include: Eric A. Hanushek, "When School Finance 'Reform' May Not Be Good Policy," *Harvard Journal on Legislation* 28 (Summer 1991): 423-456, and Ronald F. Ferguson, "Paying for Public Education: New Evidence on How and Why Money Matters," *Harvard Journal on Legislation* 28 (Summer 1991): 465-498.

30. Mary Cornelia Porter and G. Alan Tarr, "Introduction," in Mary Cornelia Porter and G. Alan Tarr, eds., *State Supreme Courts: Policymakers in the Federal System* (Westport, Conn.: Greenwood Press, 1982), p. xvii.

31. Ibid.

32. On school-finance reform in Kentucky, see Kern Alexander, "The Common School Ideal and the Limits of Legislative Authority: The Kentucky Case," *Harvard Journal on Legislation* 28 (Summer 1991): 341-366, and Bert T. Combs, "Creative Constitutional Law: The Kentucky School Reform Law," *Harvard Journal on Legislation* 28 (Summer 1991): 367-378.

33. On school-finance reform in Texas, see May, "Financing Public Schools in Texas," and William P. Hobby and Billy D. Walker, "Legislative Reform of the Texas Public School Finance System, 1973-1991," *Harvard Journal on Legislation* 28 (Summer 1991): 379-394.

34. On the politics of school-finance reform after *Robinson* v. *Cahill*, see Richard Lehne, *The Quest for Justice; The Politics of School Finance Reform* (New York: Longman, 1978).

35. The analysis here follows that in Tarr and Porter, *State Supreme Courts in State and Nation*, p. 217.

36. Useful overview of the new judicial federalism include *State Constitutions in the Federal System*, Chapters 4-6, and "Special Issue: New Developments in State Constitutional Law," *Publius: The Journal of Federalism* 17 (Winter 1987): 1-179.

37. See Barry Latzer, *State Constitutions and Criminal Justice* (Westport, Conn.: Greenwood Press, 1991).

38. Rulings enunciating distinctive state standards include: for search and seizure, *State* v. *Boland*, 800 P.2d 1112 (Wash. 1990); for double jeopardy, see *State* v. *Lachat*, 343 S.E.2d 872 (N.C. 1986); and for self-incrimination, *State* v. *Mercier*, 509 A.2d 1246 (1986).

39. *Sterling* v. *Cupp*, 625 P.2d 123 (Ore. 1981).

40. On privacy, see *In re Quinlan*, 355 A.2d 647 (N.J. 1976); on gender equality, see *Opinion of the Justices to the House of Representatives*, 371 N.E.2d 426 (Mass. 1977), and—more generally— G. Alan Tarr and Mary Cornelia Porter, "Gender Equality and Judicial Federalism: The Role of State Appellate Courts," *Hastings Constitutional Law Quarterly* 9 (Summer 1982): 919-973; on church and state, see *Fox* v. *City of Los Angeles*, 587 P.2d 663 (Cal. 1978), and—more generally— G. Alan Tarr, "Church and State in the States," *Washington Law Review* 64 (January 1989): 73-110.

41. On free speech, see *Robins* v. *Pruneyard Shopping Center*, 592 P.2d 341 (Cal. 1979); on equal protection of the laws, see *Washakie County School District* v. *Herschler*, 606 P.2d 310 (Wy. 1980).

42. See Porter and Tarr, *State Supreme Courts*, pp. xix-xx.

43. Ibid., p. xxi.

44. Tarr and Porter, *State Supreme Courts in State and Nation*, pp. 27-30.

45. This account relies on Jethro Lieberman, *The Litigious Society* (New York: Basic Books, 1981), pp. 34-36.

46. G. Edward White, *Tort Law in America; An Intellectual History* (New York: Oxford University Press, 1985), p. 61.

47. Quoted in Lieberman, *The Litigious Society*, p. 37. On the development of tort law doctrine during the second regime, see—in addition to Lieberman—Morton J. Horwitz, *The Transformation of American Law, 1780-1860* (Cambridge: Harvard University Press, 1977), and White, *Tort Law in America*, Chapters 2-4.

48. Quoted in Lieberman, *The Litigious Society*, p. 36. On the various—and at times competing—ends of tort law, see Robert E. Litan, Peter Swire, and Clifford Winston, "The U.S. Liability System: Background and Trends," in Robert E. Litan and Clifford Winston, eds., *Liability; Perspectives and Policy* (Washington, D.C.: Brookings, 1988), pp. 3-5.

49. White, *Tort Law in America*, pp. 61-62; perhaps the most important case alleviating the harshness of tort-law doctrine is *MacPherson* v. *Buick Motor Co.*, 111 N.E. 1050 (N.Y. 1916).

50. These scenarios are based on actual cases. The first scenario is discussed in G. Alan Tarr and Mary Cornelia Aldis Porter, *State Supreme Courts in State and Nation* (New Haven: Yale University Press, 1988), pp. 225-226. The second and third scenarios are drawn from Peter W. Huber, *Liability; The Legal Revolution and Its Consequences* (New York: Basic Books, 1988), pp. 38 and 81.

51. *Henningsen* v. *Bloomfield Motors*, 161 A.2d 69 (N.J. 1960).

52. *Greenman* v. *Yuma Power Products Co.*, 377 P.2d 897 (Cal. 1963).

53. Lawrence Baum and Bradley C. Canon, "State Supreme Courts as Activists: New Doctrines in the Law of Torts," in Porter and Tarr, *State Supreme Courts*, p. 88.

54. Lieberman, *The Litigious Society*, p. 43.

55. For rulings rejecting the state-of-the-art defense, see *Beshada* v. *Johns-Manville Products Corp.*, 447 A.2d 539 (N.J. 1982), and *Majdic* v. *Cincinnati Machine Co.*, 537 A.2d 334 (Pa. 1988). For a recent ruling upholding it, see *Bernier* v. *Raymond Industries*, 539 A.2d 621 (Me. 1988). For commentary on the defense and on state rulings regarding it, see "Defeat for the State-of-the-Art Defense in New Jersey Products Liability: *Beshada* v. *Johns-Manville Products Corp.*," *Rutgers Law Journal* 14 (1983): 953-975.

56. The DES case is *Sindell* v. *Abbott Laboratories*, 607 P.2d 924 (Cal. 1980).

57. This account relies on Lieberman, *The Litigious Society*, pp. 38-40, and White, *Tort Law in America*, Chapters 3-4.

58. Lawrence M. Friedman, *Total Justice* (New York: Russell Sage Foundation, 1985), Chapter 4.

59. See Lieberman, *The Litigious Society*, Chapter 1.

60. See Baum and Canon, "State Supreme Courts as Activists," pp. 87-88.

61. White, *Tort Law in America*, pp. 176-178.

62. The analysis in this paragraph relies on Robert Keeton, *Venturing to Do Justice; Reforming the Private Law* (Cambridge: Harvard University Press, 1969), and Baum and Canon, "State Supreme Courts as Activists," pp. 93-97.

63. *Cochran* v. *Keeton*, 252 So.2d 313, 318 (Ala. 1971), quoted in Baum and Canon, "State Supreme Courts as Activists," p. 96. For a more detailed assessment of the Alabama Supreme Court's changing perspective on tort law reform, see Tarr and Porter, *State Supreme Courts in State and Nation*, Chapter 3.

64. *Schipper* v. *Levitt and Sons*, 207 A.2d 314, 325 (N.J. 1965), quoted in Baum and Canon, "State Supreme Courts as Activists," p. 96. For a discussion of the New Jersey Supreme Court's orientation toward modernization of the common law, see Tarr and Porter, *State Supreme Courts in State and Nation*, Chapter 5.

65. Tarr and Porter, *State Supreme Courts in State and Nation*, pp. 39-40.

66. Litan, Swire, and Winston, "The U.S. Liability System," p. 3, and Edward J. Kionka, *Torts in a Nutshell; Injuries to Persons and Property* (St. Paul: West, 1977), pp. 12-13.

67. On the importance of the development of liability insurance to tort-law reform, see Baum and Canon, "State Supreme Courts as Activists," p. 86. Judicial recognition of its importance is found in *Henningsen* v. *Bloomfield Motors*, and *Seely* v. *White Motor Co.*, 403 P.2d 145 (Cal. 1965).

68. Huber, *Liability*, p. 154.

69. Ibid., p. 141.

70. The critics' account of how changes in products-liability policy have affected innovation is drawn from Huber, *Liability*, especially Chapters 1 and 10, and from Peter W. Huber and Robert E. Litan, "Overview," in Huber and Litan, eds., *The Liability Maze; The Impact of Liability Law on Safety and Innovation* (Washington, D.C.: Brookings, 1991).

71. See Peter W. Huber, *Galileo's Revenge; Junk Science in the Courtroom* (New York: Basic Books, 1991).

72. Robert Martin, "General Aviation Manufacturing: An Industry Under Siege," in Huber and Litan, *The Liability Maze*, pp. 483-484.

73. Reported in W. Kip Viscusi and Michael J. Moore, "An Industrial Profile of the Links Between Product Liability and Innovation," in Huber and Litan, *The Liability Maze*, p. 81.

74. R. H. Weaver, *Impact of Product Liability on the Development of New Medical Technologies* (Chicago: American Medical Association, 1988). p. 9.

75. Michael E. Porter, *The Competitive Advantage of Nations* (New York: Free Press, 1990), p. 649.

76. See generally Huber, *Liability*, and Walter K. Olson, *The Litigation Explosion: What Happened When America Unleashed the Lawsuit* (New York: Dutton, 1991).

77. See, for example, Litan, Swire, and Winston, "The U.S. Liability System: Background and Trends," in Litan and Winston, *Liability*, pp. 7-10; and Huber, *Liability*, p. 10.

78. Lieberman, *The Litigious Society*, p. 34.

79. For a summary of pertinent sources, see Stephen Daniels, "The Question of Jury Competence and the Politics of Civil Justice Reform: Symbols, Rhetoric, and Agenda-Building," *Law and Contemporary Problems* 52 (Autumn 1989), pp. 269-270.

80. Ibid., pp. 279-280.

81. James S. Kakalik and Nicholas M. Pace, *Costs and Compensation Paid in Tort Litigation* (Santa Monica, Cal.: Rand Corporation, Institute for Civil Justice, 1986), pp. ix-x.

82. Ibid.

83. See George L. Priest, "Products Liability Law and the Accident Rate," in Litan and Winston, *Liability*.

84. These data, derived from the Administrative Office of the United States Courts, are reported in ibid., p. 187, Table 7-1.

85. Deborah R. Hensler, Mary E. Vaiana, James S. Kakalik, and Mark A. Peterson, *Trends in Tort Litigation; The Story Behind the Statistics* (Santa Monica, Cal.: Rand Corporation, Institute for Civil Justice, 1987), p. 6; and *State Court Caseload Statistics: Annual Report 1990* (Williamsburg, Va.: National Center for State Courts, 1992), pp. 21-23.

86. *State Court Caseload Statistics*, p. 21.

87. Ibid., p. 25.

88. Daniels, "The Question of Jury Competence and the Politics of Civil Justice Reform," pp. 292-297.

89. Hensler et al., *Trends in Tort Litigation*, p. 19.

90. Audrey Chin and Mark A. Peterson, *Deep Pockets, Empty Pockets; Who Wins in Cook County Jury Trials* (Santa Monica, Cal.: Rand Corporation, Institute for Civil Justice, 1985), pp. 41-44.

91. See Mark A. Peterson, *Civil Juries in the 1980s: Trends in Jury Trials and Verdicts in California and Cook County, Illinois* (Santa Monica, Cal.: Rand Corporation, Institute for Civil Justice, 1987).

92. Hensler et al., *Trends in Tort Litigation*, p. 22.

93. Valerie P. Hans and William S. Lofquist, "Jurors' Judgments of Business Liability in Tort Cases: Implications for the Litigation Explosion Debate," *Law & Society Review* 26 (1992): 85-115.

94. See Priest, "Products Liability Law and the Accident Rate;" and George L. Priest, "The New Legal Structure of Risk Control," *Daedalus* (Fall 1990): 207-227.

95. Huber and Litan, "Overview," *The Liability Maze*, pp. 12-15.

96. Ibid., pp. 10-11.

97. Ibid., pp. 16-18.

98. *Kelly* v. *Gwinnel*, 476 A.2d 1219 (N.J. 1984).

99. Huber, *Liability*, p. 76.

100. Joseph Sanders and Craig Joyce, "'Off to the Races': The 1980s Tort Crisis and the Law Reform Process," *Houston Law Review* 27 (March 1990), pp. 218-223; see also Robert E. Litan and Clifford Winston, "Policy Options," in Litan and Winston *Liability*, pp. 230-231, Table 8-2.

101. Litan and Winston, "Policy Options," pp. 232-233, Table 8-3.

102. Ibid., p. 229, and Sanders and Joyce, "Off to the Races," p. 257.

103. The analysis in this paragraph relies on Teresa M. Schwartz, "Products Liability Reform by the Judiciary," *Gonzaga Law Review* 27 (1991/92): 303-334; and Joseph A. Henderson, Jr., and Theodore Eisenberg, "The Quiet Revolution in Products Liability: An Empirical Study of Legal Change," *UCLA Law Review* 37 (February 1990): 479-553.

104. Schwartz, "Products Liability Reform by the Judiciary."

105. *Feldman* v. *Lederle Laboratories*, 479 A.2d 374 (N.J. 1984), narrowing *Beshada* v. *Johns-Manville Products Corporation*, 447 A.2d 539 (N.J. 1982).

106 *Brown* v. *Superior Court*, 751 P.2d 470 (Cal. 1988).

107. These data are reported in Henderson and Eisenberg, "The Quiet Revolution in Products Liability," pp. 503-507.

108. *Georgetown College* v. *Hughes,* 130 F.2d 810 (1942). See more generally Bradley C. Canon and Dean Jaros, "The Impact of Changes in Judicial Doctrines: The Abrogation of Charitable Immunity," *Law & Society Review* 13 (1979): 969-986.

FOR FURTHER READING

This volume has provided an introduction to the judicial process and judicial policymaking. Readers interested in exploring these subjects further may wish to read pertinent judicial decisions. They may also consult the books and other materials listed below.

JUDICIAL DECISIONS

United States Reports is the official publication of United States Supreme Court decisions. Currently over 500 volumes in length, it contains the text of every Supreme Court decision. To find a case, one uses the case's citation. For example, the citation for *Gideon* v. *Wainwright* is 372 U.S. 335. The "U.S." indicates that the case is found in U.S. Reports. The number preceding "U.S." is the volume of U. S. Reports in which the case is found, and the number following it is the page number on which the case begins. Thus, *Gideon* v. *Wainwright* begins on page 335 of volume 372 of U.S. Reports. Prior to their publication in U. S. Reports, current Court rulings can be found in a loose-leaf format in *U.S. Law Week*.

The same sort of citation system is used to locate decisions of lower federal courts and of state courts. The *Federal Reporter* series includes most decisions of the United States Courts of Appeals, and the *Federal Supplement* series contains selected decisions of the United States District Courts. Some states publish an official reporter series with the text of selected state appellate rulings. These rulings may also be found in the *National Reporter* series, published by West Publishing Company, which groups the decisions of state appellate courts in regional reporters. The *South Eastern Reporter*, for example, contains state appellate rulings from Georgia, North Carolina, South Carolina, Virginia, and West Virginia.

CHAPTER 1: COURTS AND LAW

Blackstone, William. *Commentaries on the Law of England*. Chicago: University of Chicago Press, 1979.

David, Rene, and John Brierly. *Major Legal Systems of the World Today*. 2nd edition; London: Stevens & Sons, 1978.

Farnsworth, E. Allan. *An Introduction to the Legal System of the United States*. 2nd edition; London: Oceana Publications, 1983.

Friedman, Lawrence M. *A History of American Law*. 2nd ed.; New York: Simon & Schuster, 1983.

Galanter, Marc, "Reading the Landscape of Disputes: What We Know and Don't Know (and Think We Know) About Our Allegedly Contentious and Litigious Society," *UCLA Law Review* 3 (1983): 4-71.

Glendon, Mary Ann. *Rights Talk: The Impoverishment of Political Discourse.* New York: Maxwell Macmillan, 1991.

Horwitz, Morton J. *The Transformation of American Law, 1760-1860.* Cambridge: Harvard University Press, 1977.

Hurst, J. Willard. *The Growth of American Law: The Law Makers.* Boston, Little, Brown, 1950.

Merryman, John H. *The Civil Law Tradition.* Stanford, Calif.: Stanford University Press, 1969.

Plucknett, Theodore F. T. *A Concise History of the Common Law*, 5th edition; Boston: Little, Brown, 1956.

Watson, Alan. *The Making of the Civil Law.* Cambridge: Harvard University Press, 1981.

Zweigert, Konrad, and Hein Kotz. *Introduction to Comparative Law.* 2nd revised edition; Oxford: Clarendon Press, 1987.

CHAPTER 2: THE FEDERAL AND STATE COURT SYSTEMS

Ball, Howard. *Courts and Politics: The Federal Judicial System.* 2nd ed.; Englewood Cliffs, N.J.: Prentice-Hall, 1987.

Bator, Paul M., Paul J. Mishkin, David L. Shapiro, and Herbert Wechsler. *Hart and Wechsler's The Federal Courts in the Federal System.* 2nd ed.; Mineola, N.Y.: Foundation Press, 1980.

Berkson, Larry, and Susan Carbon. *Court Unification: History, Politics, and Implementation.* Washington, D.C.: National Institute of Law Enforcement and Criminal Justice, 1978.

Dubois, Philip L., ed. *The Analysis of Judicial Reform.* Lexington, Mass.: Lexington Books, 1982.

_____, ed. *The Politics of Judicial Reform.* Lexington, Mass.: Lexington Books, 1982.

Gates, John B., and Charles A. Johnson, eds. *The American Courts: A Critical Assessment.* Washington, D.C.: CQ Press, 1991.

Howard, J. Woodford, Jr. *Courts of Appeals in the Federal Judicial System.* Princeton: Princeton University Press, 1981.

Lewis, Anthony. *Gideon's Trumpet.* New York: Vintage, 1964.

Posner, Richard A. *The Federal Courts.* Cambridge: Harvard University Press, 1985.

CHAPTER 3: JUDGES

Abraham, Henry. *Justices and Presidents.* 3rd ed.; New York: Oxford University Press, 1992.

Bork, Robert H. *The Tempting of America.* New York: Free Press, 1988.

Bronner, Ethan. *Battle for Justice.* New York: W. W. Norton, 1989.

Coffin, Frank M. *The Ways of a Judge.* Boston: Houghton-Mifflin, 1980.

Danelski, David J. *A Supreme Court Justice Is Appointed.* New York: Random House, 1964.

Dubois, Philip L. *From Ballot to Bench.* Austin: University of Texas Press, 1980.

McFeeley, Neil D. *Appointment of Judges.* Austin: University of Texas Press, 1987.

Murphy, Bruce A. *Fortas: The Rise and Ruin of a Supreme Court Justice.* New York: William Morrow, 1988.

O'Brien, David. *Judicial Roulette.* New York: Priority Press, 1988.

Ryan, John Paul, Allan Ashman, Bruce D. Sales, and Sandra Shane-Dubow. *American Trial Judges.* New York: Free Press, 1980.

Schmidhauser, John. *Judges and Justices.* Boston: Little, Brown, 1979.

Watson, Richard A., and Rondal G. Downing. *The Politics of the Bench and the Bar: Judicial Selection Under the Missouri Non-Partisan Court Plan.* New York: John Wiley & Sons, 1969.

CHAPTER 4: LAWYERS

Abel, Richard L. *American Lawyers.* New York: Oxford University Press, 1989.

Auerbach, Jerold S. *Unequal Justice; Lawyers and Social Change in Modern America.* New York: Oxford University Press, 1976.

Epstein, Cynthia Fuchs. *Women in Law.* New York: Basic Books, 1981.

Heinz, John P., and Edward O. Laumann. *Chicago Lawyers; The Social Structure of the Bar.* New York: Russell Sage Foundation and American Bar Association, 1982.

Kessler, Mark. *Legal Services for the Poor.* Westport, Conn.: Greenwood Press, 1987.

Lawrence, Susan E. *The Poor in Court.* Princeton: Princeton University Press, 1990.

Luban, David. *Lawyers and Justice.* Princeton: Princeton University Press, 1988.

Olson, Susan M. *Clients and Lawyers.* Westport, Conn.: Greenwood Press, 1984.

Spangler, Eve. *Lawyers for Hire.* New Haven: Yale University Press, 1986.

Stevens, Robert. *Law School.* Chapel Hill: University of North Carolina Press, 1983.

Stewart, James B. *The Partners: Inside America's Most Powerful Law Firms.* New York: Simon & Schuster, 1983.

Wice, Paul. *Judges and Lawyers; The Human Side of Justice* (New York: Harper Collins, 1991).

CHAPTER 5: TRIALS AND APPEALS

Baum, Lawrence. *The Supreme Court.* 3rd ed.; Washington, D.C.: CQ Press, 1989.

Goldman, Sheldon, and Charles M. Lamb, eds. *Judicial Conflict and Consensus: Behavioral Studies of American Appellate Courts.* Lexington, Ky.: University of Kentucky Press, 1986.

Guide to the U. S. Supreme Court. Washington, D.C.: CQ Press, 1979.

Hans, Valerie P., and Neil Vidmar. *Judging the Jury.* New York: Plenum Press, 1986.

Hastie, Reid, Steven D. Penrod, and Nancy Pennington. *Inside the Jury.* Cambridge: Harvard University Press, 1983.

Kalven, Harry, Jr., and Hans Zeisel. *The American Jury.* Boston: Little Brown, 1966.

Kassin, Saul M., and Lawrence S. Wrightsman, eds. *The Psychology of Evidence and Trial Procedure.* Beverly Hills: Sage Publications, 1985.

Masterson, William A., ed. *Civil Trial Practice: Strategies and Techniques.* New York: Practising Law Institute, 1986.

O'Brien, David M. *Storm Center; The Supreme Court in American Politics.* 2nd ed.; New York: W.W. Norton, 1990.

Perry, H. W., Jr. *Deciding to Decide; Agenda Setting in the United States Supreme Court.* Cambridge: Harvard University Press, 1991.

Provine, Doris Marie. *Case Selection in the United States Supreme Court.* Chicago: University of Chicago Press, 1980.

Rehnquist, William H. *The Supreme Court.* New York: William Morrow, 1987.

Sales, Bruce D., ed. *The Trial Process.* New York: Plenum Press, 1981.

CHAPTER 6: CRIMINAL JUSTICE AND THE COURTS

Boland, Barbara, Catherine H. Conly, Lynn Warner, Ronald Sones, and William Martin. *The Prosecution of Felony Arrests, 1986.* Washington, D.C.: U.S. Department of Justice, Bureau of Justice Statistics, 1989.

Eisenstein, James, and Herbert Jacob. *Felony Justice; An Organizational Analysis of Criminal Courts.* Boston: Little, Brown, 1977.

Feeley, Malcolm M. *The Process Is the Punishment; Handling Cases in a Lower Criminal Court.* New York: Russell Sage Foundation, 1979.

Forst, Brian, Judith Lucianovic, and Sarah J. Cox. *What Happens After Arrest?* Washington, D.C.: National Institute of Law Enforcement and Criminal Justice, 1977.

Friedman, Lawrence M., and Robert V. Percival. *The Roots of Justice: Crime and Punishment in Alameda County, California, 1870-1919.* Chapel Hill: University of North Carolina Press, 1981.

Heumann, Milton. *Plea Bargaining.* Chicago: University of Chicago Press, 1978.

Levin, Martin A. *Urban Politics and the Criminal Courts.* Chicago: University of Chicago Press, 1977.

Nardulli, Peter F., James Eisenstein, and Roy B. Flemming. *The Tenor of Justice.* Urbana: University of Illinois Press, 1988.

Report to the Nation on Crime and Justice. 2nd ed.; Washington, D.C.: U.S. Department of Justice, Bureau of Justice Statistics, 1988.

Scheingold, Stuart A. *The Politics of Law and Order* New York: Longman, 1984.

Shane-DuBow, Sandra, Alice P. Brown, and Erik Olsen. *Sentencing Reform in the United States: History, Content, and Effect.* Washington, D.C.: Government Printing Office, 1985.

Simon, Rita J. and David E. Aaronson. *The Insanity Defense; A Critical Assessment of Law and Policy in the Post-Hinckley Era.* New York: Praeger, 1988.

CHAPTER 7: CIVIL JUSTICE AND THE COURTS

Abel, Richard, ed. *The Politics of Informal Justice.* Orlando, Fla.: Academic Press, 1982.

Bumiller, Kristin. *The Civil Rights Society; The Social Construction of Victims.* Baltimore: Johns Hopkins University Press, 1988.

Friedman, Lawrence M. *Total Justice.* New York: Russell Sage Foundation, 1985.

Harrington, Christine B. *Shadow Justice; The Ideology and Institutionalization of Alternatives to Court.* Westport, Conn.: Greenwood Press, 1985.

Lieberman, Jethro K. *The Litigious Society.* New York: Basic Books, 1981.

McGillis, Daniel. *Community Dispute Resolution Programs and Public Policy.* Washington, D.C.: U.S. Department of Justice, National Institute of Justice, 1986.

McIntosh, Wayne V. *The Appeal of Civil Law; A Political-Economic Analysis of Litigation.* Urbana: University of Illinois Press, 1990.

McLauchlan, William P. *American Legal Processes.* New York: John Wiley & Sons, 1977.

Nader, Laura, ed. *Access to Justice; Alternatives to the American Judicial System.* New York: Academic Press, 1980.

Olson, Walter K. *The Litigation Explosion; What Happened When America Unleashed the Lawsuit.* New York: Truman Talley Books, 1991.

Merry, Sally Engle. *Getting Justice and Getting Even; Legal Consciousness Among Working-Class Americans.* Chicago: University of Chicago Press, 1990.

Schuck, Peter H. *Agent Orange on Trial; Mass Toxic Disasters in the Courts.* Cambridge: Belknap Press, 1986.

Weitzman, Lenore J. *The Divorce Revolution.* New York: Free Press, 1985.

CHAPTER 8: JUDICIAL DECISIONMAKING

Cardozo, Benjamin. *The Nature of the Judicial Process.* New Haven: Yale University Press, 1921.

Carp, Robert A., and C. K. Rowland. *Policymaking and Politics in the Federal District Courts.* Knoxville: University of Tennessee Press, 1983.

Dickerson, Reed. *The Interpretation and Application of Statutes.* Boston: Little, Brown, 1975.

Levi, Edward H. *An Introduction to Legal Reasoning.* Chicago: University of Chicago Press, 1949.

Marshall, Thomas R. *Public Opinion and the Supreme Court.* Boston: Unwin Hyman, 1989.

Murphy, Walter F. *Elements of Judicial Strategy.* Chicago: University of Chicago Press, 1964.

O'Connor, Karen. *Women's Organizations' Use of the Courts.* Lexington, Mass.: Lexington Books, 1980.

Rumble, Wilfrid E., Jr. *American Legal Realism: Skepticism, Reform, and the Judicial Process.* Ithaca, N.Y.: Cornell University Press, 1968.

Wasserstrom, Richard A. *The Judicial Decision: Toward a Theory of Legal Justification.* Stanford, Calif.: Stanford University Press, 1961.

CHAPTER 9: JUDICIAL POLICYMAKING: AN INTRODUCTION

Halpern, Stephen C., and Charles M. Lamb, eds. *Supreme Court Activism and Restraint.* Lexington, Mass.: Lexington Books, 1982.

Horowitz, Donald L. *The Courts and Social Policy.* Washington, D.C.: Brookings, 1977.

Horwitz, Morton J. *The Transformation of American Law, 1780-1860.* Cambridge: Harvard University Press, 1977.

Lieberman, Jethro K. *The Litigious Society.* New York: Basic Books, 1981.

O'Brien, David M. *Storm Center; The Supreme Court in American Politics.* 2nd ed.; New York: Norton, 1990.

Shapiro, Martin. *Who Guards the Guardians? Judicial Control of Administration.* Athens, Ga.: University of Georgia Press, 1988.

Tarr, G. Alan. *Judicial Impact and State Supreme Courts.* Lexington, Mass.: Lexington Books, 1977.

Wolfe, Christopher. *The Rise of Modern Judicial Review.* New York: Basic Books, 1986.

_____. *Judicial Activism; Bulwark of Freedom or Precarious Security.* Pacific Grove, Calif.: Brooks/Cole, 1991.

Yarbrough, Tinsley E. *Judge Frank Johnson and Human Rights in Alabama.* University, Ala.: University of Alabama Press, 1981.

CHAPTER 10: FEDERAL COURT POLICYMAKING

Bell, Derrick, ed. *Shades of* Brown; *New Perspectives on School Desegregation.* New York: Teachers College Press, 1980.

Craig, Barbara H., and David M. O'Brien. *Abortion and American Politics.* Chatham, N.J.: Chatham House, 1993.

Faux, Marian. *Roe v. Wade.* New York: Macmillan, 1988.

Glendon, Mary Ann. *Abortion and Divorce in Western Law.* Cambridge: Harvard University Press, 1987.

Hochschild, Jennifer L. *The New American Dilemma.* New Haven: Yale University Press, 1984.

Johnson, Charles A., and Bradley C. Canon. *Judicial Policies; Implementation and Impact.* Washington, D. C.: CQ Press, 1984.

Kluger, Richard. *Simple Justice.* New York: Alfred A. Knopf, 1975.

Peltason, Jack W. *Fifty-Eight Lonely Men; Southern Federal Judges and School Desegregation.* 2nd ed.; Urbana: University of Illinois Press, 1971.

Rosenberg, Gerald R. *The Hollow Hope; Can Courts Bring About Social Change?* Chicago: University of Chicago Press, 1991.

Rubin, Eva R. *Abortion, Politics, and the Courts.* Westport, Conn.: Greenwood Press, 1987.

Tatalovich, Raymond, and Byron W. Daynes. *The Politics of Abortion: A Study of Community Conflict in Public Policy Making.* New York: Praeger, 1981.

Tushnet, Mark V. *The NAACP's Legal Strategy Against Segregated Education, 1925-1950.* Chapel Hill: University of North Carolina Press, 1987.

Wasby, Stephen L., Anthony D'Amato, and Rosemary Metrailer. *Desegregation from Brown to Alexander.* Carbondale, Ill.: Southern Illinois University Press, 1977.

Wilkinson, J. Harvie. *From Brown to Bakke; The Supreme Court and School Integration, 1954-1968.* New York: Oxford University Press, 1978.

Wolters, Raymond. *The Burden of Brown; Thirty Years of School Desegregation.* Knoxville: University of Tennessee Press, 1984.

CHAPTER 11: STATE COURT POLICYMAKING

Alexander, Kern, and K. Forbis Jordan, eds. *Constitutional Reform of School Finance.* Lexington, Mass.: Lexington Books, 1973.

Glick, Henry R. *Supreme Courts in State Politics.* New York: Basic Books, 1971.

Hensler, Deborah R., Mary E. Vaiana, James S. Kakalik, and Mark A. Peterson. *Trends in Tort Litigation; The Story Behind the Statistics.* Santa Monica, Cal.: Rand Corporation, Institute for Civil Justice, 1987.

Huber, Peter W. *Liability; The Legal Revolution and Its Consequences.* New York: Basic Books, 1988.

Lehne, Richard. *The Quest for Justice; The Politics of School Finance Reform.* New York: Longman, 1978.

Lieberman, Jethro. *The Litigious Society.* New York: Basic Books, 1981.

Litan, Robert E., and Clifford Winston, eds. *Liability; Perspectives and Policy.* Washington, D.C.: Brookings, 1988.

Porter, Mary Cornelia, and G. Alan Tarr, eds. *State Supreme Courts: Policymakers in the Federal System.* Westport, Conn.: Greenwood Press, 1982.

Special Issue: New Developments in State Constitutional Law. *Publius: The Journal of Federalism* 17 (Winter 1987): 1-179.

Symposium: Investing in Our Children's Future: School Finance Reform in the '90s. *Harvard Journal on Legislation* 28 (Summer 1991): 293-568.

Tarr, G. Alan, and Mary Cornelia Aldis Porter. *State Supreme Courts in State and Nation.* New Haven: Yale University Press, 1988.

White, G. Edward. *Tort Law in America; An Intellectual History.* New York: Oxford University Press, 1985.

INDEX